TRADITION
COUNTER
TRADITION

Women in Culture and Society
A Series Edited by Catharine R. Stimpson

TRADITION
COUNTER
TRADITION

Love and the Form of Fiction

Joseph Allen Boone

94-20

The University of Chicago Press
Chicago and London

The University of Chicago Press, Chicago 60637
The University of Chicago Press, Ltd., London

98 97 96 95 94 93 92 91 90 89   6 5 4 3 2

Publication of this book has been aided by
a grant from the Hyder Edward Rollins Fund.

Library of Congress Cataloging-in-Publication Data
Boone, Joseph Allen.
   Tradition counter tradition.
   (Women in culture and society)
   Includes index.
   1. English fiction—History and criticism.
2. American fiction—History and criticism.
3. Love in literature.   4. Marriage in literature.
I. Title.   II. Series.
PR830.L69B6   1987   823'.009'354   86-30911
ISBN 0-226-06464-6 (cloth)
ISBN 0-226-06465-4 (pbk.)

Contents

CONTENTS

Series Editor's Foreword

The Penguin Dictionary of Quotations has twenty-one entries for "marriage," twenty for "daughter." Perhaps the compilers of the *Penguin Dictionary* were indifferent to the closeness of these figures. English and American novelists are not. Conventionally, they have closed their books with the weddings of their daughters.

With poise, a swift intelligence, and fine aplomb, *Tradition Counter Tradition* analyzes this convention and its cultural meanings. Like many of the most vital literary critics today, Joseph A. Boone has a vision of the novel that M. M. Bakhtin has crafted. The ideology of a particular period shapes and shelters that period's texts, including its literature. As a genre, though, the novel resists rigidities. It refuses to pull a reader into the pit of orthodoxy. Instead, the novel is like a stadium in which several beliefs and aesthetic ideologies collide. "Dialogic," transcribing many voices, the novel is radical and conservative, canonical and noncanonical. It writes up the conflicts that ideology papers over.

Like their European counterparts, but in their own ways, English and American novelists were engaged with the narratives of heterosexual marriage. Boone maps out three subnarratives: those of courtship, seduction, and wedlock or sweet domesticity, which the passionate heterosexual relationship tended to replace as a symbol in the twentieth century. The English Renaissance, and the shift from Catholic to Protestant values, helped to breed ideological imperatives about marriage that dictated to fiction. Marriage was to acquire more and more status until it became the "signature of the social order." Though "wife" was a precious title, women were to be subordinate to their husbands. Despite some interest in love as the attraction of likenesses, it was more magnetically the attraction of opposites. Man and woman, husband and wife, were to be different, in character as well as power.

Yet a novel is a novel. It both sustains and subverts those ideological imperatives. The English and American novel "explained, evaded, and . . . exploded the tradition of romantic wedlock." Simultaneously, marriages themselves were shifting, breaking away from older social commands, breaking apart, reforming. The New Woman of the nineteenth century was but one rebel. The strategies of the novel, then, represent both tradition and counter-tradition.

Boone gives us traditionalists—like Austen—and counter-traditionalists. One powerful counter-line leads from Emily Brontë through George Eliot to Henry James, each socially marginal, James the most discreetly so. As they translated the "unease of marital discord" into fiction, as they became skeptical of gender polarities, they destabilized textuality itself. The revolt against the ideology of marriage was inseparable from a revolt against established principles of narrative structure, which then became a matrix of modernism.

Deftly, Boone ends with two groups of significant counter-traditionalists. The first are men—Melville, Twain, London—who write about independent men, protagonists outside of wedlock. Suggestively, Boone reads such characters as questers rather than conquesters, whose flights from marriage are challenges to traditions of the "male role" rather than manifestations of misogyny. The second group consists of women—Sarah Scott, Jewett, Barnes, Naylor—who dramatize women within female communities. Sympathetically, Boone reads these settings as centers of sustaining, alternative values.

For the past twenty years, critics from several fields have been arguing about a "core curriculum," a central body of texts and ideas that every "educated person" ought to know, and its literary equivalent, "the canon," a series of literary texts with enduring and "universal" value. Are these interlocking C's necessary, possible, and/or desirable? Though apparently about cultural and educational ideals, the argument is among conflicting political forces that seek to shape cultural and educational institutions.

Tradition Counter Tradition contributes to this forceful debate. Boone knows that various societies construct the canons that they need in order to defend the walled-up values of powerful elements within a society. "Canonical" choices can include durable goods. Nevertheless, they are choices. Sensitive to ironies, Boone is aware that his book generally takes up works that have become "canonical," whether they represent traditional or counter-traditional elements in the variegated weatherscape of fiction. However, he respectfully points to texts—from "minority," gay, or lesbian writers, for example—that are "noncanonical" now but that have revisionary power and energy. Judicious, graceful, imaginative, *Tradition Counter Tradition* exemplifies the growth of the study of gender and culture.

CATHARINE R. STIMPSON

Acknowledgments

Five years have passed since I wrote the acknowledgments to my dissertation, yet I find myself wanting to begin this page with the same words. For, as I said then, a topic such as this doesn't materialize out of mere ideas or the dusty halls of a library, but out of the care and inspiration of friends who have educated me in the value of love and given me an appreciation of its many forms. The debt for this schooling into the byways and rewards of personal relations goes back a long way, of course, beginning with my parents and with a clan of tightly knit brothers—David, Harry, John, Ben—all of whom, in multiple ways, have helped create the person who has created this book. And these lessons have continued with what I like to think of as the extended family of my adulthood, particularly with a "brotherhood" of three to whom I gratefully dedicate this book: foremost, with awe and admiration for surviving three years of manuscript pages littered across the apartment floor and for respecting the wall of books shutting me off in my corner of the living room, to Dale Wall; and, next, for maintaining enduring friendships that have spanned the years, geography, and personal change, to Bob Vorlicky and Ken Corbett. I would like to thank, as well, Debra Shostak, for her loving laughter; Jeffrey Shulman, for his warmth and intellectual generosity; Marilyn Reizbaum and Susan Winnett, for providing positive mirrors of my own aspirations; Judy Pariseau and Patricia Herrington, for being two of the most vibrantly alive people I know; Richard Ide, for serving as a professional role-model when I had only the faintest gleanings that I might need one.

This project had its beginnings as a dissertation at the University of Wisconsin–Madison under the direction of Joseph Wiesenfarth

and Susan Friedman, for whose early guidance and encouragement I cannot express enough appreciation. The combination of
intellectual and personal caring that I found at Wisconsin has been
amply matched at Harvard by Robert Kiely and Deborah Nord,
whose careful reading and criticism of this book, and interest in all
my work, has given the word "colleague" a new and special meaning for me. To all those other scholars, both here and elsewhere,
who have taken the time to read portions of this book, I also owe
my deepest thanks: among them, Debra Shostak, Susan Winnett,
Catharine Stimpson, Margaret Homans, Mary Poovey, Andrew
Delbanco, Eve Sedgwick, Marianne Hirsch, Beth McKinsey, and
Patricia Yaeger. Not least in importance has been my interaction
with the two inspiring groups of students that I taught in English
254, "The Marriage Tradition in the Novel: Plots and Counterplots," during my first two years at Harvard. These acknowledgments would be incomplete without a heartfelt salute to the
indefatigable efforts of my research assistants over the years—Will
Waters, Harry Browne, and Heather Townsend. Their meticulous
work on this manuscript augurs well for the books that they too will
someday write, as my future colleagues rather than students.

The network of family and friends who have helped infuse this
book's subject with its life and desire, with its sense of multiple
traditions and counter-traditions, is not the whole story. In terms
of material support, a welcome grant from the American Council
of Learned Societies made possible a semester's leave from teach-
ing in 1984; a Presidential Grant from Harvard University gave me
another uninterrupted semester of leave the following year. An
award from the Harvard Clark Fund not only made possible the
purchase of numerous secondary texts (whose perusal has swelled
the length of my endnotes), but also facilitated the physical production of this manuscript.

Portions of this book have appeared in earlier publications. Material from chapters 1, 3, and 4 was summarized in the article
"Wedlock as Deadlock and Beyond: Closure and the Victorian
Marriage Ideal," published in *Mosaic: A Journal for the Interdisciplin-
ary Study of Literature* 17 (Winter 1984); the James section of chapter
4 appeared as part of "Modernist Maneuverings in the Marriage
Plot: Breaking Ideologies of Gender and Genre in James's *The*

ACKNOWLEDGMENTS

Golden Bowl," published in *PMLA* (May 1986); and the analysis of the American male quest in chapter 5 appeared, in greatly abbreviated form, in *Gender Studies: New Directions in Feminist Criticism,* edited by Judith Spector (Bowling Green, Ohio: The Popular Press, 1986). I am grateful to all these publications for permission to reprint this material.

Chapter One

Wedlock as Deadlock and Beyond
An Introduction

> If every novelist could be strangled and thrown into the sea
> we should have some chance of reforming women. . . . What
> is more vulgar than the ideal of novelists? . . . In real life, how
> many men and women *fall in love*? . . . Not one married pair
> in ten thousand have felt for each other as two or three
> couples do in every novel.
> Rhoda Nunn, in George Gissing's *The Odd Women*[1]

> It [the novel] can do simply everything, and that is its
> strength and its life. Its plasticity, its elasticity are infinite.
> Henry James, "The Future of the Novel"[2]

Radically conceived yet more often than not the voice of tradition:
for more than two hundred years the Anglo-American novel has
fostered James's hopes while giving rise to Rhoda Nunn's spleen.
Opposed as such perspectives may seem, both contain truths that
are intrinsic not only to the genre but to the subject matter of this
book. For the contradictions marking the novel as a radical but
conventional literary form have simultaneously marked its representations of romantic love, generating a system of narrative strategies that have alternately explained, evaded, and (less frequently)
exploded the tradition of romantic wedlock embedded in Anglo-
American fiction since its beginnings. It is the centrality of—and
equally the divergences from—such a novelistic ideology of love
and marriage that forms the dialogue constituted by the following
chapters. How, to state the issue most simply, have the infinite
"strengths" that James associates with the genre coexisted with the
"vulgar" romantic "ideal of novelists" so abhorred by Rhoda
Nunn?

Such a focus has propelled my investigation along two complementary paths, ones that ultimately dictate the bipartite structure
of this study. First of all, I attempt to shed some light on the stranglehold of literary convention that Gissing's feminist heroine associates with the love-plot. To this end, part one, "Tradition: Marital
Ideology and Novelistic Form," explores the complex interchanges
whereby ideological structures of belief—of which the ideal of romantic wedlock is a prime example—are translated into narrative
structures that at once encode and perpetuate those beliefs. In the
process, Rhoda would have us believe, the novelistic tradition has
served a powerfully conservative function, promoting exaggerated
expectations of everlasting bliss that have enforced the subconscious acquiescence of many readers (particularly, from Rhoda's
perspective, female ones) to a limiting position within the social and
marital order.

However, as I also hope to show, the very act of deciphering the
many plots by which social ideologies of love and sexuality have
given shape to a novelistic marriage tradition uncovers a simultaneous counter-narrative: the persistent "undoing" of the dominant tradition by the contradictions concealed within the specific
forms that its representations of "life" and "love" have assumed.
The presence of such slippages in the logic governing marriage
and marriage fiction not only affords modern readers insight into
the historical values underlying the construction of the traditional
love-plot; since the pre-Richardsonian origins of the genre, such
breaks in the accepted canon have also provided avenues for a
small but subversive attack upon the evolving hegemony of the
marriage tradition in Anglo-American fiction. The narrative
modes that have emerged from these gaps in the dominant discourse—the "exceptions to the rule" that most interest me—form
the subject of part two, "Counter-Tradition: Demonstrations in
Form Breaking." When and where this revolt has succeeded in
breaking through the strictures enforced by the orthodox system
of novel making, I will be arguing, James's hopeful vision of the
"plastic" possibilities of novelistic form has not proved an empty
dream. Rather than simply "strangling" and drowning in words of
critical disapprobation the culprit-novelists at whom Rhoda Nunn
points her finger, this book shall attend to those alternative textual
voices that have tapped the genre's originally radical impulse to

subvert what (and while) it conserves. The ensuing dialogue between traditional and counter-traditional responses to love and marriage will make audible a crucial, but too often ignored, debate in the ongoing story of the making and breaking of significant form in English-speaking fiction for the past three centuries.

To argue, like James, for the novel's infinite elasticity, its ability "to do simply everything," dovetails with recent theories of the genre's origins and of its defining characteristics. M. M. Bakhtin's work is especially relevant here, for he postulates that fictional prose narrative, like no other "high genre," is by its very nature a relatively unfixed form; because it occupies the same temporal plane shared by author and audience (unlike, say, classical epic or the lyric), it necessarily remains "a genre-in-the-making," a genre lacking final rules or ironclad conventions. In this light, the novel's contact with the open-endedness of the "unfinished, still evolving contemporary reality" from which it springs has determined its very status as a verbal artifact: the heterogenous, competing, and ultimately irresolvable discourses of contemporary life are the novel's "languages" as well. Given this multiplicity and lack of fixity, Bakhtin argues, the novel genre necessarily "begins by presuming a . . . decentering of the ideological world, a certain . . . homelessness of literary consciousness, which no longer possesses a sacrosanct and unitary linguistic medium for containing ideological thought."[3] This is not to deny the effective centralizing uses to which fictional representations have been put by the dominant ideology of any given historical period. Bakhtin's theory, however, has the virtue of illuminating the manner in which the very makeup of the novel *as genre,* entailing an *inevitable* collision of systems of belief and an intermeshing of contradictory aesthetic ideologies, uniquely fits it among literary forms to express the values of the disenfranchised as well as the status quo.

Ample evidence of this many-voiced (or, in Bakhtin's phrase, dialogic) formal texture marks the beginnings of English fiction in the early eighteenth century. It is scarcely an exaggeration to visualize the formative English-language "novel" as a plebeian and somewhat scurrilous thief, swiping bits and pieces from every established genre, freely violating the boundaries hitherto separating literary and nonliterary modes of discourse, ignoring distinctions between high and popular style or subject matter—all in order to emerge in the motley guise of a self-sufficient literary form. If, on the one hand, the eighteenth-century literati tended to scoff at the beggarly and disheveled appearance of this newborn genre, the rising middle-class reading public of Defoe and Richardson's era, hungry for a literature of its own, quickly adopted the homeless vagabond as its personal possession: it alone provided a mode of discourse expansive enough to contain the visions, hopes, ideals, and fantasies of individualist capitalism and bourgeois morality. Its stolen rags thus transformed over time into showy robes, this beg-gar-king of genres had the last laugh over its original detractors, becoming the most widely read literary mode of the Victorian era, often the arbiter as well as champion of conventional bourgeois values and literary tastes. And yet, as the history of the novel has shown, fiction has never lost its latently subversive potential; in-deed, as a glance at nineteenth-century book reviews reveals, it has long been commonly assumed that "serious" imaginative fiction, however decorous, has a duty to flout popular opinion in search of higher truths. Merely disguising its innate rebelliousness under the sign of respectability, the novel thus ever remains, in Bakhtin's words, "no[n] canonical. It is plasticity itself."[4]

The idea of a genre that is potentially noncanonical, inherently multivocal, and profoundly invested in the ideological dismantling of a unitary worldview is, of course, also a feminist dream, and thus we find Virginia Woolf's language in *A Room of One's Own* uncan-nily echoing that of both James and Bakhtin, when she calls upon women novelists to seize "this most pliable of all forms" that is fic-tion and "[knock] that into [a] shape," a "new vehicle . . . for the poetry" in women hitherto thwarted by the traditional uses the genre has served.[5] Woolf's scenario is relevant to the marriage tra-dition in the novel as well as to women's fiction. For in spite of its rigorous codification of theme and form throughout the nine-teenth and early twentieth centuries, marriage fiction has never quite contained the threatening tendency of its most common sub-ject—the consequences of romantic desire—to spill over the boundaries, rather than be a mainstay, of accepted literary and so-cial structures. Not all fictions are love-plots, of course, nor is a breaking of form inevitably a cause for celebration. But by and large, the structural innovations called forth by such moments of counter-traditional discontent have helped guarantee the future of the novel itself, toppling when necessary the too-familiar house of fiction, leveling its prisons of gender, to make way for love's future structures.

I

From Austen to Eliot and Hardy, from Hawthorne to Howells and Wharton, the novel's recurring obsession with the nature of romantic relationship and its possible outcomes is clear, even if its legacy has not always been eagerly received. It has long been a critical commonplace to cite the predominance of a marriage tradition in English and American fiction. But the deeper significance of marriage as a primary shaping influence and potent symbol of order in the novel has only recently begun to receive the scrutiny it has always deserved. The early attention paid to the love-plot by E. M. Forster, Leslie Fiedler, and Evelyn J. Hinz has been expanded in an especially fruitful direction by feminist examinations of the relation of marriage to female protagonists or female plotting, in studies by Sandra M. Gilbert and Susan Gubar, Nancy K. Miller, Lee R. Edwards, and Rachel Blau DuPlessis, among others.[6] One aim of this book will be to see how these manifestations of the marriage plot both derive and deviate from a larger novelistic code of representation engaging male and female writers alike. Such an approach is meant not to disregard the difference or specificities of women's writing so much as to place that difference within a range of broader societal and literary contexts—contexts which can add to our understanding of the pivotal role assigned the ideal of romantic marriage in realistic fiction.

Chief among these contexts, as chapters 2 and 3 will show in much greater detail, was the increasingly central ideological function that marriage began to assume in the rising middle-class cultures of eighteenth- and nineteenth-century England and America. "For bourgeois society marriage is the all-subsuming, all-organizing, all-containing contract," Tony Tanner has noted, "It is the structure that maintains the Structure." Hence, Tanner continues, "the bourgeois novelist has no choice but to engage the subject of marriage. . . . He [or she] may concentrate on what makes for marriage and leads up to it, or on what threatens marriage and portends its disintegration, but [the] subject will still be marriage."[7] The specific form that this "subject" has taken in English and American fiction has relied on a conceptualization of romantic love *in* marriage not only as an achievable goal, but as a practical and an imaginative necessity for the fully experienced life. The difference between this ideal and the adulterous one practiced by the genre's more permissive, amorous Continental cousins (Tanner's eventual focus) is visible in the endings of countless Victorian novels. Of the many possible examples I might cite, the encomium to virtuous married love concluding Thackeray's *Henry Esmond* is worth quoting at length. "That happiness, which hath subsequently crowned [my life]," writes Esmond,

> 'tis of its nature sacred and secret, and not to be spoken of . . . save to Heaven and the One Ear alone—to one fond being, the truest and tenderest and purest wife ever man was blessed with. As I think of the immense happiness which was in store for me, and of the depth and intensity of that love which, for so many years, hath blessed me, I own to a transport of wonder and gratitude for such a boon. . . . Sure, love *vincit omnia;* is immeasurably above all ambition, more precious than wealth, more noble than name. He knows not life who knows not that: he hath not felt the highest faculty of the soul who hath not enjoyed it. In the name of my wife I write the completion of hope, and the summit of happiness.[8]

This extraordinary effusion to wedlock as the finality of bliss is all the more powerful for the depths of less than socially approved fantasy that, as modern readers of the novel have realized, lie barely concealed beneath its sentimental veneer. This, however, is precisely the point: the altogether incestuous and adulterous origins of this couple's desires have been successfully repressed, allowed to resurface safely in an affirmation of wedlock as the everlasting completion and summit of "happiness"—the talismanic word that echoes three times throughout Esmond's declaration.

Likewise, the Anglo-American novel's promotion of the wedlock ideal as a natural, rather than socially constructed, phenomenon has incorporated several age-old verities that we may yet recognize as constitutive of our own private romantic fantasies, even in face of a reality that often speaks otherwise: each desiring subject is destined to meet the one perfect love-object "made" for him or her; the perfect end of love is everlasting union with that individual; love will strike at first sight; sexual love transcends all material concerns; emotions are more valuable than reason in matters of the heart.[9] Despite the highly personal ring of most of these characteristics ("sacred and secret, and not to be spoken of," Esmond claims), such idealized love is far from being an exclusively private, individualized phenomenon. Within the sexual-marital economy of English and American culture, it has served an equally public function as part of the ideological apparatus ensuring social stability—it is "the structure that maintains the Structure," to repeat Tanner, the control that gives Esmond's longings for his virtual stepmother a socially acceptable label ("In the name of *my wife* I write the completion of hope"). And to the extent that the marital ideal serves as a metonymy for proper social order, it simultaneously works, as we will shortly see, to disguise the asymmetries encompassed within the trope of "balanced" order.

Implicit in these observations are certain crucial assumptions about the nature of social and literary ideology and, consequently, about the process by which beliefs and values concerning social order are transformed into precepts of fictional organization. Suffice it to say, with scores of other theorists, that the relation between ideology and literature is an extremely complex, vexed, and often indirect one; it cannot be reduced, as earlier Marxist literary critics attempted, either to a simplistic scheme of hegemonic ideas imposed from above, reproducing in the text the "false consciousness" that screens the individual from "reality," or to a model in which the work and ideology are coeval mirrors, microstructure reflecting macrostructure or form reflecting content in a clear-cut binary opposition.[10] It may therefore be helpful to start with a definition of ideology itself. For it we look at ideology, as Louis Althusser understands it, as a system of *representations,* of significations, that constitute the sphere of social relations into which each individual is fitted, we can begin to discern a series of analogies linking its operation with the theories of textual representation and the constructions of gender embedded in the novelistic marriage tradition. Foremost, ideological structures work to create the appearance of a unitary, coherent worldview by eliding the multiple social contradictions—in Bakhtin's terms, the heteroglossia of everyday life—that would challenge their dominance and power; as the construct of experience through which the individual perceives the world, ideology thus tightens its grip on its subjects by representing its system of beliefs and ideas as *natural,* as necessary, when in fact, as one critic puts it, such systems consist of "what is partial, factitious, and ineluctably social."[11]

Ideological "solutions" to social contradictions become, in a profound sense, the "resolutions" offered in traditional fiction. For the classic mode of realist narrative is also a system of representation, working to naturalize, or recuperate, the image of "reality" that it creates in the form of a coherent, intelligible whole. Presenting the reader with fictions that appear "real," but whose "realism" is predicated on a series of narrative manipulations working to present that reality as stable, ordered, and trustworthy, novelistic structures therefore undertake a mission analogous to that of society's dominant ideological structures. Predictably, then, as the genre rose to its position of preeminence in the nineteenth century, it tended to develop narrative organizations suited to the promotion of its culture's valorization of hierarchy and order within social (and sexual) relations. Alain Robbe-Grillet's explanation of this propensity for organization hints at the complexity of the various structural determinants operating in the traditional novel, ones that will be subjected to further scrutiny in chapter 3: "All the technical elements of the narrative—systematic use of the past tense and the third person, unconditional adoption of chronological development, linear plots, regular trajectory of the passions, impulse of each episode toward a conclusion, etc.—everything tended to impose the image of a stable, coherent, continuous, unequivocal, entirely decipherable universe."[12] One can begin to see how the movement toward stasis in the canonical love-plot, be the resolution comedic or tragic, functioned to preclude, by repressing from the audience's overt consciousness, any serious dismantling of the social order, the ideological grounds, underlying the fictional construct.

Which turns us back to the signifying "content" of the marriage novel: its alignments of the sexes in hierarchical patterns based on cultural assumptions about gender that are themselves powerfully ideological. As much feminist criticism has demonstrated, the entitlements to power that Marxists have traditionally associated with class hegemony can logically be extended to include those operations of male dominance and female submission encoded in the relation of the sexes.[13] Filtered through such a perspective, the presence of male authority throughout the modern history of the West, it becomes clear, is an *effect* of sexual constructions of behavior rather than a natural and immutable given. Another effect of such an unequal distribution of power has been to render the relation of the sexes profoundly asymmetrical, an asymmetry that has resulted, in Mary Jacobus's words, in the "ultimately conservative and doom-ridden concept of [sexual] difference as opposition."[14] According to such logic, "man" is what "woman" is not; attributes of "masculinity," therefore, categorically oppose and exclude those associated with "femininity." In this ideologically weighted duality, biological difference becomes the pretext for male power over women, comprising what in its broader sense may be termed a "patriarchal" sexual order.[15] Gender roles hence serve as historically specific *representations* of sexual identity, rather than signifying unitary or unchanging essences in themselves; thus, when the following chapters have occasion to refer to "masculine" and "feminine" roles, quotation marks will generally be placed around the terms to emphasize their culturally determined status. As such, sexual constructions of identity function in a manner analogous to ideological and narrative modes of signification, positing as natural "a set of potentialities . . . never unmediated by human reality."[16]

In the traditional love-plot, this sexual ideology has been most forcefully registered in the fictional idealization of the married state as the individual's one true source of earthly happiness. Likewise, the power of the fictional marriage tradition owes much of its idealizing appeal to its manipulation of form to evoke an illusion of order and resolution that, as we have seen, glosses over the contradictions, the inequities, concealed in the institution of marriage itself. One result is the tradition's appearance of an overarching unity and authority, nowhere so evident as in the codification of its narrative plots into recognizable, repeating, and contained structures. Of these, variations upon situations of courtship, seduction, and wedlock form the most common trajectories ascribed to the course of love; whether or not marriage is actually attained, these patterns almost uniformly uphold the *concept* of romantic wedlock as their symbolic center and ideal end. And, in a profound sense, as chapter 3 will demonstrate, all these formats are either reflections or inversions of each other's structural organizations. The most familiar pattern is the courtship plot whose comedic ending follows upon the systematic removal of those obstacles previously impeding union, obstacles that may range from physical separation and sociological barriers to psychological misunderstandings. A dark inversion of the courtship format, the seduction plot generally transforms would-be lovers into sexual antagonists, and division replaces union as the endpoint toward which the metonymic flow of narrative sequence is directed. The almost invariably tragic denouement that closes the seduction tale or subplot, no less than its comedic counterpart, ultimately works to uphold social norms—in particular, by mourning the abuse of virtue or by indicting those erring protagonists who have betrayed the higher dictates of morality and ideal love. The third pattern, the wedlock or domestic plot, may adapt either a comic or a tragic direction; in the former, initially troubled spouses generally undergo a series of misfortunes and threats analogous to those occurring in the courtship narrative before reuniting happily, while in the latter version, the impasse of bad marriage generally reflects the tragic misjudgments of the individual spouses. Chapter 3 will explore these patterns in detail, drawing on the courtship narratives of *Pamela* and *Pride and Prejudice,* the seduction plots of *Clarissa* and *Tess of the D'Urbervilles,* and the domestic dramas of *Amelia* and *A Modern Instance* to establish paradigms for investigating the ways in which the very dynamic of narrative, the structure of desire in traditional fiction, has been coerced into upholding a restrictive sexual-marital ideology.

Uniting all three formats, furthermore, are shared archetypes of romantic and wedded relationship which stem from cultural models evolved to explain the nature of heterosexual attraction. The development of this literary iconography, which in large part constitutes the substance of chapter 2, derives from the constructions of gender that we have already seen to be present in cultural representations of the sexes as polar "opposites." The rich folklore treating husband and wife as opposing species, for instance, is reproduced in the caricatured relations of the Bennet parents in Austen's *Pride and Prejudice* and the Tullivers in Eliot's *The Mill on the Floss.* "Mrs. Tulliver had lived fourteen years with her husband," the authorial narrator reports in the latter text, "yet she retained in all the freshness of her early married life a facility of saying things which drove him in the opposite direction to the one she desired."[17] Such opposition is only apparently symmetrical or balanced, as any reader of Eliot's text knows, since it is Mrs. Tulliver's silly "feminine" behavior, rooted in traits specifically related to her wedded role, not Mr. Tulliver's "masculine" fortitude, that is consistently made the butt of the narrator's satire. Traditional novelizations of marital opposition thus most often reflect the unequal distribution of sexual power in the larger social structure. Within this framework, wedlock is at best pictured as the harmonious union of "friends" who are complementary opposites; at worst, as a war of polar antagonists, "enemies" locked in perpetual battle due to inherently opposite natures. While the former paradigm generally characterizes the successful courtship plot and the latter the seduction and unhappy wedlock narrative, both models rest upon definitions of sexual and marital roles that, however transitory over time, are always mutually exclusive; the Victorian writer Dinah Mulock Craik's emphatic declaration, "Man and woman were made for, and *not like* one another,"[18] tersely sums up the basic principle underlying theories of complementary and antagonistic balance alike.

Craik's refutation of likeness between the sexes, however, raises the possibility of the existence of other archetypes of heterosexual romantic desire. What, for instance, are we to make of the alternatives posited by Mrs. Pryor in Charlotte Brontë's *Shirley* when she says, "I ought never to have married: mine is not the nature easily to find a *duplicate*, or likely to assimilate with a *contrast*"? Indeed, the idea of falling in love with one's "duplicate" image, rather than with a "contrast," was an increasingly familiar part of the discourse of nineteenth-century romantic ideology.[19] The degree to which the concept actually veered from prescriptions of sexual polarity, however, was often minimal. For "likeness" was most often equated with everything *but* equality of gender; moral affinity, spiritual harmony, mental compatability were fine as long as they did not upset the prevalent hierarchy empowering the male gender. Conversely, novelistic representations of "contrast" as the source of romantic attraction have almost always reduced that "contrast" to a simple binary opposition rooted in contemporary ideologies of sexual polarity; the result has been to ignore the nonsexual differences in taste and perception that can help create a degree of healthy reciprocity in relationship. One sign of counter-traditional expression to be pursued in the following chapters, therefore, involves tracing down those texts that have dared establish a "likeness" between mates in defiance of accepted hierarchical and dichotomized notions of sexual identity, or that have allowed the existence of complex differences between men and women not automatically reducible to gender stereotyping.

Contributing to novelistic representations of sexual polarity is a related archetype, deriving from Renaissance revisions of Plato, of both sexes as "half-selves" incomplete without the other. George Meredith gives a parodic example of this popularly disseminated myth in *The Egoist,* when one character notes that Sir Willoughby "is a splendid creature; only wanting a wife to complete him."[20] The inverse side of this archetype is the myth that the two halves associated with the sexes harmonize to form a wholeness, a oneness, greater than the individual self. So the married Ratignolles strike the pensive Edna Pontellier in Chopin's *The Awakening:* "If ever the fusion of two human beings into one has been accomplished on this sphere it was surely in their union." Yet Edna also realizes that this "little glimpse of domestic harmony . . . was not a condition of life which fitted her,"[21] precisely because its successful operation depends on Adèle Ratignolle's willing suspension of her individuality in favor of her wedded function as a "mother-woman." Not only is either "half-self" in this marital paradigm theoretically incomplete without the other, but the prospect of any autonomous or independent identity for the female "half" is proportionally less than that of the male. Assumptions about the inseparability of female self-diminishment and "ideal" conjugal harmony go far back into the novelistic tradition, as Flora's praise of the perfect Rose Bardwardine in *Waverley* attests: "Her very soul is in home, and in the discharge of those quiet virtues of which home is the centre. Her husband will be to her what her father now is—the object of all her care, solicitude, and affection. She will see nothing, and connect herself with nothing, but by him and through him."[22]

All these observations point toward the most problematic task facing the writer of purportedly stable marriage fictions, that of reconciling the contradictory pull between the protagonist's independent identity and sexual-marital role. The existential stakes involved in this dilemma receive a humorous but illuminating gloss in *Moby-Dick,* when Ishmael, wedded by a monkey-rope to his "mate"

Queequeg during a whaling operation, facetiously comments, "I seemed distinctly to perceive that my own individuality was now merged in a joint stock company of two: that my free will had received a mortal wound."[23] Much less a joking matter in fictional representations of women, the tension between individual freedom and corporate "married" identity takes on a note of special urgency in the case of the intelligent, strong-willed female protagonist. I will now briefly turn to a novel that vividly embodies this conflict, Brontë's *Shirley*, as a way of anticipating several of the issues that the rest of this study will be addressing. For the problematic characterization of this text's eponymous heroine, along with several inconsistencies in the plot's construction, reveals with particular intensity the potentially repressive power exerted by the novelistic marriage tradition over authorial intention and textual production.

Shirley enters the novel in chapter 11 as an economically independent and gloriously self-possessed figure; her untraditional aura of freedom is but one example of Brontë's self-conscious efforts throughout the text to break through the limitations both imposed upon and ascribed to "naturally" feminine writing.[24] Almost instantly, Shirley proclaims her difference from stifling feminine stereotypes through her playful violation of her society's polarized boundaries of gender. "I am . . . quite a woman and something more," she announces in her opening speech, "I am an esquire . . . enough to inspire me with a touch of manhood" (213); and she will later goad Robert Moore, the mill owner—"You think me a dangerous specimen of my sex. Don't you, now?"—because of her desire to take an active role in his "masculine" world of economic and political affairs (352). As Brontë makes clear, Shirley does not simply want to trade female for male privileges; she is a prototype of a mythic new type of womanhood, the living incarnation of the inspirational portrait of the mother of the universe, the woman-Titan Eve, that she draws for her friend Caroline Helstone in chapter 18.

Analogously, Shirley is romanticized by her most ardent male admirer, Louis Moore, as a creature "never to be overtaken, arrested, fixed" (584–85). In light of Louis's professed view, it is supremely ironic that it is precisely his courting of Shirley in the latter third of the novel that deprives her of this untraditional mobility, fixing her previously unconstrained responses within a traditionally static "feminine" role. During the climactic proposal scene, where Louis "the man" reveals his hitherto silent love, Shirley submissively acknowledges him as "my master"; to his ecstastic cries of possession, "I have you: you are mine," she meekly yields, "I am glad I know my keeper" (578–79). The text's conclusion completes Shirley's transformation from a "quite self-possessed, and always spirited and easy" person (291) into a "chained," "fettered," and conquered creature of the wild. Metaphorically described as "gnaw-[ing] her chain" and yearning for her "wild woods" and "virgin freedom," this pantheress nonetheless "abdicat[es] without a word or a struggle" in the presence of "her captor," Louis (584, 592). Although certain ambiguities in Shirley's stated opinions and actions can in retrospect be seen as anticipating this extreme capitulation, the submissive protagonist who ends the novel is simply not the same woman who earlier enters Caroline's life like a breath of fresh air; rather, she has become the immobile, fixed object in a masculine plot of desire. Since the ending celebrates the marriage of Louis and Shirley as a "happy" event, the unsettling tenor of the double-edged images of Shirley's engagement as a state of captivity must reflect something of Brontë's own ambivalent relation to the ideological precepts making female autonomy antithetical to marital destiny, as well as to the pressures of a fictional tradition of romance. But the problem is not simply that a romantic element has entered Shirley's story; we could happily accept Shirley in love. It is the degree to which the text goes to obscure and erase her formerly abundant strength that proves so disturbing; such elisions, indeed, reproduce the way in which ideology works to reinforce its appearance of consensus when and where none really exists.

The disquieting shifts in perspective and characterization necessary to bring about this romantic ending are also anticipated throughout Brontë's text by strategic readjustments in its organizational structure, ones that occur less as part of any organic evolution than as disruptions of its original trajectory. Beginning as an extremely critical examination of the restricted place of Victorian women in a world where power belongs to men, the narrative in its early phases locates the plot's emotional center in the special friendship of Shirley and Caroline: Shirley's arrival at Fieldhead literally brings Caroline, "wast[ing]" away (199) from a prototypically suffocating existence as a woman, back to life. Chapters 11–15 trace the personal satisfaction the two gain from each other's company. "You and I will suit," Shirley tells Caroline (226) as they together achieve a state of Dianic freedom symbolized in the private retreat or space that *Nunn*wood's virgin forest—their female bower of bliss—comes to represent for them (220–21). The only threat to their solidarity, as Shirley admits to Caroline, is that of male intrusion: "If we were but left unmolested . . . I could bear you in my presence for ever" (264). Chapters 16–21 portray the two as female allies in a broader social context, as they find themselves pitted against a male world that excludes them from its important business during the mill riot. But in chapter 22, "Two Lives," a very curious event occurs: the plot *literally* splits into two, as the arrival of Shirley's relatives, the Sympsons, separates her from Caroline and quietly displaces the summer trip that Shirley has earlier vowed she will not take without Caroline: "Ere the month of July was passed, Miss Keeldar would probably have started with Caroline on that northern tour they had planned; but just at that epoch an invasion befell Fieldhead. . . . The laws of hospitality obliged [Shirley] to give in, which she did with a facility which somewhat surprised Caroline" (374–75). The hidden subtext—never explicitly stated—that keeps Shirley away from Caroline (at the very moment that the latter undergoes a second decline that almost kills her) is most revealing: the Sympsons have included in their entourage their son's tutor, the aforementioned Louis Moore, once Shirley's schoolmaster and still her secret love. The novel, in effect, devolves into two alternating love-plots from this point on, with Caroline and Shirley overcoming the obstacles standing in the way of their respective unions with the two Moore brothers, Robert and Louis.

As Brontë's text gradually overwrites the dominant plot of female friendship with a dual one of romance and marriage, inconsistencies between the two strands begin to surface and undermine the apparent unity of the text. Such a moment occurs in chapter 26, when Caroline—and the reader—has the unsettling experience of viewing Shirley's character "under a novel aspect" (428): Shirley rather mysteriously and even rudely hints that her communications with Caroline are not as frank as we have been led to believe. Hitherto, the women have been depicted as kindred spirits "toned in [a] harmony" (231) that goes beyond words, sharing a "way of thinking and talking" (230) in all things. The newly unfolding courtship plots, however, whose suspense largely depends on Caroline's mistaken assumptions about who loves whom, demand these sudden reticences, albeit at the expense of plausibility. Even more disconcerting is the fact that Louis actually replaces Caroline as Shirley's confidant a few chapters later when the heiress, bitten by a possibly rabid dog, feels the need to confess her secret fears to a close friend: she chooses Louis over Caroline.[25]

The ultimate displacement of the plot of Shirley and Caroline's friendship, occurring as it does near the very end of the text, is so strategically handled as almost to escape notice. When Robert—now Caroline's declared lover—begins to confess his previous attraction to Shirley, Caroline preempts him by saying that Shirley has intimated all that need be known of Robert's misdirected desire on an overnight visit the week before: "We occupied the same room and bed. We did not sleep much: we talked the whole night through" (559). What is extraordinary, when one pauses to think about it, is that this climactic and revelatory scene between the two major female characters, an encounter of primary importance in the narrative of their friendship, has been relegated to indirect paraphase as part of lovers' discourse: we hear Robert's voice guessing at Shirley's confidences, while *her* voice is totally eclipsed from the text. A parallel displacement occurs in the rendering of Louis's proposal to Shirley in chapter 36. For the chapter turns out to be a first-person account written by Louis in his journal; in effect, his voice has usurped the authorial narration of the novel in a manner parallel to his usurpation of Shirley's self-possession during the encounter. The result is a deliberately partial perspective, which denies the reader any objective measure of the troubling dynamics of mastery and submission with which Louis imbues the scene. It is as if Brontë, unable to bear narrating Shirley's abdication in her own voice, places it in the mouth of the conquering hero in an attempt to deny her own hand in creating the situation. As with the never-taken trip of the two women, the missing bedroom confession, or, indeed, the destruction, described in the text's final paragraphs, of their favorite private haunt, the virgin woods of Nunnely Hollow, traces of an incompleted story of female bonding haunt the highly artificial edifice of heterosexual courtship that has been imposed on its last third. On the surface an extreme example of fictional tradition winning out over a powerful and talented writer, *Shirley* also remains, like its heroine, "something more," for the telltale gaps and dissonances marking its construction profoundly call into question the ideal coherence of all narratives and, with them, the self-proclaimed universality of the marriage plot.

The marriage tradition in the novel, it becomes increasingly clear, has exerted a tremendous power over the development of fiction, sometimes infusing its content with the spirit of life, sometimes crippling its very life-giving force under the weight of restrictive convention. The implications of this vexed relationship can begin to be summed up if we turn to a metaphor common to novelistic "happy endings"—that of the matrimonial "knot"—and look at its several variations in a cross section of texts. For the tie that binds man and woman in a match ordained from above and celebrated on earth as a portent of everlasting bliss turns out to be a very special knot indeed, bringing together social and literary representations of wedlock in a complex but common project. Hence, according to one popular nineteenth-century American novelist, marriage is "the most sacred tie on earth" because it secures not only "the peace of families, [but] the social welfare of the whole community";[26] the tie of wedlock, so perceived, bolsters the myth of a tightly knit social order. The same metaphor works as readily to express the stabilizing and coherent ends of traditional fictional form. As Trollope puts it at the end of *The Warden,* "Our tale is now done, and it only remains to us to collect the scattered threads of our little story, and to tie them into a seemly knot."[27] When the subject matter is the drama of love, the narrative metaphor becomes even more apt: thus in the final pages of *The Expedition of Humphry Clinker,* Matthew Bramble's nephew checks off the three matrimonial pacts concluding that text (unaware that as he writes, the terms of a fourth, his own, are underway) by announcing, "The fatal knots are now tied. The comedy is near a close; and the curtain is ready to drop."[28]

It would appear, however, that the knot binding narrative closure and wedlock is "fatal" in more senses than one, protecting the text's ideal vision of unchanging love from interrogation by strangling the possibility of more narrative at that very juncture where the novelist—so comments Dickens—would fain "weave, for a little longer space, the thread of these adventures."[29] The untold stories that lie beyond these foreshortened tapestries of love are among the main subjects of the Henry James essay from which one of the epigraphs to this chapter was drawn. The "immense omission in our fiction" of anything but "the most guarded treatment of the great relation between men and women," James complains, is a major culprit in the shop-worn condition of the novel, especially as these "guarded" themes keep "reappearing," garmentlike, "in forms at once ready-made and sadly the worse for wear." Indeed, this uniformity of theme and form constitutes "the particular knot the coming novelist . . . will have here to untie" in order to realize the expansive possibilities of the genre in the future.[30] In an important sense, then, we can identify one "fatal knot" blocking the novel's development with the romantic ideal of wedlock that intertwines the various strands of the novel's marriage tradition into an apparently seamless unity. The remaining pages of this introduction will turn to the means by which a counter-tradition has attempted to unloose that knot and weave from its threads the fabric of another story altogether.

II

First, one might ask, what constitutes a truly "counter-traditional" response to the ideological concerns embedded in traditional fictions of love, seduction, and marriage? A rebellion against the dictates of love-plotting in the name of greater fictional realism, for instance, does not necessarily guarantee a radical move against the love-plot's conservative sexual ideology. When Thackeray leaves the reader of *The Newcomes* to decide whether Ethel and Clive get married in the "Fable-land" where "anything you like happens," his discontent with his age's expectations of fiction exists apart from the conventional sexual politics embodied in this text (he criticizes unloving economic matches, extols sentimentally correct ones) or from its generally conventional structure.[31] In comparison, the deliberate ambiguity ending Charlotte Brontë's *Villette* is at once thematically more serious and formally more innovative than Thackeray's playful close (as I shall have occasion to mention in the conclusion to chapter 4). Nonetheless, on an overt textual level Brontë's refusal to reunite Lucy and Paul Emanuel is as much a manifesto against the illusions nurtured by bad romantic fiction as a blueprint for an ideological decentering of the contradictions embedded in the marriage tradition. "The spirit of romance would have indicated another course, far more flowery and inviting," she wrote to her publisher in defense of Paul Emanuel's presumed drowning; "it would have fashioned a paramount hero, kept faithfully to him, and made him supremely worshipful . . . but this would have been unlike real life—inconsistent with truth—at variance with probability."[32]

At different times and in different places, however, there have emerged texts whose dismantling of the patriarchal implications of marriage and marriage plots have gradually opened up the closed field of romantic representation, and which have constituted a vital counter-tradition in Anglo-American fiction. The passionate indignation with which Rhoda Nunn, Gissing's feminist heroine in *The Odd Women,* denounces "the ideal of novelists" attests to the increasing number of thoughtful writers on either side of the Atlantic beginning to rebel against the constraints imposed by the wedlock ideal on life and art alike. This literary revolt against the *thematic* limitations imposed by the novel's love ideology, however, rather like Thackeray's or Brontë's revolts in the name of greater realism, remained incomplete as long as its social criticism operated within the *structural* confines of conventional plotting. Because the wedlock ideal was so embedded in the very organization of the traditional novel, the truly successful insurrection against the tyranny of conventional marital ideology demanded a profound revision and rethinking of traditionally signifying modes of form and closure as well as content. I will be arguing that such unravelings of the marriage tradition have generally taken one of two courses. One has involved attacking the tradition from within, exposing the dangers of its socially constructed myths by following the course of wedlock beyond its expected close and into the uncertain textual realm of marital stalemate and impasse. The other has been to invent fictional trajectories for the single protagonist, male or female, whose successful existence outside the convention calls into question the viability of marital roles and arrangements. For the counter-traditional novelist, both of these plot alternatives, lying at least partially outside the boundaries demarcated by the traditional dynamics of narrative desire, have offered avenues of escape from a system of representation that by the mid-nineteenth century had come to block the "plastic" possibilities of narrative and of sexuality itself.

The subject matter and narrative manner that began to break through the hegemony of the novelistic marriage tradition, especially in the fertile period of discontent extending from approximately 1840 to 1930, dominate the second half of this book. Chapter 4 looks at four novelists—Emily Brontë, Eliot, James, and Woolf—whose response to the myth of final happiness was to express the plot of life beyond the matrimonial barrier as unhappy: in *Wuthering Heights, Daniel Deronda, The Golden Bowl,* and *To the Lighthouse,* marital conflict is no longer represented as simply a personal tragedy but as an ongoing battle that can never be resolved given the patriarchal rules and oppositional roles by which society has locked partners in wedlock into place. And, crucially, the "uneasy" schisms uncovered in all of these texts' examinations of married life are reproduced in the narrational "unease" of decentered, multivocal, and ultimately open-ended structures that refuse to give pat answers to the unsettling questions that the dislocations in the prior narratives have raised.

Chapters 5 and 6, in contrast, examine those formal innovations set into motion by depicting the marginality of the single protagonist distanced from a marital context and, hence, from marital literary tradition. These gestures toward male and female independence are less evenly matched than my pairing of chapters might first suggest: not only do male characters reject marriage for different reasons than female characters, but the cultural "reading" of the values that accrue to these separatist acts are often tellingly disparate, as the contrasting critical reception of these two sets of texts indicate. No more provocative example of independent male protagonists could be wished for than those to be found in American quest narrative and discussed in chapter 5. In contrast to Fiedler's famous discussion of the mode, I will suggest that the very gesture of fantasizing a male world outside marriage, while necessarily qualified by its exclusion of women, yielded a surprisingly positive gain for a select group of male authors; in texts by Melville and Twain, and to a much lesser extent, London, there can be found a profound exploration of the politics of "masculinity" and male bonding coexisting with a refutation of the trajectory and themes of typical love fiction. The shifting implications of the act of questing from *Moby-Dick, Huckleberry Finn,* and *Billy Budd* to *The Sea Wolf* will suggest how and why the genre lost its early potential, becoming the enclave of misogynistic endeavor in the twentieth century.

If the unceasing motion of the male quest into undefined physical and textual space is always directed away from stable narrative centers, the organizing principle in chapter 6 is that very stasis or circularity which traps the single or widowed woman, surrounded by communities of similarly unmarried women who in turn are imprisoned at the center of a society that considers them superfluous. Building on Nina Auerbach's premises,[33] I will trace the structural changes accompanying such a thematic in four widely varying texts, Sarah Scott's *Millenium Hall,* Gaskell's *Cranford,* Jewett's *Country of the Pointed Firs,* and Gilman's *Herland*—works whose generally invisible status within the Anglo-American canon has, ironically, reproduced the invisibility characterizing the female enclaves that form their subject matter. The forms of all these works are governed by the logic of incremental repetition, in which seemingly disconnected or random events circle around unchanging truths and settings, rather than by the causality of linear plotting intrinsic to the love-plot. By means of such a mode of counterplotting, the apparently negative constriction of static lives becomes a magical opening into a hidden realm of communal freedom for these self-reliant women.

Through various strategems, then, all these currents work against the ideological values instilled in dominant love fiction by embodying their critiques in form-breaking counterplots that dare to reenvision and rewrite the traditional plot of personal desire. If ideological and novelistic representations enforce their dominance, as Penny Boumelha hypothesizes, "by repressing the questions that challenge [their] limits and transposing, displacing, or eliding the felt contradictions of lived experience in a way that will permit of an apparent resolution,"[34] then the counter-tradition *begins* by reopening to question precisely those contradictions in the "lived experience" of sexual identity and married life and by forcing them into contact with its own competing agendas for change. The result is a dialogue, carried on within the counter-traditional text as well as between traditions, that necessarily works to decenter the presumed universality of the dominant sexual order—and, with it, the fictional order of marriage—by revealing its constructed and ever partial nature. And this dialogical project has also necessarily stretched the boundaries of the genre a little wider, offsetting the conservative organizing tendencies of novelistic form with the radical potential originally begetting the novel as a genre.

III

In a book that will be making much of openness as a desirable trait of literature and life, I would be remiss in appropriating the final paragraphs of this introductory chapter to create, out of all that follows, the illusion of a seamless whole. Rather, I'd like to acknowledge some of the "fatal knots" of logic that I may have drawn too tightly, and invite critics who read this book to untie and recombine those threads that may lead to richer perceptions of the interchanges of marriage, sexual ideologies, and narative form. What follows is a partial list of aspects of this work that may present problems, need qualification, invite criticism, and inspire further investigation. Along the way I will make some observations, offer some explanations, and acknowledge some debts as well.

1. To begin with, I am aware of a problem that creeps into the discourse of this book the moment I introduce the terms "tradition" and "counter-tradition" as the rallying poles of my argument: for the play of forces that forms the focus of this work is actually more dialogical than the dialectical ring of its title might first imply. These concepts of "tradition" and "counter-tradition," of course, are constructions, hermeneutic tools, imposed on a diverse genre that will always and inevitably escape tidy classification. The boundaries I erect between the two concepts are perhaps even more flexible, more open to permutations, than the shape of the following argument at times indicates; the most "radical" of the counter-traditional texts I choose to examine retain abundant traces of "traditional" sentiment, and a few of the texts I have placed "within" the tradition come close to undermining its very bases. The appearance of *Clarissa* and *Villette* on both sides of this divide, indeed, attests to its flexibility. Given the fact that one of the unspoken desires motivating this study has been that of moving our perceptions of gender beyond the sterile logic of "either/or"

AN INTRODUCTION

categories, I feel compelled to apologize for the extent to which my formulations here recapitulate that duality.

2. Some critics, on the other hand, may feel I too blithely collapse differences, particularly generic and national ones, in grouping English and American love-fictions together as part of one tradition. Certainly many of the distinctions dividing these literatures before the twentieth century are irrefutable. Too often, however, I feel that critics have artifically employed this division to impose a convenient limit on their investigations. Genre studies of the English-language novel could benefit, I think, by a wider practice of transatlantic theorization that would allow us to perceive the sometimes obscured formal and structural links rendering American fiction the legitimate (though rebellious) progeny of its English forebears. The ideal of romantic wedlock, even when differing in its specific historical adaptations to the various geographic and communal needs of England and America, seems an essential part of that literary inheritance. Chapter 2 is largely offered as an explanation of the way in which such an ideal can contain both synchronic (seemingly transhistorical) and diachronic (historically contingent) elements that make its ubiquity within related cultural groups possible.

3. A more serious question that any perusal of my table of contents may uncover concerns the relative lack of noncanonical literatures in this study. On one hand, the very focus and dates of my subject have dictated this gap as regards racially defined minorities: as the creation of a white, bourgeois culture, the wedlock ideal has simply been most visible in "white" middle-class fiction written before, say, the 1920s, at which point other voices began more insistently to break through the hegemony of dominant literary discourse. On the other hand, since several black women writers, to cite a particular group of minority writers, have made the representation and critique of marriage the nexus of highly original creations, it might be plausibly asked whether their work constitutes a part of the counter-traditional protest I will be tracing. At this point my answer is both yes and no; the fiction of Zora Neale Hurston, Dorothy West, and Toni Morrison, for instance, strikes me as inhabiting a special territory between or beside what I am calling the marriage tradition and its antithesis. Fitting these works

into chapter 4's focus on "uneasy wedlock" and open form, I decided, would reduce the complexity and contradictions of the black woman writer's doubled relation to a romantic wedlock ideal of the "other" and to an ethnic understanding of the family quite different in function and formation from the dominant class's vision of hearthside harmony. There is obviously a long chapter, if not an entire book, that remains to be written on the problematic relation of black fiction to the middle-class marriage tradition.

4. Gay and lesbian fiction forms another noncanonical tradition that may seem missing, with a few exceptions like Djuna Barnes's *Ladies Almanack* in chapter 6, from my counter-traditions. Again, the dates framing my argument have something to do with this omission; following the lead of other researchers in the field, I am reluctant to label as "homosexual" those fictions written before the turn-of-the-century construction of homosexuality as a medical and, in subsequent decades, social identity.[35] Hence it has seemed more appropriate to speak of a homoerotic element at work, for example, in the counter-traditional aspects of male bonding in the American quest. Were this book's argument extended further into the twentieth century, the increasingly vocal role played by gay and lesbian writers, or by texts with homosexual themes, in attacking the dominant sexual ideology would necessarily form an important countercurrent.

5. Given this postmodern age's deconstruction of the notion of the unified subject, some readers may find this text's references to the "self" or the "quest for selfhood" nostalgic. My use of these terms, however, is not intended to deny the psychological truth of the radical self-division upon which all human identity is founded, but rather to emphasize the ways in which specific conceptions of identity have been shaped by socially accepted constructions of gender. As the analysis of counter-traditional modes will show, the expansive "selves" that some of these fictional protagonists do attain have less to do with any *static*, traditional notion of personal coherence than with a discovery that identity is a process always in the making, multiform in potential, and open to a variety of experiences and behaviors including, but not restricted to, those associated with "masculine" and "feminine" roles. If "androgynous" at times seems the adjective that best describes certain characters' transgressions of society's gendered boundaries, it should be un-

derstood in this sense of a fluid, open, and relatively unfixed subjectivity, rather than as a prescription for a perfectly weighted balance of "male-female" traits as a possible or desirable goal for all men and women. For in certain writers, as Toril Moi suggests of Woolf, androgynous motifs function as a deconstruction, rather than a union, of the duality "masculine/feminine."[36] The problem with the latter, historically determined definition of androgyny, as has been frequently pointed out, is that it implies an equality of traits belied in cultural practice; this deceptiveness, of course, means that more often than not the concept has traditionally served to aggrandize male rather than female personality—a thorny path we will pick our way through in dealing with the American male quester's response to and incorporation of the "feminine."

6. Since I assume many of the readers of this book will be feminists, and since many of those feminists will be women, I'd like to address briefly my place as a male critic writing about the effects of gender and sexual power on literary form. It is my hope that this book will make a contribution not only to genre criticism of the novel but also to feminist literary theory by presenting a methodology whose focus sidesteps, temporarily, the debate between "feminine" and "masculine" discourse and "female" and "male" traditions to examine the ways in which writers of both genders have abetted or defied the ideological ramifications of traditional fictional order. As a man and a feminist, I have not thought it particularly appropriate to choose for exploration, for example, the possibilities of a female "difference" or "language" in texts by women; rather, I have sought to define for myself a field of literary inquiry that neither elides my own gender nor reduces the centrality of feminism to my critical practice, and for me a focus on marriage (a social institution affecting both sexes, whatever their relation to it) and on narrative structure (a component of form less gender-specific than language, at least) has provided one solution to this issue.

7. Finally, a nod to others—those critics who in multiple ways have inspired the writing of this book. Foremost, without the example of those theorists who have opened to scrutiny the study of gender in literature, this study of the novelistic bonds of men and women in and out of marriage would virtually have been impossi-

ble. Like most others working in the field, I could list the now "famous" American centerpieces of early feminist study—works by Showalter, Moers, Gilbert and Gubar, Auerbach, and so on—that have always hovered in the background of my writing, but I would also like to pay tribute to a lesser-known work by Jean E. Kennard, *Victims of Convention,* which several years ago got me seriously thinking, for the first time, about the possibility of sexist values inhering in the very form of fiction; such a kernel, also as expanded in Nancy Miller's increasingly sophisticated treatments of female plots of desire, has been intrinsic to my own formulation of how the novel incorporates the ideological organizations and desires of the dominant order into its narrative structures.

Turning to other debts, I would like to point out the formative influence of Evelyn J. Hinz's 1976 article on the marriage-plot, the first systematic overview of its kind. Also, early in my search for broader critical models, I found extremely thought-provoking the work of three critics on (primarily) Continental fiction, even as their emphases took them in directions quite different from my own: René Girard on the triangular permutations of desire that give psychological and formal shape to the "great" examples of Western fiction; Leo Bersani on the hierarchical "order of significant [realist] form" that is served by an ideology of the stable self; and, most germane to my subject matter, Tony Tanner on the form-breaking impact of adultery in three European texts. In contending that "breaks" in the social structure of marriage have precipitated the dismantling of nineteenth-century realist form, Tanner's argument and mine share identical axes; the crucial distinction between our viewpoints, as will later become clearer, hinges on my belief that literary occasions of adultery have just as often ensured novelistic stability as disrupted it, serving as a "safety valve" through which a socially approved, and literarily inscribed, masculine double standard may be vented. In this listing of debts, a final acknowledgment is due to Peter Brooks, whose theories of narrative representation and desire have confirmed my own gut feelings about the dynamics of plotting in a version more eloquent than I could ever hope to repeat.[37]

The five chapters that follow will thus begin the open-ended process of exploring the simultaneously radical and conservative impulses in the novel that have spilled over into its persistent thematizing of love. As a genre existing on the boundaries of contemporaneity, in Bakhtin's phrase, and engendered from the multiple intersections of felt realities and produced ideologies, the novel has inevitably centered on that most "lived" of human experiences, those erotic bonds with others that in a profound sense confirm our sense of personal identity while constructing the very terms by which we (mis)perceive reality, self, and others. In an analogous observation relevant to the fictions of love and self promulgated in the Anglo-American literary and social heritage, Nancy Miller has written of the "difficulty of curing plot of life, and life of certain plots."[38] All the countercurrents that will be enumerated in the following pages, in reworking these intertwined dictates of life and plot, of gender and genre, have alternately exposed and—at least for brief spaces of time—exploded the ubiquity of the marriage ideal in the novel. In the process the counter-marriage novel has also undermined the closed narrative enterprise, the stable structures, underlying the novel's marriage tradition. At such moments the doubled heritage of radical and conservative impulse informing the making of fiction becomes most transparent, revealing the importance of the issues at stake in the hypothetical "war" of perspectives assigned to Rhoda Nunn and Henry James at the beginning of this chapter. I hope that the outcome will include more of those form-breaking innovations in narrative technique that have revitalized not only the life of fiction but also the life that fiction portrays.

Part One

Tradition
Marital Ideology and Novelistic Form

Men make their own history but
they do not make it just as they please.

Marx, *The Eighteenth Brumaire*

Chapter Two

The Emergence of a Literary Ideal of Romantic Marriage

A Historical Perspective

But I am greatly surprised that you wish to misapply the term "love" [*amor*] to that marital affection [*affectio maritalis*] which husband and wife are expected to feel for each other . . . since everybody knows that love can have no place between husband and wife. . . . For what is love but an inordinate desire to receive passionately a furtive and hidden embrace?

Andreas Capellanus, *The Art of Courtly Love* (circa 1180)[1]

Love is the life and soule of marriage.

William Whately, *The Bride-bush* (1617)[2]

But as 'tis proposed here, Whether we may Marry such as we *cannot Love*, 'tis beyond all doubt, and must be Answer'd in the Negative, since such a practice wou'd be both the most *cruel* and imprudent thing in the World—*Society* is the main-End of *Marriage*, *Love* is the bond of *Society*, without which there can neither be found in that State *Pleasure*, or *Profit*, or *Honour*.

Advice column, *The Athenian Mercury* (1691)[3]

The tradition of love and marriage in the Anglo-American novel did not arise, sui generis, with the publication of *Pamela*. Behind it lies a rich history of literary precedent and lineage in Western culture extending from the twelfth-century troubadour lyric to the often lurid "amatory novellas" churned out by Samuel Richardson's near contemporaries. It would be impossible to attempt an authoritative social history of seven hundred years of evolving marital norms and all their literary manifestations here. What can be accomplished, however, in a way that bears much more directly on the interplay of tradition and counter-tradition in the comparatively brief history of the English-speaking novel, is to trace the evolution of the major literary archetypes, or paradigms, of romantic and marital relationship that the previous chapter has shown to be constitutive of the novelistic ideal of happy endings. The continuities, transformations, and contradictions that mark these representations attest to the complexity of literature's relation to history. At times the direct product of cultural and social developments and at other times the prophetic anticipation of realities to come, these literary models of love have also occasionally originated in nothing more tangible than the collective wish-fulfilling powers of an epoch's subconscious fantasies. While the following pages emphasize the imaginative, intellectual, and ultimately synchronic manifestations of this evolving love ethic—a perspective inevitably reducing the intricate causality of the economic, social, and political forces lying behind them—this should not be taken to imply that such sweeping historical change only happens in or for literature and ideas; behind literature, indeed behind history itself, there always remains the irrecoverable story of actual people who have felt emotions and acted upon desires for which there has never been an adequate word or name.

As the variety of epigraphs to this chapter might suggest, a tremendous distance separates the Continental ethos of courtly love, theoretically grounded in the irreconcilable opposition of passionate desire and utilitarian marriage, and the specifically English ideal of romantic wedlock uniting these poles—an ideal that arose as a philosophical and religious concept in the late sixteenth century and became, by and large, an accepted popular belief by the mid-eighteenth century. It goes without saying that the overt relation of the sexes, especially in regard to the status of women, underwent large-scale transformations in this span of time, as constructions of gender and the distribution of power within romantic and familial relationships shifted to accommodate evolving social, political, economic, and religious contexts. But beneath this history of seemingly constant change, a curiously static, transhistorical conception, which we have already noted, of man and woman as hierarchical "opposites" persists in cultural iconography and in literary language, archetype, and "story." Whether cast in terms of antagonistic polarity, masked in the rhetoric of complementary balance, or celebrated as "companionate" harmony—roughly the historical progression by which such constructs have evolved—the notion of sexual attraction as the product of fundamentally opposite, rather than simply different, sexual beings has infiltrated nearly all fictional conventions for representing romance. Moreover, as the discussion of ideological formations in chapter 1 has suggested, the implications of this constant dichotomization of the sexes have been twofold: to uphold as "natural" mutually exclusive definitions of "masculine" and "feminine" behavior and spheres, whatever the varying attributes allotted to either gender in any given period; and, more deviously, to conceal under the trope of oppositional "balance" the sexual asymmetries inherent in a hierarchical order based on male dominance and female suppression.

Historians of love as a social and literary phenomenon have almost uniformly proclaimed the period in which they specialize as *the* revolutionary epoch that decisively breaks from an oppressive conception of heterosexual relationship. Each age, indeed, has seen its important advances: in the High and Late Medieval periods, the elevation of women as worthy of the deepest love; in Renaissance England, the humanist focus on harmonious concord; in the age of Johnson, the valorization of friendship in marriage; in our century, the loosening of prohibitions on premarital sexual expression. But for critics to view as absolutely "new" those conceptions of romantic affiliation that have actually maintained, in ever more complicated guises, patriarchal assumptions of sexual duality and hierarchy points to a danger incurred in writing period studies: the tendency is to praise the innovations that arise in the short run rather than to measure these against larger transhistorical formations. In many ways the oversights of such criticism simply reproduce a very real tension endemic to each of the historical periods leading to the emergence of the ideal of romantic wedlock as practiced and fictive reality. For in each epoch what is a genuinely revolutionizing and antisocial aspect of an evolving love ethos is paradoxically absorbed into the very fabric of its society—a process that calls to mind the novel's simultaneous and contradictory drives toward radical expression and maintenance of the status quo. It is this tension, subtly interfused into the images of desire and archetypes of union to which we shall now turn, that is responsible for creating, as its legacy to later fiction, a gallery of love's multiple and often conflicting faces.

Permutations of the Courtly Love Tradition

For those doubting the pertinence of worshipful knights and pedestaled ladies to the novel's marriage tradition, it is instructive to take account of the parallels that have been drawn between the rise of what we now call "courtly love" in late eleventh-century Provence and of romantic love in eighteenth-century England. Both epochs witnessed a rare event in the secular history of Western thought: the breakthrough into the emotional, psychic, and social lives of their dominant classes (the aristocracy in one, the middle class in the other) of a potentially revolutionizing ethos of sexual yet sacred love. And, more relevant to our purposes, both social movements were accompanied, if not in large part instigated, by the nearly simultaneous creation of innovative modes of literary discourse (the troubadour lyric and trouvère romance in the former, the novel in the latter) for the express purpose of celebrating passion as a valid shaping force both of personality and of personal interaction between the sexes.[4]

The extent to which *amour courtois* existed as a real phenomenon beyond literary convention remains open to speculation, like its origins; our major evidence remains fifty extant manuscripts and the knowledge of about 460 troubadour poets, the majority of whom espoused the convention "that every knight must have a mistress and every married woman [her] cavalier."[5] The most "radical" implication of this new creed—even if only as an imaginative construct—was that the female sex, after centuries of official depreciation as man's inferior, the cause of his fall, and a lascivious creature of the flesh, was now viewed as worthy of his profound love. Couched both in erotic and in spiritual terms, such an attitude dominates the rhyming lyric forms devised by the troubadour poets to encapsulate their desire for and worship of the female Beloved: the lyric moment generally focuses on and fixes the image of the idealized Lady as an elevated, often unattainable object of desire. "[I] cannot keep from loving her whose favors / I shall not have," one of the most famous troubadours, Bernart de Ventadorn, confesses; "[she] left me / not a thing but my desire / and a desiring heart."[6] With the spread of the chivalric virtues and ideals promulgated by the courtly love ethic to the courts of northern France, the development of another literary form, the verse-romance of the trouvères, soon followed, projecting into time and space the narrative possibilities inherent in the courtly poet's adoration, anguish, and lust; by stressing the *active* pursuit of passion, the medieval romance became the first imaginative literature of length in Western culture to make love the motivating cause, or "desire," activating its narrative design.[7]

Such an emphasis foregrounded the theme of adultery already implicit in the convention of vassal-poet worshiping his lord's lady. Thus the plots of Chrétien de Troyes's retellings of Arthurian legend and the several versions of the Tristan and Isolde story hinge on structures of infinitely deferred because illicit desire, giving rise to a construction of passion that was to have lasting consequences for Continental fictions inheriting the medieval ethos. Although commentators have endlessly debated whether the courtly code made the actual practice of adultery a foregone conclusion, the more relevant point, as E. Talbot Donaldson has argued, is the fact that the posture—imagined or real—of worshiping a generally married paragon with whom a permanently fulfilling attachment was therefore unlikely predisposed the lover to conceive of desire as "a state of idealized frustration."[8] Likewise, Denis de Rougemont has theorized that desiring, rather than consummation, became a literary end in itself, even in later medieval romances where sexual union is achieved; it is the fragility, the doomed temporality, of Tristan and Isolde's or Lancelot and Guinevere's adulterous affair, rather than its brief fulfillment, that comes to define the motive force that generates both their grand passion and the elaborately postponed plots of their narrative recountings.[9]

The threat to established order posed by such passionate desire becomes obvious when its literary celebration is contrasted to the Christian and utilitarian concepts of marriage, which provided medieval society's accepted mode of male-female bonding.[10] The Christian symbol of "marriage" permeated medieval life on any number of levels: a "coupling" of spirit and flesh within the individual was deemed necessary for salvation; depending on the outcome of this union, the soul was figured as either the spouse of

Christ or an adulterer with the Devil; collectively, all souls partici-
pated in the "marriage" of Christ and his church, which in turn
provided the model for institutionalized marriages.[11] In accor-
dance with Pauline precept, wives were instructed to submit to
their husbands because "the husband is the head of the wife, even
as Christ is the head of the church" (Ephesians 5:22–23). The principle of subordination structuring this analogy, of course, reflected
the hierarchy of power enforced not only between husband and
wife but also between feudal lord and vassal: in a profound sense,
the marital order sanctioned by Christian doctrine, however contradiction-ridden in practice, functioned as an essential stay of medieval society itself.

Indeed, as a brief detour into sociological and anthropological
theory makes clear, the marriage rite in almost all cultures plays a
central role in sustaining a structured social order. Aside from its
sexual and sacramental functions, marriage forms a crucial socioeconomic variable because of the value placed on legitimate progeny to ensure the passage of property from one owner to the next,
a drawing of boundaries prerequisite to organized community.[12]
In addition, as Claude Lévi-Strauss argues in *The Savage Mind,* the
potentially oppositional forces of nature and culture are fragilely,
uniquely, held in check by the mediation of a system of marriage
that depends upon the harnessing of female *biological* productivity
as a form of economic exchange through *cultural* designations of
femaleness (woman as wife, daughter, whore).[13] Such a system of
exchange, moreover, is a specifically patriarchal formation, as
Gayle Rubin's widely influential extension of Lévi-Strauss's findings indicates: the "traffic in women" as "property" to be exchanged via marriage reinforces the power of men as the ruling
class of the social structure. The economic and political motives
determining marriage among the feudal aristocracy from the tenth
to the thirteenth centuries fit the criteria of Rubin's model quite
closely. For to the extent that medieval marriage in the ruling class
legally and theoretically "happened" less as a contract between a
man and a woman than as a transaction between men, solidifying
their own territorial bonds, its practice helped enforce the secondary status of women already espoused by church authorities and
enforced by popular prejudices.[14]

Given the utilitarian function of most marriages within the construct of a feudally based social system, the passionate language of courtly love thus introduced a social discourse initially foreign to its principles of order. Exactly *how* a feudal society based on contractual hierarchy managed to harness the potentially disruptive force of a love ethos advocating the violation of contractual relationships anticipates the literary recuperation of similar tensions in later novelistic representations of love. Foremost, courtly love usurped or augmented a traditional function of marriage to the extent that it too came to exist as a signifying code of civilization, a cultural medium shaping literature, language, and social modes of behavior. The system of chivalry that ensued from the formalization and ritualization of love in the decades immediately following the inception of troubadour verse, for instance, was facilitated by the many tenets of love service—dedication, faithfulness, self-sacrifice to the beloved—which simply reformulated the feudal conception of obedience to one's superior. Thus, the service of love could easily be deflected into heroic or national action, as many romances illustrate: political enemies as well as dragons could be overwhelmed in the name of one's lady.[15] The love ethos was also appropriated in the church's proliferating cults of the Virgin as a "beloved" and in the eroticized cosmographies of creation (conflating the divine creative urge and Eros) that emanated from the Chartres school of theologians.[16] The discourse of courtly love, like the code of manners that Susan B. Winnett has analyzed for a later age, hence became a vehicle allowing the unspeakable—the disruptive potential of passionate desire—"to maintain itself in the 'half-uttered' condition of imperfect repression which makes it available but not dangerous" to cultural and literary representation.[17]

By such modes of containment, courtly love therefore came to embody two paradoxical extremes at once, in that "an intensely private experience," the inner emotional life, "[was] made the ground of social well being" and the basis of public taste:[18] the same paradox, as we have seen, characterizes the novel as genre and romantic love as one of its subjects. The courtly ideal, thus socialized and integrated, was without a doubt constantly and inevitably betrayed by a much more diverse and contradictory everyday historical reality than ideological formations are wont to disclose. Nonetheless, it is exactly as an *ideal* that the idea of courtly love has left its mark, engendering a series of images and archetypes so thriving in the imagination that they have repeatedly been used as the model for the experience of love and passion in the world of Western thought.

Among the inherited archetypes important because of their continuations and transformations in later novelistic tradition, figures of total union, of desire and the obstructions engendering desire, and of sexual duality as a hierarchical balance permeate medieval romance literature. The first of these, the yearning of lovers to reach a total "oneness" of being—enduring in the courtship plot's momentum toward the "happy ending" that simultaneously functions as a return to a narrative immobility or "oneness"—is often expressed in imagistic equivalents reaching back to Plato's *Symposium*. For in Aristophanes' fable of the origin of sexual differentiation and desire, the severed "halves" of originally unified beings endlessly seek each other in an attempt to "grow into one."[19] Encapsulated in this allegory, we have, to borrow the oft-cited analogy derived from Roman Jakobson's linguistic analysis, the basic constituents of narrative and lyric: the metonymic drive, constitutive of plot itself, toward a summing up in metaphoric "wholeness-in-oneness" that is the poetic end and aim of narrative. The illusion of such oneness characterizes the moment of love's inception in Gottfried's Tristan and Isolde, for example, when their hearts instantaneously cleave together: "They who were two and divided now became one and united." The rest of the plot in effect becomes an effort to make this initial mystical merging of beings a literal reality.[20]

But the realization that the beloved will always remain a literally separate self can create despair at the height of bliss. So Chaucer's Troilus and Criseyde, no doubt like many human lovers before and since, discover at the moment of sexual congress—"syn they were oon . . . and passed wo with joie contrepeise"—and hence Troilus alternates between wishing to possess Criseyde totally and calling upon death to relieve him from his impossible desire to achieve complete fusion with her.[21] Erotic ecstasy, after all, is in many respects an obliteration of self-consciousness, or in psychoanalytical terms a displacement of the wish to return to a nondifferentiated symbiosis with the mother that would necessarily involve a kind of "death" of individual being. Desire at its most extreme, therefore,

THE COURTLY LOVE TRADITION

may paradoxically engender a suicidal longing for the *dissolution* of identity as the only means of overcoming otherness and achieving ultimate union; taken to its extreme, this self-destructive urge leads to the psychic shadowland of the literary *Liebestod,* which represents love-death as the perfection of erotic and romantic oneness. Embedded in this construction of passion is a complementary assumption equally destructive of individual autonomy: namely, that a person without a beloved is necessarily incomplete, a half-self like one of Aristophanes' sundered *androgynoi.* These self-negating facets of the archetype of passionate totality will resurface in the tensions between self and love enacted time and again in novelistic tradition.

At the same time, the inverse side of the urge toward romantic union is the equally strong compulsion, evinced throughout the courtly and later Continental canons of literature, *to avoid union* and prolong the ecstatic state of desire in and of itself. On a human level, of course, the reasons for avoiding union are manifold: a subconscious awareness that *total* union can never occur; the fear of the disappointment that often follows the attainment of a highly desired goal; a begrudging acknowledgment of the impossibility of having a complete relationship with someone else's spouse; a selfish fear of loss of self. Moreover, since desire is by definition a mental condition, a longing for that which has yet to be attained in reality, the postponing of fulfillment increases desire by nurturing in the lover an exaggerated sense of its importance; as Lotte tells Werther in Goethe's novel, "I fear that it is just the impossibility of possessing me that makes your desire for me so fascinating."[22] And if the nature of courtly love presupposes the thwarting of consummation to some unconscious extent, either the lovers in or the writer of medieval romance must invent obstacles to postpone its achievement. Thus the Tristan and Isolde story is structured by an interminable series of separations and partings, and thus the final scene of Chrétien's *Lancelot* ends with the ladies of the court, all hopelessly enamored of the tale's unattainable hero (who is already pledged to the Queen), abjuring marriage forever: better to forgo future happiness than risk the cessation of prolonged desire.

Desire waylaid by obstructions gives rise, in turn, to a complex matrix of emotions that turn upon the masochistic suffering experienced by the courtly lover, suffering undergone for the beloved's sake as well as the suffering inherent in the act of loving an object that proves unattainable. What follows is an idealization of the *pain* of love: unhappy or unsatisfied love paradoxically becomes interpreted as an ultimate expression of true feeling for one another. The fact that people today *expect* love to be frustrating—and hence idealize the suffering concomitant with that frustration—attests to the persistence of this masochistic underside of the medieval archetype of passionate love. Looking ahead to the paradigmatic formulations of the marriage plot, where seduction and rape motifs coexist with the wedlock ideal, we may press these ambivalent characteristics further. Desiring to possess for its own sake of course becomes narcissistic; the lover finds himself or herself moving in a totally egocentric world, governed only by the self-gratifying thrill of possessing *any* "other." But if desire is mediated, as in the adulterous triangle of courtly convention, emotions of envy and jealousy may easily overcome the frustrated lover, transforming love into a hatred intensified by the sadistic desire to persecute both the longed-for object and any human obstacle blocking the way to sole possession of it. So the twelfth-century commentator Richard St. Victor understood these entangled emotional states: "Often bursts of anger arise between lovers . . . and when true grounds of antagonism are not there they invent false ones, often not even probable. In this condition love often turns into hate, since nothing can satisfy their longing for each other . . . and in a wondrous, or rather in a wretched way, out of desire springs hate, and out of hate desire . . . [so that] the flame of love burns more fiercely through their opposition than it could through their being at peace."[23]

The need for obstructions to stimulate romantic longing, the proximity of love and hatred where desire is triangular, and the possibility of violence against the desired object: all these discordant notes help explain the frequency with which medieval writers and their literary heirs have tended to conceive of sexual union as a balance wrested from oppositional forces considered inherent in male and female genders. This way of conceiving sexual difference can be traced back to the cosmographical principle of *discordia concors* embedded in the most primordial of Western creation myths, which generally involve two warring godheads characterized as parents of the universe. Thus sexual dichotomization is introduced into the schema, with the hierogymous marriage of Sky and Earth,

Day and Night, yielding the harmony of created life. In the more sophisticated Greek pantheon, this sexual opposition is typically displaced onto sacred and profane elements (the love of Cupid for Psyche, Zeus's ravishment of mortal women). While this intermingling of divine and human loves derives from the deeply rooted human feeling that earthly love is in some way also a transcendent experience, it nonetheless posits male and female elements as poles in an opposition weighted in favor of the superior "masculine" forces of light, heaven, spirit. The pagan understanding of *discordia concors* intersects, moreover, with medieval Christian belief in the essential duality of soul and body within the individual subject, a duality translated into a male-female opposition of which Adam and Eve are the prototypes. If Christianity itself posited a healing of the body/soul discord through the mediation of Christ, the New Testament also conceived of human marriage (taking its model from Christ's mediating example) as a healing of a vast array of dualities brought into providential concord: the totality combining spirit and matter, divinity and mortal, lord and subject, in such a way that man and woman, however mutually aligned after the fact, seemed rooted in an *elemental* binary opposition.[24]

Even though the courtly precepts of love stand counter to those of Christian marriage in almost all other significant aspects, it is extremely telling that the language of passionate desire illustrates a similar ideological commitment to the concept of sexual polarity as the basis of romantic concord. It is not mere coincidence that love-making in both lyric and narrative courtly literature is constantly imaged as a siege or battle. The entire allegorical premise of *Roman de la Rose,* for example, leading to the Lover's climactic assault on the "castle" that is Belacueil's chastity, equates the sexual act of love with the violence of war: "I had to assail it [her maidenhead] vigorously . . . throw myself against it often. . . . If you had seen me jousting . . . you would have been reminded of Hercules when he wanted to dismember Cacus." Similarly, the rhetorical paradoxes of courtly discourse, intended to evoke the inexpressible, reveal instead a pervasive inability to conceive of love's harmony aside from terms of often violent polarity. "Love is hated peace and loving hate," the Lover complains to Lady Reason in *Roman de la Rose;* "It is disloyal loyalty and loyal disloyalty . . . [s]weet hell and heaven of sorrow. . . . It is the springtime full of cold winter."[25] Whether envisioned as antagonistic contraries or merely complementary opposites, the paradigm of the sexes common to both Christian and courtly lore stems from a dualistic conception of *discordia concors* that posits essentially different, opposed beings, incomplete without each other.

The representation of the sexes emerging from the courtly ideology concurrently maintained a hierarchy of male dominance despite the reversal ostensibly involved in elevating the lady to a position of social and spiritual superiority vis-à-vis her lover. The very generic forms of the courtly lyric and medieval romance attest to the reality disguised by this "reversal." For the male subject hypothesized by medieval love literature, by *allowing himself* to suffer mental woe and undergo trials for his lady, remained in *practical* charge of events; his very role as supplicant lover even increased the degree to which the woman became an anonymous object—now of desire rather than of scorn. In troubadour verse it is typically the male poet who addresses the woman; her representation is shaped entirely by his emotional and imaginative needs. "For her I shiver and tremble, for / the fine love that I have for her," Guillem IX writes in a solipsistic outpouring echoed nearly a century later by Arnaut Daniel: "I love her with fire / seek her with such / excess of desire / I feel I float."[26] Likewise, it is typically the knight whose valorous deeds dictate the structure of the romance-quest plot, while the lady most often remains offstage, her immobility befitting her role as exemplar of virtue. Although the literary idealization of woman as the personification of heavenliness did break from the popular conception of all women as treacherous Eves, true concern for the unpleasant realities of female existence under feudal patriarchy is by and large absent from courtly literature. As Huizinga wryly observes, "pity took on a stereotyped and factitious form, in the sentimental fiction of the knight delivering the virgin."[27] Positively, the chivalric roles accorded the sexes in the courtly tradition led to a tempering of male authoritarianism by a new emotiveness and dedication to women, while the passive situation of the female became on one level a personal source of power and, on another, part of the new estimation of her worth in male eyes. Nonetheless, the historical inequality of the sexes remained intact, with the traditional supremacy of men countering the "sentimental fiction" of woman's superiority: in literary avatars, at least, she had simply become an object for idealized desire, as opposed to sheer lust.

The Courtly Legacy in Continental Fictions of Desire and Adultery

The influence of the courtly model of all-consuming and idealizing passion on subsequent European love ideology reaches its apogee in the pervasive archetypes of triangular love and frustrated desire characterizing Continental fiction since the seventeenth century. However falsifying of actual medieval mores, Capellanus's distinction between *amor* and *affectio maritalis* determines, to large degree, both the overt themes and basic structure of such internationally diverse texts as Rousseau's *Julie, ou la nouvelle Héloïse* (1761), de Laclos's *Les liaisons dangereuses* (1782), Goethe's *Die Leiden des jungen Werthers* (1774), and Flaubert's *Madame Bovary* (1856–57). A momentary excursion into the region of passionate self-abandon demarcated by these four works will provide a useful paradigm against which to measure the wedlock ideal evolved in English fiction and its American offspring.

Like sides of a diptych, Rousseau and de Laclos's eighteenth-century epistolary novels reflect, respectively, the spiritualized and erotic faces of courtly passion. Rousseau's heroine, initially a paragon of virginal and then of maternal virtue, mirrors the womanly ideal of the French troubadours and of the later Italian school of the *dolce stil nuovo*. In a fitting symmetry, her lover performs the part of archetypally solicitous servant of love, a role enforced by economic circumstances: difference in social rank makes the aristocratic Julie as unattainable to Saint-Preux as dependent knight ever found his master's lady. Given such protagonists, it is not surprising that their lovemaking continually evokes courtly traditions, as in the scene where Julie playfully makes Saint-Preux her obedient vassal: "There, my loyal vassal, on your knees before your lady and mistress. . . . You will swear faith to her and loyalty on every occasion . . . be acknowledged as sole vassal and loyal knight."[28] The passionately mannered language of their love letters is as indicative as their actions of the specter of courtly sentiment shaping their illusory sense of reality. For whenever Saint-Preux complains to Julie that her eyes "deal death to me" (27) or that it is his wish "only to be cured or to die" (27), he is indulging in familiar if clichéd love-conceit and paradox. Similarly, at the climactic moment of separation from her, he responds in Petrarchan tropes, "Alas! She has robbed me of everything, the cruel woman, and I love her the more for it. The more miserable she makes me, the more I find her perfect" (187). Obviously, this masochistic lover revels in the idealized frustration of experiencing his beloved as an unattainable other.

The first half of the novel celebrates the mutual passion of soul mates who desire an impossibly total union of Platonic archetype. "Come, oh my soul," Saint-Preux beguiles Julie, "into your lover's arms to reunite the two halves of our single being" (75). "Come, then, heart of my heart, life of my life," Julie responds once she has decided to commit the fatal transgression, "come and be reunited to yourself" (122). True to convention, their love momentarily creates a solipsistic world that renders "[a]ll the rest of the universe . . . empty" (286), and true to the example set by the most famous medieval lovers, their extreme desire is never fulfilled except by the one tantalizing encounter. Shortly thereafter their affair is terminated by Julie's swift capitulation to the authority of her father upon his command that she marry the older, nonromantic Wolmar; this transaction, in which Julie is passed from paternal hands to the arms of a father-substitute, provides a classic example of Lévi-Strauss's claims about marriage as an essentially male commerce.[29] In the second half of the novel, Julie's middle-aged repudiation of her youthful passion and her promulgation of marriage's efficacy show the two states to be as antithetical in her mind as in Capellanus's treatise: "What has long misled me and what perhaps still misleads you [she tells Saint-Preux] is the thought that love is necessary to form a happy marriage." Opting instead for "a very tender attachment," "though not precisely love" (261), Julie divorces the very states which the English novel strives, often uneasily, to join.

Another result of Julie's arranged match is the potentially adulterous triangular situation that ensues upon Wolmar's perverse incorporaton of Saint-Preux, the rejected suitor, into the family circle to test Julie's fidelity. It is revealing that Wolmar's superficially "enlightened" philosophy of marital relationship turns out to hinge on the most traditional of frameworks, each partner serving to balance the other's opposite, gender-identified needs and lacks. "Each of us is precisely *what the other needs*," Julie explains to her old lover, "he instructs me and I enliven him. We are of greater value together, and it seems we are destined to have only a single mind between us, of which he is the understanding and I the will" (262; emphasis added).[30] Julie thus exchanges a passionate model of all-encompassing oneness, the "single being" formed with Saint-Preux, for a de-eroticized oneness of domestic being. Hence, although the text has expended half its length in celebrating the transcendent glories of illicit passion, it works in the end to uphold honorable marriage as "the true basis of society."[31] And, as such, the schizophrenic separation of passion and marriage inherited from medieval literature is reproduced in the novel's basic structure. The closest Rousseau can come to resolving these antithetical states is by embodying both of them in one figure, his heroine. He thereby exploits the contradictions already present in the eighteenth-century ideology of womanhood, inscribing Julie into the literally split body of his text both as idealized object of desire and as sentimentalized paragon of motherhood; by making the narrative's end coeval with Julie's death, he dissolves contradiction into the metaphoric stasis of eternity.

The libidinous underside of such an idealized love as Saint-Preux and Julie's becomes Laclos's focus in *Les liaisons dangereuses*. Indeed, as Denis de Rougement has astutely observed, the Don Juan seducer-figure is but a debauched Tristan,[32] and in Laclos's world of multiple sexual intrigue, Julie and Saint-Preux's chivalric ideal is relegated to a mere subplot, where it becomes the subject of erotic parody. The more prevalent attitude is exhibited by Laclos's Don Juan, vicomte de Valmont, who self-consciously manipulates the guise of suave lover to seduce his various female prey. In this mannered world, the artifice inherent in the refined game of courtly love has become *only* appearance, giving way to a war for sexual mastery that makes a plaything of passion and a trifle of love. Male and female are pitted against each other in a battle of mutual erotic destruction that receives its definitive statement in the competition of Valmont and the marquise de Merteuil, Laclos's other main principal, to see which of the two can seduce the greatest number of the opposite sex.

Valmont's two goals—to seduce the novel's virginal ingenue and

A LITERARY IDEAL OF ROMANTIC MARRIAGE

commit adultery with its paragon of married virtue—expose the sadistic underpinnings of an ideal of love based on traditional constructions of femininity. Indeed, it is the latter victim's married estate that sparks Valmont's perverse desire for revenge against the female sex for being an alien "other" that all his attempts at possession will never really suppress: "her religious devotion, her conjugal love, her austere principles. That is what I am attacking; that is the enemy worthy of me."[33] The guilt and mental disintegration of Madame de Tourvel, once Valmont's conquest succeeds, make all too apparent the paradigmatic tension between sexual love and marriage in this Continental fiction. A measure of the distance between the viewpoint of Laclos and that of the English Samuel Richardson—whose Lovelace is a similarly unremitting rake—is that the French author has chosen to stage his plot around the male's excitement in the chase itself, rather than the besieged female victim's struggle to maintain her virtue. Consequently, *Les liaisons dangereuses* depicts desire denuded of the civilized veneer that covertly permits its operation and made a weapon of violence in "this unequal struggle" of man against woman—the governing rule of which, according to the marquise de Merteuil, is strictly oppositional and gender-based: "our fortune," she says of women, "is not to lose and your misfortune not to win" (176). In the ideological framework provided by this permutation of passionate love, the deck is stacked not only against all satisfaction, but particularly against women.

While *La nouvelle Héloïse* promotes an eighteenth-century version of the ideal lady and *Les liaisons dangereuses* the carnality of sexual pursuit, Goethe's *Werther* repeats the classic triangular situation of medieval romance by situating its idealized heroine, Lotte, between young Werther, who loves her with total passionate abandon, and Albert, her sober fiancé and future husband: here, in a repeating configuration, are Julie, Saint-Preux, and Wolmar. Whereas Rousseau "solves" his love triangle with Julie's climactic drowning, it is now the man who gains the orgasm of death: since "one of us three must go," Werther eagerly acquiesces, "I sacrifice myself for you" (110). Tellingly, the morbid desire that propels Werther to suicidal despair is linked by the heroine herself, as we have seen, to his fascination with "the impossibility of ever possessing me," of realizing his love *in life* (108). The lines thus strictly drawn between love and marriage, the only alternative to adultery is the consummation of self-immolation, and in a repetition of the *Liebestod* theme of medieval romance, Werther commits suicide with the solipsistic expectation of achieving with Lotte "one eternal embrace" (121) in a sinless heaven beyond social strictures.

Madame Bovary forms a consummately self-conscious statement on the continuing influence of courtly passion upon the nineteenth-century European imagination. Emma's youthful fantasies of love have been nurtured on pulp romances and gothic tales that have preserved the conventions of medieval romance: "They were all about love, lovers, sweethearts, persecuted ladies fainting in lonely pavilions, postilions killed at every relay, horses ridden to death on every page, sombre forests, heart-aches, vows, sobs, tears and kisses, little boatrides by moonlight, nightingales in shady groves, gentlemen brave as lions, gentle as lambs, virtuous as no one ever was, always well-dressed, and weeping like fountains."[34] Her desires inflamed by these mediating images of passion, Emma falls in love with Bovary; once married to him, however, Emma seeks refuge from the disappointments of prosaic wedded life in dreams of yet a better "true love," which she in turn, and in turn again, attempts to find in a reality that only frustrates her. Rather than admit that the exhilarating passion she seeks is an impossible—or, more acutely, fictional—illusion, Emma increasingly desires love for its own sake. "Don't see them; don't go out," she peevishly remonstrates with her second lover, Léon, in an attempt to shut out all but her solipsistic dream, "only think of us; love me!" (205). The more desire overwhelms her perception of reality, the more Emma encloses herself in a fictional existence of her own creation, a point tacitly made in Léon's "reading" of his lover's self-image: "She was the mistress of all the novels, the heroine of all the dramas, the vague 'she' of all the volumes of verse" consumed in her quest to know perfect love (192). The final scenes with Léon at the inn in Rouen make painfully clear that the only consummation for Emma's insatiate longing is death, and toward that end Flaubert has structured the course of her tragic decline and his novel.

Desire and passion, then, dominate the great examples of Western European love fiction, generally arising in contexts that prohibit or disregard their fulfillment in marriage. Thus, critics generally speak of the "novel of adultery" to typify the Continental tradition for dealing with subjects of love. Tony Tanner has argued that the role of the adulteress suggests a fatal "break" in the rigid system of bourgeois realism;[35] in general, however, I would argue that the nearly universal *failure* of the adulterous affair in this tradition functions closurally to reinstate social norms, much as marriage in the English tradition comes to validate its social order. Sanctioned by a prevailing double standard that allows men outlets for their sexual dissatisfactions while punishing women for the same, adultery is permitted, both socially and fictionally speaking, within a system of containment guaranteed by the tragic outcome of the affair.[36] To see how the romanticization of love became a romanticization of marriage rather than adultery, it is necessary to turn to the Renaissance period in England, with its visions of a new ideal and new modes of relationship.

The Synthesis of Love and Marriage in Renaissance and Puritan England

A concurrence of historical circumstance, socioeconomic causation, and intellectual thought made Renaissance English culture particularly receptive to a more enlightened view of the affective possibilities of wedlock. Out of this matrix emerged two factors significant to the future development of the archetypes of love relationship we have been tracing. First, as men and women began to recognize a greater potential for lasting emotional commitment in marriage, a shift in emphasis from "polarity" to terms like "harmony," "mutuality," and, more radically, "likeness" as bases for conjugal happiness began to punctuate the language of sermons, advice manuals, and literature. Second, as the Renaissance conception of the "self" rose in prominence, literary representations of matrimony began to assume a new symbolic role, signifying the apex of the protagonist's growth and acquisition of an adult sense of identity. Although the theoretical equation of personal fulfillment with the event of marriage contained seeds enough for future revolt, the literary celebration of permanent romantic involvement in wedlock as a discovery of selfhood more immediately inaugurated a trope that was to provide the ideological center and the ideal end of the future English novel.

One cannot stress too greatly the importance of the historical shift from Catholicism to Protestantism in helping to shape the English attitude toward connubial relationship. More specifically, the turn toward a more religious glorification of matrimony as "an hie, holye, and blessed order of life, ordayned not of man, but of God," was the result of the Protestant reorientation that gained momentum after Henry VIII's break with the papacy in 1535.[37] The promotion of the idea of holy matrimony as the highest human good became a timely tool of Protestant propaganda, countering the traditional Catholic ideal of celibacy with a new ideal—that of "a state . . . farre more excellent," the Puritan William Perkins argues in his scriptural defense of wedlock, *Christian Oeconomie* (1609), "than the condition of a single life."[38] In practical terms, the rejection of priests as intercessors meant that the everyday practice of marriage was given a new significance as a living testament of one's love for, fidelity to, and relationship with God: devotion to one's mate became a potent sign of grace. Likewise, the shift from church to household as the primary agency for religious education made the success of the domestic partnership more crucial to the future salvation of the entire family.[39] These various incentives to honor marriage necessarily helped create a more affective bond between newlyweds. As a familiar Puritan adage stated the fact, "First, he must choose his love, & then he must love his choice: this is the oyle which maketh all things easie."[40] The result of the Puritan movement's concerted promulgation of marital virtues was an ideal that resounds throughout the popular sermon tracts, marriage guides, and domestic manuals of the age: "Love is the Marriage vertue, which singes Musicke to [the lovers'] whole life," the author of *Preparative to Mariage* (1591) declares; "Love is the life and soule of marriage," the *Bride-bush* (1617) echoes.[41]

However, despite the Protestant elevation of marriage and the increased significance given the wife's role as religious educator, the hierarchical arrangement of the sexes resisted substantive change. If man and woman became one in marriage, as in the medieval archetype of total union, that "oneness" nonetheless included a natural hierarchy of parts. "Nature hath placed [such] an eminency in the male," writes the Puritan popularizer William Gouge, in *Of Domesticall Duties* (1622), "[that] where they [man and woman] are linked together in one yoake, it is given by nature that he should governe, she obey."[42] The same sentiment was not only repeated in the frequently read Anglican homily on marriage, dating from 1562, but stipulated in English law, for, as Blackstone's *Commentaries* explain, "husband and wife are one person in law: that is, the very being or legal existence of the woman is *suspended* during the marriage, or at least is incorporated and consolidated into that of the husband: under whose wing, protection, and cover, she performs every thing."[43] Both the rising status of marriage and continued subordination of women within its structure were reinforced by the wholesale reorganization of the basic family unit occurring in England from the early sixteenth century onward. The gradual shift from the extended family, or kin system, to the modern nuclear or conjugal concept, in which each newly married couple became an independent unit autonomously governing its domicile and progeny, was the product of vast economic and sociological developments, including the rise of capitalist enterprise with its emphasis on economic individualism. But while this restructuring reinforced the Protestant emphasis on the importance of marriage, it also increased the possibility of unchecked exploitation of wives by their husbands, a situation formerly mitigated by the extended family group. This rise in domestic patriarchy within the nuclear unit, mirrored on the national level by the move toward authoritarian monarchy in the seventeenth century, led to a revitalized archetype of the family as a microcosmic State; whence the Puritan preachers' praise of the home as "seminary of the Church and Commonwealth," a model school "wherein the first principles and grounds of government *and subjection* are learned: whereby men are fitted to greater matters in Church and Commonwealth."[44]

The increasing importance of the marriage rite as the signature of social order thus abetted the Puritan glorification of wedlock. On the positive side, of course, the upgrading of the affective relationship of wife and husband eased many individual circumstances of domestic tension or enmity, instilling a more cooperative sense of mission between mates. On the negative side, however, the more importance people attached to wedlock, the more they venerated those traditional aspects—including gender dichotomization, hierarchy, and largely separate spheres of activity—whose alteration would have entailed real change in existing power structures. And yet, ironically, it was some of the advances inaugurated in the name of enhanced social *stability*—namely, the increased status of the wife and the growing freedom allowed children in making a choice of mate—that were eventually to open the ideal to serious question. At the heart of the evolving English ethic, one thus finds a continuation of the tensions between innovation and stabilization characterizing the rise of the courtly tradition four centuries earlier. As in that period, the incorporation of new concepts succeeded because the Renaissance idea of the good marriage was made to seem central to an already existing, normative pattern of life.

These changes in the status of marriage in the period ranging from 1550 to 1675 were mirrored in several contemporary theories of romantic attraction. Especially relevant are those paradigms emanating from within the humanist movement, the imported philosophy of Italian love theoreticians, and the literary productions of Spenser, Shakespeare, and Milton. The humanist goal of exploring the full range of the individual human's potential for development and achievement, for instance, necessarily implied equivalent changes in modes of conceiving attributes of gender (and hence heterosexual relationship) as well as of the self. The important consequences that such changes held for the iconographic, and eventually literary, representation of man and woman in relationship are much in evidence in the courtier-book tradition—those humanist treatises on how to become the perfect, universal Renaissance gentleman in service of the state. Translated into English in 1561, Baldasaare Castiglione's *Il libro del Cortegiano* or *The Book of the Courtier,* a compendium of "modern" Renaissance thought mixed with medieval ideals of chivalry and classical virtues of decorum, espouses a contemporary sexual ideology comprising at once advancements and unshakably traditional tenets. For example, Castiglione's spokesperson, Il Magnifico, eloquently refutes signor Gaspare's misogynistic views on the innate inferiority and imperfection of women ("proven," Gaspare avows, by their wish to be men) by arguing that women are created *equally* as perfect as men. "Women do not wish to become men in order to make themselves more perfect," Il Magnifico continues, "but to gain their freedom and shake off tyranny that men have imposed on them by their one-sided tyranny." However, in face of this forceful criticism of gender inequity, Il Magnifico's conservative view of the separate roles proper to each sex is all the more revealing: "Just as it is very fitting that a man should display a certain robust and sturdy manliness, so it is well for a woman to have a certain soft and delicate tenderness, with an air of feminine sweetness in her every movement." Such asymmetrical role division, it turns out, is intrinsic to Castiglione's theory of romantic heterosexual relationship as a total, encompassing union (mirroring nature's "circle" of eternity) that *completes* what would otherwise be an incomplete, halved self. For, upholding the belief that "one sex alone shows imperfection," Il Magnifico argues not only that "male and female . . . go naturally together," but that "one cannot exist without the other." Hence, Castiglione's conception of romantic union ultimately rests on a notion of the sexes as opposite complements, echoing the medieval principle of *discordia concors* while emphasizing the complementary rather than the oppositional nature of the paradigm—a qualified "advance" that looks forward to one of sentimental fiction's prototypical images of reciprocal need as the basis of lasting union.[45]

England's version of the *Courtier,* Sir Thomas Elyot's *Boke Named the Governour* (1531), promotes a similarly deceptive archetype of sexual relationship as a putative "balance" of gender-related characteristics. For Elyot "the *necessary* conjunction" of the sexes "[in] matrimony" is best signified in the circular image, not of eternity, but of the dance. Although the end result "betokeneth concord," its harmony depends upon a traditional separation of sexual attributes, for a man "in his *natural* perfection is fierce, hardy, strong in opinion," a woman "mild, timorous, tractable, benign. . . . Wherefore, when we behold a man and woman dancing together, let us suppose there to be a concord of all the said qualities, being joined together, as I have set them in order. And the moving of the man would be more vehement, of the woman more delicate . . . signifying the courage and strength that ought to be in a man, and the pleasant soberness that should in in a woman."[46] Like Castiglione, Elyot respects the female sex and grants woman an equality of perfection, but that perfection is nonetheless rooted in characteristics hierarchically "inferior" to those attributed to the male, the leader of the "dance" that is marriage.

The valorization of wedded "concord," it thus becomes clear, did not automatically signal that a marriage of true minds or sexual equals was forthcoming. A contrasting archetype of attraction, however, based on theories of likeness rather than polarity, emerged from a group of Italian writers whose *trattati d'amore* or "love commentaries" on the Italian love poets were profoundly influenced by the rediscovery of Plato. Thus Marsilio Ficino, the love theoretician whose commentary on Plato's *Symposium* most influenced English thinkers, logically extended Aristophanes' allegory of the sundered halves of the self, seeking to reunite in passionate oneness, in order to argue the untraditional premise that "likeness generates love." That is, in looking for one's missing half, the lover is attracted to someone essentially *like*—because once part of—himself or herself: "When the loved one recognizes himself in the lover, he is forced to love him."[47] Ficino himself omits any specific applications of this theory to gender, which might indeed have been revolutionary; rather, like Castiglione and Elyot, he upholds the traditional archetype of "oneness" in postulating romantic union as a "whole" greater than its parts. Nonetheless, his hypothesis of romantic attraction lays the groundwork for a theory of individual and interiorized androgyny of the sort Spenser envisions in his Veiled Venus and her human prototype, Britomart, in *The Faerie Queene*. For in the interchange of reciprocal love called forth by lovers whose likenesses literally mirror each other, not only do two become one, but "*each of the two*, instead of [becoming] one alone, *becomes two*"[48]—which, in heterosexual alignments (the homosexual possibility of Plato's original myth being excised in Renaissance versions), is to say that each becomes both man and woman. However, in influential adaptations of Ficino (or Plato) other than Spenser's, the potentially radical implications for sexual roles of gender exchange within the individual and of "likeness" between the sexes were subordinated to the more acceptable implications of oneness as a metaphysical or spiritual rather than gender-related principle. This latter view of love union dominates later English metaphysical poetry, leading Donne, for one, to write that, in the ecstasy of union, "difference of sex no more we knew."[49] It also explains the popularity of iconographic representations of "the faire Hermaphrodite" as an image of how the "whole" that is marriage transcends absolute sexual difference, rather than as a utopian metaphor for the erasure of imposed sexual categories within the "wholeness" of the individual.[50] As with other progressive formulations evolved in the medieval and Renaissance periods, the concept of passionate likeness was fitted—however contradictorily—to an already existing norm of sexual relationship.

Given the changing social practices and the climate of ideas summarized above, it is no coincidence that Spenser's verse romance, Shakespeare's romantic comedies, and Milton's epic of the world's first lovers all envisioned a harmonious intersection between passionate love and institutional marriage and that all three embody that realization in their generic forms. While English metaphysical and Cavalier love poetry, owing greatly to a Petrarchan heritage, continued to promote many of the conventions of courtly love in relatively unchanged form, it is clear that the diachronic, spatially oriented genres of epic and drama provided a more congenial home for the marital ethos inherited from Chaucer, espoused in the Puritan ideology of holy wedlock, and inspiring humanistic and neo-Platonic theories of romantic harmony. One result was a wide-reaching reformulation of previous literary paradigms of love, marriage, and sexual identity into narrative conventions that were to become standard elements in the Anglo-American novel.[51]

Books 3 and 4 of *The Faerie Queene* and nearly all of Shakespeare's comedies not only reflect the increased emphasis on mutual love and meet companionship as essential components of ideal marriage, but also emphasize the process of courtship leading to marriage as the means to individual self-knowledge: adult identity is to be found in the completion symbolically confirmed by the bonds of wedlock. Britomart's heroic quest for wholeness begins, for example, when she falls in love with the image of the knight Artegall, her mirroring complement, and disguises herself as a man to seek his counterpart in the external world; this search, meanwhile, is punctuated by other exemplary tales of love, prominently including the inset legends of Cambel-Triamond and Amyas-Placidas in book 4. Both tales conclude with best friends marrying each other's sisters, so that love literally joins friendship. As such, these marriages rehearse the two ideal ends of the paradigmatic romantic union that awaits Spenser's heroine after she and Artegall, their true identities disguised, clash in a tournament combat that produces the harmony of instant love: mistaken discord yields to rightful concord. Even though Britomart often seems to signify a wholeness that combines the best of male and female roles, the structure of her legend underscores the fact that this inner unity is a microcosm of, and a preparation for, its external embodiment in the larger concord of sexual-marital union; one state does not suffice without the other. Thus, on the whole, the world of *The Faerie Queene* illustrates that the quest for identity remains dependent on union with another, an event that Spenser represents in the age's new literary archetype of romantic wedlock. As Donald Cheney has similarly written of the first book, the Legend of Holiness, Red Cross Knight attains "wholeness not only by killing his dragon but by marrying his lady."[52]

The necessity of marriage as the means of completing the otherwise incomplete self is also pertinent to the ideology informing Shakespeare's view of wedlock. Its social implications overtly manifest themselves in *King John,* when the Citizen draws upon traditional romantic iconography to effect a political compromise, via marriage, between warring nations:

> He is the half part of a blessed man,
> Left to be finished by such as she,
> And she a fair divided excellence,
> Whose fulness of perfection lies in him.
> O, two such silver currents when they join
> Do glorify the banks that bound them in.[53]

The romantic comedies, however, generally stress the potential fullness, rather than "divided excellence," of vibrant heroines like Rosalind in *As You Like It,* Hermia and Helena in *A Midsummer Night's Dream,* and Viola in *Twelfth Night.* Sometimes blindly, sometimes unconsciously, each of these women moves toward the shared adulthood of loving marriage, for which courtship has been a necessary preparation, the trial-and-error discovery of self *and* other. Rosalind's whimsical account of the interlocking steps that link love to marriage sums up, as well, the skeletal structure of dramas and fictions for centuries to come. "Your brother and my sister no sooner met," she tells Orlando, "but they looked; no sooner looked but they loved; no sooner loved but they sighed; no sooner sighed but they asked one another the reason; no sooner knew the reason but they sought the remedy; and in these degrees have they made a pair of stairs to marriage" (5.2.31–36). Notably, the "remedy" is no longer simply sexual gratification; the proverbial stairs to heaven now simultaneously lead to a *connubial* paradise. This is not to imply, however, that the concluding nuptials of Shakespeare's romantic comedies merely function, as some critics would have it, as "the expected ending of a comedy of love";[54] rather, they represent a beginning, a rite of initiation, signaling the protagonists' successful entrance as full human beings into the ranks of adulthood. Hence the closing couplet of *As You Like It:*

> Proceed, proceed. We'll *begin* these rites
> As we do trust they'll *end*, in true delights.
> (5.4.191–92; emphasis added)

The absence of marriage or betrothal at the end of the aptly named *Love's Labor's Lost* helps make clear why the Shakespearean conclusion in marriage is so significant. In the play's final scene, the Princess and her attendants go against type by refusing to "make a world-without-end bargain" with the King and his cohorts, whose immature antics reveal that these men are not adult enough to accept the responsibility and rewards of loving wedlock (5.2.779). When the Princess imposes a one-year moratorium on all proposals of marriage, one of the consternated wooers, Berowne, wryly comments,

> Our wooing doth not end like an old play;
> Jack hath not Jill. These ladies' courtesy
> Might well have made our sport a comedy.
> (5.2.864–66)

The King remonstrates that "'twill end" in "a twelvemonth and a day," but Berowne fires back, quite wisely, "That's too long for a play" (867–68). Jack will "have" Jill only when Jack's behavior merits the honor, and Shakespeare the playwright implies that no convention of comedy will force upon his drama an ending that would signify less—a strategy of plotting we will find revived in some of the counter-traditional novels explored in this book.

Spenser and Shakespeare, then, played instrumental roles in giving literary articulation to the emerging ethos of marriage as a lasting love union. However, as the pervasive trope of women in male disguise in their canons suggests, both writers were also fascinated by and invested in exploring the constrictions facing their heroines as women; to the degree that their female protagonists disprove cultural stereotypes of femininity, both writers ultimately celebrate marriage as a union of nearly equal selves. Hence their thematic representations serve as reminders of the potentially de-stabilizing contradictions embedded within an emergent ideology of wedlock that urged companionship but not equality within its bonds, and to this degree their visions anticipate counter-traditional modes of protest in the novel as much as they overtly serve as models for its dominant tradition. In contrast, it was Milton's religiously inspired evocation of connubial love in Eden, in many ways the perfect embodiment of these contradictions, that became for the eighteenth and nineteenth centuries the most significant aesthetic paradigm for romantic marriage, lodging itself centrally in the new literary mouthpiece of that epoch, the novel.

In a vision consisting of advances away from and consolidations of the old, one forward-looking aspect of the marital ethos espoused in *Paradise Lost* is its unapologetic elevation of sexual love as part of the original paradise.[55] The delights of procreative sex are a good, Milton intimates, once placed in the proper context of loving wedlock:

> Hail wedded Love, mysterious Law, true source
> Of human offspring, sole propriety
> In Paradise of all things common else.[56]

Milton is equally the advocate of true friendship, rather than enmity, between husband and wife; in *The Doctrine and Discipline of Divorce* he identifies the most noble aim of marital union as a *mutual* discourse that is "meet and happy."[57] Before the fall in *Paradise Lost*, Adam and Eve exemplify this compatibility, "happy in our mutual help / And mutual love" (2.727–28). Such mutuality, however, does not imply the identification of similar selves that both Ficino and Spenser intend in their use of the term. Rather, because Milton believes that order and hierarchy govern sexual relations as well as the spiritual ones wedding God and humanity, Eve willingly accepts an inferior position as Adam's mate:

> God is thy law, thou mine: to know no more
> Is woman's happiness, knowledge, and her praise.
>
> (4.637–38)

Only man, indeed, is created in God's image, woman being godly solely in reference to her created source, man, a fact which explains the (in)famous line, "Hee for God only, shee for God in him" (4.299). It is a subversion of natural sexual hierarchy, indeed, that occasions the fall.

The importance of hierarchy thus necessitates a sharp differentiation of the sexes, according to behavior and role, in Milton's Eden and the world that lies beyond. Extending the typology promulgated by biblical commentators since the early medieval period, Adam represents superior reason, as Eve does inferior natural appetite and sensuous appreciation, attributes "Not equal, as thir sex not equal seem'd" (4.296). The differences marked by gender are signified in the descriptions of their hair, for whereas Adam's sublime "front" designates "Absolute rule," Eve's wanton tresses imply her need for "Subjection" (4.300–301, 307). In so distinguishing the sexes, Milton stands by the traditional demarcations voiced in Castiglione and Elyot; like them he also contributes to the image of marriage as a symbolic uniting of deceptively complementary halves which together create a wholeness encompassing both sexes. "Part of my soul I seek thee," Eve says to her husband, "and thee claim / My other half" (4.487–88). The only problem, betrayed by the contradiction inherent in any discourse of "half" selves, is that Eve's "part" is ideologically, as well as practically, inferior to Adam's. Thus, while admirable in its intent, Milton's elevation of friendship in marriage not only developed an idealized paradigm of heterosexual relationship in which sexual differentiation is the norm, but *made attractive* the whole notion of hierarchical difference as the path to true happiness.[58] A similar strategy, as we shall now see, underlies the sentimental concept of companionate marriage that was to become the goal of countless fictional protagonists in the post-epic age of rising middle-class morality in England and, shortly thereafter, America.

Eighteenth-Century Sentimentalism and the Bourgeois Ideal of Companionate Marriage

In 1781 Boswell observed that "there has perhaps been no period when Marriage was more the general topick of conversation than at present," a comment that could have been expanded to include the preceding hundred years.[59] For in the wake of the Restoration, the Puritan ideal of "holy matrimony" underwent a wide-ranging pro-

EIGHTEENTH-CENTURY COMPANIONATE MARRIAGE

cess of secularization that issued in a middle-class sexual ideology consciously working to legitimize romantic passion *within* approved social bonds as a necessary and intrinsic aspect of the human economy; the translation of the spiritual into a secular model rendered "domestic happiness," according to more than one marriage manual, "the completest image of heaven we can receive in this life."[60] The result, well summarized in an advice column of the popular *Athenian Mercury*, was that if the propagation of society were "the main end of marriage," then love, increasingly seen as the correct path to wedlock, had become "the bond of society" as well. The historian Lawrence Stone uses the term "companionate marriage" to encompass the developing social vision of wedlock as a union of friends taking place in England and its American colonies after the 1660s. Perhaps most instrumental in popularizing the archetype of connubial "friendship" were its advocates in the presses, the literary genres, and the coffeehouses—advocates such as Addison, Steele, Richardson, Defoe, products of an enterprising and optimistic middle class eager to produce and possess its own images of culture and success.[61]

The concurrent development of a contractual, secular definition of marriage in the civil sphere—reflecting the political reformulation of monarchy after the Glorious Revolution as a voluntary agreement between subjects and king—also helped validate the practice and claims of companionate marriage.[62] Simultaneously, however, such enlightened views raised some rather troubling questions about the nature of authority within wedlock's traditionally hierarchical framework. As the early feminist Mary Astell perceived, "If Absolute Sovereignty be not necessary in a State, how comes it to be so in a Family?"[63] On the one hand, anything *but* friendship in marriage was derided as tyranny;[64] on the other, most contemporaries failed to realize that the shift from absolute patriarchal authority to a benevolent paternalism did not change the fundamental hierarchy of power in the marital estate. The contradictions inherent in the friendship ideal are perfectly crystallized in some of Hester Chapone's writings. Celebrating the "conjugal happiness" that ensues when a husband elevates his wife "to the rank of his *first* and *dearest friend*," she simultaneously upholds the husband's "*divine right* to the absolute obedience of his wife, in all cases where the first duties do not interfere."[65] Given this affirmation of male prerogative, it becomes obvious why it is the husband who confers the elevating status of friendship in the first proposition: it is his right. Like many others, Chapone simply ignores the political demise of the "divine right" model upon which she bases her portrait of ideal domestic arrangement, and in so doing her work mirrors the process by which social ideology attempts to repress, while actually revealing, the contradictions that constitute its appearance of unity and equity.

The double message—equal but not equal—instilled in the public understanding of companionate relationship also permeated the standards of male and female conduct issuing from the age's evolving sentimental love ethos. The sentimental revolution has been described as the middle class's cultural awakening to the gentle, tender, and softening emotions "most amenable to domestic needs and desires"—a turning, that is, to values traditionally associated with the "feminine" sphere and as such not unlike the chivalric elevation of women in the High Medieval period.[66] To a great extent the insecurities bred of the bourgeoisie's sense of having just "arrived" created their desire for a more civilized and refined existence; companionate marriage became a fashionable vehicle by which a husband could advertise his successful achievement of a domestic kingdom presided over by that most visible sign of status, a delicate, "ladylike" wife. Such idealization of the female role, however, simultaneously intensified those stereotypes of feminine delicacy circumscribing women's independence and economic utility. A much stricter code of acceptable female behavior, endlessly refined in series of popular conduct books, was therefore one result of the new premium placed on a wife's delicacy and leisure as signifiers of middle-class achievement; a parallel myth—and pervasive novelistic archetype—arising from the sentimentalization of woman's role invoked her saving "feminine" graces as the only virtue capable of taming the "unregenerate Adam" lurking in every man—a concept reinscribing the polarity of the sexes along moral lines that, more than ever, demanded female chastity while excusing male promiscuity.[67]

Ironically, given the historical view of female concupiscence, women were now denied any sexual feelings at all. The result placed women in a rather difficult bind, as Ian Watt has perceptively noted, since the pure maiden was nonetheless expected to exude the sexual attractiveness necessary to lure those "unregenerate Adams" to the paths of righteousness and matrimony.[68] The paradoxical tension between virginal and coquettish roles thus gave rise to a complex and schizophrenic image of femininity that early fictional heroines such as Pamela—a paradoxical combination of chaste innocence, sexual overtures, and economic opportunism—illustrate in abundance. A balancing stereotype of masculinity, with similar implications for fictional and dramatic representation, also emerged, in which the libertine pursuits of the youthful male are accepted as an inevitable stage in his development, preceding but not incompatible with his subsequent role as the benevolent family provider and hero of the hearth.[69] Given this widening rift in the behavioral roles allotted men and women within sentimental ideology, it was inevitable that the teasingly coy game of courtship often disastrously blurred into the sex warfare of seducer and virgin. The Congreve verse that Eliza Haywood selected as an epigraph to her seduction novella, *The Rash Resolve* (1724), serves to gloss the proximity between such sentimental sexual stereotyping and potential sexual exploitation:

> Woman is soft, and of a tender Heart,
> Apt to receive, and to retain Love's Dart:
> Man has a Breast robust, and more secure;
> It wounds him not so deep, nor hits so sure.[70]

Specifically at issue in the sex combat of seducer-virgin, of course, was the issue of female chastity, an originally religiously inspired ideal which had now come, as Christopher Hill has noted, to be identified as a property value in and of itself: "in the world of capitalist production expensive goods must not be shop-soiled or tarnished."[71] Not far beneath the surface of the sentimental doctrine of the sexes, that is, one finds the monetary imperatives of the middle class at work. And market price was a real and growing issue for women in a society where the rising practice of economic individualism necessitated their greater dependence on marriage and men; to attract worthy providers, money in the form of a dowry was more important than ever. Given the disproportionate number of eligible women in eighteenth-century England (creating what worried observers termed a crisis spinster-state), men could afford to be selective, opting to marry for attraction *and* money. As the frequently husband-hunting narrator of Defoe's *The Fortunes and Misfortunes of the Famous Moll Flanders* (1722) expostulates, "But for a wife . . . the money was the thing . . . [and] the market is against our sex now."[72]

While the bourgeois context of the sentimental ethos thus helped create a capitalist "market" out of marriage, the middle class's individualistic bent, coupled with its investment in the companionate ideal, helped encourage the development of a mating process designed to ensure its ends. Thus, another tangible effect of the age's cultivation of "tender" feelings, implicit in the above discussion of sexual roles, was the evolution of increasingly elaborate rituals of courtship in the early eighteenth century, a historical development rife with literary implications for the nascent novel and its wedlock ideal. If marriage were to be a true union of friends, then it followed that young lovers must be trained in mutual affection and tested for lifelong compatibility. As Addison put it, "The passion should strike root and gather strength before marriage be grafted on to it," a sentiment repeated throughout the periodical literature of his age.[73] In the literary sphere such an attitude was most visibly reproduced in thematic versions of the "free choice" versus "arranged marriage" issue structuring drama from Restoration comedy to early eighteenth-century sentimental examples of the genre.[74] Such drama reflected popular sentiment and a growing reality, for although marriages among the beleaguered aristocracy were increasingly used for the aggrandizement of familial and political power, the evolving middle-class ethos evinced a slow but steady shift toward the child's right of choice, given parental veto power, in the hundred years following the Interregnum. Just as the child's increasing participation in mate selection abetted the growing practice of courtship, so too the development of philosophical concepts of personal autonomy and political doctrines espousing the individual's inalienable right to personal happiness helped foster a more lenient attitude toward emotional commitment as a respectable, not merely ideal, motive for marriage.[75]

By the mid-eighteenth century, these loosening strictures led to a phenomenal outbreak in passionate manifestations of romantic feeling: young ladies actually swooned, youths fell "madly" in love and eloped to Gretna Green in Scotland, dejected lovers committed Werther-like suicide, all in the name of irresistible passion. As in the courtly ethos, passion had become a prevailing "fashion," with the notable difference that the expanded courtship process, oriented toward an ideal of lifelong conjugal love, provided a framework large enough to accommodate and contain the potentially disruptive intensity of such overflow of emotion. Romantic love, in short, had become yet another signature of social stability.[76] Nonetheless, such an ideological construction of "passion" invited a great deal of abuse, increasing the risk of women's sexual exploitation at the hands of male "lust" masked as "love": hence Mary Wollstonecraft's denunciation of the doctrine of irresistible passion as artifice, "a plausible excuse to the voluptuary who disguises sheer sensuality under a sentimental veil."[77] Such subconscious fears, as well as desires, were played out in the lowbrow and often lurid fictions consumed with increasing frequency between 1700 and 1740, whose narratives of rape and betrayal, as we shall see in the following chapter, attest to a darker underside to the myth of benign happiness promoted in the companionate ideal.

The novelistic genre of post-Richardsonian fame, presenting stories of courtship and seduction as alternating faces of the same sexual-marital ideology, thus came of age at the same time that the vogue of romantic passion was flowering in the second half of the eighteenth century, and this convergence understandably prompted several contemporary observers to accuse the new fiction not only of promulgating the social trend but of helping to create it by encouraging belief in the validity of such emotion as a viable mode of plotting one's own destiny. Nonetheless, despite the moralists and social critics who, like Wollstonecraft, derided the new fashion of romantic love as an "artificial"—that is, "fictional"—emotion, it was an accepted social fact that romance simply for its own sake was on the way to becoming an acceptable, even admirable reason for marrying.[78] The result was a scenario that included both an initial stage of "falling in love" and an extended period of courtship, all in the name of establishing a lasting conjugal happiness that would in turn support the economic prerogatives of an emerging capitalistic and individualistic social order. The yearnings of "frustrated desire" inherited from the courtly tradition were thus ideally deflected into a trajectory whose consummation could safely be anticipated. And one can recognize in this trajectory the parallel contours of the love-plot formulas concurrently being worked out in the incipient novel of the age and coming to define its marriage tradition. To these "fatal knots" we shall now turn.

Chapter Three

Narrative Structure in the Marriage Tradition
Paradigmatic Plots of Courtship, Seduction, and Wedlock

> If you think of a novel in the vague you think of a love
> interest—of a man and a woman who want to be united and
> perhaps succeed. . . . The perfect person is to come along, or
> the person we know already is to become perfect. There are
> to be no changes, no necessity for alertness. We are to be
> happy or even perhaps miserable for ever and ever.
>
> E. M. Forster, *Aspects of the Novel*[1]

> It has often surprised me, said the author . . . to find that all
> the distresses of a novel proceeds from a passion, which is, in
> general, supposed to contribute to our chief happiness. . . . I
> wonder that the novel readers are not tired of reading one
> story so many times, with only the variation of its being told
> different ways.
>
> Susanna Rowson, *The Inquisitor*[2]

The novelistic tradition of love and marriage emerging in mid-eighteenth-century England and overtaking the mainstream of "respectable" nineteenth-century fiction has come to be seen as axiomatic of the genre, and with good reason. For as the previous pages have begun to show, the history of the English-language novel cannot really be separated from the history of the romantic wedlock ideal whose rise we have been tracing: the new genre gained its formal coherence, in large part, by becoming the repository of the marital ethos increasingly cultivated among the Protestant middle classes of England and America. E. M. Forster's whimsical description of the minimal expectations that the twentieth-century reader brings to the canon, cited as the first epigraph to this chapter, conveys something of the widely held belief that a "love interest" is intrinsic to the novel. But, as his qualifying adverb "perhaps" twice concedes, the fictional trajectory of desire is neither always smooth nor its outcome in union certain. "For aught that I could ever read," Lysander remarks in a telling conflation of art and life in *A Midsummer Night's Dream,* "the course of true love never did run smooth" (1.1.132–34).

On the one hand, it is this very note of uncertainty, epitomized by the deferrals and obstructions at least temporarily interfering with a final outcome, that makes *any* narrative act possible; on the other, these hesitancies begin to betray the contradictions embedded in marriage fictions that attempt to reconcile the desires of the individual with the very institutions regulating and proscribing those desires. Nonetheless, because such narrative *détours* in English fiction have by and large been predicated on the unquestioned, and monolithic, centrality of romanticized marriage as *the* ultimate signifier of personal and social well-being, the result has been a series of structural paradigms that, however apparently differing in their representations of passion, have upheld essentially the same dominant sexual ideology. As Susanna Rowson, the early American writer of didactic seduction tragedies, puts it in the passage cited as the second epigraph above, our love fiction tells "one story" over and over, "with only the variation of its being told different ways." To read the transhistorical contours of this "story," as I now propose to do, we must exchange the diachronic emphases of the previous chapter for a more or less synchronic focus on plot variations-within-sameness.

In the English and American traditions, these variations have most frequently grouped around themes of courtship, seduction, and wedlock, paradigms of which have been present in English fiction since its pre-Richardsonian origins. Moreover—as I will argue in a comparison of the courtship plots of *Pamela* and *Pride and Prejudice,* the seduction plots of *Clarissa* and *Tess of the D'Urbervilles,* and the wedlock plots of *Amelia* and *A Modern Instance*—these three narrative patterns exist to a great degree as either reflections or inversions of each other's organizations; they interlock to form a code of implicit formal rules and defensive strategies that attempt to limit the genre's intrinsically heterogeneous play of meaning— and analogously the variable scope of human desire—by imposing a "center" of meaning, of coherence, in the name of romantic wedlock, Anglo-American culture's version of the Lacanian *nom du*

PARADIGMATIC PLOTS

père. To this very fact may be ascribed the tremendous ideological power that the novelistic marriage tradition has wielded over popular belief for more than two centuries. For the metamorphosis of social conventions of love into narrative conventions of form has, metaphorically speaking, inscribed around the dominant fictional treatments of love and marriage a nearly inviolable circle within whose boundaries the traditional novel has generated its own self-sustaining truths about the sexes and their proper relations. The imposition of such boundaries, that is, has since the beginning of the genre helped to ensure that the begetting of subsequent thematic or narrative patterns, contained by a common point of origin in the connubial ideal, will repeat the ideological maxims necessary to promote the illusion of sexual hierarchy as the basis of societal, and ultimately fictional, order.

Just how these characteristic variations upon the love-plot contribute to the monologic of representation in the marriage tradition from the 1740s to early twentieth century will provide the focus of this chapter. In delineating the "one story," as Rowson puts it, comprising this tradition, I do not mean to give short shrift to the evolving novel's variety or complexity. What an examination of the codification of form in marriage fiction reveals, rather, is a multiplicity of results: novelists creating highly sophisticated structures within the tradition, novelists blindly following its conventions or unconsciously promulgating its ethos, novelists using its paradigms as convenient frames on which to hang loosely connected episodes, novelists actively struggling against its thematic and formal strictures without breaking loose of them. Likewise, my division of marriage-related novels into courtship, seduction, and wedlock patterns is not meant to imply that these paradigms have only occurred separately of one another; quite to the contrary, I have differentiated among these paradigmatic plots—which quite often overlap within a single text—in order to emphasize how profoundly these three major variants of the love-to-marriage development either mirror or reverse each other's structural organizations. The way in which these stabilizing narrative structures reinforce each other lies at the core of the marriage tradition's formidable influence, as I have already suggested, and can be traced back to the genre's origins in pre-Richardsonian fictional narrative. Since I will frequently be referring to these predecessor texts, the next section will briefly summarize the salient features of this early body of fiction. The following section will categorize several general structural features relevant to the narrative representation of love in the marriage tradition, after which I will address the courtship, seduction, and wedlock variations of the love-plot each in turn.

Pre-Richardsonian Models

The early eighteenth century witnessed an explosion into the popular literary market of fictional prose narratives that preceded by more than three decades the 1740 publication of *Pamela*. Highly melodramatic and sometimes painfully unsophisticated in technique, these narratives of tortured love provide simplified, easily disassembled models of the complex representational and ideological structures characterizing the marriage tradition in later fiction. Moreover, the very origins of these novelistic forerunners, as their foremost critic, John J. Richetti, has demonstrated, are intimately linked to the sexual and social issues whose literary manifestations we have been following. The female-authored pre-Richardsonian narrative, in particular, arose in reaction to a very tangible, early eighteenth-century cultural mythology rooted in sexual antagonism and economic conflict: with near uniformity, innocent female virtue is persecuted by a malign masculine ethos to whom power and possession have become the natural accoutrements of a worldview that Ian Watt associates with the rise of economic individualism.[3] The dark and usually tragic picture that emerges from these novellas, as I suggested at the end of the previous chapter, intimates a disturbing kinship within the period's sexual-marital economy between the idealization of romantic love and female victimization, and this kinship is equally evident in the rudimentary structural patterns used to evoke the trajectories of love and lust in these fictions.

According to Richetti, narratives with a love theme written between 1700 and 1739 fall into three roughly chronological thematic categories—the scandal chronicle, the amatory novella, and the pious text—that are repeated in the early American canon almost exactly one hundred years later. What these gradations suggest, for both nations, is the gradual transformation of a popular definition

PRE-RICHARDSONIAN MODELS

of "true love" as irresistible, scandalous passion into the didactic rubric of "true *married* love" as piously respectable passion—a transformation, however, that (like the love-plot) never quite covers the traces of its origins. The titillating, passionate ethos found in these pre-Richardsonian texts can be seen as an extreme manifestation of the age's growing cultivation of sensibility; in its fictional avatars, such "love" is viewed as an involuntary and overpowering emotion whose transcendent and everlasting blessing women are inherently more capable than men of experiencing. As in the Christian precepts that this love religion mirrors, self-effacing submission to the force of love thus becomes a sign of superior virtue and, in the usual event of love's tragic betrayal at the hands of male lust, a woman's means to heavenly martyrdom.[4] The most blatant perversion of the ideal sanctity of love is represented in the early-century scandal chronicle, *romans à clef* or "secret histories"—such as Manley's *The New Atalantis* (1709)—set in decadent court atmospheres rife with political and sexual intrigue. Less relevant to our structural concerns than its subsequent avatars, the scandal narrative typically runs through a series of loosely structured, semipornographic scenes that repeat with scant variation the same tale: unregenerate, politically powerful, often aristocratic men corrupt virtuous maidens whose tragic ends are hastened by the fact that they generally fall in love with their seducers.

The amatory variation, ushered into being in the twenties by Eliza Haywood, Mary Davys, and others, continues the dichotomization of innocent heroine and evil world, but shifts the narrative emphasis to the pathetic and erotic sides of seduced virtue that would preoccupy later writers from Richardson to Hardy. Adapting a structural pattern of separation and flight as old as Greek prose romance, these novellas focus as much on the heroine's tears as on her flesh during the "warm" seduction scenes, and her corrupter is often portrayed as a potentially true lover, torn between higher emotions and brute desire. The "plot," accordingly, derives from the stratagems of deferral and postponement that the heroine, who recognizes the dangers of her own capacity for passion, must invent to fend off the advances and wiles of her sexual antagonist. "The heroine can only find love and happiness by resisting, by running away from love, by attempting with heroic determination to suppress it," Richetti notes, for in so doing, "she will one day be rewarded for ever by a tragic apotheosis, or by the legalizing [in marriage] of that which she has avoided but desired all along."[5] The amatory tale's tendency to spiritualize the inner purity of the persecuted female becomes even more pronounced in the moralistic pious fables that gained popularity in the 1730s, foreshadowing the emergence of "respectable" love fiction in the 1740s; as Richetti notes, in this variation the Christian heroine's repeated escapes from erotic dangers *without* succumbing or being overpowered come to symbolize "the power of faith and Providence," and the improbable plot coincidences that result in the salvation of the heroine can be justified as evidence of the inscrutability of God's plan. Since marriage or a commitment to marriage often forms the initial circumstance in the pious narrative, the heroine's trials upon being separated from her actual or destined mate serve a double duty, testing her sexual fidelity and Christian fortitude alike. This didactic function also summoned into being a new masculine prototype: the heroic Christian male who can love purely and, in so doing, use his male strength to *protect* rather than persecute female virtue.[6]

In all three formulations of the myth of persecuted female innocence, then, one finds a concomitant belief in the efficacy of true love, be it destined to tragedy or the means of earthly salvation in marriage. To their credit, these early fictions protest in unambivalent terms the victimization of women. Yet, paradoxically, while nearly all attack the bifurcated sexual ethos of their age as the culprit endangering true love's existence, the sexual stereotyping that pervades their narratives upholds the very imbalance of power that makes possible the situation they deplore. Male dominance, for instance, is in itself never questioned; rather, it is depicted at its most negative as an inevitably overpowering evil that cannot be avoided, and at its most positive as the heroic strength that saves helpless virtue. And, in turn, feminine passivity is accepted as a given—represented at its least moralistic level as an "excuse" for succumbing to the vibrating embraces of the seducer and at its most moralistic as a reflection of Christian submission to God's providence. As Richetti sums up the compromised element of protest in these works, "the elaborate insistence upon the absolutely compulsive nature of passion, which is the main feature of the [genre's] many definitions of love, is a way of avoiding an active subversion of the male world."[7] Such lurid fictional representations, one begins to perceive, are not so far removed from the sexual constructions rising from the "enlightened" sentimental ideology in which chastened coquettes magically become ennobling wives and reformed rakes benevolent husbands. Turning now to the codification of theme and form in the novel's marriage tradition, we shall see how the blatant contradictions in these pre-Richardsonian novellas foreshadow the more invisible schisms hidden within the sophisticated formulations of the modern love-plot.

Traditional Structures of Desire and Theories of Narrative Equilibrium

The paradigms of courtship, seduction, and wedlock that we will be examining shortly share a number of formal and structural features that have traditionally served to reinforce the ideological power of the marriage tradition. The use of developmental and perspectival structures to inscribe erotic "meaning" into the body of the text, the differing valences of male and female forms of bildungsroman, the deployment of various techniques (such as linearity, repetition, circularity) to create an impression of the novelistic world as a hierarchically ordered "whole," and especially the valorization of the closed ending—all these aspects of eighteenth- and nineteenth-century narrative structure are worth our review at this point: they shed invaluable light on the way in which the marriage tradition successfully managed, for so many years, to circumscribe its thematized desires and curtail its narrative energies in the name, ironically, of readerly satisfaction.

The developmental component of plot, for example, is essential to any narrative, and, since the Greek Alexandrian romance, has held special relevance to the representation of erotic desire in narrative. From Richardson to the early modern period, furthermore, novelistic treatments of love's wayward course have been channeled into comic or tragic sequences sharing a developmental grammar which Robert Kiely has concisely summarized as "encounter, attraction, union, break, and resolution in either final reunion or separation."[8] Any story consists of at least a beginning and an ending, and the transformation from the initial term ("encounter") to the latter ("reunion or separation") implies a minimal sequencing of events or phases of change; as Terry Eagleton has remarked, "if everything stayed in place there would be no story to tell."9 And on a simple psychological level the very appeal of narrative resides in the various developmental strategies of complication and suspense that have been evolved to prolong the pleasures of reading by deferring the equally strong impulse to reach an end that will satisfy the reader's expectations. Thus Peter Brooks, drawing on the Freudian hypothesis of the dynamics of desire and death shaping the narrative of each individual life, defines literary plot as the tension maintained by the elaboration of a narrative "middle" that is "an ever more complicated postponement or *détour*" over-determined by "the terminal quiesence of the end." Echoing the highly sexualized metaphors of "tumescence"/"detumescence" and "pleasurable discharge" that Brooks uses to describe the textual erotics of narrative climax and closure, Eagleton adds that in the "classical" text our "readerly" satisfaction is "gratifyingly released" by its resolution, for "our energies [are] cunningly 'bound' by the suspenses and repetitions of the narrative only as a preparation for their pleasurable expenditure."10 In this notion of the reader's erotic pleasure in textual excitation, deferral, and release one can perceive a pattern not dissimilar to the stages of attraction, break, and resolution outlined by Kiely: the developmental trajectory of the traditional love-plot, it would appear, reflects the trajectory ascribed to the reader's own displaced desires. Yet, as the sexual imagery pointed out above suggests, the reader hypothesized by Brooks and Eagleton is male; the pattern of desire being evoked follows a linear model of sexual excitation and final discharge most often associated, in both psychological and physiological terms, with men. If this is so, the erotic dynamic of the traditional love-plot, however much it may play to female desire, nonetheless would seem to encode at the most elementary level of narrative a highly specific, male-oriented norm of sexuality fostering the illusion that all pleasure (of reading or of sex) is ejaculatory.11

Several theories about the "proper" function of prose fiction, moreover, have been built on this metaphoric equation of erotic pleasure with narrative suspense, as well as on the sexual biases underlying it. For instance, Robert Scholes and Robert Kellogg view narrative as a rhythmic sequencing of event and crisis geared to move toward a final relaxation of tension analogous to Brooks's "discharge" and Eagleton's "expenditure": "the reader of a narrative can expect to finish his reading having achieved a state of equilibrium—something approaching calm of mind, *all passion spent.*" Given the italicized metaphor, it is not surprising that these two theorists suggest that the love-plot, "inevitably" moving toward "the consummation of . . . love in marriage," is especially well suited to narrative representation, since romantic desire and its fulfillment are, in their view, among "the most obvious correlatives for the tension and resolution *which a plot demands.*"[12] The unquestioned assumption that narrative structure "demands" a climactic "consummation" or "resolution" of its tension, of course, also characterizes those critical schools, usually grounded in Aristotelean or formalist methodology, that advocate formal coherence or "wholeness" as the desideratum of all literature; whence the presuppositions underlying theories of structure developed by critics as diverse as Monroe Beardsley, Sheldon Sacks, and Frank Kermode.[13] As we will later see in discussing modes of closure, such hypotheses about the prerequisites of plotting are in themselves at least partially products of ideological concerns analogous to those constrictive ones promulgated by the marriage tradition.

Novelistic structure, of course, consists of more than the developmental plotting of event or sequence; equally important is its perspectival format, which Beardsley has defined as the narrator's spatial and temporal relation to the material being described, and versions of which Gérard Genette uses to describe the reader's relation to the narrated material.[14] The emerging novel in the English tradition was set apart from its pre-Richardsonian forebears precisely in its superimposition of such perspectival formulations on its inherited developmental structures: the addition of narrative distance between author and text, and between intratextual points of view, added a wealth of epistemological density to the new genre in general and to the love-plot in particular. The question of who truly desires whom (and for what reason), the degree to which lovers understand or miscomprehend each other's intentions, the knowledge available to the reader and subordinate characters but unperceived by one or both romantic leads, the authorial insights imparted to or strategically withheld from the reader—all these variables in the perspectival design made possible a much more intricate, as well as psychologically dense, play of dynamics involving novelist, protagonists, and reader in the narrative process leading to the attainment or withholding of ideal love.

Within these developmental and perspectival parameters, most fictional expositions of love have to some degree followed the time-honored form of the bildungsroman, for the story of a youth's progress from innocence to adulthood, from the realm of illusion to the world of reality, is often marked by the vicissitudes and trials of love. Yet a general distinction can be made between the function of the love-plot in male and female stories of maturation.[15] Because in female variations of the form the climactic event of marriage confers on the heroine her entire personal identity (as wife) as well as her social "vocation" (as mother), the growth of the female protagonist has come to be seen as synonymous with the action of courtship: until very recently the only female bildungsroman has been a love-plot. The female success story is thus marked, according to Nancy Miller, by a "trajectory of ascent" (and, one might add, assent): "the heroine . . . moves in her negotiation with the world of men and money from 'nothing' to 'all' in a feminine variant of *Bildung*."[16] And that "all" is the recompense of a marriage that satisfies on conventionally personal, social, and material levels. The unconventional Zenobia, doomed heroine of Hawthorne's *The Blithedale Romance* (1852), puts it another way, however: "Fate has assigned" the grown woman "but one single event, which she must contrive to make the substance of her whole life," she complains, while "a man has his choice of innumerable events."[17]

And, indeed, the typical male bildungsroman often merely uses the love-plot as a kind of narrative scaffolding upon which to hang the various independent concerns, the "innumerable events," of the hero's growth to adulthood and social integration. Such a device can be traced back to Greek New Comedy—the source of many of the love-plot conventions incorporated into the early novel—where the separation of young hero and heroine most often serves as a pretext for the stratagems of the blocking characters, antics, or foils; in the space between the lovers' separation and reunion, one or even both may drop out of the picture altogether with little violence to the overall plot.[18] Fielding's *The History of Tom Jones, a Foundling* (1749) uses the courtship format somewhat analogously in adapting it to a comic bildungsroman trajectory. For the physical separation of Tom and "his Sophia" forms the starting point of journeys in search of each other which, crisscrossing in neatly symmetrical patterns, give to the gargantuan novel a coherent external design. Because this is Tom's story, Fielding relegates most of Sophia's travels and travails to the offstage action or summary and thus makes the misadventures that waylay Tom on the eventual path to matrimony the source of a running commentary on the experiences, exploits, and ideal virtues constitutive of a "normal" young man's personal and social self. The event of marriage at text's end hence serves a largely symbolic role, underlining Tom's already acquired identity rather than standing as the sum of his whole being; indeed, the discovery of his "true identity" as Bridget Allworthy's genteel son (a stock New Comedy device) *precedes* his achievement of romantic satisfaction, not in the reverse order mandated by the female bildungsroman, where marriage confers all identity.[19]

The differing ideological values accruing to male and female variants of the bildungsroman are also registered in another important structural facet of many love-plots—the double suitor convention. Jean E. Kennard has convincingly argued that the two-suitor version of the female courtship plot reinforces through its very form a belief in female inferiority: the heroine must be weaned from an initially mistaken male object of desire by a second, more responsible wooer, who, as her mentor figure, provides a model of the correct behavior to which she herself needs to aspire in order to become an autonomous adult.[20] But no matter how immense the heroine's positive gains in self-assertion, as Austen's *Emma* (1816) perhaps best illustrates, she can only remain hierarchically secondary to the husband, who, having authored her very identity as an adult, inevitably remains her superior. On the other hand, while the developmental trajectories tracing the growth of male figures like Edward in Scott's *Waverley* (1814), David in Dickens's *David Copperfield* (1849–50), or Henry in Thackeray's *Henry Esmond* (1852) are structured around successive love affairs (the first signifying the youthful romanticism that must be renounced for the adult reality promised by the second), the love interest remains only one of several aspects defining these men's careers. Agnes may appear to the grateful David as his angelic guide, directing him ever onward and upward, but, in contrast to the male mentor prototype, Agnes never creates or "authorizes" David's experience; to the contrary, she is a product of *his* vision of the goal he wishes to attain, and thus she comes to symbolize an inner principle within David himself.

With these differences in mind, we can turn to some of the lines of affiliation binding the narratives of courtship, seduction, and wedlock together under the aegis of the marriage tradition. I have already suggested that all three paradigms to a large degree either mirror or invert each other's structures, an observation verified in part by the findings of other critics. Evelyn Hinz, for example, has demonstrated a specific link between representations of comedic courtship and tragic wedlock as complementary versions of the same myth of "wed/lock": the former pattern, tracing the process of the lovers' conversion to a socially viable perspective, emphasizes the "wed" of wedlock as its goal, while the latter variant focuses on the "locked" condition of marriage as that which generates the complications to be resolved. But the "thematic function of marriage in both," Hinz summarizes, "is the same: it symbolizes the entrance into society of the individual, the acquisition or restoration of a realistic attitude toward life, the movement . . . to a *novelistic* sense of reality."[21] From a different angle of vision, Nancy Miller traces the rising and falling trajectories that link female-centered sequences of courtship and seduction within the "ideologically delimited space of an either/or closure" as complementary versions of the same "heroine's text."[22] In regard to the fates of male rather than female protagonists, the reversibility of courtship plotting and what Fiedler has identified as "its travesty, seduction," is supported by de Rougement's analysis of the link between the mythic Tristan and Don Juan figures as idealized and eroticized projections, respectively, of the same masculine ideological matrix.[23] More generally, Kiely's previously cited description of the stages making up the traditional love-plot, ending in "resolution in either final reunion or separation," intimates the alliance between comedic and tragic versions of these narrative sequences. For even in "tragic or pathetic abortions of realized love," Hagstrum writes of eighteenth-century literature, there "shine glimpses of the Miltonic [connubial] ideal, sometimes for no other purpose than to make the tragic loss of Eden more poignant and to show how pitifully short of the ideal human substitutions fall."[24] On the other hand—and here the ideological contradictions underlying the ideal rise to the surface—sexual tragedy need only be followed by marriage, in society's eyes, to be transformed into its seeming opposite, comedy: "Is not the catastrophe of every story that ends in wedlock accounted happy, be the difficulties in the progress to it ever so great?" Lovelace facetiously gloats to Belford after Clarissa's rape.[25]

Each of these three plot paradigms generally reinforces its meaning by organizing its steps toward a tragic or comedic ending into a hierarchically ordered sequence of intensifying crises, wherein each new event presents a larger, more potentially catastrophic version of the crisis point that has just been passed—which in the love-plot generally means making the eventual union of lovers *appear* more and more remote. Closely related to such sequencing is the way in which the various phases of the developmental structure often seem to become repetitions of each other; that is, viewed synchronically, the same situation of impasse in a given text (say, an unsuccessful declaration of love) is enacted time and again, in various guises, until its intensified replay finally leads to a breakthrough, reversal, and resolution. This mode of structural repetition in the traditional love-plot thus serves an ultimately familiarizing and stabilizing function, binding and connecting scattered parts of the text for its "proper" and ultimately conservative expenditure of energy in a seemingly unified climax and release.[26] At the same time, internal structures of parallelism and chiasmus often contribute to the symmetrically balanced patterns that imbue many "classic" novels with their illusion of completeness and stability. The way in which the overall movements of many such narratives seem to come full circle, the end repeating the beginning with the difference of the narrative space traversed between, becomes yet another specific strategy exploited by the marriage tradition to validate its own ideal.

What Coleridge has to say about the function of poetic narrative in this regard is illuminating, for the "common end" of the traditional marriage novel is also "to convert a *series* into a *Whole:* to make those events, which in real or imagined History move on in a *strait* Line, assume to our Understandings a *circular* motion—the snake with its Tail in its Mouth."[27] In other words, the metonymic alignment of narrative events seeks its "end" in the luminary stasis of the metaphoric "wholeness" that the marriage tradition associates with the harmony of wedlock. Within the textual field of fiction so defined and so contained, the specific placement of the turning points, threshold moments, and climaxes of self-discovery typically associated with stages of young love, sexual disgrace, or domestic life become crucial signifiers of meaning; these major events, moreover, are strategically interwoven with subplots featuring complementary or foil themes, fates, and characters to construct the illusion of a coherently ordered, enclosed, and entire fictional world. This created wholeness, in turn, fosters the illusion of a fixed external "reality" whose natural operation or order is not open to question or contradiction.

These various strategies of narrative organization point toward the privileged role played by modes of closure in the traditional love-plot. As we have already seen in chapter 1, the impetus toward concluding stasis in courtship, seduction, and wedlock variations upon the marriage theme, whether tragic or comic in outcome, functions like the structuralist concept of the naturalizing sign to cut short any serious or prolonged inquiry into the ideological framework informing the fictional construct. For by leaving the reader in a state of unquestioning repose and acceptance, the self-contained or "classic" text inculcates a vision of a coherence or stability underlying social reality and cultural convention alike: the finality of the end becomes the ultimate signifier of this immutable worldview. And, inevitably, as the discussion of ideological formations in chapter 1 suggested, the reader who unconsciously accepts such a fictional representation of reality as unproblematic or "natural" remains prey to its ideological constructions.[28] In the eighteenth- and nineteenth-century novel, therefore, the closed plot became a perfect vehicle for reinforcing the middle-class belief in romantic wedlock as a virtually unassailable "truth"; not only the "happy ending" concluding the usual trajectory of courtship, but its inverse, the tragically closed outcome befalling those who abuse the ideal, worked to uphold the wedlock ideal as the *desired* goal and *natural* end, even if maliciously thwarted, of love's progress. Hence Forster's quip, "We are to be happy or even perhaps miserable for ever and ever."

Such plot formulations, moreover, underscore the teleological assumptions inherent in a traditional ordering of narrative as an inevitable movement from instability to equilibrium. In this regard, as Annette Niemtzow has remarked in the spirit of Kermode's *The Sense of an Ending*, "The marital apocalypse . . . was expected to reorder time, structure its random flow and provide it with meaning."[29] One of the pre-Richardsonian novellas that we will be examining as a precursor of the Austenian courtship plot, *Luck at Last* (1723), provides an example of this deliberate "reordering" as its author proceeds to equate the achievement of "the most solid happiness" of wedlock "concluded upon . . . [the] bottom" of true love with narrative stasis itself:

> And thus we have brought this relation to a conclusion, which though it was black enough and melancholy in the beginning, though it had not the least glimpse of light at first, . . . and promising nothing but a *continued series* of misfortunes, with a *long and dismal chain* of galling miseries attending it, at last *broke forth* into a dawn, and emerging itself into a glorious unexpected *calm,* the lovely sunshine of a cloudless *serenity.*[30]

The author thus envisions the event of marriage as the happy ending beyond which no comment is necessary because nothing more happens: all is serene. Yet, as we have seen, the impulse toward such stability, consonance, or equilibrium—whatever one's metaphor—is almost necessarily a falsification of the mimetic claim of fiction purporting to record "reality." This is the point of Bersani's warning that the placement of significance on the particular fictional moment (or absence) of marriage in order to achieve a "suitable conclusion" is ultimately a coercion of reality.[31] For poetic justice rarely falls from the skies with such appropriate timing or with such "just rewards" as it does in traditional novelistic conclusions—whence the modern reader's uncomfortable sense of the artificiality of the flurry of concluding weddings (and untimely deaths or deportations) dotting the novel's marriage tradition: its claim to represent social order "as is" is exposed in the very structural manipulations necessary to present and naturalize that claim.

Paying attention to the specific narrative techniques used to construct the illusion of closural finality will reveal, then, how the dispensation of final rewards in the shape of upcoming nuptials and dimpled babies often had more to do with the public demand for "moral" fiction—that is, a kind of *social* fiction—than with the author's aesthetic commitment to verisimilitude.[32] Nineteenth-century novelists developed an ending device that Marianna

Torgovnick calls the "conventional epilogue" expressly to answer this purpose—a summary paragraph or chapter following the concluding action. Its various functions included tying up loose plot-threads, projecting the protagonists into predictably satisfying or appropriately dismal futures, bidding the reader a tranquil farewell, and frequently shifting into present tense in order to intimate a sense of attained perpetuity and final stasis.[33] All these strategies for achieving traditional closure attempt to limit the inherent possibilities of fictional narrative and of human desire by imposing a "center" that governs the subsequent circulation of textual meanings and values. And in regard to the marriage tradition, that center—"the structure that maintains the Structure," to repeat Tanner's formula[34]—is the ideal of romantic wedlock around which the plot formulations of courtship, seduction, and wedlock began to coalesce with the emergence of the genre.

"Uniting Them" Ever After: The Courtship Narratives of *Pamela* and *Pride and Prejudice*

The most familiar pattern in Anglo-American romantic fiction, of course, is that of courtship, whose ideal goal approximates the companionate union of loving friends described by Stone. As in the paradigms provided by Greek New Comedy and the later Alexandrian romance, lovers are sundered by a score of obstacles—including parents, wrong suitors, geography, personal prejudice, and class barriers—all of which must be removed to facilitate a successful alliance.[35] On a thematic level, the ending in marriage that follows upon courtship (whether as dramatized or implied event) thus at once affirms the existing or revitalized social order and symbolizes the lovers' completion in each other: as two "halves" become one "whole," in accord with Platonic archetype, they form a microcosm that in turn reflects the "whole" of society. On a textual level, moreover, the courtship novel's fundamental structure of frustration and fulfillment is built around the principle of delayed gratification—for only as long as the lovers are kept apart or the desired condition is deferred will the story keep moving forward or the reader continue reading. Once the possibility of a straight line between the romantically attracted protagonists has been established and "two" become "one," the plot in effect returns to the one-dimensionality from which it arose; hence the appropriateness of the final words of *Pride and Prejudice,* "uniting them," in which the verbal signifier of union is made to coincide with the cessation of all narrative movement.

An excellent prototype of the way in which the content of courtship has successfully availed itself of the element of duration characterizing all narrative exists in Longus's *Daphnis and Chloe,* the A.D. 100–300 prose romance most familiar to early English audiences. The Prologue begins with the narrator-persona's discovery in a grove of the Nymphs of a two-dimensional piece of art, "the painted picture of a tale of love," which so delightfully "[speaks] of love" that the narrator "conceive[s] a strong desire" to animate, to bring to life, its scenes by "compos[ing] a literary pendant to that painted picture."[36] This allegory of the birth of linear narrative desire is fittingly recapitulated by the text itself, as the narration moves out of the static frame provided by the Prologue into the spatially conceived world of pastoral love inhabited by Daphnis and Chloe. The subject of Longus's text being the ideal maturation of these two young lovers, its idealized setting becomes a protected space within which their childish affections can blossom into an untainted natural eroticism. A requisite number of separations and obstructions transpire—including kidnapings by pirates and jealous suitors of all sexual persuasions—but none ever really poses a serious threat to the lovers' eventual fulfillment. Such plot devices, rather, merely accent the erotic rhythm of approach-and-deferral threading its way throughout the whole text, by which means the narrative enacts a kind of linguistic striptease, especially in its verbalization of the fumbling stages characterizing Daphnis and Chloe's sexual initiation: Longus's description lingers lovingly over their wonder as they attempt to read the undeciphered mystery of each other's bodies, then over their bewilderment as they turn toward the world of natural signs in attempts to discover *how* to make love. That is, external "event" or "action" takes its cue from the internal dynamic of "erotic" deferral at work between the protagonists and within the narrating act itself. This is an aspect of romantic plotting that we shall also find in the less obviously sexualized Anglo-American novel, where externalized forms of discourse, including postponements of and obstructions to union, at once mask and reveal the text's play of sublimated erotic desire.[37]

Appropriately the conclusion of Longus's narrative hinges on the impending sexual act that will consummate Daphnis and Chloe's romance. For the last sentence brings the reader to a threshold—that of the bridal chamber into which the two lovers have disappeared. Here, Longus tells us, "for the first time Chloe learned that their pastime in the woods had been mere pastoral play" (68), as Daphnis (now, tellingly, Chloe's superior in sexual knowledge) initiates her into the mysteries of hymen. The ending, therefore, is a culmination that, in marking the passage from youth to adulthood, from the world of pastoral to the real, transforms the preceding narrative movement into a completed aesthetic whole; abetted by the retroactive privileging inherent in any conclusion, this text in effect becomes a static work of art analogous to that "painted picture of a tale of love" from which the narrative originally took its inspiration and momentum.

It is not irrelevant that Mr. B similarly characterizes his pursuit of Pamela as "a pretty story in romance"[38]—one, however, whose ending remains unwritten as long as Mr. B pursues and Pamela desists by making the writing of her letters an act of narrative postponement. While it would be fallacious to confuse the unabashed eroticism of Longus's "pagan" tale with the English-speaking novel's "civilized" version of courtship, the very dynamic by which the former unfolds sheds light on the psychological imperatives that in shaping fictions of love in general have consequently shaped later conceptions of how love *should* be represented in fictional form. In this regard, two pre-Richardsonian amatory novellas, Arthur Blackamore's *Luck at Last; or, The Happy Unfortunate* (1723) and Eliza Haywood's *Love in Excess; or, The Fatal Inquiry* (1719–20), provide illuminating examples of the various narrative principles—and contradictions—incorporated in the paradigmatic love plot of *Pamela* (1740).

Underpinning the Cinderella-like courtship structure that Blackamore's tale shares with *Pamela* is the bourgeois dream of rising in status through an advantageous love match that, as the last chapter demonstrated, was one product of the burgeoning capitalistic ethos beginning to restructure eighteenth-century English society. The motivating cause of action, hence plot, in Blackamore's text, is also class-related: the heroine, Sylvia, decides that the only way to avoid an arranged match (as we have seen, a continuing prerogative of the upper classes) continually likened to a hateful "siege" (11, 15) is to run away from her parents. Her subsequent road adventures form a metonymic "chain" of "misfortunes" and "galling miseries" (80) that culminate in her employment as the servant of a philanthropic noble couple who serve as foils to her own parents. Under their watchful care, Sylvia suddenly finds herself courted by a neighboring young gentleman raised "never [to] regard pedigree so much as virtue"—Pamela's titular quality—in choosing a wife (54); the descending curve of the heroine's progress, in a neat reversal of direction, turns out to be a rising one after all as the two fall in love. One final obstacle to Sylvia's ascent is surpassed when she is reconciled with her parents. Culminating with the "instructive lesson" that parents ought not to "interpose their authority" unduly in the affections of their children, Blackamore thus espouses an enlightened ethos of romantic love in line with the age's progressive marital ideology. For the text's final assertions echo the middle-class journals and advice manuals of the day in advocating freely chosen love over parentally arranged matches: "A love grounded upon such a basis [as tried and true affection] can never miscarry; it is founded upon right reason; and the effect of wedlock concluded upon such a bottom is the most solid happiness this world can produce" (80). Such a happiness, furthermore, is figured in the language of harmonious balance intrinsic to the Miltonic archetype of marital "oneness" reviewed in the previous chapter; hence the chiasmic construction of the wording used to sum up the newlyweds' identical satisfaction: "he in her, and she in him, being mutually happy," they find "a perfect harmony in both their affections" (65).

Such a construction of "perfect harmony," however, is not without its disturbing implications when the suitor is less nicely behaved. In this regard, Haywood's *Love in Excess* sheds light on a dimension of *Pamela*'s plotting that attests to the patriarchal presuppositions hidden within the ideal of "mutually happy" harmony. For just as the double standard embedded in the age's sentimental image of companionate marriage permitted the metamorphosis of male seducers into sincere mates without social or authorial disapprobation, Haywood's text gradually transforms itself from a lurid seduction narrative into a sentimental fable of courtship without any sense of contradiction. The impulse to accuse Haywood of authorial incompetence, of mixing two modes into one, is checked by the fact that the mechanics governing the organizational structure of Richardson's *Pamela* are nearly identical to her own. What is at stake is not so much technical incompetence as a shared ideological framework imposing its own contradictions on Haywood and Richardson's visions of romantic love.

The three volumes making up the accurately named *Love in Excess* chart the libertine-hero Count D'Elmont's progress from vice to reformation and marital reward; each volume thus also becomes a significant structural marker in the transformation of its seduction narrative into a supposedly benign courtship plot. Haywood opens with a classic love triangle in part 1, in which D'Elmont, reveling in the seducer's aggressive code, is doggedly pursuing an innocent maiden (Amena) who has fallen irresistibly in love with him, while Amena's foil, the wicked Alovisa, schemes to get D'Elmont into her bed. The developmental format of this section, patterned on a series of titillating "near-climaxes," in effect mirrors the seducer's code, for the consequence of these deferrals of actual conquest, these postponements of completed "story," is to conflate the rake's sexual frustration with the reader's desire for narrative closure. "The novel itself becomes a paradigm of sexual play," Ruth Perry writes, "building up the audience for the big moment, delaying it, and building it up again."[39] At the end of part 1, the tormented Amena is left utterly miserable ("Oh! to what am I reduced by my too soft and easie nature"[40]), betrayed by love, by D'Elmont, and ultimately by Alovisa, whom she thought her best friend; as Amena's angry father commits her to a nunnery, Alovisa and D'Elmont ironically contract a marriage of utter convenience.

Part 2 reinstitutes movement as the now remorsefully married D'Elmont plots a new assault on female virtue, this time in the form of his angelic ward Melliora. What first seems a mere repetition of Amena's story, however, turns out to be a repetition with a significant difference: having always mocked the power of Love, D'Elmont now becomes its victim as he falls head-over-heels for Melliora. D'Elmont's original plan of removing to his country estate in order to stage Melliora's seduction in relative isolation is thus counterbalanced by his awakening moral sensibilities. The characteristic elements of the fictional modes of seduction and courtship are thrown into quickening juxtaposition—barely averted rape scenes succeeded by tearful declarations of undying love—and the seesaw-ing narrative pace now replicates not only D'Elmont's sexual frustra-tion but his inner turmoil as he is torn between pathetic and erotic urges. In contrast to the tragic lot befalling Amena at the end of part 1, the conclusion of this section forestalls closure by imposing a maximum separation between the now all-but-declared lovers: Melliora escapes to a convent to protect herself from her own attrac-tion to D'Elmont, whereas at the end of part 1 Amena's retirement to a convent figures as a sign of her living death.

The pattern of reversals initiated in part 2 is completed in part 3 as the abandoned (and fortuitously widowed) D'Elmont submits ut-terly to love's sway, abjuring the aggressive pursuit of lustful desire for helpless longing. At this crucial juncture—what does one do with a *male* hero who is utterly *passive?*—Haywood injects into the plot a fresh set of obstacles that channel the former rhythm of male sexual menace into a more worthy course of action. For when Melliora is kidnaped from the convent, D'Elmont must resurrect his prowess in service of a different cause, that of overcoming all sorts of external obstructions in order to save Melliora from the very sexual threat he has hitherto embodied. In the process he be-comes the hero, in effect, of a courtship plot. Thus, when united in marriage with Melliora at text's end, D'Elmont is invoked without any irony on Haywood's part as *the* example of pure "Conjugal Affection" (3:156). Under the all-absolving sign of romantic mar-riage, any apparent contradictions in his behavior—or in Hay-wood's narrative patterning—are summarily dismissed. The "happiness" of this climax is oddly reinforced by the tragic denoue-ment of a subplot involving the unrequited love and subsequent death of Violetta, a woman so madly in love with D'Elmont that she has disguised herself as his page to be near him. As Richetti percep-tively notes, *both* endings "bring release from the heroic tribula-tions of love"—D'Elmont and Melliora's by channeling love toward its proper goal in "Conjugal Affection," Viola's, by permitting the orgasm of death when love cannot be honorably requited.[41] Hay-wood's instinctive preference for this double ending reveals a rather damning similarity between conventionally tragic and come-dic ends of love, one that suggests the contradictions hidden within this text's thematic conflation of seduction and courtship modes as well. In a word, the narrative "logic" embodied in Haywood's courtship plot depends—as we shall also find in more sophisticated variations of the love-plot—on glossing over the cultural and sexual "illogic" embodied in the myth of the reformed rake.

In Richardson's epistolary version of the bourgeois Cinderella fable in *Pamela,* the major obstacle to marital union is not simply class or rank but, as in *Love in Excess,* the sexual prerogatives assumed by the upper class and given concrete representation in Mr. B's pursuit and Pamela's defense of her most precious "jewel" (6). Hence the structure of *Pamela,* like that of Haywood's novella, must trace the process of trial and conversion by which Pamela's would-be "violator" ultimately becomes, in the language of the novel, her avowed "protector" and "generous friend" (351). It does so by repeating and intensifying Pamela's central dilemma in situations of constraint that finally achieve release in a complete reversal of literal and figurative direction. Insofar as maximum discord yields to the reconciling "balance" of marital "oneness," the figure of *discordia concors* encoded in the novel's archetype of love relationship also becomes an apt metaphor for the chiasmic structure of its courtship plot. But if Pamela's Protestant ethic of wedlock is allowed a triumph over Mr. B's aristocratic libertinism, its victory comes at the price, as Watt has pointed out, of an even more rigid construction of "femininity" than ever: Pamela must simultaneously be passive, duplicitous, sexless, and sexy to win Mr. B's lifelong admiration.[42] "Love" in *Pamela,* as its narrative dynamics make clear, turns out to be a contest of dichotomous and unequal sexual roles from beginning to end, first eroticized as an antagonistic struggle between "feminine" virtue and "masculine" vice, and subsequently as a complementary alliance of male "master" and female "servant" in the socially approved sexual hierarchy of marriage.

The first phase of Richardson's plot, like Haywood's before him, follows a pattern of attraction and frustration inscribed by the force of male desire. As the naive postscript of Pamela's first letter reveals, the novel's opening moment coincides with the onset of Mr. B's passion: thus Richardson makes his love theme the originating "cause" of the novel, and erotic desire the impetus for all further narrative action. The narrational tension that marks the first stage of *Pamela*'s structure derives from the irony that neither the Andrews (the recipients of Pamela's letters) nor Richardson's readers (their "purchasers") are deceived about the sexual motives underlying Mr. B's overtures to the young girl. A gap in perspective is thus generated that, despite the text's proleptic subtitle, heightens the suspense regarding Pamela's fate: exactly *when* "will she or won't she"?[43] The narrative quickly moves from Mr. B's failure to reap sexual favors from his *verbal* sparring (for Pamela refuses to respond to the obligation his language of flattery attempts to impose) to his equally frustrated attempts at *physical* confrontation (springing from his hiding place in Pamela's closet, he is frightened off when Pamela faints dead away at his touch). The ironically "impotent" culminations to these escalating acts of aggression deliberately toy with both the reader's and Mr. B's expectations by forestalling an immediate convergence between the two protagonists.

The second stage of Pamela's tribulation and Mr. B's conversion repeats and ultimately reverses the first. It begins with an ironic rite of passage as Pamela resolves to leave the estate and reports in her letters that she has won her point as Mr. B orders a carriage to carry her home. Without her knowledge, however, her resolve has been countermanded by the more duplicitous plotting of her master, for Mr. B has ordered the carriage to pirate Pamela away to his secluded Lincolnshire estate, where she will become his literal prisoner. Thus, at the very moment Pamela thinks she is putting the greatest possible distance between herself and Mr. B, she is being directed into closer proximity to danger than ever. In this new and defamiliarizing setting, Pamela records a series of mental and physical tortures that seem to repeat the circumstances of the Bedfordshire experience in an increasingly feverish key: the claustrophobia of Mr. B's announced approach; an abortive escape attempt; an even more serious physical assault (this time Mr. B makes it to Pamela's bed disguised as her sleeping partner Nan); Pamela's deadly faint and (again) Mr. B's contrition; a second leave-taking. The latter event, however, reversing the associations of the first departure, becomes the novel's major turning point. For whereas Pamela's exit from Bedfordshire led her into actual physical captivity, her unimpeded departure from Lincolnshire only leaves her the prisoner of her own desires; by now she realizes that she loves her keeper more than her freedom. The turns of Richardson's plot have brought us almost exactly to the midpoint reversal of Haywood's novella, where Melliora's self-knowledge becomes reason enough for fleeing D'Elmont's presence.

Not only has repeated contact with Mr. B convinced Pamela of his potential for reformation; in a parallel reversal, he has begun to esteem Pamela's embattled virtue in spite of himself. This would-be seducer in effect authorizes—and, in the text's own language, authors—the courtship novel that the narrative of his and Pamela's life henceforth becomes. Even before she leaves Lincolnshire, Pamela's doubts about the "end" to which events are moving have begun to anticipate this change in genre. "If . . . I am not destined more surely than ever for ruin," she confides to her parents, "I . . . am either nearer my *happiness,* or my misery, than I ever was" (221). Thus, when Mr. B now writes Pamela that "all will end happily" (263) if she voluntarily returns to Lincolnshire, he lives up to his word by transforming an earlier taunt—"we shall make out between us, before we have done, a pretty story in romance, I warrant ye" (26)—into a literal truth. For he has facetiously undertaken to read Pamela's letters to know "in what manner to wind up the catastrophe of the pretty novel" (242) that he calls her life. And in being "touched . . . sensibly" (252) by its story, he writes the above-mentioned letter that summons Pamela to retrace her steps to a happier end.

The courtship theme hinges on this complete reversal of the literal and figurative directions, respectively, of Pamela's steps and of the narrative itself: due to Mr. B's change of heart, the obstacles represented by Pamela's lack of upper-class status and his own lack of middle-class morals are removed or mediated, and what has appeared a movement toward ultimate obstruction—epitomized by Pamela's leave-taking—turns out, as the reader has long suspected, to have been gradual convergence all along. As part of these reversals in narrative direction, the newly revealed lovers settle into the conventional roles proper to their sexes in the courtship ritual. Pamela submits in total trust to Mr. B's commands, saying she has "no will but yours" (291), and he chivalrously declares himself a "prisoner" accepting "the most agreeable fetters that ever man wore" (307)—an ironic choice of wording from a man who has forcibly kept the object of his desire under lock and key until sexual antagonism becomes sexual attraction.

For, courtly language aside, Mr. B remains "master" to Pamela's "servant" even in their companionate union. Erotic domination, as the psychoanalytic theorist Jessica Benjamin would say, is intrinsic to Pamela's essentially masochistic definition of her "feminine" identity and desires.[44] No longer overt signifiers of unbreachable class distinctions, as at the text's opening, the terms "master/servant" have become, ironically, *affectionate labels* designating the roles to be observed within the sexual hierarchy institutionalized by matrimony. It is not without due cause, therefore, that Pamela concludes the wedding ceremony with a gratefully submissive "Thank you sir" (364); she *must* be grateful for the social fiction that allows for the transformation of would-be rapists into merely "naughty" assailers and thence into fortuitously available husbands: "And thus, my dearest, dear parents, is your happy, happy, thrice happy Pamela, at last married; and to whom?—Why, to her beloved, gracious *master!* . . . And thus the dear, *once naughty assailer* of her innocence, by a blessed turn of Providence, is become the kind, the generous protector and rewarder of it" (364; emphasis added). Once the final obstacle, Pamela's integration into the country gentry, is removed in the post-wedding narration, Richardson finally brings plot and themes to a simultaneous close by returning the couple to Bedfordshire, the original "scene of the crime" where Pamela's textual existence began. As if to underline this circular repetition, Pamela pays a nostalgic visit to the summer house that, as Nancy Miller has noted, served as the occasion of Mr. B's "first violence to her virtue."[45] The vantage point of her newly acquired identity now allows Pamela *fondly* to reorder the past by recuperating those trials as part of an always operative, only unperceived, providential plan. Such repetition-with-a-difference, allowing both reader and Pamela a synchronic measure of the distance she has traversed in her rise from servant to mistress, draws a circle around her achievement that at once "freezes" her maturation at this point in time, completes the middle-class fantasy motivating this novel, and shields the marital ideal upon which her rewarded virtue pivots from further interrogation. Pamela's "reward" is ultimately the reader's gratification.

The wit, irony, and general knowingness of Jane Austen's canon is, technically speaking, worlds removed from Richardson's "to the moment" epistolary method. Nonetheless, as in *Pamela,* the narrative dynamic structuring *Pride and Prejudice* (1813) also consists of two parallel stages of courtship; in the latter, too, the repetition of frustration confers the hindsight necessary to reverse the negative effects of an initially mistaken discord and bring about the happy harmony of marriage. The feeling of most readers that this union *truly* balances the claims of self and society for its protagonists—a rare feat in the history of the marriage tradition—has to do with at least three factors. First, every stage of Austen's form so closely reinforces her themes that there is figuratively little space left to doubt the success of Elizabeth and Darcy. Second, Elizabeth's lively intelligence and "self-sufficiency without fashion"[46] bolsters one's conviction that she is Darcy's equal in all but social status, while her sheer energy of movement suggests the degree to which the plot of her story, in contrast to Pamela's, is the inscription of the heroine's own desires and its ending the consequence of her own choices. And third, Austen takes care never to create expectations for her protagonists that an enlightened understanding of marriage cannot fulfill. On one hand, Austen is as stern a critic of wedlock as the novel tradition would ever see; her impatience with the conventional wisdom labeling marriage, "however uncertain of giving happiness," as woman's "pleasantest preservative from want" (93) exacts its revenge in the counter-examples that shape Elizabeth's better judgment: Charlotte's mercenary match, Lydia's imprudent elopement, the Bennets' union of antithetical natures. On the other hand, as part of her inherited "classical" vision of the world, Austen instinctively felt that the right correctives applied to the worst abuses of society would make life within its framework not only possible but congenial; thus, as one critic points out, her female characters—even including Elizabeth—generally accept some curbing of their energies for the sake of the social structure.[47] So, too, with marriage as a social form. In Sandra Gilbert and Susan Gubar's words, "Austen admits the limits and discomforts of the paternal roof, but learns to live beneath it."[48] The same observation may be applied to Austen's adaptation and further refining of the courtship plot: on the level of the individual sentence (indeed, from the text's famous opening sentence onward), there exist many a devious inflection and glancing blow at sexual roles and marital institutions, but these barbs are safely loosed within a closed framework or superstructure designed to affirm a progressive vision of marriage as a viable social good.

The process by which Darcy and Elizabeth reach this point is unfolded within a symmetrically balanced structure that turns on the mid-novel rupture caused by Darcy's ill-advised proposal of marriage, an event paralleled but reversed at novel's end when his proposal is repeated and accepted. While the content differs in significant ways from *Pamela's*, the pattern of rupture and reversal, one might note, is nearly the same. Within this developmental frame, the energy driving the first half of Austen's text is created by comic situations in which the physical proximity between Darcy and Elizabeth is countered by the mental distance that separates them; the second half of the text reverses this scheme, staging situations in which external circumstances keep separating characters whose minds are increasingly attuned to one another. The "task" of the ending becomes one of balancing these unequal equations, so that physical and mental convergence can occur simultaneously. Just how and why Elizabeth and Darcy get off on the wrong footing, the raison d'être of this courtship plot, forms the subject of volume 1, which is constructed around a series of balls that evoke the traditional metaphor (which we have observed in Sir Thomas Elyot) of the dance as the "necessary conjunction" of the sexes. But the union that "betokeneth concord," according to Elyot, is in this instance caught in a protracted state of discord in which Darcy's precipitous prejudice finds its opposing force in Elizabeth's wounded pride. Thus the tenor of Elizabeth and Darcy's first meeting at the Assembly Ball in chapter 3 turns on her overhearing his unflattering reasons for refusing to dance with her; several days later, at Sir Lucas's in chapter 6, Elizabeth exacts the pleasurable revenge of refusing *his* invitation to dance; and, finally, when the two *do* dance at the Netherfield Ball of chapter 18, it is ironically to the displeasure of both—two opposing halves do not yet a whole make, in this case.

The linear sequence bridging the balls of chapters 3–6 and chapter 18 graphically illustrates the comedy of misperception that holds the two apart. For in chapters 7–12, the event of her sister Jane's illness at Netherfield has forced Elizabeth into an unwonted daily proximity with Darcy that has escalated into a verbal "war of wits" evocative of Beatrice and Benedick's adversarial wooing in *Much Ado about Nothing*. The hilarious irony of the situation that develops involves not only Elizabeth's stubborn blindness to Darcy's better qualities, but also his self-important confidence that she must look on him with as much favor as he has begun to see her. Thus, although neither is aware of it, their perspectival views are already locked in potential combat. The sequence binding chapters 13–17, in contrast, introduces Elizabeth's two suitors, Collins and Wickham; these subplots forewarn of the dangers of marriage for the sake of material security or sexual attraction alone. By the time of the disastrous Netherfield Ball in chapter 18, Austen's structure has thus laid bare all the marital options likely to present themselves to a woman of Elizabeth's standing, which makes all the more ironic the lack of rapprochement between the now-interested Darcy and the disaffected heroine.

This pattern of unmatched feelings within situations of forced proximity repeats itself when Elizabeth and Darcy renew contact at Rosings in volume 2. In the ensuing comedy of manners Darcy's all-but-avowed feelings again completely escape Elizabeth's notice until the famous proposal scene where Darcy's haughty offer is met by Elizabeth's immediate refusal. Exploding their parallel misperceptions and leaving both aghast, the event presents a mannered equivalent of the initial sexual impasse created in *Pamela* by Mr. B's pursuits and Pamela's deferrals. The scene also functions to bring all the obstacles to any future union between the two out into the open: on Elizabeth's part, Darcy's ungentlemanly manner, interference in Jane and Bingley's courtship, and unexplained behavior to Wickham; on his, the inferiority of her family connections. As hitherto internal barriers come to dictate the external course of action, the remaining plot becomes, in effect, a working out of the obstructions articulated in this mid-novel moment of rupture rather than rapture. With such a shift of focus, the irony of misperceptions governing the sequence of events up to this point is superseded, in a symmetrical reversal, by the ironies of external circumstance that will continue to divide Elizabeth and Darcy just when the situations in which they are being placed make both feel the most empathy yet for each other's viewpoints.

These reversals begin immediately after the ill-fated proposal as Elizabeth, receiving Darcy's letter explaining the Bingley and Wickham affairs, realizes his behavior is "capable of a turn" (154); the consequent revision of her misperceptions, in turn, revises the direction of the plot. The humiliation of facing her unfounded prejudices begins a process of self-knowledge ("Till this moment," Elizabeth admits, "I never knew myself" [156]) that culminates in her recognition of Darcy's actual worth as a suitor. On one hand, the very grammar of this epiphanic moment, in which Elizabeth is both subject and object, attests to the degree to which this heroine is an unconventionally active shaper of the plot of her self-awakening; a matured sensibility precedes her acceptance of a marital identity. And, yet, on the level of plot, the *context* of this moment of self-discovery speaks to the subtle limitations that the narrative structure of courtship imposes on female self-definition. For Elizabeth's awakening is irrefutably made contingent upon an event involving the dynamics of courtship—namely, Darcy's declaration of love and her own blindness to his desire—and her growth will be measured by her future responsiveness to possibilities of romantic affiliation. As the subject of a female bildungsroman, therefore, Elizabeth remains inscribed within the one arena, the one destiny, permitted by the mechanics of love-plotting.

The next stage of the text's repeating pattern of frustrated movements toward romantic union quickly follows this crucial turning point, as the unexpected encounter of the two protagonists at Pemberley (reported in vol. 3, ch. 1) gives Elizabeth the chance literally to "see" Darcy, framed by his own context, with new eyes. Just as Darcy's renewed attentions seem to augur a fresh accord, conventional expectation is quickly dashed by the climactic news (again registered in a letter) of Lydia's elopement with Darcy's enemy Wickham. In yet another of the symmetrical reversals staged by the narrative, the disappointment that was Darcy's at the moment of his proposal is now replayed as Elizabeth's despair. For— as with Pamela's penultimate rupture with Mr. B midway through Richardson's text—the heroine's recognition of a "gulf impassable" (231) simultaneously triggers an acknowledgment of her deepest feelings: "never had she so honestly felt that she could have loved him, as now, when all love must be vain" (206). As absence breeds desire, impasse again forestalls the movement to alliance, and the necessary, the only possible, result is the generation of yet more plot.

At this point, exactly one year having passed since the text's opening, the novel seems to repeat its beginning: as in the opening chapters, Bingley returns to the neighborhood of the Bennet home, again in Darcy's company, still unmarried and still, presumably, "in want of a wife" (1). Subjected to the same foolish predictions of her mother, Elizabeth is persuaded that everything is "hastening to the same vexatious conclusion" (251) as before—which is to say, continued disappointment. But as with the circularity bringing *Pamela* to a close, this repetition of event becomes a measure of the growth in individual perspectives that will allow a revision of the former plot of events. Thus, when Bingley and Jane meet at dinner, a literally straight line signaling an end to their uncertainties is drawn: "On entering the room, he seemed to hesitate; but Jane happened to look round, and happened to smile: it was decided. He placed himself by her" (253); shortly thereafter, Elizabeth has occasion to congratulate Jane on achieving "the happiest, wisest, most reasonable end!" (259). On the other hand, dinner only seems to increase the metaphoric distance separating Elizabeth and Darcy, try as she may to close the gap: "Mr. Darcy was almost as far from her, as the table could divide them" (253). For a final obstacle remains in the path of their union, materializing in the immediately following chapter in the arrogant person of Lady Catherine. In yet another ironic reversal, however, Lady Catherine's attempt to force a wedge between her nephew and Elizabeth on the ground of social inequality creates the peripeteia bringing the two together: not only does Lady Catherine's rude behavior remove the obstacle posed by Elizabeth's inferior connections by revealing Darcy's relatives to be just as disagreeable, but her prying questions give Elizabeth reason to hope that Darcy still cares for her. The deflation of Lady Catherine's expectation becomes the source of the reader's pleasure in satisfying his or her own.

Therefore, when next alone with Darcy in the immediately following chapter, Elizabeth begins to execute her own "resolution"—as well as set the course for the text's resolution—by initiating a conversation "for the sake of giving relief to my own feelings" (273). This evidence of Elizabeth's active desire is worlds removed from Pamela's obliging passivity. Yet at the same time Elizabeth's carefully couched words—which ostensibly refer to feelings less immediate than her desire for Darcy—abide by the male rules of the game of courtship. Like Jane's smile to Bingley, they allow the man to make an informed rather than mistaken guess, hence nominally to remain in control of events. The upshot, of course, is that this time Darcy's renewed proposal is met with Elizabeth's heartfelt acceptance. Such repetition-with-a-difference, measuring the narrative transformations wrought from beginning to ending propositions, thus becomes the means of "uniting them" in the happy synthesis signaled by the text's last two words. The equipoise that the structure attains in its conclusion reproduces, on the level of discourse, the complementary balance achieved in Elizabeth and Darcy's marriage; apparently mistaken discord has yielded to the *shared* viewpoints of equally intelligent counterparts.

What, then, of the sexual politics embedded in this companionate union, so strikingly different from the inequities persisting in the marriages of D'Elmont and Melliora, of Pamela and Mr. B? To large degree, of course, the erotic threat embodied in masterful suitors of the likes of D'Elmont and Mr. B has been displaced, in Austen's text, onto the sexually attractive but morally reprehensible Wickham. In contrast, Darcy's desires are never expressed in terms of sexual power; rather—and more importantly—his presumptive "mastery" imposes itself in terms of social and economic codes, as in the abortive proposal scene, and in the dynamics of the plot itself. For if Elizabeth, despite her self-assertion, finds her identity developing within a form of plotting that limits her to traditionally "feminine" alternatives, Darcy's development is largely excused from the vicissitudes of narrative duration: his transformation into a worthy suitor, unlike Elizabeth's, depends only on our "seeing" him in a changed context after the fact, a tactic easily provided for by a narrative ellipsis; Elizabeth, meanwhile, must undergo the cause and effect of personal growth in narrative time. Other traces of sexual inequity linger in the actual relationship established by the two lovers. Despite Austen's advocacy of similarities of temperament as the true test of attraction, to some degree the two also remain complementary opposites: thus Elizabeth sees Darcy's sober disposition, "though unlike her own," as one which can be softened by her contrasting "liveliness" (232). Tellingly, however, immediately following her acceptance of Darcy's proposal, she "checks" her impulse to tease him, "remember[ing] that he had yet to learn to be laught at" (278). The impulse to give Darcy time to grow, of course, is both endearingly human and humane, but it subtly reinforces Elizabeth's future role, as wife, to wait rather than initiate.[49]

Such hints of an asymmetrical marital dynamic, however, are overshadowed by the degree to which Elizabeth and Darcy truly appear suited for each other. The fiction of this suitability, in turn, is created and reinforced by the degree to which the novel's design of repetition and frustration seems to come full circle in the understanding achieved by these originally misunderstanding protagonists. For the carefully orchestrated sequence of final events imposes a sense of closure that ensures the happiness of Elizabeth and Darcy and the perpetuation of a better world (hence the harmony of the microcosmic community shown grouping around the two). If Elizabeth expands the range of female possibility through her activity and energy, she does so without radically challenging the structures of power governing her society; in this she is like her creator as an artist. Within the superstructure imposed by the mechanics of courtship plotting, admittedly enlarged and expanded to give her heroines the space to develop more freely than in prior love fiction, Austen creates the illusion of an ordered world that is contained and complete, and, insofar as her text reproduces this ideology, she stops short of questioning the necessity of marriage as the primary ordering desire of society itself.

Certainly the major nineteenth-century novelists after Austen—the Brontës, Hawthorne, Dickens, Thackeray, Trollope, Eliot, to name a few—made the story of love's progress a major unifying thread of their narrative formats. Nonetheless, the satisfying alignment that *Pride and Prejudice* creates between its form and content, not unlike its successful negotiation between the dictates of self and society, is a fairly rare accomplishment in the history of the English and American marriage tradition. The major impediment to successful courtship plotting, predictably, was the sexual ideology structuring its ends. It became increasingly difficult for subsequent novelists lacking Austen's neoclassical worldview—and particularly for serious women novelists—to repress from representation the conflict between a heroine's desire for growth and those social and marital institutions limiting the terms in which her adult identity as a woman could be expressed.

Despite the signs of this increasing strain infiltrating their texts, Charlotte Brontë's *Jane Eyre* (1847) and George Eliot's *Middlemarch* (1871–72) provide examples of the post-Austen courtship tradition at its best and brightest.[50] In *Jane Eyre* both perspectival and developmental facets of the novel's form are carefully governed by a univocal goal: Jane's achievement of a balanced, "full" identity that attains thematic and narrative synthesis in marriage to her "likeness," Rochester. As Peter Garrett has pointed out, the novel's dialectical movement between geographic settings associated with extremes of passionate rebellion and spiritual repression (Gateshead and Lowood, Thornfield and Moor House) forms a virtual graph of Jane's psychological progression toward a synthesis of these strands of personality in the adult freedom of self and love that her final destination, Ferndean and marriage to her "beloved master," is meant to represent.[51] However, the sheer difficulty of Bronte's attempt to create a final union of relative parity, one that will not wholly compromise Jane's insistent desire for a less stereotypically "feminine" completeness of being, can be inferred in the discomfort that many critics, both feminists and nonfeminists, have expressed over the maiming of Rochester as a necessary prelude to the lovers' reunion. Likewise, in spite of the satisfaction that the narrative of Dorothea's personal growth in *Middlemarch* yields, the disappointment many readers and critics have felt over the terms of her final alignment with Will Ladislaw—whatever one's view of his ultimate suitability for Dorothea—attests to the problems embedded in an inherited plot dynamic in which the heroine's quest for fulfillment cannot be separated from issues of love and marriage, from dynamics of gender and power.

As much about marriage as the wooing process, *Middlemarch* also illustrates a version of the courtship format appearing with increased frequency after the 1850s, one in which an initial courtship and "bad" marriage (such as Dorothea's to the tyrannical Casaubon) forms a preparatory stage for the rewards of true love; as such the formula operates similarly to the schema that Kennard has dubbed the double-suitor convention. The paradigm appears as early as Eliza Haywood's *The Padlock; or, No Guard without Virtue*

(1726) in which an ill-used wife receives her reward in the form of a truly devoted second husband. But for the Victorian novelist this plot formulation held particular appeal as a way of responding to the strained literary realism of presenting all married life as one happy end, as well as a way of giving recognition to the growing public discourse on the legal and psychological abuses perpetuated by real-life marriage; in addition to Eliot's example, Wilkie Collins's melodramatic *The Woman in White* (1860), DeForest's Civil War romance *Miss Ravenel's Conversion* (1867), and Meredith's *Diana of the Crossways* (1885) illustrate some of the possibilities to which the formula lent itself. Yet, as an application of Kennard's analysis of the ideological values embedded in the double-suitor convention would imply, the final relationships established in even the most progressive of these texts retain traces of the asymmetrical alignments of gender within matrimony that the two-marriage formula was at least in part an attempt to escape.

Less frequently, as in the case of Brontë's *Villette* (1853) or the original version of Dickens's *Great Expectations* (1861), novelists have chosen to represent the trajectory of *unsuccessful* courtship. Such plots, however, generally contain their unhappy reverberations within tragically closed formats as ideologically delimited as that of the courtship paradigm. Thus, in the intended conclusion to *Great Expectations*, Pip's failure in love is meliorated by a tragic suffering that bestows the emotional integrity and saddened maturity that facilitates his abjuration of romantic illusions and his adult integration into society. That the novel's "second" ending, a subdued reunion of the estranged lovers demanded by Dickens's publishers, almost equally well rounds out the themes and design of the novel attests to the reversibility of comedic and tragic endings to the courtship narrative. In either case there is a final synthesis to Pip's acquisition of adult maturity, an achievement of a seemingly stable identity that will resist future vacillation; in neither is the ideal of romantic wedlock questioned in and of itself. The tragic plot of *Villette* is made more complex by the feminist impulse lying behind Brontë's characterization of Lucy Snowe's inner erotic life, as I will suggest in the conclusion to the next chapter. Nonetheless, with the loss at sea of her betrothed (an ending as much disputed by Brontë's publisher as Dickens's original conclusion by his own),[52] the text may be seen as bringing to an aching but elegiacally fitting close the strains of renunciation and essential aloneness that have shaped Lucy's external emotional life from its outset. For Brontë the choice to depict the tragic frustration of a true love becomes a strategic move allowing her to sidestep the issues we have seen disturbing the intended final symmetry of other courtship plots—in this case, whether Lucy's hard-earned selfhood would have eventually come into conflict with her inclination toward emotional bondage in love, and with Paul Emmanuel's toward total mastery, had the two actually married. Ambiguous and open as *Villette*'s ending to some degree is, its overt courtship format unconsciously serves the conservative purpose of naturalizing the romantic ideal by averting an exploration of its potential contradictions in practice.[53]

The problems embedded in literary and social conventions of love become even more pronounced in examples of the female bildungsroman that end in the independently minded heroine's death. As several critics have illuminatingly demonstrated in regard to Eliot's *The Mill on the Floss* (1860) and Edith Wharton's *The House of Mirth* (1905), the extremity of such a solution writes into the form of these two texts a devastating critique of cultural institutions regulating women and passion.[54] But death as the final "end," no less than marriage, simultaneously enforces a closural pattern of transcendence, of an end to human desire, that works to reinforce both cultural standards of morality and literary ideals of poetic justice: the female rebel against the prescribed destiny and rules of her sex, no matter her degree of inner integrity, is demonstrated to have no place, literally, in the contained fictional world of the hierarchically structured novel, or in the hypothetical order it reproduces. The tragic love-plot thus effectually writes the problematic Maggie Tullivers of fiction out of existence, and in the process the social order that has motivated her eviction is left, like the closed narrative pattern of her life and death, intact.

Trajectories of Doom: The Seducer's Plot in *Clarissa* and *Tess of the D'Urbervilles*

The tragedy of love, however, most often occurs as a tragedy of sex in the Anglo-American tradition, taking the form of "gothic" seduction narrative; the defamiliarizing traits of the gothic allow for a psychodramatic rendering of the torments of sexual victimization less likely to be ventured in strictly realistic fiction. On its most basic level, the seduction plot reads like a tale of courtship gone awry: stripped of the veil of social propriety or moral constraints, would-be lovers are revealed as sexual antagonists and the witty verbal sparring of suitors is transformed into ritualized physical combat. In the polarized figures of seducer and pure maiden, the metaphoric "war of the sexes" becomes a grim *literal* reality, a fight to the death over female chastity: "War always with my foe," one seduced heroine sounds its battle cry, "war to the knife, war to the last!"[55] As our prior readings of the seduction-to-courtship formula in Haywood's *Love in Excess* and Richardson's *Pamela* might suggest, the objectification and subjugation of woman inherent in idealized versions of romantic love are simply carried to their logical extreme in the pure seduction narrative: by reducing women to anonymous objects of sexual conquest, the seducer no less than the legitimate suitor attempts to erase those signs of female autonomy and otherness that threaten his own identity as the superior and more powerful sex.[56]

In the process, the developmental pattern of separation/union typifying courtship plotting is subsumed in seduction fiction into one of pursuit/division as a series of scenes of ever-narrowing entrapment rivet attention on the impending sexual violation—and psychic fragmentation—of the female protagonist. Accordingly, narrative movement becomes the province of the male figure, who expends his libidinal energies in devising multiple stratagems, and therefore creating more and more "plot," till his desire—the deflowering and breaking of his victim's will—is attained. The female protagonist, in contrast, typically attempts to *halt* action, to remove herself from the hazards of narrative time and narrative desire, in order to escape the seducer's plots. But the only "out" from such a dynamic is the death that is the end of narrative itself, and hence, in contrast to the comedic ending that predominates in courtship movements, the inverted text of seduction most often enforces closure through tragedies of death or exile. Ostensibly mourning the abuse of virtue by indicting those antagonists—the rapacious seducer, the fallen woman—who have betrayed the higher dictates of morality and married love, the seduction narrative justifies its disturbing, often voyeuristic content by situating it within tragic formats whose function is to transform its metonymic representation of illicit sexuality into static moral exempla. Such overdetermining ends implicitly endorse romantic wedlock, by its absence or subordination to a secondary plot line, as the only viable economy of female desire.

But the authorial distribution of poetic justice meted out in novelistic tragedies of seduction simultaneously betrays some of the contradictory values invested in its ideology and form. For the double standard by which even innocent female victims of male sexual violence are made to suffer fates worse than those of their seducers attests to the ideological and psychological inequities buried in a cultural standard of male superiority. The woman who *willingly* lapses from a moral code that upholds the sanctity of marriage, of course, suffers the worst punishments. She threatens, indeed, an even more damaging exposure of the contradictions embedded in the social order—first, because she co-opts the male prerogative of desiring, and second, because her very existence outside the accepted male–female hierarchy recapitulated in marriage disproves its universal applicability.[57] In telling contrast, the male seducer often exudes an attractiveness that his villainy can never quite dispel, and as such he embodies a fastidious culture's self-exposing fear yet envy of the power of desire: he is dangerous not only in his sexual prowess, but also in his liberating—and appealing—exercise of an imaginative solipsism that threatens to spill over the "fixed" boundaries of stable, socially defined identity.[58] Thus, like the seduced maiden or impure woman—embarrassing signifiers of a lapse in the patriarchal logic of paternal benevolence—the male seducer, although allowed a short exercise of his sexual prerogative, must ultimately be reined in by the appropriate masculine authorities lest his unregulated energy disrupt the illusion of order necessary to social harmony.

This double-edged valorization of male power (as natural sexual force, as legal authority) inscribes itself into the narrative rhythm of the seduction text in revealing ways. For instance, the author's control over the reader's participation in the unfolding narrative parallels the manipulative control asserted by the seducer, who is not infrequently figured as the "author" of the heroine's destiny: within this dynamic the reader (whether male or female) becomes the victim, like the female protagonist, of a power beyond his or her control. Yet at the same time the ingress the text grants its readers into scene after scene of sexual temptation and titillation, exploiting the erotic dynamic involved in the very act of reading, ultimately implicates the reader in the narrated action as voyeur: our "position" in the text as distanced yet privileged onlooker transforms us into yet another of the heroine's victimizers.[59] By simultaneously enforcing these dual identifications, the very construction of the seduction plot thus makes its audience complicit in a textual design of mastery and submission that is necessarily ideological—and I would suggest that this contradictory double identification applies equally to male and female readers, although there may well be significant differences in how the reading experience of finding oneself in the position of "victim" or "violator" is assimilated into and exploited by the psychology of the reader. The following pages will attest to the various ways in which three representative texts—Haywood's *The Mercenary Lover* (1726), Richardson's *Clarissa; or, the History of a Young Lady* (1747–48), and Hardy's *Tess of the D'Urbervilles* (1891)—have promulgated this dynamic, even while criticizing it, and, in so doing, have perpetuated the sexual values intrinsic to a patriarchal social order.

In the classic seduction plot, the male's physical and psychological combat with the virginal heroine invariably unlocks the story of her fall, abandonment, broken heart, and death: its trajectory of decline and descent is as tragic as the ascendant star of successful courtship is generally comedic. Many seduction fictions—*Charlotte Temple, Ruth, Tess of the D'Urbervilles*, to name a few—stage the woman's initial fall quite early in the narrative in order to dwell at greater length on the protracted stages of her degradation (and less frequently, as in Gaskell's *Ruth*, on her tragic redemption). An exemplary case is Haywood's *The Mercenary Lover; or, The Unfortunate Heiress*, whose sexual adversaries, Clitander and Althea, are pure representations of unregenerate male lust and cloistered female virtue. The first fifteen pages of this novella rush toward the climactic pronouncement, signaled in one of Haywood's few paragraph markings, "The Scene of Ruin now over . . ."[60] Significantly, however, this prototypical fable of seduction begins with a wedding, that of Clitander to Althea's sister in what *appears* to all the world to be "the most exemplary [of] patterns of Conjugal Affection" (11)—a verbal echo of that state Haywood asks us to believe the ex-libertine D'Elmont has achieved at the end of *Love in Excess*. Almost immediately Clitander sets into motion his evil designs on Althea, his sister-in-law, and the incestuous implications of the resulting triangular configuration are meant to drive home to the reader the enormity of Clitander's dual crime against ideal love and family: he is no mere seducer and enemy of pure love but a breaker of the taboos upon which the foundations of organized society depend.[61] It is also telling that Clitander desires not only Althea's body but her sizable inheritance; the monetary gain that so pronouncedly rewards virtue in the paradigmatic courtship plot is grotesquely conflated with sexual expenditure in this gothically inverted world. In contrast, Althea's serious turn of mind and belief in goodness (characteristics that would make her an admirable heroine in Austen) become the very traits that blind her to Clitander's dissembling wiles until his persuasive manipulation of the fawning *language* of love, emotionally placing her "absolutely in his power" (13), has moved her over "the Brink" (15) of rational control. The threshold moment that brings self-knowledge for Elizabeth Bennet is figured as loss of reason, a fall into the chasm of irrational passion, for Althea.

In the post-seduction sequence of events, Althea's pregnancy, perversely "arousing" Clitander's hatred and fear of discovery, engenders his plot to murder her. Within the logic of the marriage tradition, the progression is less improbable than it may initially seem: unsanctioned male desire *is* deadly, phallic sexuality always borders on the murderous. This scheme Clitander sets into motion in an instance of narrative repetition: once again playing the lover to the wretched girl, he writes "artful" letters of conciliation that move her to a fatal "second yielding" in spirit. Ironically, Clitander's greatest tactic in regaining Althea's affection is entirely verbal and nonphysical, as he draws upon the imagery of the sentimental love ethic to represent their union as a mating of "Minds . . . pair'd by Heaven, [as if] we two were chosen from the unnumber'd Millions . . . to prove the Immortality of a perfect Passion" (47). As Althea "melts" before such language, the script of her doom is again being written by her society's definition of the roles and desires "natural" to both sexes. For it is Clitander's inherently "masculine" power to be so designing and artful an "Author of her Ruin" (40), while Althea's

confused acquiescence is the natural consequence of "the Irresolution of a Female Mind when agitated by that undoing Passion"
(45)—a fact that Clitander as "Author" so well knows.

As the villain moves to complete his murderous plot, the ritualistic sex-combat of seduction in effect becomes a literal fight to
the death; the erotics of narrative, the enticements which spur the
act of reading, become ominously necrophilic as the plot's "climax"
is figured (as in Monk Lewis's later *The Monk*) as a sexual death:
beyond this point the plot, lacking a victim, can go no further.
Moreover, to italicize the enormity of the tragic end to which unbridled sexuality leads even a virtuous woman, the narrative closes
with a melodramatically gothic depiction, extended for several
paragraphs, of the mad ravings and horrific death of Althea: she
undergoes all the agonies of the damned in what is at least subconsciously a perverted figure of female orgasm. Clitander, on the
other hand, enjoys a certain "triumph" (62) in never being pros-
ecuted for his crimes. Hence, just as Haywood's seduction plot begins with the premise of an unbridgeable male-female dichotomy,
it ends by maintaining the gulf between the sexes in this unequal
dispensation of legal and poetic justice.

Richardson's deeply psychological and self-consciously critical
probing into the motivations of seducer and victim in *Clarissa*
(1747–48) places his text on an entirely different imaginative and
emotional plane than the combination of voyeuristic delight and
moralistic horror animating Haywood's text. In effect, *Clarissa*
turns the plot of *Pamela* on its head, offering in its themes and form
a harsh critique of the gendered system of power that the former
novel often seems to take for granted. Nonetheless, this monumental study of the mechanics of erotic domination triggered in its
hordes of imitators, in Leslie Fiedler's words, a "notion of love as
[an ultimate] war of the sexes," whatever Richardson's intentions.[62]
Reading and rewriting the novel through the lens of cultural
norms, subsequent writers of conventional seduction tragedies
found in its subject and design ample testimony supporting their
belief in a "natural" opposition between men and women as the
basis of heterosexual relationship, be it expressed in legitimate or
illegitimate forms.

In presenting the inverse image of *Pamela*'s euphoric trajectory,

THE SEDUCER'S PLOT

Clarissa reads at times like a palimpsest of its predecessor: Lovelace's assaults on Clarissa's virtue repeat the stages of Mr. B's persecution of Pamela (flattery, linguistic manipulation, kidnaping, confinement) with the crucial exception that there is no implicit guarantee of virtue being "rewarded" as the final result of this sexual confrontation of opposing wills. It is, rather, part of the text's strategy that the opening action blur the thin line separating the courtship and seduction plot; Lovelace appears both attractive and vaguely menacing as he attempts to insinuate himself into Clarissa's favor through his covert letters. The problem facing Clarissa as she struggles to interpret his overtures—simultaneously the reader's dilemma until Lovelace's self-revealing letters to Belford begin—is therefore initially an epistemological one. Hence the first phase of Richardson's developmental structure consists of Clarissa's withholding of either commitment or judgment as she desperately attempts to gain time to establish a correct "reading" of Lovelace's character. She is less a character in search of a plot than, in a sense, one who needs to determine the kind of narrative into which her author has already placed her. "Whatever course I shall be *permitted* or be *forced* to steer, I must be considered as a person out of her own direction" (1:345–46), she writes Anna; her task is to find whether there are alternatives to the two "romantic" scenarios (one being the offer of Solmes, her family's economically motivated choice of suitor, and the other that of Lovelace) that block her own choice (which is that of removing to the literal "plot" of the estate she has inherited from her grandfather, there to achieve "the desired port" of "the single state" [1:346]).

The effort to forestall action, however, is shattered as Lovelace's stratagems precipitate her unthinking escape from the Harlowe family garden into the confinement of his coach. With its rapid movement toward an unknown end hurling Clarissa out of the metaphoric stasis of innocence into narrative time, Richardson inaugurates the metonymic chain of events, figured as a series of symbolic enclosures (like this coach), that constitute the "erotic" dynamic of seduction narrative—movement within an ever-narrowing space from which there is no true escape. In contrast to the pivotal turning points of courtship formulas, which often hinge on the separation of potential lovers, the literal *convergence* of Clarissa and Lovelace in rushing out of the garden together (a calculated reference to the ending of *Paradise Lost*) ironically marks the point of greatest psychological *division* between their perspective to this point. This distance is precisely what Clarissa must close if she is to learn in time how to read the plot of Lovelace's designs in regard to her future.

Thus, the second stage of Clarissa's dawning knowledge is inaugurated as she becomes aware of the extent of Lovelace's calculations to bring her into his "power" (one of the text's most repeated phrases) and out of her own. The ensuing structural alternation between Clarissa's letters to Anna and those of Lovelace to Belford at once reveals to the reader the disparity between Lovelace's words and intentions and measures Clarissa's progress in breaking down epistemological barriers to truth; in turn, the reader's greater knowledge of the closing gap between Lovelace's desires and deeds generates a narrational tension that structurally functions to rivet our attention upon, while increasing our horror at, Clarissa's vulnerable situation. For Clarissa, too, the collapse of perspectival distance that she has sought only spells out the inevitability of her approaching doom as Lovelace's intentions become all too clear: his goal, most simply, hinges on destroying not merely her "virtue" but also the sensed autonomy of one who withholds from him the psychological recognition upon which his own sense of being, his "masculine" élan, rests. The irony here, of course, is that if Lovelace's power depends on Clarissa's recognition, then his sadistic persecutions undercut the myth of his superior power by revealing that his mastery is the slave of constructed desires, hence an assumed—and ambivalent—*role* rather than a natural force.[63]

The sense of menace intrinsic to the plotting of seduction narrative is also reproduced in Richardson's text by its delineation of the stages of Clarissa's forced removal from the world of the familiar. Progressively stripped of geographic, moral, and psychological props and placed in increasingly stifling situations of confinement, she is left fighting off Lovelace's advances only on the grounds of her increasingly diminished self. The nightmarish narrative dynamic of continual assault is counterpointed—in a strategy typical of seduction fiction—by Clarissa's determination to plot a way out of Lovelace's deadly masterplot, a task complicated (again, without her knowledge) by his interception of her correspondence. Near escapes finally culminate in the actual escape to Hampstead, but the distance Clarissa believes finally to have put between herself and her tormentor turns out to be an illusion. For, immediately after Richardson presents Clarissa's letter informing Anna of her "success," he juxtaposes it with Lovelace's renewed correspondence to Belford revealing his knowledge of Clarissa's whereabouts and his diabolic scheme to recapture her: he has again seized authorial control from Clarissa's hands. The quickening narrative pace as Lovelace's voice (and desire) almost exclusively appropriates the text reveals both his power of the moment and the proximity of a textual climax that looms as a verbal equivalent of Lovelace's own impending orgasm. The height of this linguistic frenzy is cut short, however, in a disconcertingly abrupt cessation of forward momentum, as Lovelace reports in the novel's shortest letter that the anticipated conquest *has already passed:* "And now, Belford, I can go no farther. The affair is over. Clarissa lives" (3:196).

The structural orchestration that has been leading to this moment is profoundly disturbing on several levels. Primarily, it illuminates the degree to which a text's "pornographic" element exists as much in its plotting as in any concrete representation of an act of rape. For the readerly desire to press forward and discover the outcome of Lovelace's attempt approximates the very dynamic of textual and physical appropriation by which Lovelace enforces his own desire, while the *absence* of that very moment from the text compels the reader imaginatively to fill in the missing picture and therefore *re*create the scene of the rape. But to the extent that its literal absence deprives us (and perhaps, as Judith Wilt has argued, even Lovelace)[64] of the "satisfaction" promised by traditional narrative climaxes, this *void* in the text also approximates the violence done to Clarissa, senseless or "voided" during the assault and temporarily crazed, her rational memory erased, immediately after. The perverse dynamics of this seduction narrative thus enforce the reader's participation as both master and victim in the representation of the un(re)presentable crime of rape.

Once this point has been reached, the direction of the narrative is inevitably reversed. Having expended his desire, Lovelace literally can "go no farther" in instigating plot or directing action; Belford's letters of reproach and, eventually, the reemergence of Clarissa's temporarily suppressed voice signal the beginning of a counter-movement toward an ending in which seducer is mentally punished and victim is spiritually rewarded. For, ironically, Lovelace's violation of Clarissa, the ultimate moment of their *union,* has inaugurated their total *division,* both mentally and physically, for the remainder of the text; as in the earlier garden-escape scene, the text's structural climax inverts the usual turning point of courtship narrative, where seemingly irreconcilable division is actually the pretext for impending union. Moreover, as the crucial last words of Lovelace's letter, "Clarissa lives," tacitly admit, he has failed to master her essential will, and the emptiness of his sexual conquest only underscores for him—and the reader—the inviolate superiority of Clarissa's virtue to his merely temporal power. In turn, the rape confirms Clarissa in her personal resolution never to marry her seducer, despite the appeals of both his and her friends. Her subsequent flight from Mrs. Sinclair's "inner" house of horror, this time successful, foreshadows the spiritual liberation for which she now begins to prepare herself as she wills herself to die to the world that has abused her. The stasis of death has, ironically, become Clarissa's final freedom and pleasure; her narrative desire has become the desire for an absolute "ending."

In the eyes of the general eighteenth-century reading public, Clarissa's tragic apotheosis and heavenly gain of a bridegroom in Christ provided the only possible resolution to her defilement. And in the telling double logic that the very form of the classic love-plot ensures, the paradox of the pure spirit of woman triumphing over victimization by the agency of her death confirmed not only the prevailing sentimental archetype of the spiritually superior but static nature of "femininity," but also its practically *inferior* status in face of the diachronically represented realms of "masculine" domination and of narrative plot.

Nearly a century and a half later, Thomas Hardy was to attempt a similar defense of the sexually violated but morally pure woman in *Tess of the D'Urbervilles* (1891). However, despite his eloquent defense of Tess's essential purity (the subtitle is "A Pure Woman Faithfully Presented"), he, like Richardson, upholds many of the sexual stereotypes and structural conventions embedded in the closed format of seduction. Beginning with the foreshadowing of Tess's sexual fall in the early scene when Prince is stabbed by the "pointed shaft" of the mail-cart,[65] the tightly interlocked sequence of events constituting the substance of Hardy's tragedy and Tess's short life is directly traceable to and repeats the violence of her sexual violation by Alec D'Urberville. Pitting rakish pseudo-aristocrat against morally superior servant in this plot nexus, Hardy of course revives the *Pamela* archetype and, in doing so, underlines the economic correlatives of sexual power; it is concern for her family's financial situation upon Prince's death, after all, that has brought Tess within Alec's orbit. As in Haywood's *The Mercenary Lover,* the actual seduction or rape (Hardy purposefully creates an ambiguity as to which) occurs early in the text, at the end of the first of the novel's seven "phases." Significantly, the event is not described beyond Alec's approach to Tess's sleeping body, for at this point the authorial narrator pulls back from the immediate scene to muse over the inexplicable fatality of the "coarse pattern" that this "beautiful feminine tissue" is "doomed to receive" (63). In an image meant to turn the reader's attention from the material to the philosophical, Hardy's language of sympathy virtually commits the violence his direct representation avoids: the metaphoric inscription of the seducer's "coarse pattern" or plot over the unwritten text of Tess's objectified body—tissue "blank as snow" (63)—forcefully reminds us of the psychological convergence between acts of narrative and physical violation in seduction plotting.

The result in *Tess* is a linear narrative organization that is bracketed by murderous acts (Prince's death, the stabbing of Alec, both repeating the irreversible harm done to Tess) and that is structured, like Richardson's text and other examples of the mode, by a relentless rhythm of pursuit and flight; for however much Tess attempts to escape the past and start a new life, her loss of virtue returns in one form or another (an illegitimate child; overheard rumors; her guilt-induced confession to Angel Clare; Alec's reappearance) to pursue her to the grave. As Hardy says in the last lines of phase one, "The Maiden," in an image of rupture that echoes the language of Haywood and Richardson, "An immeasurable social *chasm* was *to divide* our heroine's personality thereafter from that previous self of hers" (64; emphasis added), and it is the translation of these social divisions inward that will leave Tess at the end of her life so psychically splintered that she will even lack the conscious inner integrity that serves as the dying Clarissa's recompense for worldly suffering.

The pathos of Tess's situation is heightened by the parallel plot of her courtship by and eventual marriage to Angel Clare, who cannot accept her "sin" and deserts her on their wedding night. Reported in the overlap between the pointedly titled phases "The Consequence" and "The Woman Pays," Angel's desertion forms another kind of violation of Tess, mirrored in the text's division into the two books at this point. While Hardy argues forcefully and eloquently against the moral prescriptions of his age rendering a woman's sexuality, a natural process, into an irreversible crime ("Was once lost always lost really true of chastity? . . . The recuperative power which pervaded organic nature was surely not denied to maidenhood alone" [87]), his debunking of conventional moral standards does not really call into question the dualistic nature of the sexual ethos underlying either Tess's victimization or Angel's avowal of the double standard; what Hardy sees as Tess's innate virtue, as well as her self-destructive acquiescence to fate ("this feminine loss of courage at the last and critical moment" [267]), are traditionally female attributes, after all. Penny Boumelha notes that Tess's tragedy "turns on an ideological basis, projecting a polarity of sex and intellect, body and mind, upon an equally fixed polarity of gender" in which "sex and nature are assigned to the female."[66] As a symbol of Nature, moreover, Tess becomes a passive victim like the wounded pheasants she finds in the forest; as such her situation resembles Clarissa's, another hunted prey fallen victim to the "sportive cruelty" that Lovelace explicitly associates with men: "We begin, when boys, with birds, and when grown up, go on to women" (2:245).

One result of the basic dualisms structuring Hardy's philosophy and unconsciously obstructing his impassioned critique of social mores is to be found in the point of view the text establishes vis-à-vis Tess as its passive subject. For the very concern with maligned female sexuality that leads Hardy to make Tess's consciousness the center of his narration ironically turns her into a recumbent object of the text's and thence the reader's fetishizing desire, as the oblique presentation of the seduction/rape scene has already indicated. "And so it is that all the passionate commitment to exhibiting Tess as the subject of her own experience," Boumelha says of the sexual imagery pervading the representation of Tess, "evokes . . . in the narrative voice . . . erotic fantasies of penetration and engulfment [that] enact a pursuit, violation and persecution of Tess in parallel with those she suffers at the hands of her two lovers."[67] The *subject* of any narrative act is in some sense an object to be consumed, but when the *subject matter* is female seduction, the potential for a kind of ideological abuse of the reader soars exponentially as the erotics of narration veer in and out of the experiential reality described within the text.

The series of symbolic enclosures ending the novel reinforces Hardy's sympathetic but ultimately conservative view of the sexes. Once Tess murders Alec (a literalization of the motif of sexual warfare characterizing the seduction narrative in general), she temporarily escapes with Angel to experience the honeymoon she was previously denied in what Alan Friedman calls "a ghastly parody of the classic ending of a novel,"[68] but which (like Clarissa's anticipated "marriage" to Christ) serves at least partially as a nostalgic reminder of the forfeited ideal, of what could and should have been a better story of love. This dreamlike moment of stasis in the shut-up country estate, however, is broken, true to the form of the seduction narrative, by a resumed pursuit that ends in yet another enclosure: Tess's circumscription and capture within Stonehenge's symbolic circle. Her role as sacrificial victim, like Althea's and Clarissa's, is completed in the final scene, her hanging. To this ending, moreover, as if to underscore the relation between his tale and the abused ideal motivating it, Hardy appends the disconcerting event of Angel and Tess's sister romantically joined in an image of closure derived from the final lines of *Paradise Lost:* "they arose, joined hands again, and went on" (355). Once again, the story of sexual fall is linked to the myth of a greater fall, with the emphasis this time on the restorative properties of the "paradise regained" in true love. Via the agency of this double ending, Hardy's text maintains an ethos identical to the double standard previously condemned in Angel's behavior to Tess: for it permits the male survivor of this tragedy the reward of a second, this time unsullied, feminine ideal of love made in the image of his first.

While *Clarissa* and *Tess of the D'Urbervilles* illustrate with particular vividness the narrative dynamics at work in sophisticated examples of the seduction plot, neither comes close to matching the blatant thematic and textual exploitation characterizing most of the popular fictions of sex written between Richardson's and Hardy's time. Before turning to this chapter's third paradigm, the wedlock plot, the following paragraphs will simply sketch the contours and fate of the seduction narrative in these intervening decades. In England, the Richardsonian seduction theme was quickly assimilated into the evolving antirealist gothic tradition as one of its staple sources of nightmare: in a bourgeois culture whose keepers of morality tended to view all unlicensed sexuality with a kind of horror, the gothic novel's perverse equation of the *frissons* of terror and of unbridled sexual desire seemed quite "natural" (indeed, we see it continuing in current pornography). The labyrinthine plots of confinement and escape, of pursuit and discovery, characterizing such gothic prototypes as Walpole's *The Castle of Otranto* (1765), Radcliffe's *The Mysteries of Udolpho* (1794) and Lewis's *The Monk* (1796), provide provocative evidence of the patriarchal worldview encoded in the dynamics of the seduction format and the marriage tradition as a whole. Hence Radcliffe's female protagonist, Clarissa-like in her sufferings, remains utterly passive in the face of her tormentors, with both menace and rescue falling to the lot of the dominant male. In contrast, once Lewis's male protagonist is seduced and becomes a seducer, his unleashed desire breeds dreams of total phallic power and conquest that generate the remainder of the plot. The frenzied culmination of his desires, in a narrative climax in which the double act of rape and murder conflates sex and death as one event, becomes a graphic illumination of the consequences of a cultural ethos reading sexual difference as essential opposition.

In addition to its propensities for gothic display, the paradigm of seduction also lent itself to highly sentimentalized themes, as the origins of American fiction attest: W. H. Brown's *The Power of Sympathy* (1789), Susanna Rowson's *Charlotte Temple* (1791), and Hannah Foster's *The Coquette* (1797) all derive their pathetic appeal from the example of Richardson. Whereas Rowson's and Foster's heroines, dying in childbirth near their text's ends, illustrate the near-tragic uniformity befalling the female victim of seduction, the trajectory of seduction often collapses into its mirror opposite, courtship—a process we have already noted in *Pamela*'s plot—in the women's fictional tradition especially strong in mid-nineteenth-century America.[69] In Augusta Jane Evans's best-selling melodrama, *St. Elmo* (1866), for instance, the orphaned Edna Earl is pursued by a veritable moustache-twirling villain (of the sort Hardy satirized in his characterization of Alec D'Urberville), who is made to renounce his wayward behavior and become a clergyman (again foreshadowing Hardy's satiric representation of Alec's conversion). At this point, Edna Earl can comfortably accept her former persecutor as "my first and my last and my only love" in a declaration that exposes, yet again, the shared ideological values linking courtship and seduction under the auspices of the marriage tradition.[70]

Although Gaskell's *Ruth* (1853) forms a notable exception, Victorian realists were in general content to incorporate seduction into their texts as admonitory subplots (hence Em'ly's story in *David Copperfield*, Hetty's in *Adam Bede*). Its secondary status as such could thus "safely" be used to enhance the exemplary status and appeal of the wedlock ideal touted in the narrative's major development. In contrast, Hardy's controversial publication of *Tess* heralded a return of the "dangerous" theme of overt female sexuality to serious fiction. But while versions of the seduction topos have continued in the twentieth century, the lifting of the sexual taboo has stripped the classic archetype of embattled seducer/virgin of much of its former power to horrify and titillate. If the seduced heroine—like Dreiser's Carrie Meeber—is no longer devastated by her loss of virginity, the narrative of seduction ceases to produce the same kind of voyeuristic sexual gratification cum tragic moral. This is not to deny the persisting tragedy of sexual combat and female victimization enacted in modern fiction—novels by Hemingway, Faulkner, and Henry Miller, by Jean Rhys and Anaïs Nin, leap to mind—but such destructive dynamics typically unfold on the grounds of the mutually entered sexual relationship or the extramarital affair. To speak of adultery, however, is to encroach on the home territory encompassed by paradigmatic plots of wedlock, and to these we shall now turn.

The Dynamics of Domesticity: The Wedlock Plot in *Amelia* and *A Modern Instance*

Wedlock versions of the love-plot have always held a more tenuous position than either courtship or seduction paradigms in the marriage tradition—partly because the narrative of wedded life lacks the teleological finality of courtship and seduction movements, and partly because too complete a representation of the married state runs the risk of becoming, as we shall see in the next chapter, a deconstruction of its ideality. As Thackeray satirically notes in *Vanity Fair* (1847–48), it is far safer for the writer to close his or her eyes to the "drama" of married life unfolding on the other side of the novel's countless "happy endings" in marriage: "As his hero and heroine pass the matrimonial barrier, the novelist generally drops the curtain, as if the drama were over then: the doubts and struggles of life ended: as if, once landed in the marriage country, all were green and pleasant there: and wife and husband had nothing but link each other's arms together, and wander gently downwards towards old age in happy and perfect fruition."[71]

Carolyn Heilbrun has argued that before the watershed date of 1873 (when Hardy's *Far from the Madding Crowd* was published and Butler's *The Way of All Flesh* begun), conjugal life was a tacitly forbidden fictional subject, and that once Eliot and Meredith helped lift the taboo, it was overwhelmingly depicted as a failed institution. Although it is true that the later three decades of the century witnessed a tremendous increase in both social and fictional attacks on wedlock, this scheme somewhat oversimplifies the case. Ever since Richardson's faltering attempt to fit a narratable form to Pamela's married life in *Pamela II* (1741), to say nothing of the pious novellas preceding Richardson's sequel, a number of English and American texts have undertaken to depict the problematic state of wedded life in their primary as well as secondary plots.[72] For novelists interested in the subject of wedlock, there remained the challenge of devising a dramatic conflict and developing a framework of obstruction and resolution that would activate the "story" of marriage without ultimately compromising its idealized status or its conventional sexual ideology. The two most common solutions were that of focusing (1) on the tribulations of the long-suffering wife caught in an adulterous triangle (who must contend either, like Fielding's Amelia, with her husband's waywardness or, like Penelope Aubin's Lady Lucy, with his unwarranted suspicions of her virtue) and (2) on the impasse of the totally mismatched union (such as that of the Hubbards in Howells's *A Modern Instance*). The former variation, often lending itself to popular and sentimental treatments, usually reaches one of two basically comedic resolutions: the erring husband reforms (like the would-be rake of courtship fiction) or, if too tyrannical, dies, freeing the wife to enter a happier second marriage (as occurs in Wilkie Collins's *The Woman in White*). Misplaced monetary values, initially mistaken perceptions of the other, former romantic liaisons or indiscretions—issues often figured as the obstacles that must be overcome before marriage can take place in the courtship formula—number among the most frequent causes of tragic impasse between mismatched mates.

The shape of the drama of domesticity unfolding from these subjects, one notes, tends to separate into rising or falling lines of development whose contrasting movements—like the trajectories of happy courtship and tragic seduction—equally uphold the conventional marital economy. Hence, in the wedlock narrative that moves toward a comic resolution, the organization of events often reproduces the format of courtship, its narrative dynamic arising out of the obstacles and threats temporarily barring the way to happy reunion. On the other hand, the structure of the tragic wedlock plot, as Hinz has demonstrated, inverts the progress of lovers toward a unified goal in marriage; it begins with the unhappy condition of wedlock itself and proceeds to school the protagonists in their own tragic misjudgments and illusions.[73] The fictive goal of marriage, quite literally, has now become its semantic opposite, a "gaol" or prison. But within the logic of the novelistic tradition of marriage, as Kiely has noted, even when the outcome is tragic a bad union is "never to be blamed on the institution itself."[74] It is the individual, not the institution, that is to be held accountable: for sinning against the ideal (as in the case of the philandering husband); for maintaining those Bovaryesque illusions that limit one's tolerance for the realities of shared life; or, finally, for allowing the imperatives of economic need, or greed, to overrun the sacred ends of "true love" as the primary justification for marrying.

Many of the textual problems and strategies developed in post-Richardsonian fictions attempting to thematize the situation of wedlock are already present in Penelope Aubin's *The Life and Adventures of the Lady Lucy* (1726), whose providential formula of "Adventures . . . deliverance . . . and reconciliation"[75] sheds light on the pattern developed by Fielding in *Amelia* and ironically reversed

NARRATIVE STRUCTURE IN THE MARRIAGE TRADITION

by Howells in *A Modern Instance*. Turning on a husband's mistaken supposition of his virtuous wife's infidelity, the skeletal structure of this moralistic fable of marriage begins with Lucy's wooing by and marriage to Albertus. The male protagonist, not coincidentally, is captain of the troops that have just killed Lucy's father and ransacked his castle as part of the Glorious Revolution; the implicit message is that a daughter's transition from the paternal home takes no less than victory by another conquering male.[76] Three years later, the stasis of the newlyweds' dyadic bliss is disrupted by the arrival of an unwelcome "third" in the form of Albertus's cousin Frederick: promptly falling in love with the unsuspecting Lucy, the new arrival incites Albertus's irrational mistrust and jealousy in a classic triangular situation. Frederick's sexual schemes against Lucy's person are succeeded by Albertus's murderous "designs" against both, the end of which is Lucy's supposed death and removal from the text. Hence the last third of the novel focuses on Albertus, whose life of sexual wantonness—ironically replicating the crime of adultery of which he has accused Lucy—is followed by his miraculous Christian conversion and (even more miraculous) reunion with a "resurrected" Lucy. For Lucy, not dead but awaiting "patiently the Events Time might produce" (74) on the suggestion of her spiritual adviser, has been hiding for eighteen years in a convent. And as her pious patience pays off "in the End" (117), Aubin's textual design, beginning with the anticipation of marital union and reaching a temporary climax in its opposite (violent separation), effects a kind of circular return by granting Lucy and Albertus the satisfaction of a providential reunion.

That is, if one can term "satisfactory" a reward that depends upon some *eighteen* years of suffering, immobility, and inaction by the heroine. For Aubin's wedlock narrative, designed to illustrate a wife's true calling in the exercise of the superior Christian virtues of patience and passivity, not only ends up calling into question such values, but also unconsciously renders ambivalent the very idea of designing a narrative: the active dynamic of plot itself becomes antithetical to the eternal repose that Aubin aligns with perfect marriage. If Albertus initially illustrates "wrong" action by implementing a "cruel Design" (64) against personified innocence, Lucy herself, *she* remains a correct model of *in*action, "wait[ing] upon God" (74) to implement *his* design. Ironically, however, and revelatory of the ambiguities pervading Aubin's aesthetic, it is the sinning Albertus (rather than the sinned-against Lucy) who becomes God's active instrument in the providential plot that draws the novella to its coincidence-ridden close.[77] Having withdrawn from the world upon his conversion and become a holy hermit, Albertus is allowed to inaugurate *positive* action, obfuscating his former heinous acts, when he intercedes in the plight of the wronged Arminda (a character introduced in chapter 9); he uses his power as God's emissary to effect her reunion with her jealous husband. Narratologically speaking, since Arminda's tale of woe in wedlock "so much resemble[s] his own" (118), Albertus's participation in bringing about her happy end psychically frees him to experience his own reunion with Lucy (which occurs several years but only a few paragraphs later). We have seen how both Richardson and Austen use circular repetition at the end of their courtship plots to convey a sense of their protagonists' growth. So too Aubin's use of parallel plots of unhappy wedlock provides a measure of Albertus's moral education; these repetitions facilitate the text's, hence wedlock's, return to stasis, to narrative nonbeing. The rewards of Providence, however, voice a morally ambiguous and contradiction-ridden message: for by "forgiving" Albertus his former transgressions while applauding his Lady's patient suffering as admirable behavior, Aubin's concluding sleights-of-hand at once cover over the very *cause* of marital discord in the main plot—Albertus's unfair persecution of Lucy—and reinforce a continuing stratification of the sexes along unequal axes dictated by gender.

If the whole notion of action and design is rendered ambivalent on a thematic level, so too is the novella's external design self-revealing. For it is highly suggestive that the *bulk* of a story about its titular heroine primarily consists of five inset tales related by characters only peripherally connected to the skeletal marriage plot. The very presence of such "filler" material—which far exceeds the eighteenth-century novelist's propensity for interpolated tales—indicates, I would suggest, a fundamental uncertainty on Aubin's part about the ability of her primary subject, marital strife, to generate "plot" enough on its own. On one level, these digressive tales are cautionary, anticipating Aubin's own moral. The long set-piece involving the Hermit in chapter 3, for instance, turns out to foreshadow Albertus's own religious conversion (although at this point we have no indication he will prove a husband in need of such drastic reform). Very closely repeating the wiles of Clitander in Haywood's *The Mercenary Lover,* published the same year, the Hermit narrates how he has raped his wife's younger sister, gotten her pregnant, then poisoned her, before conveniently "imploring the Almighty's Pardon as I ought" (38); the universal admiration that his story incites suggests the double standard that will also allow Albertus his conversion and restitution as a "good" husband despite his past murderous intentions. Arminda's narrative, mentioned in the previous paragraph, is the fifth and final interpolated narrative; a story of triangular desire and a husband's unwarranted jealously that, as I have indicated, echoes Albertus's own, it both recapitulates what has gone before and anticipates in its happy resolution what is to come. But, like all of these digressions, it also *fills in* for the main plot's *lack* of development, in this case by giving the reader a replay of that same plot; it postpones the only end the Albertus-Lucy narration can have, intensifying the anticipation of that very event by holding it at bay. Aubin's text of wedlock thus curiously exposes its own paucity, creating a final satisfaction that hinges on reestablishing a marital bliss ambiguously equated with the deathliness of "eternal repose" (x). The ultimate "lie" to which this text gives testimony can be located in its claim that its satisfaction originates in a linear model of narrative organization—"Oh, who would not tread in *the most rigid Steps* that lead to Virtue's Temple, to be so rewarded?" (123; emphasis added); such a model, needless to say, is worlds apart from the digressive meanderings that have been necessary to give this tale any substance. As long as its subtexts endanger its overt ideality, then, the wedlock plot remains, for Aubin and other writers, essentially plotless, an untold tale.

The first major post-Richardsonian work of fiction to disregard the illusion of the happy end by traveling beyond it, Henry Fielding's *Amelia* (1751) opens with an announcement of the intention to examine the "accidents which [befall] a very worthy couple after their uniting in the state of matrimony."[78] Foreshadowing Thackeray's metaphor of the "matrimonial barrier" barring access to the drama of the "marriage country," an early reviewer noted that Fielding was acting "in defiance of . . . established custom" by beginning his text "at the very point at which all his predecessors have dropped their capital personages. It has been heretofore a general practice to conduct the lover and his mistress to the doors of matrimony, and there leave them, as if after that ceremony the whole interest of them was at end, and nothing could remain beyond it worthy of exciting or keeping up the curiosity of the reader." Yet, as the same reviewer also astutely commented, Fielding's aim in probing the narrative possibilities of married life remained quite identical to that of the chronicler of courtship—namely, "to inculcate the superiority of virtuous conjugal love to all other joys."[79] While the novel's trajectory dismantles the myth of wedlock as a paradise of inaction by revealing its possible plots, the authorial voice nonetheless betrays a belief in stasis as the ideal goal of a perfect marriage. Thus the romantic ideal to which Booth and Amelia aspire (and which they have temporarily lost because of Booth's financial difficulties) is figured as an "earthly paradise" (1:164), a pastoral state of "love, health, and tranquility" in which life "resemble[s] a calm sea" (1:167). And, as we shall see, it is precisely at this promised land of undifferentiated "serenity" (2:341), of non-narratability, that the last paragraph of the text will triumphantly announce as having arrived.

The degree to which the Booths exemplify a secularized version of the Miltonic ideal of "virtuous conjugal love" is clearly illustrated in their marital roles as wife and husband. Amelia, like Lady Lucy, is a paragon of virtue and "perfect innocence" (1:186), explicitly compared by the narrator to Milton's unfallen Eve (1:276). Her husband extols her in sentimental terms that anticipate Coventry Patmore's evocation of the Victorian Angel of the House: "Thou heavenly angel . . . art thou really human, or art thou not rather an angel in a human form? O no . . . thou art my dearest woman, my best, my beloved wife" (2:215–16). Lest she seem too immaterial to his bourgeois audience, Fielding makes explicit the *middle-class* efficiency of this angel with encomiums such as that addressed to her splendid cookery, which office she performs "with as much pleasure as a fine lady generally enjoys in dressing herself out for a ball" (1:284). And Booth, despite his many lapses, fills the complementary connubial function of the newly sensitized male. His declaration that "tenderness for women is so far from lessening [one's masculinity] that it proves a true manly character" (1:147), like his pride at having assisted at one of Amelia's lyings-in (1:144), places him in a line of heroic types descended from Dryden's hearthside hero, expounded in the pious novella, and culminating in the nineteenth-century woman writer's projected fantasy of what Showalter has called the woman's man or feminine hero.[80]

Fielding's plot—situated between this marital ideal and the movement toward its actualization—arises out of the difficulties that impede the course of "virtuous conjugal love." To this end the opening paragraph of the text self-consciously places the married protagonists in the Greek Romance tradition of separated lovers, tallying the "various accidents," including "distresses . . . so exquisite" and "incidents . . . so extraordinary" (1:13), that will serve as roadblocks to perfect united happiness. Within this schema, as A. R. Towers notes, it will be Booth's role to pose the problems, Amelia's to pose the solutions.[81] Given this premise, the dramatic action begins with a crisis that precipitates all further obstructions—Booth's unjust imprisonment for debt upon his arrival in London and subsequent separation from Amelia. The appearance among the inmates of Miss Matthews, a former acquaintance once enamored of Booth, precipitates a further obstacle to the Booths' marital well-being: namely, the adulterous affair that ensues once the two prisoners have exchanged their lengthy personal histories in books 1–4. While most critics have simply noted that this opening device affords Fielding a clever appropriation of the *in medias res* beginning of classical epic, Miss Matthews's and Booth's retrospective narratives are inextricably tied to the saga of wedlock that follows, for their stories exemplify two of the love-plot's most paradigmatic alternatives at work. Miss Matthews's tale is a variant of the seduction story, recounting the path by which her various illicit and triangular passions, early culminating in her sexual "fall," have doomed her to continual frustration; Booth's fable of "the particulars of [his] courtship" (1:66), in contrast, is an archetypal rendition of the mediating obstacles that the sheer force of purely conceived passion can overcome.

In the process, the art of telling becomes, for both Miss Matthews and Booth, an elaborate act of erotic enticement and deferral. First, to stimulate further Booth's "*ardent* desire of knowing her story" (1:40; emphasis added), Miss Matthews creates a sexually teasing narrative that transforms herself into the predominant object of his perception. In turn, the many "scenes of tenderness" (1:110) that next unfold from Booth's courtship narrative only whet Miss Matthews's desire for Booth, as her flirtatious asides and leers increasingly intimate. The process of telling becomes even more erotically entangled, however. For if the encouragement that Booth receives to tell "every step of [his] amour" (1:70) stems from Miss Matthews's certainty that the moment will then be hers when his story is finished, it becomes humorously clear that Booth, in Scheherazade fashion, "immediately complie[s]" (1:108) with the request to go into more detail for the exactly opposite reason: that is, to avoid the inevitable "conclusion" to be drawn from Miss Matthews's behavior, "which could not convey a very agreeable idea to a constant husband" (1:108). Booth's defense, however, backfires, as the story-telling of his virtuous passion becomes for him a displacement of moral responsibility that makes room for the seduction that soon follows: at this moment actual conversation becomes, in Fielding's wordplay, the "criminal conversation" (1:175) of sexual intimacy. While Booth's following lapse forms part of a larger moral pattern inveighing against extramarital sexuality, the titillating and comic method of its presentation betrays an unconscious double standard at work on the authorial level of narration. Ironically, it is in the text's definitive repudiation of the libertine ethos that this bias becomes most clear; at the same time that Fielding pauses to denounce male lust, he upholds its occurrence as a "natural," hence uncontrollable, characteristic of the male species. The measure of a man's virtue resides, most simply, in repression: "To run away [from inevitable temptations] is all that is in our power" (1:279). The schism between male and female sexuality pervading eighteenth-century sexual discourse remains intact, despite Fielding's "enlightened" promotion of male fidelity, in the novel's ideological framework.

If Booth momentarily falls prey to his own "nature," Amelia is constantly menaced by the brute desires of the very men who claim they are Booth's best friends: indeed, as the structure of the wedlock narrative that follows Booth's release from prison indicates, the threat of adultery looms for either spouse as their greatest obstacle to "domestic happiness" and stability. For while Booth's momentary affair (and his subsequent desire to conceal it from Amelia) generates further plot by setting into motion a chain of seemingly inescapable and escalating misfortunes, so too does an elaborate series of structural repetitions involving attempts on Amelia's virtue maintain the forward momentum and tension of the narrative. One instance involves the duplicities of a lord who pretends to befriend Booth with promises of preferment while plotting Amelia's downfall by inviting her to a masquerade at Ranelegh. The lord's scheme is foiled at the last minute when one of his former victims, Mrs. Bennet, reveals the identical machinations by which he ruined her. Significantly, Mrs. Bennet's interpolated narrative—an inset seduction tale lasting nearly all of book 7—is an almost exact replica, in miniature, of the Booths' trajectory to this point. Like Amelia she has been cheated of an inheritance and marries against her family's will; like the Booths the Bennets remove to London in search of fortune, only to find themselves in worsening straits until their landlady—now the Booths' landlady—introduces them to a "protector" in his lordship. With horror Amelia discovers that the stages by which the lord has ingratiated himself with the Bennets, exactly paralleling the tactics he has used with her and Booth, have also culminated in an invitation to Ranelegh, where a spiked drink leads Mrs. Bennet to "a ruin to which I can truly say I never consented" (2:48). This inset fable thus becomes a powerful object lesson instructing the Booths in the depths of the deception by which worldly evil will effect its ends.[82] But one lesson and one instance of repetition aren't enough; even before the lord's scheme has been exposed, the reader discerns its replication in the growing attraction of another of Booth's "friends," Colonel James, to Amelia. For Amelia finds herself trapped in an uncannily similar scenario as James invites the Booths to yet another costume ball: this time Amelia recognizes the duplicitous sign of false appearance (aptly conveyed in the masquerade metaphor) for what it is worth, and averts the crisis.

The penultimate events leading to a reversal of this series of trials also originate in the moral threat that sexual intrigue poses to marriage. For the obstructions barring the Booths from happiness reach a climactic nadir at the end of book 11 when Miss Matthews blackmails Booth into visiting her while the duped lord simultaneously exacts his revenge by having Booth arrested—the third repetition of the plot's initiatory event—for his gambling debts. But now that the marital situation seems to have reached its maximum discord, a rapid series of surprise revelations—equivalent to those creating the illusion of final consonance in courtship plotting—reverse the wheel of fortune's downward movement. First, the imprisoned and penitent Booth finally confesses his past sexual transgression to Amelia, only to discover (along with the reader) that she has long ago learned of and forgiven him the affair. The twofold moral that Fielding implicitly draws from this revelation is quite telling in the contradiction it embraces: most obviously, that Booth's lack of openness has been as much an obstacle to marital happiness as external misfortune, and, implicitly, that Amelia's quiet forebearance is well rewarded by Booth's penitence. The irony, however, is that Amelia's model behaviour—bringing to mind Lady Lucy's similar patience—depends precisely on concealing what *she* knows, a situation that curiously perpetuates the very noncommunication within marriage that Fielding is putatively criticizing in Booth's behavior. It becomes evident there is a hierarchy of values at work here that, in implicitly endorsing different codes of behavior for husbands and wives, also reinforces a double standard of poetic justice not unlike that granting Albertus an unproblematic restitution at the end of Aubin's novella.

The second last-minute reversal that Fielding introduces into his plot also recalls a trait his text shares with Aubin's novella. For Booth experiences an overdue conversion to Christianity, an event leading—providentially, of course, now that he is weaned from an un-Christian belief in Fortune—to his release from prison.[83] His spiritual gain, moreover, is quickly followed by concrete material rewards in a third reversal as Amelia recoups her stolen inheritance, an event thereby resolving the family's financial crisis. What this last fortuitous turn manages to elide, once again, is Booth's total failure to provide the support that social and marital convention demands of husbands (it is Amelia's fortune, not Booth's ingenuity, that saves the day). Thus the meting out of final rewards that ends the novel, creating the illusion of the Booths' perfect happiness, of the ideal attained, depends on a series of authorial manipulations disguised as acts of Providence.[84] As in countless other love-plots, Fielding's final chapter, set up as an epilogue, brings its projections of characters' futures to a close by assuring us that the Booths enjoy "an *uninterrupted* course of health and happiness" upon their retirement to the pastoral countryside; "Nothing can equal *the serenity* of their lives," the narrator declares in an image of final stasis that depends on the *perceived* symmetry of Amelia and Booth's love: for if Booth has "the best of wives," Amelia proudly avows to the narrator that it is because her husband has "made her the happiest of women" (2:340–41; emphasis added). Rather ironically, Amelia offers as a sop to the reader's peace of mind a proposition that in fact contradicts the truth of the plot (her exemplary status has in fact preceded and made possible Booth's exertions in the name of goodness). But the entire text has so schooled us in a view of Amelia's utterly "feminine" guilelessness that we accept her invitation to forget and forgive Booth's lapses as she herself has so successfully done, and in thus following Amelia's lead we recuperate for the text the romantic ideology Fielding's comedic dynamic has worked to ensure.

It is perhaps not surprising to find such an unquestioning acceptance of marital values reflected in a format governed by an overabundance of coincidence, climax, and conciliation. But similar formal manipulations executed in the name of a unitary social order can also be found governing the avowed realist's depiction of unhappy and less ideal wedlock. William Dean Howells's *A Modern Instance* (1882), for example, provides a classic case study of the often unconscious, conventional constraints operative in a novel otherwise boldly representing the "modern instance" of miserable marriage and possible divorce. On the one hand, Howells's desire to promote greater realism in American letters committed him to a realistic assessment of "what married life generally comes to"[85] when a marriage based on false expectations awakens from illusion. On the other hand, Howells's equally deep allegiance to Victorian social order and the good life prevented his piercing to the core of the sexual assumptions spurring the marital warfare of Bartley and Marcia Hubbard—and this allegiance ultimately dictates the closed field of his tragic narrative organization every bit as much as it does the comedic format of Fielding's *Amelia*.

On the positive side, Howells uses the courtship and elopement of Bartley and Marcia to expose the dangers of the excessive idealization fostered by sentimentalizing ideologies of romantic marriage. It is Bartley's illusion to expect that his future wife's "ennobling and elevating" womanly nature will "influenc[e him] for good" (15)—a sentimental precept encoded in the very structure of *Amelia,* where the heroine's example indeed precipitates Booth's transformation—just as it is Marcia's illusion that Bartley can become her entire "world" (225). "You're better for me than the best man in the world, dear," Marcia will protest in romantic rhetoric coeval to Amelia's final asseveration of happiness, "and even if you were not, I should love you the best" (262). What Howells makes clear, however, is that womanly sentiment alone is not enough to reform Bartley, his modern-day and democratized version of the eighteenth-century aristocratic rake. When proclamations of total love depend on a jealousy as ferocious as Marcia's, the result is bound to be problematic if the man involved is as much a philanderer as Bartley. (Although adultery is never a *real* threat in this wedlock text, the suspicion of its shadow is enough, at crucial turning points in the plot, to add to the forces of disintegration at work in the Hubbards' marriage.)[86] Howells thus implies that it is the willed blindness of Marcia and Hubbard to their intrinsically incompatible natures—a blindness itself the byproduct of sentimentally fostered conceptions of romance—that will eventually transform what was mistaken for "love" into a mutual enmity and contempt potentially damaging to all society.

Yet despite Howells's realistic assessment of the illusions underlying the couple's initial attraction, he fixes the blame on their individual failure to perceive the truth of their situation in time to remedy it, rather than calling into doubt the values lying behind the romantic ideal of marriage they aspire to fulfill. In this regard it is telling that the text fails to link its criticism of Bartley's self-love and Marcia's self-effacing adoration to the masculine and feminine constructions of social behavior that the two are clearly if unconsciously imitating; Howells overlooks the degree to which these instances stem from an ideology of sexual power to which he, too, unconsciously subscribes. Hence, for example, the novel's criticism of the "canonizing compassion" by which women turn their husbands into gods (58) is carefully qualified by the fact that Marcia's devotion is mistakenly directed to a man *not worth* her worship—a better husband might prove a more worthy god. The text is strewn with similarly generalizing statements about the "nature" of women: the authorial narrator lauds "the daring, the archness, and caprice that make coquetry in some women, and lurk a divine possibility in all" (45); looks askance at "that wearisome persistence with which women torment the men they love" (179); and is convinced that a manly hug presents "an argument that no woman can answer . . . it seems to deprive her of her reasoning faculties" (384). Telling, also, is the novel's only successful model of marriage, that of the lawyer Atherton and socialite Clara: Atherton's sober rationality molds Clara's former flightiness into properly worshipful submissiveness in yet another novelistic instance of complementary opposition rooted in asymmetrical difference.

In this framework, the question of *what to do* about an unfortunate, deteriorating marriage like the Hubbards' becomes a question of what is ultimately best—and safest—for society. Divorce is deemed an unacceptable solution, since, to Atherton's mind, it is a tool of scoundrels to "lure women from their duty, ruin homes, and destroy society" (369). Thus, in the novel's climax, Marcia is forced to undergo the public humiliation of a court appearance, once Bartley deserts her, to keep him from slipping a divorce suit through the lenient Indiana courts. Otherwise, the societal ideal of womanhood might be sullied—despite the fact that the neurotic Marcia only superficially fits that ideal. Nonetheless, because her society can only see men and women in either/or terms, public opinion transforms Marcia into "the heroine of so tragic a fact" (363) as desertion and demands that the villain responsible for her tragedy must pay: "It's the cause of an innocent woman against a wicked oppression" (389–90), Clara Atherton righteously says in defense of Marcia's avenging trip to Indiana. If Howells adds a knowing note of irony to Clara's oversimplification, the terms of his conclusion, as we shall see, turn the irony against his own insights.

The structure of *A Modern Instance* reinforces this ultimately conservative social vision of wedlock, delineating a tragic curve and falling apart as inexorably as the inversed comedic plotting of successful courtship and marriage. The fact that nearly every significant plateau in Bartley's and Marcia's careers is activated by an improbable coincidence indicates the extent to which Howells, like Aubin and Fielding, is willing to manipulate the arrangement of his material to make the characters' march to success or doom seem "inevitable."[87] And the circular fates visited on the "broken lives" (416) of each of the main characters appropriately brings the tragic patterning to a complete halt: Marcia returns to the stifling town of her youth, shutting herself away from the world in a penultimately submissive gesture of self-punishment that calls to mind Tess Durbeyfield's internalized masochism; Bartley's downward slide into the traditionally masculine vices of lechery and dissipation ends when an irate husband shoots him, an act of ironic poetic justice that serves as "penalty or consequence, as we choose to consider it, of all that had gone before" (418); a third character, Halleck, resigns himself to the religious illusions ("He accepted everything" [418]) against which he has spent his life rebelling, becoming a minister rather than facing the consequences of his repressed passion for Marcia. The finality with which these lives of "tragic occurrences" (418) are uniformly locked into place on the last pages of the novel deflects attention away from the social circumstances shaping their actions and to the flawed perceptions and weaknesses of character that they as individuals have contributed in making their relationships unhappy.

The promulgation of the social good at the expense of the individual also forms the keynote of the final scene, an argument between Atherton and Clara that concerns the propriety of Halleck's asking for Marcia's hand now that Bartley is dead. Atherton takes the hard "masculine" line, arguing that the fact of Halleck's prior passion for Marcia while she was married is an "indelible stain" that makes a proposal impossible, a "lapse from the ideal" (420–21). Clara, just as predictably, reacts emotionally, arguing that the suffering undergone by Halleck merits the reintegration into society that marriage alone can confer. Howells purposely leaves the debate up in the air in what has been mistakenly labeled an "open ending."[88] More significant than this final ambiguity is the unambiguous fact that *both* perspectives uphold the status quo: Atherton opts for the morally edifying tragedy of self-sacrifice; Clara, for the morally redemptive comedy of a "happy ending." Whatever Atherton finally chooses to advise Halleck, the pattern of Howells's novel remains closed, the disturbances of this "modern instance" of unhappy marriage safely brought to rest within the tragic framework of its structure.

This narrative recuperation of the contradictions inherent in the late nineteenth-century ideology of wedlock is essentially the pattern reproduced in other texts of tragic wedlock throughout the history of the Anglo-American novel. For example, although its tone is more satiric than the prior examples, the marital separation that ensues in Susan Ferrier's *Marriage* (1818) after Lady Juliana's precipitous elopement points only to her own foolishness, and this didactic message is repeated in the stories of her twin daughters, whose fates provide final examples of "wise" and "foolish" marital fortunes. Another early Victorian novel, Dickens's *Dombey and Son* (1846–48), is in great part a scathing exposé of a wife's nightmarish entrapment in a tyrannical marriage. Dickens, however, unconsciously undermines the legitimacy of Edith's rebellion against her husband Dombey—and hence against the larger social system he represents—at the point at which her anger threatens the author's own idealizing vision of marriage and of women; thus the narrator explains away Edith's hatred of Dombey as an inherent character flaw preceding her uninnocent entrance into a marriage of convenience, and he makes her avenue of escape (running away with the despicable Carker) *morally* reprehensible. While Edith's fate is foreshadowed, even glorified, throughout as "doomed" and "tragic," Dickens simultaneously employs a double standard of poetic judgment—echoing Aubin's and Fielding's—that allows Dombey to undergo a moral rehabilitation and, in this case, to regain not a wife but the substitutive love of his much-abused daughter.

The relative sophistication with which *A Modern Instance* deals with conjugal tragedy is more than matched by the penetrating analyses of marital relationship in James's *The Portrait of a Lady* (1881), in several of Meredith's novels, and in Hardy's *Jude the Obscure* (1895). The questioning of the ideological ramifications of the marital ideal implicit in all these texts, however, is ultimately forestalled by their enclosure within structural paradigms whose movement toward tragic frustration or tragic resignation conserves the social beliefs they purport to eschew. A brief glance at a few examples makes this clear. Although James's criticism of marriage was to become progressively counter-traditional, as the next chapter will demonstrate, his resolution of Isabel Archer's fate in *The Portrait* depends on her martyrlike assumption of responsibility for her deadlocked marriage. Refusing the comic salvation that the suitor Caspar Goodwood foolishly thinks he is offering, Isabel instead opts for the tragic alternative, the "very straight path" that will lead back to Rome, her husband Osmond, and stepdaughter Pansy, in a much interpreted and controversial ending scene.[89] But even though James wisely chooses not to comment on the specifics of Isabel's future and to leave its details uncertain, open to conjecture, nonetheless the tragic pattern of whatever this experience will be has *already* been determined by Isabel's ironclad commitment to see the doomed marriage through to the end: the trajectory of the entire novel has been moving all along to this paradoxical redefinition of Isabel's touted freedom to choose.

Meredith's late novels obsessively return to the theme of unfair tyranny in wedlock and attempt to stage positive alternatives, but his closed endings almost uniformly reveal an inability to free himself of romantic convention. In *One of Our Conquerors* (1891), the unhappily married Nataly enters an idealized common-law union with Victor, only to undergo years of social ostracism that end in her death; in *Lord Ormont and His Aminta* (1894), the heroine's sufferings in a tyrannous, ugly marriage are alleviated when she forms an idealized relationship with a new lover, which supplies the novel with a kind of facsimile of the traditionally happy ending; in *The Amazing Marriage* (1895), self-sacrifice closes the separate careers undertaken by its unhappily married protagonists.

Hardy shares with Meredith an intuitive sense of the patriarchal biases dooming "modern marriage" to unhappiness, but his texts of unhappy marriage simultaneously work to cover the contradictions they expose. Thus, despite his severe attack on the legal institution underwriting the societal ideal of wedlock in *Jude the Obscure* (1894–95), the novel's sense of inevitable cosmic doom overshadows and shapes the lives of its protagonists in such a way as to support—as the prior discussion of *Tess* also demonstrated—an ultimately pessimistic view of *all* sexuality as tragic, and of flesh and spirit, man and woman, humanity and universal malignity, as irreconcilable binary oppositions. The chiasmic patterning of interchanging relationships that forms the basis of the organization of *Jude* also upholds a conventional message, for the marriages end up exactly where they began, inscribing circular patterns that negate forward progress and that illustrate the degree to which the protagonists are trapped by "natural" instincts stronger than their wills. Returning to the cold-blooded Phillotson to punish her own "transgressions," Sue ensures her frigid spirituality; reclaimed by Arabella, Jude gives himself over completely to the "grosser" aspects of his body. "Hardy is more bound than he knows," writes A. O. J. Cockshut, "by the convention he is attacking."[90] Indeed, Hardy's appeal to essential "natures" hides the culturally formulated preconceptions about sexuality and the body/mind split that underlie his characters' motivations. In such irrevocable movements toward tragic closure, pessimistic and even self-questioning wedlock plots like *Jude* participate along with more obviously conventional texts in the ideological indoctrination common to the novelistic marriage tradition.

The "New Woman" Novel and the Fiction of Sex: Compromising Positions

In ironic counterpoint to the vision of social order, however illusory, imposed on conventional novelistic forms via plots of courtship, seduction, and wedlock, the latter decades of the nineteenth century produced an increasingly articulate, demystifying public discourse about the failings of real-life marriage, particularly in regard to the position of women within its institutionalized strictures. This historical phenomenon lies behind Hardy's talk of the "shop-soiled" condition of the marriage theme in his day[91] as well as behind his use of the emancipated-woman motif in the representation of Sue Bridehead in *Jude the Obscure*. For in both Britain and America the growing agitation for specific legislative reform in regard to marriage laws, divorce proceedings, and suffrage that characterized the fledgling feminist movement gave rise to a generation of self-consciously styled "New Women," young women whose declarations of independence and advocacy of free union spurred what was popularly known as the "marriage debate" or "marriage crisis" in the press and topical literature of the 1880s and 1890s. Fiction followed not far behind, testing out the potential of the New Woman as heroine and her cause as theme in a series of "problem novels," among which *Jude the Obscure* was immediately classed by its reviewers. What is telling about even the most radical of these novels is the degree to which their content and form reproduce the conservative sexual ideologies against which they seem to rebel; underlying the "radical" theme of free union, one finds a familiar ideal of lifelong, permanent, and even hierarchically ordered love that has simply been stripped, in one critic's words, of the "deadwood" of religious and legal sanctions obscuring the priority of individual loving commitment.[92] Likewise, even the most stylistically experimental of these texts—and female writers of New Woman fiction in particular showed their discomfort with realistic modes by mixing forms of allegory, impressionistic monologue, and the political tract[93]—fail to break out of a narrative dynamic of either/or closure that circumscribes their heroines within morally edifying structures predicated on traditional constructions of "feminine" martyrdom and "masculine" power. As Boumelha rightly observes, "the free union's exact reproduction of the [contemporary] ideology of marriage (loving, lasting, monogamous)" is exposed in "the female role of loving self-sacrifice" assumed by the many New Woman heroines who willingly, masochistically, look forward to martrydom in the name of their cause.[94]

One of the most experimentally as well as thematically "daring" of these fictional protests, Olive Schreiner's *The Story of an African Farm* (1883), exemplifies this self-subverting tendency. Its disturbing heroine is an independent-minded woman, Lyndall, whose articulations of protest against "the position of women," like her actions, are grand but vague, riddled with internal contradiction. Thus, while she passionately disclaims traditional sexual roles as demeaning, she reveals an unconscious predilection to view as intrinsic to romantic relationship a binarism based on essentialist stereotypes of gender ("Men are like the earth and we are the moon").[95] Likewise, while Lyndall rejects the legal tie of marriage as ignoble entrapment, the narrative she chooses for the plot of her life remains tied to an extremely idealized erotics of love; in the same breath that she tells the mysterious stranger with whom she has a passionate sexual affair that "I cannot marry you," she adds, "If you wish, you may take me away with you, and take care of me" (239), and despite her fears that his kind of love seeks only to "master," she admits from her deathbed that he is the one person who arouses her deepest desire for "something nobler, stronger than I, before which I can kneel down" (279). If on the one hand Schreiner, like other New Woman writers, distinguishes her text from that of seduction by making it clear that Lyndall is the initiator rather than victim of sexual adventure, nonetheless the end of Lyndall's freely chosen but psychologically circumscribed independence reproduces that of several of her fallen sisters: the tragic closure of death in childbirth.

Aside from Schreiner's best-selling novel, two of the following decades' most popular treatments of the independent heroine and the free union sanctioned by love alone, William Barry's *The New Antigone* (1887) and Grant Allen's *The Woman Who Did* (1895), illustrate the way in which deceptively conservative precepts of gender are reinforced by tragic narrative formats. The heroine of the former pays for her sexual freedom by becoming a nun, an exchange of metaphoric movement for absolute stasis and an act of tragic renunciation fixing her within a traditionally "feminine" mode of self-sacrifice and unrequited suffering. In *The Woman Who Did*—which, along with Hardy's *Jude,* was the most widely read novel of 1895—Herminia Barton's denunciation of marriage as "vile slavery" finds its counterpart in the declaration of "freedom" she makes as she hands herself over to her lover, Alan, on her own terms, "*I* am *yours* this moment. *You* may do what you would with *me*" (emphasis added).[96] In a single, swift grammatical transformation, Herminia's avowal of subjecthood ("I am . . .") unwittingly reveals itself as having entered a new state of objectified possession ("yours . . . me"); and, indeed, the subsequent terms used to describe their relationship do little to counter the sexual norms that led Herminia to denounce marriage as vile slavery. As the author approvingly notes when Herminia, now pregnant, yields to Alan's decision to go abroad to escape scandal, "She would be less a woman, and he less a man, were any other result possible. Deep down in the very roots of the idea of sex we come on that prime antithesis,—the male, active and aggressive; the female, sedentary, passive, and receptive" (82). The scientific biologism of late nineteenth-century thought has simply come to reinforce an archetype of gender asymmetry reaching back to the Renaissance humanist treatise and the Puritan conjugal guide.

In terms of the novel's narrative logic, the "willing martyrdom for humanity's sake" (10) that has marked Herminia's fate from her first appearance begins to fulfill itself when, upon Alan's sudden death in Perugia, Herminia is left stranded with a newborn daughter and no financial support. For the rest of the text, the trials of motherhood substitute for the truncated love story. In the process Allen *uses* Herminia's maternal love—as a "sign" of her natural femininity—to compensate for what some readers might think her radical, and hence "unwomanly," flouting of sexual convention. "Every good woman is by nature a mother," Allen unequivocally declares, adding that "Herminia was far removed indeed from that blatant and decadent sect of 'advanced women' who talk as if motherhood were a disgrace and a burden" (138). Although Allen's lack of sympathy with the feminist movement differentiates his text from the impulse inspiring much New Woman fiction written by women, it is telling that women's stories of free union also almost uniformly uphold an essentialist ideology of motherhood, a defensive literary strategy that at least partially undermines the radical intention of their fiction.[97] In *The Woman Who Did*, Herminia like a "true" mother literally ends renouncing "all" for the sake of her illegitimate child—committing suicide to free the grown-up daughter from the shame of her mother's unconventional past and to enable the daughter's entrance into the legal marriage Herminia herself had avoided. In New Woman fiction by women as well as by men, then, the attribution of traditional "feminine" personality traits to all of these "emancipated" heroines dovetailed with the use of didactic, tragic structural paradigms to curtail the effectiveness of these works as counter-traditional expressions.

Even in Sarah Grand's euphoric portrait of a New Woman in *The Beth Book* (1898), the protagonist's survival and success as an independent woman is conventionally signaled by the equally last-minute gain of a worthy mate. Following Beth's climactic break from an unhappy marriage and the successful publication of her feminist manifesto, the "book" of the title, the final pages of the novel focus on Beth's epiphanic discovery of her true vocation as a public orator; but at the very same moment she feels that "something was wanting," and it is as "an augury, the fulfillment of a promise," that the "Knight of her daily vision, her saviour" of whom she has dreamed, quite literally rides into her vision in the novel's last paragraph.[98] Tellingly, Grand's female bildungsroman ends by pronouncing *his* name: thus, the last word in this trajectory of female growth and liberation, belying the title "Beth's Book," reorders the preceding events into what might be called a slightly new variation on a very old theme: female adversity rewarded by true love.

In examining comparable American novels of the 1890s, Larzer Ziff sums up the conflict at the core of such resolutions: "The new theme of the independent woman called for a new plot that would not resistlessly flow to the magnetic terminal of marriage, but the young lady writers of the nineties dared enough when they dared the theme. . . . They cannot break free of the marriage pattern."[99] A few novels influenced by the feminist movement and incorporating independent women did, however, succeed in transcending the marriage pattern of which Ziff speaks: Louisa May Alcott's *Work* (1872–73); Sarah Orne Jewett's *A Country Doctor* (1884), whose female protagonist turns down marriage to a man she loves in order to practice medicine; James's *The Bostonians* (1886), in which Basil Ransom's "courtship" of Verena Tarrant sardonically parodies the possibilities of happy conclusions; and Gissing's *The Odd Women* (1893), which juxtaposes a tragic subplot of patriarchal wedlock with the comedy of Rhoda Nunn's refusal of a marriage proposal in order to maintain her independent status and continue her missionary work rehabilitating single women for the business world. In novels such as these, one finds traces of the counter-traditional expression whose contours we will begin exploring in the next chapter.

What, finally, becomes of the marriage tradition in the twentieth century? Its constricting impact on significant form in the novel abated, of course, with the advance of a modernist aesthetic that devalued the plot linearity, narrative coherence, and realistic modes of representation that had underwritten the formal rules of nineteenth-century fiction. Nonetheless, traces of the love-plot format, along with its themes and ideological values, have continued to inhabit (and inhibit) the genre to the present day. Nowhere are these manifestations so subtly present as in the modern "fictions of sex" marking the rise of modernist literature around the outbreak of World War II. This new novelistic frankness about and glorification of the subject of sexuality has frequently been lauded as a belated reaction to repressive Victorian literary convention and as a truly liberating strike against the romantic ideology embedded in the marital ideal. But in fact nearly the opposite is true. The New Woman novels at which we have already looked, foreshadowing the emergence of sexuality outside of wedlock as a "modern" literary subject, provide a clue to this reality. For, as one critic has written of *The Woman Who Did,* Allen attempted not to break tradition so much as to ennoble *existing* constructs of male and female sexual "nature," bringing sex into the fold of *accepted* human behavior: the liberation of sexual passion, many early twentieth-century writers were similarly convinced, could improve society by restoring a mystical harmony between flesh and spirit, nature and humanity.[100]

In effect, with the modern redefinition of eros as the unrepressed Truth and natural Center of personal well-being,[101] the (hetero)sexual relation has come to occupy a symbolic role analogous to that formerly fulfilled by romantic wedlock, both in social and literary representations. The displacement of one ideal by the other, moreover, has served to maintain an essentially contiguous sexual order. As the sexism underlying the putatively "emancipated" 1960s reminds us, the historical substitution of sexual freedom for conjugal relationship does not automatically transform the transhistorical "rules" of sexual hierarchy, of dichotomization into mutually exclusive and hierarchical roles, or of the exploitation encoded in institutionalized marriage. This contiguity, in turn, is directly related to the way woman is defined in both marital and nonmarital economies of desire. Central to marital and sexual idealizing processes alike is a definition of woman as an item of "commerce" in the bargains struck of heterosexual coupling: an item desired for its commercial value as an untainted good when passed from paternal to husbandly keeping, for its pleasure-producing value as tainted but infinitely receptive body when passed among male lovers. Thus, although the context, the terms of bonding, in modern life may have changed, the idealized sexual affair of modern literature has remained a repository for many of the values and assumptions once associated with the romantic ideal of wedlock.

Likewise, many of the thematic conventions and formats characterizing the nineteenth-century marriage tradition resurface in only slightly differing contexts in twentieth-century erotic plots. Perhaps the greatest continuity between old and new formats exists in the plotting of tragic wedlock, with the major distinction being a less overtly moralistic use of adultery as a measure of marriage's failure. When texts such as Ford's *The Good Soldier* (1915) or Fitz-gerald's *Tender is the Night* (1934), for instance, focus on the break-down of communication between spouses, marital tragedy also becomes a vehicle for expressing the quintessentially modernist theme of alienation, division, and unhappiness in a meaningless universe. As already noted, the seduction plot per se ceased to exist once female chastity ceased to be a "jewel" to be protected at all costs and became a gift that modern standards "permitted" the woman to give to its eventual (male) receiver. However, the ideo-logical subtext of the seduction tale—capitalizing on sexual pursuit and combat—is continued in sundry novels of sexual relationships, ranging from Henry Miller's compulsively repetitious chronicles of masculine conquest to Jean Rhys's pursued and masochistic hero-ines.

Although the courtship narrative culminating in happy mar-riage more or less faded from serious fiction after World War I—Forster's *A Room with a View* (1908) is one of the last relatively successful novels working in a forthrightly Austenian mode—vari-ous comedic formulations of love relationship have persisted. Fied-ler's facetious but accurate comment on the love ethos of Hemingway's heros is relevant in this regard: "The rejection of the sentimental happy ending of marriage involves the acceptance of the sentimental happy beginning of innocent and inconsequential sex."[102] For D. H. Lawrence, too, the development of totally sexual relationships outside marriage provides several of his female pro-tagonists—Lady Chatterley, Yvette—with a modern equivalent of the happy ending. Yet, as critics have begun to realize, Lawrence's manipulations of perspective, imagistic patterns, and narrative se-quence to authorize his female protagonists' sexual awakenings re-stricts them to an ultimately phallic economy of plot and sexual desire (the female takes as a model for her own libidinal subjectivity the lessons learned from her darkly mysterious male other). The ideological entrapments of these "transformed" courtship for-mulas pertain not only to the modern male writer, as Kennard and Heilbrun have demonstrated in regard to trends in contemporary women's fiction. The plot substitution of the "abandonment of marriage" for "the achievement of it"[103] in such women's writing does not automatically answer the question of how the sexually lib-erated female protagonist is to establish an autonomous identity, nor does such a change of focus necessarily constitute an insurrection against the gynophobic values often underlying modern sexual "liberation." In sum, the text where the female protagonist achieves a subjectivity outside the strictures of some form of the age-old love story has, until recently, remained rare indeed.

Some novelists, however, since the rise of the genre, have made inroads against the sexual-marital economy underlying the novel's dominant tradition. These advances they have accomplished by coupling their thematic expressions of discontent with form-breaking narrative structures. And it is this more fully counter-traditional impulse whose evolution the following chapters will pursue, from novels that manipulate the subject of marriage to explode the formal and closural restraints of wedlock plotting, to those texts which reinvent a course of action and of plot for those both courageously and timorously self-reliant protagonists venturing outside the realm of married life and marriage plots altogether.

Part Two

Counter-Tradition
Demonstrations in Form Breaking

the story shall be changed . . .
A Midsummer Night's Dream

Chapter Four

Uneasy Wedlock and the Counter-Tradition's Contribution to Open Form

Beyond the "Happy Ending" in *Wuthering Heights, Daniel Deronda, The Golden Bowl,* and *To the Lighthouse*

> Every limit is a beginning as well as an ending. Who can quit young lives, after being long in company with them, and not desire to know what befell them in their after-years? . . . Marriage, which has been the bourne of so many narratives, is still a great beginning, as it was to Adam and Eve. . . . It is still the beginning of the home epic—the gradual conquest or irremediable loss of that complete union which makes the advancing years a climax, and age the harvest of sweet memories in common.
>
> George Eliot, *Middlemarch*[1]

> A gulf had opened between them over which they looked at each other with eyes that were on either side a declaration of the deception suffered. It was a strange opposition, of the like of which she had never dreamed—an opposition in which the vital principle of the one was a thing of contempt to the other. . . . She had taken all the first steps in the purest confidence, and then she had suddenly found the infinite vista of a multiplied life to be a dark, narrow alley with a dead wall at the end.
>
> Henry James, *The Portrait of a Lady*[2]

One of the last great marriage novels to conform to the Shakespearean dictum that "journeys end with lovers meeting,"[3] Eliot's *Middlemarch* (1872) begins its Finale with what now seems the swan song of the courtship tradition that had dominated novelistic explorations of love and marriage for nearly a hundred years. "Every limit is a beginning as well as an ending," Eliot states in an implicit admission of the arbitrary nature of all conclusions, then proceeds to defend the structural paradigm upon which her own closing depends with the assertion that hers is the threshold to a yet better, though unnarrated, story: "Marriage, which has been the bourne of so many narratives, is still a great beginning." However, for those of Eliot's successors venturing into the less familiar territory of the "home epic," wedded life proved less a hopeful beginning than an emphatic dead end, a state of moral and narrative impasse. James's metaphoric expression of Isabel Archer's marital experience in *The Portrait of a Lady* (1881) provides a riveting instance of this viewpoint: "then she . . . suddenly found the infinite vista of a multiplied life to be a dark, narrow alley with a dead wall at the end." The contrast between these two images of wedded horizons may seem greater than one would expect, given the single decade separating Eliot's and James's texts, but it captures with dramatic vividness the rapid shift in literary decorum and public attitude that culminated in the displacement of courtship by wedlock themes as the major focus of the novel's marriage tradition; indeed, the tragic wedlock plot came into its own in the decades in which Eliot's career was ending and James's beginning. However, as I have already argued, the prototypical gesture of representing failed marriage as a *closed* tragedy tended to preclude a thoroughgoing interrogation of the sexual and social ideologies of power perpetuating wedded discord: the stabilization of narrative impulse and granting of readerly repose inherent in the tragic endings of serious and popular love-fictions alike confirmed a fairly benign, if illusory, view of the social universe.

What recourse, then, remained for the novelist who wished to break loose of the formal constraints of the marriage plot in order to expose the irresolvable conflicts built into a code of conjugal love that defined the sexes as complementary but unequal partners, partners linked in a lifelong oppositional play of power masquerading as pleasure? The subject matter and narrative manner that began to dislodge the hegemony of the fictional marriage tradition with particular force in the second half of the nineteenth century, in fact, had already been set into motion before the "debate" over marriage became a popular topic of dissension in the 1870s and 1880s. Eliot and James were to join a select group of novelists whose reaction was to translate the unease of marital discord into the text itself. By developing techniques that involved the temporal and spatial dislocation, duplication, juxtaposition, and irresolution of various narrative "parts," their texts began to counter the formulaic trajectories, converging lines, and climactic "discharge" endemic to the protypical Anglo-American love-plot. This chapter will argue that such a development links the early innovations of Emily Brontë's *Wuthering Heights* (1847) and Eliot's *Daniel Deronda* (1876) with the modernist experiments of James's *The Golden Bowl* (1904) and Woolf's *To the Lighthouse* (1927): all four texts ultimately refuse to simplify the unsettling contradictions exposed by their narration of the "secret stings," as A. D. Blackamore put it in *Luck at Last,* "which ever render life and wedlock both uneasy" (81). The destabilizing strategies evolved in all four of these novels attest that a truly empowering revolt against the strictures of wedlock ideology has entailed, indeed demanded, a radical rethinking of the dynamics of narrative structure, of narrative desire, itself.

The unsettling thematic implications of what was to become the counter-tradition's main metaphor of wedlock can be inferred from a review of "modern" fiction written by the sometimes novelist Mrs. Oliphant in 1855. Focusing on the example of *Jane Eyre,* she warns of the threat posed to the "orthodox system of novel-making" by a fictional "revolution" that has undertaken to challenge the traditional hierarchy of the sexes by espousing female "equality" in relationship. "Here is a battle which must always be going forward—a balance of power only to be decided by single combat, deadly and uncompromising, where the combatants, so far from being guided by the old punctilios of the duello, make no secret of their ferocity."[4] The unending combat that Mrs. Oliphant mocks as an abrasive "new" mode of wooing, other writers found to be an accurate metaphor for the antagonistic opposition underlying the sentimental code of conjugal love—"an opposition," as James's Isabel Archer thinks, "the like of which she had never dreamed. . . in which the vital principle of the one was a thing of contempt to the other." For the sex war becomes a central issue and image in the counter-traditional reevaluation of romantic and marital companionship. Of course, the concept of love as war, as the previous chapters have shown, was not an unfamiliar one; seduction plots made explicit use of often violent martial imagery to depict sexual pursuit and conquest, while courtship narratives often displayed suitors as more or less civilized foes battling each other with wit and words. The scene of ritualistic swordplay in Hardy's

Far From the Madding Crowd, for example, illustrates the traditional archetype of mating as a kind of male-instigated war, with Sergeant Troy's phallic thrusts leaving Bathsheba pleasurably "powerless."[5] For a small number of novelists, however, the tableau of the embattled sexes functioned not as a sign of a natural dichotomy separating men and women, but rather as the unnatural consequence of social constructions of sexual roles and power within wedlock. The less easily resolved potentialities of such a representation may be inferred from the direction the warring metaphor takes for the newly married heroine of Meredith's *Diana of the Crossways:* "We walked a dozen steps in stupified union, and hit upon crossways. From that moment it was tug and tug, he me, I him. By resisting I made him a tyrant, and he, by insisting, made me a rebel."[6] The linguistic structure of Meredith's phrasing, mirroring yet parodying the idealized balance of wedlock in its chiasmic patterns, implicitly becomes an indictment of the adversarial roles of male "tyrant" and female "rebel" encouraged and intensified by this "tug of war." The gap can only widen given these definitions, never resolve itself, save through the total overthrow of one sex or the other.

Such warfare becomes particularly invidious within a legalized context of relationship based on the assumption of permanency. In this regard, Roland Barthes's insight into the nature of the domestic "scene" and the aim toward which its violence is directed brilliantly glosses what Victorian fiction generally managed to hide: Barthes tells us he has "always regarded the (domestic) 'scene' as a pure experience of violence. . . . The retorts engender one another, *without any possible conclusion,* save that of murder, and it is because the scene is entirely bent on, aims toward this ultimate violence, *which nonetheless it never assumes* (at least among 'civilized' people), that it is an essential violence, a violence *which delights in sustaining itself.*" The socially constructed myth of marital perpetuity, that is, engenders within the institution a self-sustaining and unending degree of emotional and psychological violence that reinforces the concomitant myth of sexual opposition. A graphic illustration of these intersecting myths occurs in the diary of Steven Marcus's "other Victorian," who so loathes being tied to his wife that he writes, "I felt I could murder her with my prick, and drove, and drove, and drove, and spent her up with cursing": here, the impossible "ultimate" act of murder referred to by Barthes has been displaced onto sexual climax in a legalized act of violent sexual mastery. What aesthetic forms have done, Barthes continues, is to create the *illusion* that such scenarios can have a resolution; traditional dramatic plotting generally attempts to "domesticate," or tame, its represented violence by "*oblig[ing]* it to end." Such impositions of authorial fiat call to mind the tendency of the conventional wedlock plot to end in melodramatic climaxes involving death or reconciliation—climaxes identified in chapter 3 as at least metaphorically masculine "spendings" of narrative and erotic energy—in face of the fact that domestic warfare, as Barthes reveals, normally lacks "any possible conclusion," one quarrel begetting another in an ever-widening circle of discord.[7]

Perceived in this light, the novelistic depiction of husband and wife as covertly—if not openly—hostile combatants, locked in an unending battle of personal and societal dimension, may begin to imply a radical critique of the ideological forms underlying the presumed order of marriage. The "unease" emanating from such deadlocked representations of conjugal impasse becomes an almost inevitable consequence of exposing the irresolvable conflicts and contrary attitudes—between self and social role, between alternative possibilities of relationship, between the sexes themselves—that we have already observed insinuating themselves into standard fictional portrayals of marriage. Hence, to the novelist rebelling against this tradition, the arena of life beyond the "happy ending" most often appeared, to borrow Mrs. Oliphant's wording, "a battle which must always be going forward." Consequently the problem became *how*—or *whether*—to attempt to contain, in narrative terms, such uneasy experience. What if one's protagonists, locked together in a legally or morally binding bond, cannot remove themselves without social disapprobation from the "unstable relationships" that various theorists have judged a proper beginning but an antithetical resolution to the "inevitable" stasis universally "demanded" by fictional narrative?[8] How, for instance, to give meaningful shape to the unhappy marriage in which the erring mate is not reclaimed by a faithful wife (as in *Amelia*) or removed by timely death (as in *Middlemarch*)? Or what if conflicts of constricting marital roles and personal integrity are not neatly resolved by the total collapse of a relationship as a tragically "appropriate" index of individual failure? Where else can the representation of marriage *go*, as it were?

In creating the uncharted and uncertain world of marital impasse, writers such as Emily Brontë, Eliot, and James thus faced a number of narratological obstacles. The structural solutions that they evolved anticipate the techniques that contemporary critics, with modernists like Woolf in mind, have gathered together under the rubric of "open-ended" narrative form. Often viewed as the twentieth century's "answer" to the seemingly closed system of Victorian thought and literature, the prototypically open-ended text refuses to bring its multiple narrative lines together in one univocal pattern, because, as Robert Adams puts it, "unresolvedness" is part of the meaning;[9] themes may or may not reach a temporary end, Alan Friedman notes, but the underlying, expanding stream of experience does not.[10] A typical signature of the form, these critics avow, is its "open ending," stripped bare of authorial commentary and judgment and therefore disruptive of the reader's traditional expectation of repose and relaxation of tension; forced to engage with the text beyond its actual close, the reader loses the ability to recuperate, hence naturalize, the text's manifold possible meanings or contradictions into a centrally unifying statement and must therefore actively struggle to reach an even tentative judgment.[11]

Some recent theorists have dismissed "openness" as a useful critical distinction given the degree to which the repressed "discontents" of *any* narrative ultimately violate its sense of finality; and, insofar as simplistic categorization of novelistic closure is concerned, their point is well taken.[12] But as the prior discussion of the codification of form in the marriage tradition has suggested, the degree to which a fictional construct attempts to enclose its meanings and thereby create the appearance of a totalizing simulacrum of "order" can be measured in terms of specific textual strategies and techniques, which in turn illuminate the writer's allegiances or infidelities to reigning narrative and social conventions: there are infinite degrees of not only "closing" but "opening up" a text. With these caveats in mind, the terms "closed" and "open" remain useful as general signposts for evaluating the impact of the marriage tradition on novelistic form. For the counter-traditional exposure of wedlock as a state of often irresolvable impasse advances a cause as well suited to the *avowed* purposes of open narrative as vindication of the conjugal ideal is suited to the tradition's *attempts* at closed form.

Thus, although the frequent explanation of the inconclusive text as an intellectual and aesthetic product of the modernist movement has its validity, it is only a partial picture; not only do some varieties of open fictional narrative reach as far back as Sterne's *The Life and Opinions of Tristram Shandy* (1760–1767), but other explorations of the form may be traced to a long-standing discontent with the gender- and power-related implications of wedlock and with the inherited strictures of literary tradition on the genre's themes and form. Indeed, in an early work like Richardson's *Clarissa,* a partial prototype of the counter-traditional marriage novel coexists with the rise of the tradition itself, as we shall shortly see. The modernist breakthrough, especially characterized by thematic and formal irresolution, was the result of many converging forces; of these, the revolt against marriage themes had an impact, both in helping to create this breakthrough and in appropriating open-ended structures for its own purposes, which have yet adequately to be measured.

As novels that strive to come to grips with the importance of love, the nature of relationship, the potential for destruction in traditional conjugal alignments, and the impact of constructions of gender on identity, *Wuthering Heights, Daniel Deronda, The Golden Bowl,* and *To the Lighthouse* share themes that elicit similar formal responses, especially in the effort to translate the uneasy tension of marital "war" into principles of narrative structure. Before enumerating the tactical and textual means by which these formats attempt to defuse the ideological precepts of standard love-fiction, it is illuminating to return to a text we have already examined that anticipates their counter-traditional maneuvers: Richardson's *Clarissa.* Even though this epistolary novel is situated on the battlefield of seduction rather than wedlock, its devastating view of sexual combat arises from its implicit condemnation of the abuse of sexual power institutionalized in patriarchal marriage.

First of all, the alternation of letters between Clarissa and Anna, on the one hand, and between Lovelace and Bedford, on the other, inscribes in the text's structure an irremediable—and widening—division between the worlds and perspectives of the sexes. In the process, the "battle" between Clarissa's will and Lovelace's desire to "triumph over the whole sex" (1:153) in seducing her is exposed as the inevitable result of a sexual code that permits Clarissa's sufferings in the name of male power. As in the counter-traditional marriage novel, this external dichotomization of the sexes precipitates internal divisions between social and personal identities. Clarissa's fight for chastity is not simply, as Fiedler would have it, the stock response of the Virgin archetype; her resistance, rather, expresses a desperate desire to maintain a coherent sense of subjectivity, epitomized in her plea to her family, in face of their effort to force her to accept Solmes in marriage, "Only leave me myself" (2:109). Inversely, Lovelace's dehumanizing attitude toward women, like his revulsion for marriage, ensues from a narcissistic entrapment within a code of masculine superiority that dictates his monomaniacal desire to conquer or be proven inferior—a self-destructive solipsism we will find enunciated by several male characters throughout this and the next chapter. In the narrative stages that form the plot of Clarissa's rebellion against such tyranny, schism follows schism in an unending pattern of disaster that even her containment in death does not completely check; the world she leaves behind in choosing to die apart from her family is in complete disarray, the house of the Harlowes disintegrating in a chaos of "confusion" (4:482) that echoes Lovelace's vision of "the whole world [as] but one great Bedlam" (4:136). While the novel existing in the imagination of its readership became a quintessential model of the seduction narrative, as I have suggested in chapter 3, the *Clarissa* that Richardson wrote simultaneously anticipates in its themes and patterns of unchecked discord the counter-traditional presentation of wedlock as "a battle which must always be going forward."

The way in which the dying Clarissa's wishes parody the concluding nuptials of love fiction ("As for me, never bride was so ready as I am" [4:303]) also points to one of the basic strategies of developmental plotting employed by the counter-tradition: the methodic undermining, reversal, or withholding of the threshold moments and narrative climaxes associated with phases of courtship, marriage, and domestic life in conventional fiction. Thus, typically signifying structural markers like the passage into adolescence, proposals and weddings, conferrals of adult status, births, and deaths are manipulated through the duplication, juxtaposition, and displacement of their usual linear arrangement in such a way as to rob them, at least partially, of their ideological force. Rising movements become "falls," courtings turn out to be false starts, wedding scenes are replaced with disturbing counterforces, deaths escape the stabilizing logic of the courtly *Liebestod.* The effects that such "tampering with the expected sequence" portend for the reader are well described by Virginia Woolf in *A Room of One's Own:* "For whenever I was about to feel the usual things in the usual places, about love, about death," she says of the hypothetical Mary Carmichael's formbreaking novel, "the annoying creature twitched me away, as if the important point were just a little farther on" (85, 95). In the depiction of uneasy wedlock, then, such a deflation of expectations provokes a sense of textual dislocation parallel to the situational disjunctions unfolding on the level of content.

In regard to perspectival rather than developmental textual operations, several of these novels use elements of structural repetition to introduce a temporal "unease" into their representations of the course of unhappy love and marriage. Traditional love-plots, such as those reviewed in chapter 3, often use repetition to underscore the reversals necessary to effect an ending whose balance recapitulates the state of complementary equipoise desired in marriage. But in novels like *Wuthering Heights* or *To the Lighthouse,* the eerie and unsettling repetition of events, actions, and characters underlines an unbridgeable gap between cause and effect, between marital ideal and outcome, that cannot be univocally resolved. Closely related to and often the agent of such destabilizing repetition is the use of some form of double plot or dual structure to keep the direction of the counter-traditional text always slightly "off-center," as opposed to "end-directed." Relevant in this regard is Peter Garrett's theory of the irresolution often generated by the format of the Victorian multiplot novel. Borrowing his terms from Bakhtin, Garrett argues that in such texts the simultaneous existence of multiple and singular foci creates an ongoing *dialogue* —rather than dialectic—of structural perspectives that inhibits resolution into any single pattern of meaning. "In place of the defensive strategies that attempt to limit the play of meaning by imposing a center," Garrett notes, "such a conception of dialogical form can open our reading to the multiplicity and instability of decentered structure."[13] It can also, we might add, free the erotic dynamic of narrative from a linear model of excitation and release by opening the reader to a more diffuse, circuitous course of textual "pleasure."

Similarly destabilizing strategies underlie the variety of double-plots characterizing the four novels to be examined in this chapter: in the story of two generations in *Wuthering Heights*, the narrative of the second Cathy, unsettlingly recalling her mother's life, is held in check by the concurrent plot of Heathcliff's revenge and death; the two largely separate and alternating plots of *Daniel Deronda* imply a dialogue over diverging female and male destinies for which there is no "final" answer or narrative synthesis; *The Golden Bowl*'s structural division into two parts and into two centers of consciousness (one the husband's and the other the wife's) reminds the reader that half the story is always unfolding offstage; the ten-year lapse between segments of *To the Lighthouse* only accentuates the continuing disruptions created by the issues left unresolved during the Ramsays' marriage. In all these works, then, the multiplicity of developmental or perspectival foci becomes an often radically de-centering structural ploy, creating a narrative expansiveness, a multiplication of differences, that opens to question the stability and coherence espoused in traditional marriage fiction.

Given these various strategies for opening up the counter-traditional text, some preliminary distinctions between types of closural irresolution can be drawn. In *The Golden Bowl* and the Gwendolen plot of *Daniel Deronda*, for instance, the greatest impact of irresolution is made simultaneous with the actual conclusion, where characters and situations are quite literally left, in James's phrase, *en l'air*. Eschewing the conventional summary-oriented "epilogue" (of which the Finale to *Middlemarch* is a version), both these plots culminate in scenic dramatizations, stripped of authorial commentary and judgment, which break off ambiguously.[14] The critical personal relationships in *Wuthering Heights* and *To the Lighthouse*, in contrast, are abruptly terminated *mid-novel*, despite the fact that half the "story" remains to be told; the premature deaths of Catherine and Mrs. Ramsay serve to open their narratives to expanding visions of disturbance registered on both thematic and textual levels. Although these latter two texts end in densely charged symbolic tableaus that are aesthetically satisfying, the promise of each looks toward an unknown, untested, and unspecified future coexisting in open suspension with unresolved lines of action in which the ghosts of the past refuse to be laid to rest.

The counter-tradition's contributions to the development of open-ended form, thus, exist as a consequence of its refusal to give easy answers to the often irresolvable contradictions that its critiques of wedlock reveal to be operative in the very ideal of conjugal happiness. Whether the novel's effect of irresolution is achieved by leaving characters or situations climactically suspended *en l'air,* by foregoing a final dispensation of rewards, by leaving the reader poised on the brink of a visionary unknown, or by creating a welter of plots and perspectives upon which no all-encompassing resolution may impose itself, the final effect of such uncontained expansions, in Marianna Torgovnick's phrase, is to "unsettle" the reader, who must also become a critic of the conventions residing in the marital ideal. Thereby enforcing the reader's active engagement in the unease of wedlock unhappily embarked upon, all these novels set into motion organizational formats that forego the repose traditionally associated with fictional closure as well as with domestic felicity. The message, rather, is in the unease with which these narrative formats attempt to replicate the ongoing battle of marital conflict, a war waged within and outside the self that cannot be resolved in terms of the conventional rules and roles by which society and narrative have locked partners in wedlock into place.

·*Wuthering Heights*·
Uneasy Wedlock and Unquiet Slumbers

Although now recognized as a nineteenth-century classic, *Wuthering Heights* (1847) has always impressed its critics as something of an anomaly in the English tradition of the novel, and its difference is nowhere so marked as in its unconventional attitudes toward love and marriage. Indeed, the "disjointed" and "strangely original" qualities of the text's form that its initial reviewers found unsettling have everything to do with its equally strange and original representation of love.[15] In pitting its vision of life-affirming relationship against the destructive course of identity frustrated, violated, and sundered by societal norms of wedlock, Emily Brontë's unconventional tale of passion unfolds onto multiple planes of plot, reality, and perspective that defy the boundaries of traditional fictional order. The result is a textual openness, an explosiveness of possibility, that flouts the proper "end of fictitious writings"[16] prescribed by the novel's Victorian critics and readers alike. Its final denial of the easy moral, in turn, becomes Brontë's strategy for affirming a radical paradigm of self-in-relationship that runs counter to the sexual polarity, self-limitation, and inequality endemic to most English marriage fiction.

That Brontë's unorthodox critique establishes itself, in some degree, in opposition to her society's dominant sexual ideology is a fact established in the best of recent criticism of *Wuthering Heights*. One might look, for example, at the novel's recurrent figure of the oppressive male "master" for a clue to this dimension of Brontë's vision. The correlation between male control of the family and excessive and often arbitrary displays of power first surfaces in old Earnshaw, who despite his kindness is thrown "into fits" by "slights of his authority,"[17] and continues in his son and heir Hindley, who, from the safety of his domestic "paradise on the hearth" (27), mercilessly persecutes the young Heathcliff and Catherine; it will resurface in the very different personalities of Edgar Linton, Heathcliff, and Heathcliff Linton. In turn, Brontë measures the negative consequences of male tyranny in the novel's accumulating pattern of forcibly sundered relationships, as well as in the internal divisions of identity that mirror such losses. And, crucially, this thematic pattern of division is registered in the structural schisms or ruptures that make up so much of the fabric of *Wuthering Heights,* beginning with its dual narrators and continuing in its divisions between the worlds of "reality" and ghosts, between recollected and anticipated levels of time, between modes of ending. Coexisting with this multiplication of parts is another, more radical kind of narrative doubleness engendered by the constant duplication of characters, events, gestures, settings: everything seems uneasily to replicate itself in similar but different forms, progressively upsetting readerly assumptions of stable reality and narrative coherence alike. Standing against this structural pattern of division and doubling, moreover, is a single thematic constant, the image of oneness and difference embodied in the passionate bond of Catherine and Heathcliff. Moving from an overview of this pivotal relationship to the multiplication of developmental and perspectival strategies that envelop it, we may begin to see how both these patterns participate in a subversion of the traditional marriage plot and the tenets underlying its construction.

I

Brontë's reworking of received notions of romantic affiliation is given its fullest expression in the affinity uniting Catherine and Heathcliff as untraditional soul mates: "He's more myself than I am," Catherine will say of this uniquely nonpolar attraction in her famous speech of chapter 9, "Whatever our souls are made of, his and mine are *the same*. . . . Nelly, *I am* Heathcliff" (68, 70; emphasis added). The mystical intensity of this assertion of "like" selves, it is essential to realize, originates in a childhood inseparability so powerfully conveyed that, despite its fleeting nature and representation in only a very few pages, it colors the reader's impression of their adult passion and of the rest of the novel. The singularity of being that ensues from the youths' absolute identification comes alive in a series of vivid figures of oneness, union, and merger; these range from the diary entry in which Catherine tells of pinning her and Heathcliff's pinafores together in the arc of the dresser to create a shelter from their oppressors, to recollections of their moorland escapes joined "under [the] shelter" of a single cloak (27, 50). No image, however, is as evocative of their oneness as the enclosed oak-paneled bed that the two share at the Heights until Heathcliff is fourteen and Catherine twelve. This womblike structure, to which the narrative keeps returning at pivotal moments, at once suggests their umbilical closeness, serves as a private "space" within which each can nurture the other's nascent identity, and hints at the highly charged eroticism that will seem to unfold naturally, almost imperceptibly, from these moments of early physical intimacy.

As such an image also suggests, the children seem to share a siblinglike affinity; even their adult passion will retain this sense of a brother-sister relationship. The intimation of kinship, however, is less suggestive of literal incest than of Brontë's attempt to redefine romantic attraction in terms of erotic identification rather than sexual antagonism. One mark of such an intention may lie in a plaintive comment the younger Cathy later makes: "People hate their

wives, sometimes; but not their sisters and brothers" (192).[18]
Cathy, of course, oversentimentalizes the reality of the typical sibling bond—a wishful fallacy shared by a variety of Victorian novelists including Austen, Dickens, Eliot, and Gaskell, and exposed in
Brontë's text by the negative relations of actual brothers and sisters. But Cathy's articulation nonetheless holds an intensely real
meaning as a *metaphoric* expression of an alternative to reigning
preconceptions of marriage as the union of opposingly gendered,
and hence inevitably antagonistic, factions. For, unlike the hatred
visible between many husbands and wives, brother and sister ideally participate in a noncombative mode of male–female relationship, one that is unthreatening because gender difference is
rendered secondary to the bond of blood-likeness, familiarity, and
friendship. By characterizing the future lovers Catherine and
Heathcliff as foster siblings, then, Brontë begins to undermine the
ideology of sexual attraction embedded in traditional conjugal
arrangements.

At the same time, to the degree that the blood tie of kinship
points to a common source greater than the difference of gender,
sibling "oneness" becomes a symbol for a potential state of psychological integration. Hence, Catherine's youthful representation as
Heathcliff's "rough-headed counterpart" (51) has suggested to
readers since the novel's publication a working out of the Platonic
myth of androgyny: "He and she are, so to speak, but a single person," wrote a French essayist in 1857, "he is the male soul of the
monster, she the female."[19] One needs to be careful, however, in
applying the slippery term "androgyny" to these two characters.
For readings that designate Heathcliff the sundered "masculine"
component and Catherine the "female" half of a Platonic (or even
"monstrous") whole mistakenly transform the nearly identical personalities of Catherine and Heathcliff into sexually defined opposites. This is precisely the conventional notion of love against
which Brontë pits her vision. Rather, what one finds in the young
Catherine and Heathcliff are states remarkably free of the constraints typically imposed by social constructions of "masculinity"
or "femininity"; theirs is the place of difference vis-à-vis the exacting geography of gender mapped out by their world. Nelly's narration, for example, calls attention time and again to the defiant,

unsubmissive side of Catherine's unrestrained childhood personality that has led Patricia Spacks to label her "an anti-heroine, in every respect opposed to her century's ideal prototype of the adolescent woman." Conversely, Gilbert and Gubar have suggestively demonstrated some of the ways in which Heathcliff's youthful status at the Heights—as victim of oppression, as unnamed "it" (39) without rights or birthright, as mediator marking the boundary between natural and cultural realms—replicates the anthropological status of women in patriarchal social organizations. The psychological continuum connecting Catherine and Heathcliff as symbiotic and symbolic twins tantalizingly subverts traditional demarcations of sexual identity.[20]

The affinity that Catherine and Heathcliff discover in the wild Eden of their preadolescent years also has specifically external origins, ones which reinforce Brontë's critique of conventional romantic norms. To the extent that Catherine's *real* brother, Hindley, mercilessly persecutes them, they are drawn together in empathy and rebellion as equals whose cause lies in human rather than sexual values;[21] to the extent that Hindley totally neglects their upbringing, the two are granted a temporary respite from the socializing pressures of nuclear family life that would more readily fix them in restrictively gendered modes of behavior. The social and psychological freedom that they gain as "unfriended" orphan "creatures" (46) is epitomized in the unconstrained, savage life they lead on the moors, their haven from the values of the dominant order. As such, they inhabit that "free territory" or "wild zone" that recent feminist criticism has made a compelling metaphor for those overlooked gaps in patriarchal logic where invisibility becomes the avenue to autonomy and power.[22] Privy to this "space" as youths, Catherine and Heathcliff, classic outsider figures, become the insiders, free to exist on their beloved moors as self-sufficient allies and unconscious equals who define as their antagonists the world's representatives, not each other.

In opposition to this bond of "like" selves, Brontë uses the social marriage of Catherine and Edgar to depict the consequences of a relationship based on conventional polarity: Catherine's soul is lightning, Linton's moonbeam; her blood feverous, his ice-water (72, 101). Since "opposites" are supposed to attract according to popular love ideology, to surface appearance the newly-wed Lintons have achieved the golden mean requisite to the conventional wedlock ideal. But as the disharmony that erupts upon Heathcliff's return betrays, Catherine and Edgar's conjugal happiness exists only as long as their precarious balancing of disparate wills manages to exclude all conflict or personal desire. Furthermore, this uneasy balance of opposites is doomed because it is rooted in basic inequality. "There were no mutual concessions," Nelly says of Catherine's domineering and Edgar's mild personalities, "one stood erect and the other yielded" (81). Once roles reverse, and Edgar decides to wield his legal right as "master," it will be *his* preemptory command that Catherine choose between himself and Heathcliff that explodes once and for all Nelly's wishful assertion that they are "in possession of a deep and growing happiness" (81). The sentimental ideal of love, touted as the source of peaceful concord, is thus exposed to be the opposite, a breeding ground of violence and hatred, because its basic premise, the union of contraries, is rooted in a sense of initial and unequal antagonism.

Hindley's marriage to Frances, Isabella's elopement with Heathcliff, and Lockwood's sterile romantic fantasies all reveal a similar lesson: the dominant social order promotes conceptions of love that, whether insipid, erotic, or voyeuristic, allow men access to power through their control of women. It is with the petulant Frances perched on his knee that Hindley feels the strength to begin his retaliatory persecution of Heathcliff. Isabella's illusory conception of Heathcliff as a Byronic "hero of romance" (126), which results in her becoming the sexual instrument of his scheme of revenge, issues in a hatred as destructive as her mistaken love. Lockwood's coolly teasing game of glances with the "fascinating creature" (15) at the seaside prefigures his equally sterile fantasies of becoming the younger Cathy's "favoured possessor" (21). "Something more romantic than a fairy tale it would have been . . . had she and I struck up an attachment" (240–41), Lockwood can *safely* fantasize at the very moment he is taking leave of the region. In exposing the politics of sexual power hidden within such "fairy tale[s]" of sentimental romantic "attachment," the novel highlights, by contrast, the radical difference of a love based on likeness and equality.

II

As I have already intimated, the web of interrelationships giving substance to Brontë's critique of love relationship is complemented by an extremely complex narrative structure, one in which the doubling and division of developmental lines of plotting become a powerful agent adding to the novel's uneasy and explosive tensions. On the most apparent level, the division of the text into two halves after its midpoint—the moment of Catherine's death and of the second Cathy's birth in chapter 16—suggests a "classic" double plot structure governed by the sequentially ordered trajectories of mother and daughter. But if one chooses to evaluate the novel's organization in terms of a singular focus on Heathcliff's development, *Wuthering Heights* may appear as *one* continuous plot which overlaps and encloses the generational stories of the two Catherines. Because of this overlapping of developmental structures, a truly synchronous rather than sequential double plot may also be seen operating after chapter 16: the unresolved story of Heathcliff's frustrated love, becoming that of his revenge and agony, develops beside the history of the second Cathy. All these modes of "doubling," moreover, occur within a narrative format in which the disruption of temporal sequence through the use of dual narrators makes the two "halves" of the text seem almost to unfold simultaneously (the latter stages of the second Cathy's history, observed and narrated by Lockwood at the beginning of the novel, are happening while Nelly narrates the history of the first Catherine). The fact that no one has ever been able to argue successfully that only one "plot," or for that matter one character, dominates *Wuthering Heights* should alert us, indeed, to the multivocal principles underlying its structure.[23]

Within this doubling framework, the clash between the desiring self and marital identity is most graphically represented in the bildungsroman variations that structure the mother–daughter history. In contrast to the traditional female bildungsroman, in which the heroine's acquisition of mature identity is confirmed by marriage, the trajectories of courtship and wedlock forming the narrative of the two Catherines become the means of raising profoundly disturbing questions about the social institution of

marriage. For by methodically undermining the threshold moments, rites of passage, significant scenes, and climactic actions of
conventional romantic fiction, Brontë's text italicizes its damning
portrait of the harrowing effects of wedlock on female identity by
presenting it in repeating plots that mirror each other in an uneasy
blend of parallel and chiasmic structures as disorienting as they are
gripping.

The original Catherine first "enters" the text in Lockwood's
opening narration not as a living character but as a disembodied
name, tracings of which Lockwood finds etched on the windowsill
of her former bedchamber: "*Catherine Earnshaw,* here and there
varied to *Catherine Heathcliff,* and then again to *Catherine Linton*"
(25). These markings not only suggest Catherine's fundamental
uncertainty about who she is or will become, but also forecast, in
exact order, the successive crises of identity shaping the plot of her
life and, in inversed order, her daughter's development from Linton to Earnshaw status. As Lockwood's overnight experience at the
Heights opens into Nelly's retrospective narrative in the immediately following chapter, the text presents the "real" Catherine—as
opposed to the tracings that remain on the windowsill—in a fairytale-like tableau equally prophetic of her destiny. Asking her father
to bring her a riding whip from Liverpool, a present critics have
associated with the "ungirlish" power she delights in wielding,
Catherine instead gets Heathcliff.[24] Not insignificantly, then, Nelly's narrative originates in the very event that triggers the most
formative stage of Cathy's youthful development—the brief but
idyllic blossoming of a rebellious self-sufficiency that unfolds on
the moors with Heathcliff as her comrade.

The loss of freedom that brings this narrative stage to a halt at
Thrushcross Grange in chapter 6 forms the decisive turning point
in Catherine's story and in the novel as a whole. This loss, indeed, is
underscored in that the event precipitating it is literally absent
from the present-time of Nelly's narration, reported to her only
after the fact by Heathcliff.[25] One moment he and Catherine are
joined together—another image of their oneness—in the act of
spying into the alien, civilized world of the Linton family; the next,
forcibly separated as Catherine, wounded by the watchdog
Skulker, is detained within. As a significant threshold in the
bildungsroman of Catherine's youth, this event ironically reverses

the rising pattern of most fictions of female growth: twelve years of age and on the verge of sexual maturation, incapacitated by her wound and forced to undergo a six weeks' confinement, the pubescent Catherine is initiated by the Lintons into superficially appealing modes of "feminine" social privilege—a rite of passage into female sexuality that, significantly, is recorded as a "fall" from the sufficiency of her prior existence.[26] Emerging from her symbolic captivity at the Grange as "quite a beauty . . . a lady now" (50–51), Catherine manifests an internal division of self and sexual role that results, as even Nelly notes, in her "adopt[ing] a double character without exactly intending to deceive anyone" (62). For although she and Heathcliff attempt to remain "constant companions still" (63), her feminized self increasingly inclines toward Edgar Linton in what becomes a compressed courtship narrative. The tightly interwoven sequence of action in chapters 7, 8, and 9, charting the gradual evolution of their attraction in face of Heathcliff's prior claim, culminates in Catherine's decision to marry Edgar, her complementary opposite and hence conventionally appropriate suitor. The specific event of Catherine and Edgar's engagement, moreover, is structured to expose their sentimental romance for what it is—a relationship rooted in an antagonism that portends its own violent end. Ironically, it is Catherine's slapping of Edgar in a moment of anger that elicits her suitor's immediate, offstage proposal: "I saw the quarrel had merely effected a closer intimacy," Nelly reports, ". . . and enabled them . . . to confess themselves lovers" (66). One could hardly ask for a more perfect example of the *discordia concors* principle discussed above in chapter 2 as a historical model for traditionally conceived romantic attraction.

Yet strategically juxtaposed with this rapprochement, and antithetical to conventional courtship plotting in several ways, is Catherine's "confessional" speech to Nelly in chapter 9. For what she has to say of her two "suitors" brings to a head the conflict between social role and personal identity that she is undergoing. The dream she reports to Nelly of being cast out of heaven (which she associates with the Grange, Linton's home) and of waking "sobbing for joy" on the "heath" that is her true "home" (and, by synecdoche, Heathcliff) reveals an intuitive recognition of the self-deprivation involved in accepting Edgar (72), as do the contrasting types of language she uses to describe her feelings for both youths. Furthermore, in contrast to the temporary obstructions blocking union in traditional courtship formulas, Catherine's answer to Nelly's question, "All seems smooth and easy—where is the obstacle?" reveals that barrier to be something more than temporary: *"Here!* and *here!* . . . in my soul, and in my heart" (71). The obstacle, that is, is her authentic self, which by analogy is also the self of Heathcliff ("Nelly, I am Heathcliff," Catherine continues). It is inevitable, then, that marriage to Edgar spells a permanent alienation from "heath" and "home" for Catherine, canceling the personal sense of wholeness that her bond of identification with Heathcliff has represented.

Given this fact, it is ironically appropriate that the narrative climax of the plot of Catherine's presumed "courtship" should ignore the situation of the betrothed suitors, focusing rather on the psychological impasse created by the sundering of Catherine and Heathcliff's relationship. For when she learns that Heathcliff has run away, Catherine undergoes an immediate *internal* breakdown (mirroring their *external* severance) that leaves her a literally debilitated, more capriciously "feminine" ghost of her former fierce self, "broken" for her place in the marital order. The displacement of the subsequent espousals of Catherine and Edgar to an ambiguously worded, one-sentence paragraph near chapter's end cooperates in upending the rhythm of climax and smooth succession that propels the traditional erotic narrative; the gap of three years that intervenes before the marriage is finalized, moreover, further renders its occurrence anticlimactic by intimating, among other things, that Catherine has been silently, desperately, holding out for Heathcliff's return.

In the wedlock plot that unfolds in the following chapter, the dialectic between marital destiny and selfhood almost instantly resurfaces in acts of psychic and narrative violence. For in Brontë's careful arrangement of Nelly's narrative, the return of Heathcliff is made to seem nearly simultaneous with Catherine's marriage; thus, his mysterious reappearance becomes, like the welling up of the forbidden, an external manifestation of Catherine's hitherto suppressed acknowledgment of her forfeited identity. The geometric configuration that results as Catherine finds herself torn between the demands of her husband and Heathcliff nightmarishly repeats the premarital struggle leading to her emotional collapse in chapter 9. The consequence, again, is internal fragmentation. Locking herself into her bedroom at the end of chapter 11 in a despairing assertion of autonomy, Catherine actually reenacts her self-imprisonment in wed/lock, in the process precipitating a descent into schizophrenia, the ultimate loss of identity. Hence, in the psychodramatic "mad" scene of chapter 12, Catherine is unable to recognize her reflection in the mirror as "Mrs. Linton" (106) because, in becoming Edgar's wife and complement, she has lost her true mirroring self, Heathcliff. It is entirely appropriate, then, that in her mad reveries the "whole last seven years" have grown a "blank"; she returns, in a striking instance of narrative analepsis, to the memory of being "enclosed in the oak-panelled bed" at the Heights and "*laid alone* for the first time, . . . wrenched from . . . my all in all, Heathcliff" (107; emphasis added). This traumatically repressed (and hitherto narratively suppressed) event, it dawns on the reader, was the *immediate* consequence of Catherine's initiation, exactly seven years ago, into the Grange and womanhood. The desire to erase these intervening years and return in memory to an undivided state is less a regressive turning away *from* reality, therefore, than an affirmation of the reality of a lost identity, "savage, and hardy, and free," preexisting the fiction of self she has assumed in marriage; as Catherine says in a statement where madness speaks the words of truth, "I should *be myself* were I once among the heather on those hills" (107; emphasis added). Instead, as "Mrs. Linton, the lady of Thrushcross Grange," the maddened Catherine finds herself inhabiting an alien role in an alien plot as "the wife of a stranger" and as an "exile, and outcast" (107) from her previous life with Heathcliff. Ironically, it is at this point that Edgar finally enters Catherine's sickroom, and her reaction—"I'm past wanting you" (109)—marks a sobering conclusion to the ill-fated narrative of their marriage.

In terms of the bildungsroman structure of the narrative of Catherine's life, the issue of her illness is a "permanent alienation of intellect" (112) and loss of the will to live: like Clarissa Harlowe, Catherine discovers that death, the elimination of self, becomes the only liberation from a fragmented existence. The end of Catherine's devolving trajectory, then, is quite the opposite of the glorified and idealized *Liebestod*, or death-longing, of Continental love literature; her death neither fulfills nor resolves anything, and it simultaneously frustrates the conventional assumption that mature female identity lies in marriage, marking, to the contrary, an ultimate fragmentation of identity.[27] And as a narrative "exit," Catherine's demise not only imposes an unbridgeable chasm between herself and the living Heathcliff but violently ruptures the text at its midpoint, the consequences of which are manifest in the uneasily multiplying levels of narration and nightmare that follow.

Out of this splintering of lives, of text, the novel seems to begin again with the birth of the second Cathy—in a sense, Brontë's third opening, following Lockwood's beginning in chapter 1 and Nelly's in chapter 4. The uncanny doubling of "Catherines" that ensues, creating an atemporal as well as genealogical relation between the two plots, serves to bring into perspectival alignment the unchanging system of oppression against which the violated self must struggle. For within the brackets of Nelly's retelling, the stages of Cathy's growth to adulthood, like Catherine's before her, chart an education into female powerlessness—an education whose inevitable end, as glimpsed in the narrative time occupied by Lockwood, seems to be the embittered self-division of one who "feel[s] like death" (233).

Drawing upon a complex pattern of repetitions and reversals, the second phase of Brontë's demystification of the cultural ideal of sheltered womanhood begins by reversing the literal direction of the first Catherine's trajectory. Thus, the plot of young Cathy's unconscious quest for identity begins where her mother's ended, in the Victorian world of the Grange, and moves toward the Heights. Raised to believe herself everyone's "'love,' and 'darling,' and 'queen,' and 'angel'" (162), Cathy's growing adolescent longing to explore the moors beyond the Grange's walled-in gardens signals a strong unconscious desire to differentiate, to break out of the constraints of a limiting storybook identity (as "'love' and 'darling,'" etc.), and a return of the rebellious spirit that was once her mother's. Cathy's rebellious desires, however, are circumscribed by her Edenic confinement in "innocence," a fact directly linked to the next stage of developmental plotting. It is precisely her inability to recognize "evil," to perceive the network of power controlling the world of the Heights as well as her home, that transforms her eventual escape from the park into an entrance into an even worse prison. Blind to Heathcliff's design in abetting her moorland rambles, Cathy finds herself embroiled in an exploitative affair with her cousin Linton Heathcliff, a "fiction" of romance based on sentimental norms in which the differences that existed between her parents have become totally antithetical extremes. From the first moment of their reacquaintance at the Heights—Cathy's "whole aspect sparkling" and Linton's "languid" (175)—their opposing natures portend mutual disaster. Worse, Cathy's dutiful upbringing, repressing her sparks of self-assertion, traps her in a destructive mode of erotic masochism as she selflessly submits to the misery—and mastery—of Linton's peevish moods.

This courtship variation reaches a climax in a rite of passage as pivotal as the older Catherine's adolescent detainment by the Lintons at the Grange. Mirroring that event in reverse direction, Cathy leaves the Grange world of her youth irrevocably behind as Heathcliff dupes Nelly and herself into crossing the forbidden threshold of the Heights, where they become his literal prisoners. What follows is an unending nightmare as Cathy's most vital relationship (to her dying father) is severed and any sense of autonomy crushed as Heathcliff forces her to agree to marry his son Linton. The plot thus replicates the situation of the first Catherine—confinement in an alien environment, marriage as a tool of self-diminishment— but with a difference that makes clear the social ethos underlying the trials of both: for the older Catherine's more subtle seduction by the trappings of privilege becomes, in the younger Cathy's experience, a blatant rape of her individual will by male-sanctioned powers of authority. And as Cathy's new husband fulfills his father's prophecy that he "can play the little tyrant well" (219) despite his physical weakness, his litanic repetition of the phrase, "It's mine" (223), in a terrifyingly solipsistic speech claiming all of his wife's belongings as his own, confirms the degree to which Cathy's victimization is coterminous with her sex. Through the strategic placement of such unnerving "domestic" scenarios, the patriarchal ideal of wedlock is shown to mask a state of absolute female captivity; the sentimental notion of a complementary union of opposites, exposed as an instrument of sexual domination and a perversion of human love.

The plot of Cathy's "education" into female adulthood reaches its nadir when after her father's funeral Heathcliff assumes control of the Grange as its new master: "He made no ceremony of knocking or announcing his name; he was master, and availed himself of the master's privilege to walk straight in, without saying a word" (227). Just as the women's crucial threshold entrances have entailed losses of authority, Heathcliff's signifies successful mastery: structure again becomes a comment on gender. By sundering young Cathy from her last familiar associations with this action, Heathcliff willfully perpetuates the pattern of expanding disaster that began with his own separation from Catherine. First held captive against her will, Cathy now becomes, again like her mother, a victim of negative self-enclosure; withdrawal from others becomes at once her only protection and a formidable obstacle to any recovery of her violated self-esteem. In bringing this "story" to a close, Nelly perceives that the only solution (or, textually speaking, *re*solution) for Cathy lies in the very institution that has debilitated her: "and I can see no remedy at present, unless she could marry again; and that scheme, it does not come within my province to arrange" (236). The irony implicit in this reversal of the expectations associated with marital "schemes" in fictional plotting could not be greater, for it will take an "arranger" far more innovative than Nelly—or the writer of conventional romances—to extract Cathy from the impasse of her deadlocked and deathly situation.

But Cathy's history is only one consequence of her mother's unsettling death; structurally juxtaposed and intersecting with her linear development is the adjacent developmental plot of Heathcliff's life following Catherine's death. Heathcliff's trajectory echoes Catherine's in that external separation—now made final by death—completes a process of internal division, a "fall" into what Carolyn Heilbrun has called an "anti-androgynous world."[28] From an initially marginal and noncategorizable position of difference, Heathcliff transforms himself after Catherine's death into what Isabella calls "half a man" (149)—that is, a prototypically "masculine" oppressor who unfeelingly appropriates people's lives and possessions as a way of avenging himself on the social caste system responsible for his initial separation from Catherine.[29] But the final irony is that for all his acquired "power" as master and tyrant, he also ends up leading an imprisoned inner existence, one epitomized in the plot of his unceasing unrest in the last half of the novel.

While the dual foci of the novel's second half pit Heathcliff's actions against those of his primary victim, the younger Cathy, another structural effect—the splintering of perspective that emerges between the violent present-time of his revenge and the timeless eternity of his agony—forestalls a totally negative condemnation of his increasingly diabolic role. For the more he lives in the past (mourning his lost unity with Catherine) and the more he anticipates the future (envisioning that opening in time that will allow their unworldly reunion), Heathcliff is propelled out of a temporal framework altogether; this technique works to suspend our judgment of his present actions and to point us instead toward their cause. A vivid example occurs in chapter 29, where the developmental plots involving Heathcliff and Cathy jarringly intersect with Heathcliff's crossing the threshold of Cathy's home as its new master. For the eventfulness of the moment—representing the ostensible apex of Heathcliff's drive toward revenge in one plot and the nadir of Cathy's loss of self-possession in the other—is very nearly nonexistent from Heathcliff's perspective. His mind, rather, is fixed on the unbearable frustration of his eighteen-year separation from the *other* Catherine, which has led him the night before, as he confides to Nelly, to reopen her grave in an impossible attempt to erase the division between the living and the dead (one recalls Catherine's analogous attempt to erase seven years of time in chapter 12). Coming to epitomize all the years of unrest that Heathcliff has suffered without his "life" and "soul" (139), his action is itself a repetition of a hitherto suppressed narrative event, his parallel attempt to unearth Catherine's corpse the evening of her burial.[30] The latter structural displacement gains all the more power from the present circumstance of its telling: for, at the greatest moment of his revenge upon the Lintons, Heathcliff is ironically for all purposes *absent,* living entirely in the past moment of Catherine's death. The separation between temporal realms could not be greater, a structurally juxtaposed effect that is reiterated in the following chapter as Nelly's story unexpectedly enters "present" narrative time; the past has caught up with the present that involves Lockwood, yet the Heathcliff whom Lockwood visits in the current novel-time of chapter 31 is by now almost entirely an inhabitant of the past.

These jarring narrative shifts are, of course, part of the novel's larger perspectival structure, in which the temporal and spatial dislocations caused by the presence of multiple narrators ultimately strengthen the reader's awareness of an uneasy past whose effects continue to disrupt the present. For Brontë's complex manipulation of multiple frames of narration not only mediates between reader and text but also works, significantly, to disturb any semblance of the univocal recuperation characteristic of conventional ficitional closure. The effect is a tension similar to that created by the division and doubling within the novel's developmental structures.

Such disorientations in perspective predominantly occur as a result of the continual "flashes" of present narrative time that punctuate Nelly's history, forcing the reader to assimilate great leaps in time and space. One such significant dislocating moment occurs when the crisis of chapter 9—Catherine and Heathcliff's separation—is cut short by a return to Lockwood's first-person narration. However brief and seemingly incidental, his account of his illness brings the two narrative levels into sudden, disturbing proximity: the same doctor who treats Catherine the page before is now taking care of Lockwood; Heathcliff, who has just disappeared from the text of Nelly's tale, reappears at Lockwood's bedside. And even more unsettling is Lockwood's failure to connect the living reality of his visitor with the "hero" (80) of the story he immediately asks Nelly to continue, treating the past as an impersonal fiction that does not touch his safe reality. The intrusion of living representatives of the past—Dr. Kenneth, Heathcliff—into current time, of course, underlines the *radically altered* circumstances of the present that have resulted from the cataclysmic rupture of the lovers just narrated.

With the exception of the novel's final chapters, the greatest number of such interruptions in continuity occur in the sequence (chapters 12–15) detailing the stages of Catherine's decline from madness to death. Her internal fragmentation, therefore, is heightened by these jumps back and forth in the spatial and temporal frames. A further dislocation occurs when at the beginning of chapter 15 the reader suddenly learns that Lockwood is no longer listening to, but *re*telling, what has been told him; Nelly has finished her tale, which, "only a little condensed" (130), Lockwood now claims to pass faithfully on to *his* audience, a decentering device whereby the once-removed past becomes twice-removed, qualifying still further the judgments of its various narrators.[31] In contrast to the spatial fragmentation of the Catherine plot, the trajectory of young Cathy's experience forms an almost unbroken narrative line of descent into nightmare—the horror of which is brought home to the reader, with a shock, with Nelly's interjected comment, "These things happened last winter, sir" (204). Upon Heathcliff's removal of Cathy from Nelly's field of observation, her narration (temporarily kept in motion by the insertion of Zillah's account of Cathy's miserable life at the Heights) necessarily draws to an inconclusive close. "Thus ended Mrs. Dean's story," Lockwood recounts, then promptly decides to bring his sojourn in the region to an "end" as well, an act simultaneously terminating his own narrative.

Yet it is Lockwood's "re-entrance" into the text in chapter 32— the novel's fourth "beginning"—that reopens the spatial structure of the novel as well as the temporal possibility of more story. The opening of the chapter, marked by the date "1802," circles the reader back to the novel's first sentence, also designated by a date, "1801." The events enclosed within this year-long cycle are thus shut away, so to speak, into the past, while the chapters that follow form a separate unit that in fact becomes an eerie repetition, in miniature, of the *whole* novel: Lockwood comes to the region; Nelly tells him another two-part story (this time, of the young lovers Cathy and Hareton and of the strange death of Heathcliff); Lockwood passes judgment and leaves. Once again, a kind of sequential double plotting is achieved as the novel seems to repeat itself, with the significant difference that this doubling-back simultaneously functions as coda and conclusion to all that has gone before—a conclusion, as we shall now see, that maintains a doubleness worthy of Brontë's radical rewriting of the traditional love-plot.

III

It is commonly said that *Wuthering Heights* consists of two endings, not necessarily reconcilable, in its dual movement toward earthly and unearthly union.[32] In chapter 32, Nelly recounts for the returned Lockwood (who has already stumbled into Cathy and Hareton reading together) the story of the young couple's courtship, which she ends with a prototypically Victorian affirmation of wedlock ("The crown of all my wishes will be the union of these two" [250]). Nelly's conventional hopes, however, should not necessarily pass as Brontë's own, as they have for generations of critics. The critical gesture of summarily dismissing the Cathy-Hareton romance as "a rather sugary frill" unconsciously repeats the sexism underlying Thomas Moser's judgment that its love interest is "simply a superficial stereotyped tale of feminine longings" belonging "with countless pieces of sub-literary fiction in women's magazines."[33] In contrast to such views, I would like to suggest that this final love story is essential to the revisionary cast of Brontë's structural and thematic designs. Not only does the anticipation of this union, happy as it is, strategically share narrative time with the very different plot of Heathcliff's end; its paradigm of romantic bonding equally serves, as we shall see, to propel the narrative forward into an unknown and unwritten future.

In crucial ways Cathy and Hareton's relationship hauntingly evokes yet revises that of the first generation of lovers. Like their forebears, they also come to share an attraction grounded in affinities of situation and inherited similarities of temperament—"opposition" between them is a mistaken, not an elementally gendered, condition. Foremost, as Heathcliff's victims, both discover an essential sameness in their experiences of degradation: the widowed Cathy's stultifying captivity at the Heights, echoing her mother's adult deprivations at the Grange, parallels Hareton's keenly suffered entrapment in brutish ignorance, a condition that Heathcliff perversely enforces in order to repeat his own debasement at Hindley's hands. Hence, since both youths have been stripped of their rightful identities by Heathcliff, the first stage of their growth toward mutual love details, appropriately, how each becomes the other's avenue to regained autonomy. Hareton serves as Cathy's lifeline to the world of the living as she finally breaks out of her self-imprisoning despair to acknowledge his presence for the first time, simultaneously admitting her sense of loss and static self-enclosure: "Oh, I'm tired—I'm *stalled*, Hareton!" (237). In a parallel movement, Hareton's yearning to escape his own "stalled" condition ("Will you ask her to read to us, Zillah? I'm stalled of doing naught" [235]) reaches a poignant climax when Cathy teaches him to read, an act of mental liberation (not of feminization, as too many critics have claimed)[34] that symbolically gives Hareton back his robbed identity as he learns to spell his name, Earnshaw, inscribed above the Heights' entrance. Likewise, it should be noted —to counter critics leaping to "obvious" interpretations of "Freudian" symbols—that Brontë does not rob Hareton of his phallic potency when he chooses to forgo his gun and pipe for Cathy's company; rather, he is stripped of his *learned* masculine defenses, of the tactics of withdrawal into a privileged male realm, that have stood in the way of his achievement of adult humanity.

Second, the sameness binding the second generation of lovers is also registered in their kinship as cousins, a literal "return" of the sibling ideal once uniting Heathcliff and Catherine. The structure of the sequence in chapter 32 leading to the convergence of the two—both tellingly identified by Nelly as "my children" (254)— makes clear the link between bloodlike affinity and romantic love in the novel's revisionary erotics. Breaking from feminine norms of passivity by actively campaigning for Hareton's attentions, Cathy first presses upon him the claim of actual kinship ("I should like you to be my cousin now"), then follows it with the claim of friendship ("And you'll be my friend?"). A paragraph later the two have become "sworn allies" and thence, in Nelly's proleptic summation, declared lovers whose minds, "tending to the same point, contrived . . . to reach it" (247–49). If the ensuing childlike playfulness of the lovers is worlds removed from the tumultuous and troubled passion of the first generation, hence more "conventional," its calm register should not negate for the reader the radical difference that their love, tempered by the context of their preceding oppression, has made: in Brontë's vision, identification with rather than against each other has created a common ground, transcending normative boundaries of class and gender, that allows for the rebirth of child-like joy, the foundation of a new Eden of possibility located in the world rather than on the moors, that is aptly signified by the lovers' playful (but never again naive) innocence.

Therefore, as friends who share a natural and erotic affinity that does not deny their differences, as adults and equals not defined solely in terms of gender roles, and, finally, as comrades in a common cause against Heathcliff's tyranny, Cathy and Hareton create a relationship that goes far in repudiating the Victorian stereotype of ethereal love. In its place their hard-earned alliance gives birth to a dynamic ideal, one that like Brontë's narrative is neither "stalled" nor rigidly defined but poised on the brink of realization. Hence the end is also a beginning for these two lovers. Planning to marry on New Year's Day, they will leave the Heights behind to begin the future in a new year and a new world in which nothing is certain but the united strength of their alliance. "*They* are afraid of nothing," Lockwood grudgingly admits, as Cathy and Hareton ramble into the Heights and out of his narration: "Together they would brave Satan and all his legions" (265–66). In a final movement worthy of the text's manifold entrances and openings, Cathy and Hareton prepare to cross the threshold of an open future.

This sense of visionary possibility, however, is posited against a very different kind of fulfillment simultaneously occurring in Nelly's tale of Heathcliff's "'queer' end" (245), one that presupposes a mode of irresolution in which ambiguity and unrest predominate. Again, the message lies in the structural sequence, for the organization of chapters 33 and 34 demonstrates that Heathcliff cannot achieve his desired reunion in death with Catherine as long as he lives to avenge himself on his enemies and thus tacitly accepts a definition of manhood antithetical to the united difference he once shared with Catherine. Appropriately, then, it is the doubled visual image of his lost love, reflected in the newly allied Cathy and Hareton, that leads to Heathcliff's abjuration of revenge and makes possible his unearthly reunion: "[T]hey lifted their eyes together to encounter Mr. Heathcliff," Nelly tells Lockwood, "Perhaps you have never remarked that their eyes are precisely similar, and they are those of Catherine Earnshaw. . . . I supposed this resemblance disarmed Mr. Heathcliff" (254).[35] Within minutes, Heathcliff confesses that "I don't care for striking, I can't take the trouble to raise my hand . . . where is the use?" (255). In proportion to the lessening grip of his constricting obsession with mastery, the "disarmed" and metaphorically unmanned Heathcliff conversely expands in a newly receptive passivity that, in rewriting the erotic dynamic of traditional novelistic terms of masculine "fulfillment," will *make possible* his and Catherine's reunion. "*I am swallowed* in anticipation of its fulfillment" (256; emphasis added), he thus says as he acquiesces to the promise of death and reunion.

The two final days of Heathcliff's life, recounted in chapter 34, record the surreal process by which the "other" world, where Catherine waits, moves into and begins to coexist with commonplace reality for a few moments before reversing direction and leading Heathcliff outward in its wake. For, as the window "swinging open" (264) by his deathbed—Catherine's enclosed bed—suggests, death has become that opening in the wall, a final entrance into another and uncertain realm where their twin phantoms ceaselessly roam the moors. Resting neither in heaven nor in hell, they occupy, once again, the purgatorial "wild zone" that once made possible their most essential selves. While the Heathcliff plot thus attains an aesthetically satisfying close, the fact that such satisfaction comes at the expense of life underlines, in a way no reader can ignore, the severity of the actual conditions that have made fulfillment impossible in his and Catherine's lives: if the tenor of their doomed desire ultimately seems metaphysical, it has been raised to such a pitch by the specifically cultural and psychological origins of their tragedy. This sense of thwarted love haunts the text in the concluding hints of unease—do their ghosts *really* roam the moors?—that can never be answered.

Not only do these conclusions in earthly union and unearthly reunion play off each other, but the several self-contradicting denouements offered by each narrator also prevent *Wuthering Heights* from resolving into a univocal pattern. Both Nelly and Lockwood attempt—for their *own* peace of minds—to impose closed patterns on the sequence of final events. Nelly, for example, first offers Lockwood the closed, conventionally worded assurance of the young lovers' bliss at the end of chapter 32; then she moves on to narrate Heathcliff's "poor conclusion" (254) in the final chapter, at first expressing the hope that Heathcliff rests "soundly" in his grave but qualifying and unsettling her own interpretation as she relates the rumors that his and Catherine's ghosts walk the moors (265). Lockwood's narrative voice resumes, and he too first turns to the lovers, as if confirming one type of plot, yet he also moves on to the concurrent plot involving the first generation as he visits their graves. Here, like Nelly, he also attempts to paint a reconciliatory picture of repose. But, again like Nelly, he qualifies his own attempt in the penultimate moment of closure; for his dismissal of "unquiet slumbers" for "the sleepers in that quiet earth" (266) is belied by the supernatural imagery inundating the novel's final paragraph—moths, harebells, and soft wind all signify the presence of restless ghosts in folklore.[36] This repeating pattern of assertion followed by qualification in Nelly and Lockwood's final statements, in itself meticulously crafted and aesthetically perfect, holds Brontë's text in open suspension to its very end.

Thus, Heathcliff's entrance into an undefined and indefinable perpetuity in death, like Cathy and Hareton's movement across the threshold of a visionary future in life, ultimately turns outward to the reader, who is left to grapple with the thematic reverberations emanating from the repeating, multiple levels of structure in the novel; the final diffusion of both sets of protagonists into worlds beyond the text suggests at once the deathly hazards of identity razed by societal and sexual expectations and left forever uneasy, and the possibility of a mode of love that by guaranteeing autonomy and mutuality may create a new world. Suspending the promise of the one union against the ghostly reverberations of the other, Brontë instills in her text a difference, and in its ending an endless double movement, that reaffirms her unorthodox vision of a love that is passionate—and yet more.

·*Daniel Deronda*·
Conclusions "But a Dipping Onward"

The ending of *Wuthering Heights,* marked as it is by a radical openness, nonetheless includes a promise of happiness in the anticipated union of Cathy and Hareton, even in the uncertain ghostly reunion of Catherine and Heathcliff. George Eliot's *Daniel Deronda* (1876), on the other hand, rejects "happiness" altogether at the end of its heroine's plot. For Gwendolen's disastrous experience of wedlock culminates in a fate unique among Victorian heroines: despite her husband Grandcourt's death, she is denied the chance (such as Brontë gives her second Cathy, or Eliot her own Dorothea) of a more satisfactory second marriage. Rather, at text's end she is left quite alone, deprived even of her friendship with the newly married Daniel, the direction of her life beyond the final pages open to conjecture. Such an unusual situation has led Barbara

DANIEL DERONDA

Hardy to call *Deronda* a "love story with a difference" that "touch-[es] the limits of Victorian fiction." Eliot's protomodernist innovations, however, go beyond the fact, cited by Hardy, of the *absence* of romance between her ostensible "hero" and "heroine."[37] For Gwendolen's uneasy fate is registered in the uneasy structural arrangement of the *whole* novel; both the dislocations caused by courtship and marriage in the heroine's plot and its intersections with Daniel's simultaneously unfolding quest for identity are arranged to anticipate the novel's unsettling, open ending. In the process, Eliot's analysis of unhappy wedlock expands into an indictment of the power structure of Victorian life itself and—whatever her mixed personal feelings about her society and the limitations of marriage—provides in *Deronda,* as Lloyd Fernando has argued, "a great instance [in which] an author in rebellion against the conventions of society rebel[s] against the orthodox conventions of her art as well."[38]

Fernando's point is especially relevant in light of the entire Eliot canon, for critics since Henry James have argued that Eliot had difficulty ending her novels convincingly; her tendency to conform to conventional closural formulas involving "marriages and rescues in the nick of time as a matter of course" (so James complained of *Adam Bede*) often sets oddly with the social implications of her detailed portrayals of women's constricted lives.[39] Nonetheless, if not always successful in wedding form and content, Eliot remained acutely aware of the demands of form and the implications of conclusions throughout her career. On the one hand, her aesthetic concern with developing the most complex possible web of "inner relations" led to dissatisfaction with its bracketing in either beginnings or endings, which she saw as "at best . . . negation[s]" of the text's organic totality: "Only, endings are inevitably the least satisfactory part of any work in which there is any merit of development."[40] On the other hand, Eliot's evolving definition of form included speculation about the text's connection to extrinsic relations. For, like the self-maintaining organism that contains its own system *yet* exists within a larger network of relations, Eliot argued in "Notes on Form in Art" (1868), the "multiplex interdependent parts" of a well-formed literary work must achieve "a wholeness which again has the most varied relationship with all other phenomena"—including those external to itself. Given such a premise, a literary text can never be "complete" in the sense implied by traditional modes of closure: its formal relations must inevitably extend outward into the unknown beyond the printed word.[41]

It is in *Deronda* that Eliot most successfully achieves a self-regulating yet diffusive wholeness that does not sever its outward-reaching threads. She accomplishes this "multiplex" aim, in large part, by refusing for once in her career what she herself termed "the artificial necessities of . . . denouement,"[42] which in the case of *Deronda* meant allowing the disturbances raised in its undermining portrait of conventional love and wedlock to build toward an end that is uncertain but logically and aesthetically appropriate. Three aspects of the novel's structural innovations, in particular, cooperate in effecting a subtle but irrevocable subversion of the traditional authority of marriage and marriage plots: the strategic orchestration of the Gwendolen-Daniel encounters, which generates an implicit commentary between the two plots and between male and female destiny; the deliberate undermining of fictional expectations, romantic conventions, and threshold experiences in the developmental plotting of the Gwendolen story; and, finally, the irresolution of the text's conclusion as fitting climax to its narrative and thematic concerns.

I

The two foci of the largely independent trajectories inscribed in Eliot's double-plot structure, Gwendolen Harleth and Daniel Deronda, are highly complex individuals whose characterizations—like the text's structure—withstand simplification into pat formulas: "Character too is a process and an unfolding," Eliot wrote in *Middlemarch* (178). Contemporary reviewers praised the fine psychological nuances with which Eliot brought Gwendolen to life, but they often remained unsure of how to categorize or judge her behavior; she was neither the blameless ingenue nor the poisonous femme fatale, neither the maiden deceived in love nor the patiently suffering wife, of Victorian iconography.[43] The truth of the matter is that Gwendolen is filled with dreams of autonomy rendered ambivalent by the fact that they are based on an illusion of freedom and power for which her pampered, solipsistic upbringing is alone responsible. Underneath Gwendolen's restless egotism, however, one finds these same desires also expressing a submerged, desperate yearning for self, any self, not automatically defined by expectations of gender. She repeatedly tells herself that, whether or not she eventually marries, "she was not going to renounce her freedom, or according to her favorite formula, 'not going to do as other women did'" (168), and she warily parries one of Grandcourt's near declarations with the comment, "Oh, I am not sure that I want to be taken care of: if I choose to risk breaking my neck, I should like to be at liberty to do it" (169). Similarly, having observed in her mother's life the "domestic fetters" rendering matrimony "a rather dreary state," Gwendolen imagines for herself a destiny in vague realms beyond wedlock: "the dramas in which she imagined herself a heroine were not wrought up to that close" (68). It is telling, however, that she voices her rebellion against conventional female destiny in purely fictive terms ("the dramas in which she imagined herself") or in "favorite formula[s]," for she is *already* the fettered prisoner she fears becoming in marriage, an embodiment of upper-class Victorian femininity "held captive by the ordinary network of social forms" and rendered incapable of imagining life outside "the sphere of fashion" (83). Attempting to suppress the conflict between her realistic assessment of married life for many women and the subconscious knowledge that her fate will be no different, Gwendolen undergoes a crisis of identity similar to that culminating in Catherine Earnshaw's schizophrenia in *Wuthering Heights*.

Daniel's initial perception of this unknown woman as a "problematic sylph" accurately captures a sense of Gwendolen's contradictions, but it also attests to an "inward debate" (38) occurring in Daniel himself, one that renders him much more complex than his morally earnest exterior might indicate: he attempts to suppress the sexual attraction aroused in him by Gwendolen's disturbing beauty at the gaming table, for instance, by establishing a never quite successful "objective" evaluation of her character as a disinterested observer.[44] This self-deceiving facet of Daniel's generally forthright personality demonstrates, like Gwendolen's illusions of autonomy, an intense desire to control fears that, in his case, ensue from an essential uncertainty about his origins, his ambiguous status as Sir Hugo's "ward," and his growing suspicions of a marginal racial heritage that will culminate in the discovery of his Jewish ancestry. If Gwendolen compensates for her inadequacies by imposing her ego on all others, Daniel controls his fears by an egoless giving of himself that, virtually placing him above human contact as paragon of perfection, becomes a strangely self-serving gesture in itself. As vague in imagining the future as Gwendolen, the Daniel we first see also attempts to suppress those contradictory desires that would prematurely force him to relinquish his tenuous hold on a safe world.

With such thematic similarities uniting the novel's major protagonists, one might expect to find, as in a Dickensian or Trollopean multiplot, an elaborate structural interweaving of lives and fates in closely related patterns of cause and effect. To the contrary, Eliot creates a discontinuous double-plot format in *Deronda*, in which the stories of Gwendolen and Daniel proceed along largely independent tracks that touch at only a few carefully chosen moments.[45] One effect is to create a gap between Gwendolen and Daniel's spheres of action that seems to widen rather than narrow. And if the reduction of literal links between these juxtaposed lines of development creates an ongoing extratextual "dialogue" of perspectives, to use Garrett's term, its subject concerns the diverging possibilities of selfhood available to men and women in Victorian England—a dialogue that for Gwendolen can lead to no conclusive answer given the limited alternatives her world offers women.

The few structural intersections of these plots, furthermore, point to the originality of Eliot's plan in *not* making her protagonists lovers. The epigram preceding the first chapter's opening *in medias res* ("Men can do nothing without the make-believe of a beginning") calls attention to the manipulation of the narrative sequence that has been necessary to open with Daniel and Gwendolen's initial meeting at Leubronn, and this heightening of the moment's significance, in turn, deliberately teases forth expectations of a narrative payoff in the predictable form of romance. In spite of Eliot's repeated (though sometimes equivocal) declarations to the contrary, the insinuation that these two protagonists appear to *others* as potential lovers strategically functions to keep the possibility, however unlikely, alive. Only gradually does the reader, as is Eliot's whole purpose, realize that such a desire reveals an imagination no less conventional than Sir Hugo's, to whom a marriage between Daniel and Gwendolen would be "as pretty *a story* as need be" (834; emphasis added)—a fiction not unlike Nelly's unrealistic projection of romance between Lockwood and Cathy in *Wuthering Heights*. The reader, thus, is made an accomplice in the act of conventional fiction-making and as such becomes part of *Deronda*'s education in another mode of reading and writing lives.

Eliot, of course, implants these misleading romantic cues precisely to italicize the relationship that Gwendolen and Daniel *do* finally establish for what it is: an unconventional friendship of man and woman based on an equal vulnerability and noncombative concern for the other contrasting vividly to the Victorian martial ideal that permits Grandcourt's antagonistic mastery of Gwendolen and encourages her submission. Indeed, the second intersection of Gwendolen and Daniel's lots, postponed for nearly four hundred pages and strategically placed just after her engagement to Grandcourt in book 4, forces a comparison of the two men and the differing potential of her relationship to each. Likewise, the third conjunction of the two plots, occurring at the opening of book 5, further underscores this difference: chapter 35's summary of the sadistic mastery that Grandcourt has established over his wife in seven weeks, "nullify[ing]" any hope of marital "interchange" (480), is immediately juxtaposed with Daniel's New Year's Eve visit and the three very different encounters of chapter 36 that succeed in opening the way to a difficult but ultimately rewarding communication between himself and Gwendolen.[46]

Notably, it is Daniel's capacity for sympathy and lack of the aggressiveness traditionally associated with men that makes his friendship so valuable to Gwendolen. His "difference" as a man can be measured in Gwendolen's reaction to the only time he touches her, during the crisis at Genoa: "The grasp was an entirely new experience to Gwendolen: she had never before had from any man a sign of tenderness which her own being needed" (755). Eliot has taken pains, in fact, to portray in Daniel a transcendence of gender norms; he is shown to possess "an affectionateness such as we are apt to call feminine" as well as the stern judgment and mental independence "held to be rightfully masculine" (367). Moreover, it is Daniel's capacity to feel for others with "perhaps more than a woman's acuteness of compassion" (747) that enables him to respond positively not only to Gwendolen but also to his mentor Mordecai, to a hitherto unknown racial heritage, and eventually to an epic vision of a new Jewish nation. In Eliot's revisionary perspective, that is, Daniel's "feminine" sympathies make the literary world of epic possible once again—a bold assertion, given the epic's traditionally "masculine" associations.

In regard to the overall function of the double plot, Leon Gottfried has argued that Daniel's accomplishments are meant to instill the hope that Gwendolen's "narrow world of daily life" will not remain immune to "that of possible heroic fulfillment."[47] Yet the "gap" that exists between the two plots, literally represented by the large textual spaces separating the relatively few encounters of Gwendolen and Daniel, also suggests an impasse between the worlds in which each is allowed to move. This difference lies behind Eliot's choice of contrasting generic modes to represent the action of the two plots; Gwendolen's story unfolds in a highly "realistic" mode befitting its deterministic logic of cause and effect, whereas Daniel's career gradually assumes the trajectory of a romantic quest, in which prophecy and vision subsume realistic truths.[48] Given this modal contrast, one can begin to infer Eliot's commentary concerning the unequal possibilities of self-discovery open to the sexes, for as Gwendolen complains early in her courtship, "We women can't go in search of adventures. . . . We must stay where we grow" (171). Consequently, although Gwendolen and Daniel are both in a sense marginal members of their societies, Gwendolen's "inferior" status (as a woman) leads to her psychological imprisonment *within* social forms, while Daniel's (first as an orphan, later as a Jew) makes possible his freely chosen *exclusion from* society, which in turn leads to his final breadth of vision. The modal tension between Gwendolen and Daniel's worlds, despite their special bond of mutual sympathy, thus adds to the structural dialogue in which the question of self-fulfillment as regards Gwendolen's future remains unanswered.

II·

The open end toward which the stages of Gwendolen's experience build is also consistently anticipated by a developmental structure which (like the bildungsroman variations in *Wuthering Heights*) parodies and reverses the converging patterns traditionally associated with courtship and wedlock movements in fiction. Thus the flashback to Gwendolen's life prior to the Leubronn episode of chapters

1 and 2 invites us, via its tone, to expect a love story in which courtship leads to marriage. And, indeed, both Gwendolen and the reader are quickly caught up in a whirl of social events so arranged as to suggest that they are building toward "the beginning of that end—the beginning of her acceptance" of the eminently eligible Grandcourt (184). Hence, it is no coincidence that Grandcourt's arrival in the vicinity is heralded in language that echoes—with irony—the famous opening lines of *Pride and Prejudice:* "Some readers of this history will doubtless regard it as incredible that people should construct matrimonial prospects on the mere report that a bachelor of good fortune and possibilities was coming within reach" (123). Nonetheless, this is exactly what Gwendolen's family does, as the young woman realizes ("you all intend him to fall in love with me," she says with some delight [127]), and the concluding lines of the first book of *Deronda* anticipate such a plot as well, ending with the formal introduction—and hence initial convergence—between this man and this woman.[49]

The certitude with which a conventional courtship plot seems about to unfold, however, is subtly qualified by a series of disturbances—one of the first being Gwendolen's abrupt dismissal of her first suitor, Rex, on the grounds that she hates being made love to, an event ironically confirming the epigraph to chapter 4, which warns that if the writer presses too quickly to a conclusion in marriage, "un roman serait bientôt fini!" (67). Gwendolen's subsequent acceptance of Grandcourt's attentions because of his very *lack* of passion inserts another jarring note in her growingly complex characterization, countering the emotional commitment presumed to bind romantic protagonists in indissoluble bonds. Indeed, part of the problem seems to lie in the *fiction* of love itself, as Gwendolen confesses to her mother: "I wonder how girls manage to fall in love. It is easy to make them do it in books. But men [in real life] are too ridiculous" (110). Counterpoised with this idealized fiction is the brutal reality epitomized by her uncle's argument that "the point is to get her well married" as soon as possible because she has "a little too much fire in her" (111). And, in her heart of hearts, Gwendolen knows that her life cannot escape society's preconceived plots. Hence, the great irony of the epigraph (created by Eliot) preceding the chapter in which Gwendolen meets her future husband:

1st Gent. What women should be? Sir, consult the taste
Of marriageable men . . .
             Our daughters must be wives,
And to be wives must be what men will choose;
Men's taste is woman's test. (132)

The truth of this disturbing observation is narratively borne out
with Grandcourt's cold-blooded announcement, in the immediately juxtaposed scene, that he is wooing this girl to master her: power
rather than passion turns out to be the motive that Grandcourt's
perverse pleasure, or "taste," is intent on dictating.

It is part of Eliot's overall strategy that these negative notes hardly
have time to make an impression before being shunted aside by the
pace of events pressing forward to the archery match of chapter 14,
where Gwendolen as well as her relatives eagerly anticipate Grandcourt's proposal. But at this pivotal threshold the courtship breaks
apart—and the narrative similarly breaks, shifting plots abruptly—
with the unexpected revelation of Grandcourt's illegitimate children. What in a more conventional love-plot might be melodramatic
highlighting of a temporary obstacle blocking the path to happiness
forms a very real obstruction for Gwendolen, shattering her protected view of the world, determining the guilt that haunts her for
the rest of the novel, and, more specifically, leading to the section's
anticlimactic culmination—the heroine's renunciation of conventional wedlock expectations: "I don't care if I never marry anyone.
There is *nothing* worth caring for" (192; emphasis added). Such an
attitude, circling the reader back to the present-time of the novel's
beginning, retroactively explains Gwendolen's disillusioned attitude
at Leubronn; its negative effect is underscored by Gwendolen's
immediate disappearance from the text for nearly a hundred
pages.

The second phase of Gwendolen's uneasy courtship, however,
has already been set into motion by the failure of her widowed
mother's investments, the event that draws Gwendolen away from
the gambling table and back home to gamble for her economic
future at the end of the opening Leubronn sequence. For, as the
oldest and most beautiful of five fortuneless sisters, she is *expected* to
make the solvent match that will resolve the family's financial crisis.
When the Gwendolen plot resumes, the sequence of tightly interlocked scenes emphasizes the inevitability of her fate: she arrives

DANIEL DERONDA

home, the musician Klesmer dashes her hopes of an independent artistic career, she is forced to accept a position as governess, and— *voilà!*—Grandcourt's note arrives, asking permission to renew his suit. The relentless logic of these events renders any illusion of free choice in the matter a moot point, just as it renders Gwendolen's cry, "I *must* decide" in regard to seeing Grandcourt or not, without meaning (338). Hence her climactic "yes" to Grandcourt, in a proposal scene of claustrophobic intensity, echoes like a sentence "in a court of justice" (348), and book 3 draws to a close with an ironic facsimile of concluding stasis as Gwendolen emerges to announce to her mother that "Everything is *settled* . . . everything is to be as I like" (350; emphasis added).

But as the very tone of the title of the following and fourth book ("Gwendolen Gets Her Choice") betrays, life beyond the nuptial threshold proves to be anything but settling for Gwendolen. The opening note is set within the same chapter that records her transformation from single to married status when, on the evening of the wedding, Gwendolen is overcome by a maddened hysteria that echoes Catherine's in *Wuthering Heights*; even the idealized honeymoon of Victorian marital manuals has become a nightmare. And in the following pages, the domestic scene dear to sentimental fiction is exposed as a vicious battleground, the site of a psychologically debilitating war for sexual power in which Grandcourt uses his socially superior status as male and master to force Gwendolen into wifely submission. As Grandcourt gloatingly thinks, "She had been brought to accept him in spite of everything—brought to kneel down like a horse. . . . In any case she would have to submit" as "his . . . wife" (365). Grandcourt's perception of his "wife" as an antagonist who must be subdued, stemming from his fear of losing power and thus being exposed as an inadequate man, forms a damning link between the masculine problematic of identity underlying the cultural doctrine of submissive womanhood and the abuses fostered within conventional wedlock ideology by its idealization of male–female polarity. The irony that Grandcourt is characterized by a vacancy, a nullity of being, not only reveals the essential hollowness of his mastery over others, but makes all the more glaring the power that lies in male status and social discourse alone. All Grandcourt has to do to quell Gwendolen's feeble attempts at resistance is to remind her of his power and her accepted role—"You have married *me*, and must be guided by my opinion"—for Gwendolen to realize she is "helpless against the argument that lay in [those words]" (655). When Grandcourt puts the seal on his sadistic mastery by forcing Gwendolen to accept his kiss (thereby destroying yet another of the wedlock ideal's sacred signifiers of devout everlasting love), she resigns herself to the devastating knowledge that "He was using her as he liked" (659). Any sensual pleasure, for either Gwendolen or her husband, has been replaced by the perverse gratification of erotic domination.

After the novel's midpoint marriage, moreover, the segments of the Gwendolen plot alternating with the Daniel plot become much shorter, fragmented, like her now-diminished existence: her textual presence is reduced to a discontinuous series of abbreviated scenes that form mere interstices in the rest of the narrative. In telling contrast, the Daniel plot becomes more fully fleshed, taking on positive direction with its increased length. Each of the book divisions in the second half of the novel, indeed, ends upon a major threshold moment in Daniel's search for identity and vocation, a structural reversal that underlines the fact that Gwendolen's entrance into marriage, supposedly the zenith of a woman's experience, is rather its close. The placement of Gwendolen's story within a double-plot structure, therefore, constantly brings her experience of uneasy wedlock and diminished selfhood into sharper focus. As "an imprisoned dumb creature" trapped "in the painted gilded prison" (651) of wedlock and wedlock plotting, Gwendolen moves toward self-negation (again recalling *Wuthering Heights*) from which the only escape seems destruction either for herself or for Grandcourt: the marital battle has become a fight to the death, that "ultimate violence" which Barthes describes as the unspeakable desire shaping the "domestic scene."

The violent death-by-drowning of Grandcourt in book 7, bringing the deadlocked Gwendolen plot to its climax, thus forms a psychologically appropriate conclusion to the warfare waged by these antagonists, yoked as they are in a deathly mésalliance of power and gender. But while the specific situation of uneasy wedlock terminates, its disruptive effects linger on without conclusion or compensation; that is, even though an "ultimate" act of violence has been reached, the inner or "essential violence" that Gwendolen's being has sustained continues to repeat itself, in Barthes's phrase, "without any possible conclusion." For Gwendolen is not released from her trials into the blissful rewards of conventional fictional widowhood; rather, her long-standing guilt (for having married Grandcourt at all) is increased by specific remorse at having maintained murderous thoughts about him. On such a note Eliot begins to intimate her break from the novelistic tradition of "just rewards," preparing the way for the open ending of the eighth and final book of *Deronda*.

III

Although the attention given the novel's controversial Jewish theme during its serial publication overshadowed the discomfiting implications of the Gwendolen plot, its lack of a romantic denouement did not go unnoted. An unauthorized sequel named *Gwendolen: Reclaimed,* penned by an anonymous admirer in America, vividly attests to the fact that most of Eliot's readers *expected* a traditional marriage ending as Gwendolen's compensation for suffering. In this version, following a series of totally conventional plot complications and character misunderstandings, Gwendolen appears on the last page fainting submissively, gratefully, and graciously, into Daniel's manly arms as his declaration of love reclaims her from no less than deathly illness:

> What a reclamation! Those only who, like them, have stood upon the brink of despair, who, like them, have been restored—unexpectedly restored—to life, to hope, and to happiness, can judge their emotions and sentiments at this time. And when, at last, Deronda confessed his undying devotion and love, she sank beneath gratitude and joy, into the expanded arms of her adored lover,—RECLAIMED.

In undertaking to "correct" Eliot's plot by supplying such a romance, this author claimed to be motivated by the "almost universal disappointment at the unanticipated conclusion of the story—a conclusion which many readers have resented as though it were a personal affront."[50] And, indeed, the uncertainty about the relation of Eliot's concluding intentions to the novel's ultimate function and meaning is also reflected in the opinion of her publisher. "I am puzzling greatly as to how Mrs. Lewes is to wind up in one more book," Blackwood wrote Eliot's common-law husband; "I am certain the public after reading book 7 will sympathize with me in wishing that there were to be more." Upon the manuscript's completion, Blackwood tactfully hinted to Eliot that "There will I know be disappointment at not hearing more of the failure of Gwendolen and the mysterious destiny of Deronda, but I am sure you are right to leave all grand and vague."[51] What Blackwood, along with other readers, failed to realize was the degree to which Eliot's "grand and vague" conclusion has been anticipated by the text's themes and structural rhythms all along.

In addition, the end of book 8 has been self-reflexively foreshadowed in the fable of Berenice that Daniel's artist friend Hans tells: "The story is chipped off, so to speak, and passes with a ragged edge into nothing—*le néant*" (514). Because Berenice is a Jewish martyr, the incompletion of her story reflects the uncertainty of Daniel's penultimate Eastern venture. More specifically, however, Berenice's fate as a beautiful and ambitious woman—cast out of a socially enviable marriage, left solitary, and finally disappearing from sight—suggests the situation facing Gwendolen after Grandcourt's death. Not only does Eliot deny Gwendolen a happy remarriage upon her husband's death; neither does she supply any definite reassurances of the rebirth of Gwendolen's razed identity. Before the vague stirrings of a "new existence" (840) that Gwendolen feels can take root, she must first experience her essential separateness, however painful solitude may be, and learn to trust her own worth without relying on the guidance of a mentor like Daniel. And it is the crucial function of her first encounter with Daniel since Grandcourt's death to illustrate this formidable truth. The principle of "separateness with communication" (792) that Daniel has in mind for the emergent Jewish national identity must also become part of Gwendolen's personal creed and the model for their own relationship. Thus Eliot reintroduces Rex Gaiscoigne, still hopelessly in love with Gwendolen, into the text at precisely this juncture to reemphasize the fact that remarriage is not the right solution for Gwendolen at this point in time; rather, her remaining sense of self, not "boxed" into yet another marriage or another kind of dependent relationship, may at least have a *chance* of recovery, of redefining itself in relation to the openness of the future.

Gwendolen's most challenging lesson in separateness occurs

when Daniel pays her his final visit, a scene that simultaneously marks the last intersection of their trajectories and closes Gwendolen's history. With Daniel's explanation that he is not only leaving England but that his future is tied to Mirah as his bride-to-be, Gwendolen feels "reduced to a mere speck" in his "wide-stretching purposes" (875). But, in contrast to the negative reduction of self she has undergone in marital deadlock, this sensation of diminishment gives way to a potentially affirmative perception of a larger reality: "she was for the first time being dislodged from her supremacy in her own world, and getting a sense that her horizon was but a dipping onward" (876). This inner transformation in perspective is signaled in outer action as Gwendolen moves from an initially solipsistic reaction to an attempt to be positive for Daniel's sake rather than her own: "I said . . . I said . . . it should be better . . . better with me . . . for having known you" (878). Her last words repeat this wishful affirmation ("I will try—try to live . . . It shall be the better for me—") but as Eliot notes, "She could not finish" (878).

This breaking-off of speech, leaving the future hanging in the space after the pronoun "me," appropriately symbolizes Eliot's narrative technique as she proceeds to "break off" Gwendolen's story without further authorial speculation on the direction her life will take. The reader is privy to a very brief last view of Gwendolen hysterically sobbing to her mother her last words to Daniel, and the fact that it is impossible to tell whether she is blindly repeating his advice in desperation or taking to heart the resolve "to live" makes it impossible for the reader to simplify the terms of her future. It is thus thematically and structurally appropriate that in the novel's final chapter Gwendolen's presence is reduced to the letter, printed on the next to last page, that she generously sends Daniel on his wedding day.[52] Already removed in person from the text, she has begun to live a separate life and travel into her unknown future. And even while she reasserts her hope that "it shall be better with me" (882), she admits that she does not yet see the shape in which she will carry out his hopeful prophecy that she become "among the best of women, such as make others glad that they were born" (840). Instead, her horizon remains "but a dipping onward"—uncertain, uneasy, unresolved—as the reverberations of her past, echoing into the future, help create what has generally been recognized as a new kind of novelistic ending.[53]

Closure in the Daniel plot, in contrast, might appear entirely traditional—there is a marriage (Daniel and Mirah's) and a death (Mordecai's)—and in this instance the text perhaps most clearly illustrates the sentimental and Victorian side of Eliot. But as in *Wuthering Heights* these events may also serve some interestingly unconventional functions worth our speculation. First, it is important to realize the degree to which the cloying representation of Daniel's love affair with Mirah beguiled the contemporary reader into accepting, at least partially, the potentially alienating Jewish element of Eliot's story: Jews fall in love like everyone else, Eliot seems to imply. In a sense, then, Daniel's conventional marriage makes his unconventional mission more palatable. Similarly, the presence of this predictable love-angle creates a "cover" for the radical critique of marital ideology in the Gwendolen story. By playing one plot off the other, therefore, the text suggests new possibilities while deflecting criticism by keeping the traditional in view. Meanwhile, the typically "Victorian" handling of Mordecai's death, which completes the transference of his vision of a Jewish homeland to his pupil Daniel, becomes, in an even more unconventional twist than Eliot may realize, the novel's closest approximation to a convincing "romantic" close, bringing as it does the plot of Daniel's search for identity to its climax through the spiritual union of the two men's souls in one.[54] And, finally, the visionary quality encompassing the ending of the Daniel plot has certain, though circumscribed, affinities with what is "open" about Gwendolen's uncertain future. For, although the *structural* movement of Daniel's story reaches a point of stabilization in his simultaneous discoveries of identity, love, and vocation, the *thematic* implications of his on-going quest do not: to Eliot's Victorian reader the mission on which Daniel embarks can only remain uncertain, incomplete, given the historical reality that there was no Jewish homeland in the 1870s.

Therefore, despite their modal differences, a certain complementarity exists between the separate futures facing Gwendolen and Daniel as each strives, in Jenni Calder's words, to create new worlds "beyond community, beyond the recognized anchors of life."[55] Seen in conjunction, their experiences emphasize the implicit lesson that meaningful destiny and self-definition (for Daniel as a racial alien, for Gwendolen as a single woman) lie outside social prescriptions of normality. Hence, Eliot's structure—refusing the seductive ease of the happy end in the Gwendolen narrative, leaving behind the English world of the reading audience altogether in Daniel's story—plots different modes of rebellion against the norm in which freedom ultimately lies *outside* the secure brackets of the text. The densely textured structure of *Deronda*, so monumentally Victorian on its surface, turns out to be unexpectedly modern not far beneath. By exposing wedlock as something less than a happy conclusion, this rich and innovative novel succeeds in calling into question the social order underlying the traditional order of fiction itself.

·*The Golden Bowl*·
Maggie's Maneuverings in the Marriage Plot

To move from Eliot's revision of the wedlock plot to Henry James's is an easy step and a natural transition. James rather acerbically noted of Eliot's earlier canon that marriage "is all very well in its place," but "by itself makes no conclusion." Given such a view, it is not surprising that he spent his novelistic career plotting fictions that chipped away at the constraints imposed on theme and form by the marriage tradition. Truly "modern" fiction—the novel of the future—would not develop, James often argued, until more English and American novelists abandoned the thematically safe "region[s] of virtuous love" and skirted the formally restrictive "rigour[s] of convention" dictated by dominant nineteenth-century fictional ideology. For James realized that the power of tradition was the true culprit in maintaining novelistic laws that, ironically, contradicted the mimetic foundation of the realistic novel; hence his disdain of "the 'fatal Conclusion'" perpetuated by "the old tradition . . . which exacts that a serious story of manners shall close with the factitious happiness of a fairytale."[56]

It has been argued that James's concern with formal issues dictated his criticism of conventional love-plots and predictable conclusions. Such a view, however, overlooks the wealth of recent criticism that has emerged to suggest James's acute if sometimes ambivalent responsiveness to the social issues of his day involving women, gender, and sexuality.[57] The degree to which his artistic ethos incorporated such sympathies surfaces eloquently in the aptly named essay "The Future of the Novel," written on the eve of the new century. Here he prophesies that "nothing [will be] more salient" in sparking the needed "renewal" of the novel "than the revolution taking place in the position and outlook of women—and taking place much more deeply in the quiet than ever the noise on the surface demonstrates."[58] Whatever his ambivalences toward "noisy" public movements, feminist or otherwise, such an articulation makes it clear that James's agenda for fictional "revolution" was intimately tied to the upsetting of social hierarchies and sexual inequities as well. As Annette Niemtzow puts it, James's objection to fictional endings in marriage may have been aesthetic, but it was an "aesthetic commitment in consonance with newly visible . . . social reality and with James's quiet, albeit anti-social and critical, sympathies."[59]

Among his literary predecessors, James perhaps found himself most indebted to Eliot, despite his criticism of her "fatal Conclusions," for his insight into the related narratological problematics of misbegotten desire and deadlocked marriage. The legacy is most direct in *The Portrait of a Lady*, where Isabel Archer's marital situation echoes Gwendolen's in *Daniel Deronda* (written five years earlier in 1876 and much admired by James).[60] The conflict between an authoritarian husband's tyrannical will and a wife's constricted selfhood suggested to James, as it had to Eliot, a situational impasse for which traditional lines of plot and modes of closure seemed inappropriate. The overall shape of Isabel's trajectory of experience, as I have suggested in chapter 3, culminates in a kind of "tragic" finality, given her resolve to return to Osmond; nonetheless, by deliberately suspending Isabel's specific fate *"en l'air,"* James begins moving toward the structural diffuseness that marks Eliot's ending.[61] For, while the aim of aesthetic completeness—the organic "whole" of what "groups together"—would continue to be an important consideration in the novels following *The Portrait*, James's later canon manifests progressively open-ended plots in which characters with necessarily limited points of view are left in ambiguous positions that bring the reader face-to-face with the issues implicit in their concluding uncertainty. The result of James's structural innovations is well summarized by a fellow pioneer of early modernist technique, Joseph Conrad: "One is never set at rest by Mr. Henry James's novels. His books end as an episode in life ends. You remain with the sense of life still going on. . . . It is eminently satisfying, but it is not final."[62]

And it is exactly this infinite sense of unrest that characterizes the relational patterns, both narrative and personal, left unresolved in *The Golden Bowl* (1904)—like Eliot's *Deronda*, James's last completed novel. James considered calling his text "The Marriages."[63] This title would certainly have pinpointed James's unsettling subject matter, for the plot traces the deepeningly ambiguous maneuvers by which Maggie Verver, having discovered the flaw in her own and her father's socially perfect matches to be the sexual affair carried on by their spouses, attempts to wrest the form and content of married life into a nonthreatening equilibrium—that is, into a narrative that would approximate the traditional form of fiction itself. Out of this essentially melodramatic premise, James evolves a devastating commentary on the conventions underlying romantic and marital union—be the motivation of relationship economic, sexual, or conventionally sentimental—by making every stage of his counterplot an opening up of the narrative assumptions underlying the fictional tradition of wedlock. This textual diffusiveness is marked, finally, by the irresolution of the novel's ending. For, in contrast to Eliot's *Deronda,* where the destiny of the widowed Gwendolen is left *"en l'air,"* the very marriage that forms the center of *The Golden Bowl,* that of Maggie and Prince Amerigo, is left ambiguously suspended, open to question, at text's end. Maggie may physically "reclaim" her Prince in the last paragraph of the text, but her triumph is no redemption of fairytale-like proportion, as some critics have mistakenly assumed. Rather, as Ruth Yeazell incisively demonstrates, "what we really witness here is less a closed fiction than a character struggling to will such a fiction." Against Maggie's self-interested "passion for closure," Yeazell points out, James has instilled in his text "an openness which stubbornly persists."[64] By means of this dislocating narrative principle and its destabilizing effect on the novel's relationships, roles, and structure, James perfected his version of indeterminate form as a way of charting the ambiguous course of marital strife.

UNEASY WEDLOCK AND OPEN FORM

I

Particularly prominent in James's early fiction, his brother William complained, are "those male *vs.* female subjects you have so often treated."[65] Nearly thirty years later, James had not yet exhausted the subject, as evinced by the wide spectrum of male–female relationships in *The Golden Bowl:* two marriages, one clandestine love affair, and a father–daughter bond that passes for a marriage. And in each relationship the keynote most often sounded is the division between the sexes, a division italicized by constantly shifting plays for power over and possession of each other. The two most obvious cases of predation involve the social matches made by Maggie and her father Adam Verver, both of whose mates figure as "the kind of human furniture required aesthetically by such a scene, . . . attestations of a rare power of purchase."[66] In an ironic reversal of expected sexual roles, the opening pages of the text establish the Prince as an "object of price" (1:12) pursued and captured for his aristocratic pedigree. The Prince, however, is no innocent victim; he complacently accepts the fact that he has sold himself for material rather than marital ease. Indeed, the manner in which the Ververs' desire for European lineage "complements" the Prince's need of Maggie's American millions belies the seemingly ideal, magically perfect surface of the anticipated union: the popular myth of complementary opposition as the basis of romantic attraction has become an object of grim parody. Adam's marriage to his daughter's childhood friend, Charlotte Stant, is also a calculated arrangement, a "majestic scheme" and "deliberation of a plan" (1:210–11) based on utility rather than love. It is telling that Adam's interest in Charlotte is roused during his business trip to Brighton to buy antiques for his museum collection; gaining her assent becomes analogous to bidding for the valuable tiles he wishes to add to his list of possessions. Like the Prince, Charlotte accepts the implications—and limitations—of this arrangement because she desires financial security.

The fact that Adam tacitly admits to gaining "another daughter" (1:222) in marrying Charlotte casts a revealing if disquieting light on the nature of his relationship to his *real* daughter, Maggie. For the uncomfortably incestuous undertones that emerge from this "decent little old-time union" (1:135) of father and daughter, fondly figured by both as a kind of marriage, become a damning commentary on the sentimental ideology encouraging women to be docile child-wives and men paternal rulers in wedlock. It is precisely such an ethos that is responsible for idealizing the May–December archetype of union reproduced in Charlotte and Adam's less than ideal marriage. Moreover, the incestuous insularity of Maggie and Adam's domestic intimacy conveniently provides Charlotte and the Prince the excuse with which to justify their similarly self-involving affair: they argue that neglect by their *sposi*, away engaging in "make believe renewals of their old life" (1:252), has "forced" them "face to face in a freedom that partook, extraordinarily, of ideal perfection, since the magic web had spun itself without their toil, almost without their touch" (1:298). This solipsistic passion, however, confirming the pattern of frustrated desire linked in chapter 2 to Continental fictions of adultery, loses its momentum once the obstructions to its fulfillment are overcome and a sense of reality begins intruding upon the idyl. Hence, the Prince's passion wavers as soon as his greater self-interest (that of keeping in Maggie's good graces) intervenes; Charlotte's doomed desire, ironically, increases in proportion to the frustration of her calculations to keep the Prince for herself. The adulterous affair, James demonstrates, is as empty of disinterested notions of romantic love as is the Victorian connubial ideal.

In making all these relationships throw into question aspects of the age's marital ethos, the text simultaneously implicates the hierarchy of male and female roles that too often transforms love relationship into a battle for mastery and possession. The Jamesian ideal of selfhood exists only through negative counterpoint in *The Golden Bowl:* Maggie, Charlotte, the Prince, and Adam all exemplify the limitations of socially constructed identities rooted in sexual differentiation. Maggie, at first glance, might seem to be the one character to acquire an empowering sense of identity as she progresses, like young Cathy Linton of *Wuthering Heights,* from the "helpless, obliging passivity" of a dutiful daughter "[not] born to know evil" (1:78) to an adult knowledge of the world. In truth, however, Maggie inhabits one feminine stereotype after the other. Despite gains in self-assertion, she remains trapped in limiting social definitions of her role. Telling in this regard is the fact that those critics who view Maggie's growth as positive equate female maturity with *wifely* responsibility—a role that, in their eyes, Maggie champions in "saving" her marriage.[67] Yet Maggie's "womanly" machinations in the name of reestablishing domestic order and conventional propriety are consistently called into question by the darker implications of her expanding "desire to possess and use" others (2:49); in becoming an active crusader for her marriage she may rebel against the proscription of "feminine" passivity, but only by accepting the terms of aggression and conquest valued by a power-obsessed society. Adding to the uneasiness with which Maggie's endeavors unfold is her claim that she does all "for love" (2:46). However, in conflating her possessive desire to dominate with "her appointed, her expected, her imposed character" (2:71) as loving wife, Maggie ultimately lies to herself about her own motives. As James tells us, "it was only a question of not, by a hair's breadth, deflecting into the truth" (2:250–51) that becomes Maggie's guiding principle. Her claim only to want "happiness without a hole in it, . . . the golden bowl without the crack" (2:216–17), reveals the illusory constructions of wholeness, regarding both her marriage and her identity as wife, for which Maggie settles.

Despite the fact that the Prince's obsequiousness to the Ververs makes him appear "a lamb tied up with a pink ribbon" (1:113), he uses his male status to attain his own end, marital security, every bit as much as Maggie does her maidenly and wifely personae. Amerigo's unquestioning assumption that masculine privilege is his natural right surfaces most visibly in the way he manipulates his sexual appeal to control Maggie as well as Charlotte, both of whom he views as members of that species of "wonderful creatures" who try "to outdo each other in his interest" (1:351).[68] And, in truth, simply because he is male, the schemes of both women eventually do work to his advantage: "That was *his*, the man's, any man's, position and strength—he had necessarily the advantage, that he only had to wait with a decent patience, to be placed, in spite of himself, it might really be said, in the right" (1:49–50). Amerigo may have to make some choices in the end, but he nonetheless retains a control of his future not open to the women in the novel.

The paradoxically enormous power that resides in calculated passivity when exercised by a man is glossed by the contrasting experience of Charlotte. Although she, like the Prince, has also sold herself on the marriage market, she becomes *victim* of her decision to a degree that never affects him. If the Prince at first seems inordinately passive, waiting to be "placed" in other's narratives, Charlotte by juxtaposition first appears an uncharacteristically energetic woman determined to make her "place." Beneath her aggressive camouflage, however, Charlotte remains utterly passive in her surrender to worldly conventions and standards, for she has imbibed society's belief that true female independence is abnormal: "'Miss,' among us all, is too dreadful. . . . I don't want to be a horrible English old-maid" (1:219). But when she attains the alternative state of decorative wife, Charlotte finds herself *completely* stripped of control, a caged "prisoner" (2:230) trapped like the similarly "imprisoned" Gwendolen (*Deronda* 651) in the unsatisfying (and inescapable) stasis of her husband's marriage plot. Charlotte's victimization is inevitable, given her acceptance of social definitions of her options; all the roles she has occupied—"old maid," "adulteress," "wife"—are grounded in assumptions of female inferiority or capitulation to male whims and power.

Charlotte's ultimate submission is most powerfully registered in her husband Adam's successful exercise of authority over her. This consummately capitalistic collector of valuable objects and people, ruthlessly aggressive behind a placid and even boring exterior, is also the quintessential Victorian patriarch, making his proposal of marriage an act of conquest that demands Charlotte's assent be a woman's moment of "supreme surrender" (1:239–40). Thus, it comes as no surprise when he completely takes control of her married existence: "the likeness of their [marital] connexion would n't have been wrongly figured," the narrator reports, "if he had been thought of as holding in one of his pocketed hands the end of a long silken halter looped around her beautiful neck" (2:287)—an image of male mastery that underlines the role of sexual differentiation in upholding the power structure of matrimony and patriarchal society.

II

It remains to be seen how the narratological innovations characterizing *The Golden Bowl* work to subvert these ideological structures of institutionalized wedlock by outmaneuvering the spatial and developmental "rules" that govern the traditional marriage plot. James's commentary on destructive sexual roles is, for example, deflected into one of his most basic narrative strategies, that of dividing the text into two halves, titled "The Prince" and "The Princess." Presenting the marriage from roughly opposing viewpoints, this perspectival dialectic draws attention to the sexual division that separates husband and wife, locks them into antagonistic roles, and bars each access to the other's subjective thoughts, feelings, and needs. Different from but comparable to Brontë's manipulation of sequential double-plotting to suggest timeless repetition in *Wuthering Heights* and Eliot's diverging plots in *Daniel Deronda*, James's bipartite structure also functions as a decentering device, averting simplistic closure by accentuating the widening rifts between the two points of view. In the process, the erotic dynamic of the narrative is channeled into a more diffuse, circuitous course that breaks from the linear model of excitation and release characterizing traditionally satisfying fictions. Hence, although Maggie's consciousness—concentrated on healing the marital breach—eventually comes to dominate the action, the doubleness of possibility sustained by the novel's dual structure keeps the reader uneasily aware that Maggie's efforts constitute only a *partial* view of the wedlock situation; the offstage presence of the Prince's implicit perspective throughout the second half suggests the presence of a larger plot in which all the protagonists are puppets of multiple narrative lines and tangents that refuse assimilation into one univocal pattern.[69]

Once again we find such open ambiguity prepared for by a developmental structure that reverses the traditional threshold moments and climaxes associated with courtship and marriage processes in fiction. The undermining process begins in the very first chapter, which opens just after the Prince signs his marriage agreements; his immediately following walk about town, its direction "sufficiently vague" (1:3) and "restless" (1:4), foreshadows the dislocations that the "locked" condition in which he now finds himself are setting into motion. The structural arrangement of the three sections composing book 1 confirms this sense of uneasiness. The first section ostensibly moves from the signing of the marriage settlement to the union itself, creating a minuscule courtship pattern. The legitimacy of this pattern, however, is undercut at the one end by the Prince's opening uncertainties ("I've now but to wait to see the monster [marriage] come," he facetiously yet seriously confides to Fanny Assingham, adding that "One does n't know what still may happen" [1:25–26]), and at the other by the climax of the section, which turns out to be *not* the final moments of the Prince and Maggie's convergence but his reunion with Charlotte—an event that ironically transpires under the pretext of seeking a wedding gift for Maggie. The second section repeats the first one's surface movement, courtship to marriage, in tracing Adam's calculated wooing of Charlotte, who is "purchased" as the Prince has just been purchased for Maggie. Again, the reasons prompting the union are totally misplaced, since Adam primarily conceives the idea of marrying Charlotte to assuage Maggie's filial guilt in abandoning him for Amerigo. The section's climactic proposal scene is devastatingly undermined as Adam mistakes the "strange" expression (1:239) lighting Charlotte's face for "feminine" joy, a disturbing sign that another mistaken union has been initiated.

The third and final section of book 1 charts the adulterous convergence of the two new additions to the Verver family. From the perspective of structure alone, this movement toward adultery, coming on the heels of two "courtship" sequences, implies a rather damning critique of the way these arranged matches have steered Charlotte and the Prince into each other's arms. In this light, the entire third section forms an anticlimax to the action, marriage, inaugurated in the first two sections. Ironically juxtaposed with Charlotte and the Prince's climactic vows of renewed (and now illicit) devotion in chapter 22, moreover, is a two-chapter coda, an extended bedtime conversation between Fanny and her husband, that undermines the affair's apparent closure, just as the movement toward adultery has in its turn undermined the prior double movement toward marriage. Although the sequence first shows Fanny transparently attempting to deny the truth ("I was uneasy—but I'm satisfied now. . . . There's nothing [going on]" [1:366]), her resurgent suspicions ultimately become a fearful "open[ing] out" of possibility "into the region of the understood" (1:378). Her refusal, nonetheless, to verbalize the "understood" ("Nothing—in spite of everything—*will* happen. Nothing *has* happened. Nothing *is* happening" [1:400]) only confirms the uneasiness of the dislocations, both thematic and textual, that the representative marriages of the Ververs have set into motion. The result, significantly, is to render the final statement of the first half of the novel completely ambiguous.

The three parallel sections that make up the second half of the novel, centered on Maggie's dawning consciousness of the affair, trace the stages by which she sets a counterplot into motion in order to realize her own desire "to be *with* him [the Prince] again" (2:27). Because her scheme depends on placing each of her "antagonists"—first the Prince and then Charlotte—in the dark, its implementation adds to the expanding uncertainties that culminate in the text's ambiguous conclusion. In the crucial fourth section, Maggie's struggle to restore a "proper" and superficially peaceful equilibrium between the couples entails, ironically, a mute warfare with her husband as her "adversary" (2:142)—a warfare that reaches a decisive climax only when Maggie gains the certain evidence of the affair that tips the scale in her favor and consequently places the "discovered" Prince in her power. The deliberate ambiguity ending the section, in which the Prince meets Maggie's implicit accusation by indicating that he will "depend on her" for future direction, exposes the struggle for dominance that underlies the connubial ideal—indeed, that is inherent in its ideological consruction of sexuality—and that has opened the text, stage by stage, to multiple motivations and interpretations, both within the world of the text and on the level of the reader. For in this penultimate moment Maggie leaves the Prince totally in the air as to her final intentions:

> "I know nothing but what you tell me" [the Prince states].
> "Then I've told you all I intended. Find out the rest!"
> "Find it out—?" He waited.

And Maggie leaves him waiting: she knows his dependence resides in the fact that it is now he, "absolutely, who is at sea" (2:203) and not she herself.

This pattern of irremediable division glossed over by surface unanimity—like the sexual dichotomization hidden under the unifying sign of marital harmony—is repeated in the structural arrangement of section five, which details the stages of Maggie's conquest of her second "antagonist," Charlotte. In the section's last chapter, Maggie forces Charlotte—who has been left in the dark by the Prince's defection—to accept the appearance of victory by pretending to "save" Adam, *her* husband, from Maggie's filial clutches. Maggie's nobility in appearing the loser is exploded by the dramatic irony that the two women's "opening" into apparent accord

(2:317) is based on an absolute denial of reality—the truth of the matter is that Maggie is "saving" her own husband by dictating what Charlotte's response is to be.

Maggie reaches this point of control over the lovers by perfecting her acting skills, learning to read between the lines, making imaginative leaps, imposing her omniscience on others—as often noted, characteristics associated with the modern artist's unsettling enterprise. As a creator, however, Maggie ironically pictures in herself the opposite, a maker of stability. Ominously self-absorbed, she wills into being a traditionally romantic fiction—replete with sentimental ending—"of which she herself" is "author" (2:235) as well as "far-off harassed heroine" (2:307). Emblematic of her attempt to "rewrite" (as well as re-right) the plot of their lives is the excuse that brings her to the garden in chapter 39 in search of Charlotte. Charlotte has been reading an "old novel," a three-volume romance, but (as Maggie notes) has carried off the wrong volume. Therefore Maggie seeks her out under the pretext of reasserting the traditional fictional order, an act with multiple resonances for James's own fiction: "*This* is the beginning; you've got the wrong volume, and I've brought you out the right" (2:311). In the process Maggie also reasserts the "right" moral order by masterminding the Ververs' removal to America. In accomplishing this understanding with Charlotte, Maggie sets the stage for reunion with Amerigo. The subjectivity with which Maggie has plotted these ends, however, makes the reader uneasily aware that her fiction may only be one plot among several. Indeed, her very *authority* to plot has been opened to question by the ambiguous nature of her enterprise—a situation generating for Maggie a degree of authorial anxiety that James manages to avert for himself by making his plastic design contain an infinite number of co-plotters. All of the characters, in fact, are shown hatching "plans" by which to act; yet all, too, are shown operating in the dark, "groping soundlessly among . . . questions" and doubts (2:139). The very absence of communication among all these plotters, otherwise so verbose, is one of the most telling indications of the failure of their relationships.

Two varieties of ambiguity, thus, are promulgated in increasing proportion throughout book 2 of *The Golden Bowl:* a vertical probing into internal motivations and attitudes, which only unearths deeper ambiguities of character; and a linear multiplication of implicit/explicit plot lines and perspectival structures, which only complicates the reader's task of determining the objective "truth" of any reported incident or action. Both modes of ambiguity contribute to the uncertainties that infuse—and defuse—the marriages reestablished in the sixth and final section. Maggie's entire effort to this point, that of seeing the Prince through to "the right end" (2:322), has depended on the hope of transforming herself "from being nothing to him to being all" (2:228)—a desire that can be seen not only as consuming Maggie's entire being but as devouring the Prince's individuality in the process. Indeed, the ambiguity surrounding Maggie's gamble to win back her husband's love reopens the question of *who* really has the upper hand in this war for marital supremacy as, in the last chapter, she awaits the Prince's return from seeing the Ververs off: "She had thrown the dice, but his hand was over her cast" (2:367). The "great gambling loss" sealed by Gwendolen's marriage in *Deronda* (496) remains in process in Maggie's text.

Among the welter of critical interpretations attempting to measure the degree of Maggie's success, F. W. Dupee represents the traditional view that the sentiment "*Amor omnia vincit* . . . certainly dictated [its] structure and movement."[70] Such a literalist reading of the ending, however, failing to distinguish the "marriage plot" that is Maggie's fiction from James's counterplot, overlooks the destabilizing ironies embedded in the text's developmental and perspectival structures, as well as the series of disturbing notes occasioned by the Prince's return to Maggie in the novel's final scene. Maggie's extreme emphasis on the significance of this moment, indeed, ends interrogatively: "Here it was then, the moment, the golden fruit that had shone from afar; only what *were* these things, in the fact . . . as a reward?" (2:367). Given James's repeated attacks on fictional rewards, the appearance of the word in terms of the approaching union of the Prince and Maggie strikes a warning note; moreover, as a financial rather than narrative metaphor, the idea of "rewards" also reflects ominously on Maggie's erotic expectations: she wonders whether her patience is about to be "paid in full," then in relief interprets the Prince's countenance upon his reentrance to mean he is "holding out the money-bag to her" (2:368). But her personal gain also uneasily brings to mind the eco-

The Golden Bowl

nomic basis of the original union as well as the guaranteed security "on the score of his bank account" (1:292) that the Prince has protected in opting for Maggie over Charlotte. And, finally, to the extent that these financial metaphors conjure forth images of sexual expenditure, we also return to the narratological implications of final "rewards": for if the Prince decides to "spend" himself at this climactic moment, as Maggie's marriage plot demands, she will assume that she has succeeded—when in effect she will have simply won a place for herself in an essentially masculine "plot" of desire whose linear trajectory must inevitably curtail the "loosening" and "float[ing]" tide (2:239–40) that figures her own wished-for release.

Another unsettling element in this final scene is Maggie's method of letting the Prince know that she does not expect a confession but considers the subject of his affair finished once and for all: " 'Is n't she [Charlotte] too splendid?' she simply said, offering it to explain *and to finish*" (2:368; emphasis added). Thus, rather curiously, Maggie calls attention to the one person that the Prince at this crucial juncture would probably rather not be thinking about. Maggie's closing "gift" to her husband, like so many of her seemingly benevolent actions, becomes a subtle means of inflicting punishment, the results of which may be measured in the novel's final sentences (in both senses of the word), whereupon Maggie and the Prince meet in an embrace that Yeazell accurately labels an act of literal as well as literary containment:

> "That's our help, you see," she added—to point further her moral.
>
> It kept him before her therefore, taking in—or trying to—what she so wonderfully gave. He tried, too clearly, to please her, to meet her in her own way; but with the result only that, close to her, her face kept before him, his hands holding her shoulders, his whole act enclosing her, he presently echoed: " 'See?' I see nothing but *you*." And the truth of it had, with this force, after a moment, so strangely lighted his eyes that, as for pity and dread of them, she buried her own in his breast. (2:368–69)

The gap that still exists between these two partners locked in marriage can be sensed in the lack of communication pervading their dialogue at this point: Maggie must "add" explanations, the Prince must "try" to take it in, but as the ambiguous word *see* indicates, they remain speaking different languages. The declaration of love, the final seal of the traditional marriage plot, is also an admission of defeat.

It is Maggie's penultimate realization of this irremediable breach that is finally so disquieting. The "truth" that she sees strangely lighting Amerigo's eyes is, most simply, that although she now totally possesses him—to the point that she has literally become *all* he sees—she remains in the dark about how he feels toward her or toward the leave-takings of the previous hour.[71] At the end of Maggie's fiction, indeed, nothing is as stable as it once seemed; the hard-won knowledge that in conventional fictions would guarantee the certitude of the "happy end" makes certitude in this narrative impossible. Whatever their many ambiguous feelings, Maggie and the Prince are now irremediably locked in an uneasy alliance that, unlike the novel, cannot stop at this point: in this regard James's ambiguously open form has become the perfect vehicle to represent the unsettling effects of sexual dichotomization within that "steel hoop of an intimacy" (2:141) constituting adversarial marital relationship. And the most disconcerting, saddest part of this *ongoing* rather than closed tragedy is that Maggie must bury her eyes to the truth that she has just gleaned. To look at the Prince directly—that is, to establish any communication at all—would be to face the failure of their marriage; therefore, it follows, wedlock must remain a mutual pact of *non*communication and self-deception.

Paradoxically, the indirections by which Maggie has attempted to execute her plan of bringing herself and her husband together have not only guaranteed this continuing gap in their personal relations but also opened up the narrative relations of the text. In Maggie, the traditional author has unwittingly become a modernist who deconstructs her own designs; the modernist in James, conversely, allays his ambivalences about "designing" at all by making the self-betraying designs of marital power and sexual discord the very subject of his modernist deconstruction. As James puts it in a statement that could stand as an analogy for his organizational principle in charting the course of wedlock-gone-wrong in *The Golden Bowl*, "Maggie had so shuffled away every link between consequence and cause that the intention remained, like some famous poetic line in a dead language, subject to varieties of interpretation" (2:345). For the novel's multiple structures and open ending, in exploding Maggie's effort to make her marriage a closed fiction, simultaneously open up for the reader's interpretation the contradictions embedded in "the dead language" circumscribing the social and fictional myth of romantic wedlock. Thus demonstrating the infinite "plasticity" and "elasticity" he celebrates as the "strength and . . . life" of representational art in the essay "The Future of Fiction" cited at the very beginning of this book, James's text of marital designs gives a further shake to the discrepancies between life and plot that led writers following in this footsteps, like Woolf, to abandon thematic regions of "safety" and, in so doing, to create new forms, new plots, for both life and fiction.

·*To The Lighthouse*·
A Modernist Dismantling of the Victorian Marriage Ideal

When toward the end of *To the Lighthouse* (1927) Lily Briscoe muses, "Could it be, even for elderly people, that this was life?—startling, unexpected, unknown?"[72] her thoughts cogently sum up a sense of the fluidity and openness of modern existence that Virginia Woolf's experimental techniques have set out to capture. Accordingly, *To the Lighthouse* has gained prominence as a classic example of modernist fiction. This status, however, has until recently obscured other thematic concerns equally important in motivating Woolf's innovations in form, particularly her choice of the very traditional and unmodern marriage of the Ramsays as her subject matter. For Woolf's revision of the wedlock plot in *To the Lighthouse* is both modernist and feminist in conception; by means of the same narrative devices that violate conventions of fictional realism, Woolf simultaneously dismantles the Victorian marital ideal embodied in the Ramsays' union of complementary opposition. Like *Wuthering Heights, Daniel Deronda,* and *The Golden Bowl,* Woolf's text grounds its destabilizing representation of uneasy married life in the conflict between personal identity and marital role—a conflict expressed in the dialogical interplay of subjective perspectives defining the Ramsay marriage internally and externally. But, unlike its predecessors, this counterplot goes even further in flouting readerly expectations of what properly constitutes marital "drama," first by depicting unglamorously middle-aged protagonists, seemingly content in their static relationship, then by presenting a single nondescript day in their shared life (in "The Window") before unexpectedly cutting short the possibility of its continued story with Mrs. Ramsay's death (parenthetically reported in the following "Time Passes" section). When the narrative action picks up ten years later, the "marriage plot," such as it were, exists only as retrospective commentary in the minds of Mrs. Ramsay's survivors. "Non-eventful" as such a focus might seem, it uncovers a hidden wealth of drama in the unspoken and quickly repressed instances of "domestic violence"—to summon up Barthes's term once more—that lie at the heart of the romantic ideal perpetuated by the Ramsays, exacting its toll daily over the years. In an echo of the double plot of *Wuthering Heights*, this silent antagonism outlasts death and separation, leaving as its legacy an aftermath of unresolved tensions mirrored in the splintering and finally visionary structure of the final section ("The Lighthouse").

Feminist criticism of the past decade, having focused on Woolf's call for a women's literary tradition in *A Room of One's Own* (published two years after *To the Lighthouse*), has directed most of its energy into tracing the development of a distinctively "female" tradition or voice in the Woolf canon.[73] But as *A Room* also intimates, the repudiation of what Woolf identifies as "patriarchal" discourse is also a rebellion against an inherited novelistic tradition whose narrative "shape" or design "has been made by men out of their own needs for their own uses" (77, 80). And in this regard Woolf's aesthetic response intersects with the concerns of other writers, male and female, attempting to write against a dominant literary and social ideology of love and marriage. Anticipating Bakhtin, as we have seen in chapter 1, in her designation of the genre as "this most pliable of all forms," Woolf was convinced that it was possible for women to break down the strictures of tradition and "[knock] into shape . . . new vehicles" of fictional discourse (80). Her diary charts her personal odyssey toward a "new form," the "*Unwritten Novel*" in which events repudiate traditional linear order by "open[ing] out" of each other, and her critical essays extend the challenge by exhorting the reader to become a partner, rather than judge, in the increasingly open process of fictional creation.[74] While such attitudes are indubitably "modernistic," they also exemplify Woolf's desire, as she put it in *A Room*, to detonate the restrictive view of men and women implicit in "the whole structure" (77) of the nineteenth-century novel and, in the process, to discover a style, a voice, and a form of her own.[75]

I

Because of its elegiac nature, critics long believed Woolf's portrait of the Ramsays to be an uncritical celebration of her parents' union, and the Ramsays' differences a representation of inherently separate masculine and feminine principles. Even as readers have gradually come to acknowledge the imperfections in Mr. and Mrs. Ramsay's marriage, the couple's polar viewpoints have frequently been explained away as a metaphor of modern alienation rather than as part of a specific critique of marriage in and of itself.[76] Woolf's depiction of the responses of the Ramsays to their existential situations, however, illustrates the degree to which societal concepts of gender have contributed to the gulf in communication holding them apart even in the most intimate of relationships. And simultaneously Woolf implies that the learned "masculine" response of Mr. Ramsay is inadequate in ways that Mrs. Ramsay's "feminine" reaction, however stereotypical and entrapping, is ultimately not. Although both Ramsays share a strikingly similar vision of "this thing . . . called life" as a hostile enemy ready "to pounce" (92), Mr. Ramsay assumes a prototypically masculine defiance in face of humanity's essential isolation, epitomized in his pose as lone romantic quester braving the void as he stands on his little spit of land surrounded by the encroaching sea, quoting Tennyson and Cowper in solipsistic raptures of despair. Mrs. Ramsay's perception of human solitude, in contrast, repeatedly causes her to perceive the unity or oneness underlying nature; it becomes the impetus for her to forge human connections, to will an order and coherence out of flux by at least providing the illusion of a maternal center around which others' perceptions may gather. If Mr. and Mrs. Ramsay fail to meet each other fully in marriage, Woolf suggests, it is the fault not only of an alienating universe but of the alienated marital roles that they have embraced in embracing each other in a quintessentially Victorian union.

Indeed, *To the Lighthouse* presents a detailed anatomy of the irresolvable ambiguities inherent in the Victorian ideology of wedlock

lying behind the "essential . . . thing" (93) that Mrs. Ramsay pur-
ports to share with her husband.[77] Above all else, their relationship
aspires to an illusory oneness that Woolf figures as "that solace
which two different notes, one high, one low . . . give to each other
as they combine" (61). That such concord derives from an essential
asymmetry ("one high, one low") and hides an essential discord is
exposed not only with the deflating observation, a page later, that
the sound of the two notes dies "with a dismal flatness" in Mrs.
Ramsay's ears, but with the fact that marital harmony for both depends on a continual balancing of oppositional viewpoints that neither *wants* to resolve. As their garden walk in the twelfth part of the
first section graphically illustrates, they are most comfortable talking to each other as long as they know their views will never intersect: "They disagreed always about this, *but it did not matter.* She
liked [Mr. Ramsay] to believe in scholarships [for their son An-
drew], and he liked her to be proud of Andrew whatever he did"
(103; emphasis added). By silently agreeing to disagree, they in fact
bolster each other's limiting assumptions about the opposite sex
(hence Mr. Ramsay is equated with "factual" accomplishment, Mrs.
Ramsay with nondiscriminating maternal pride). It is what they
cannot presently talk about—their private feelings—that reveals
the flaw undermining the idealized "wholeness" of their relationship: "They both felt uncomfortable. . . . No, they could not
share that; they could not say that" (104). It is one of Woolf's most
telling verbal strategies that the "that" which can never be shared
between the Ramsays is never named but always referred to by
indefinite pronouns; for example, a moment earlier Mrs. Ramsay
has mused that "marriage needed—oh, all sorts of qualities . . .
one—she need not name *it*—*that* was essential; the *thing* she had
with her husband. Had they *that*?" (93; emphasis added). But if the
"thing" that makes marriage worthwhile cannot be spoken, its silence, of course, admits the possibility that these indefinite references have been emptied of any meaningful content.

The degree to which the Ramsays' dichotomized roles in marriage fulfill needs traditionally linked to gender also plays into the
text's deconstruction of the conventional romantic ideal in two
ways. Without fail, Mr. Ramsay demands, Mrs. Ramsay gives: if
Mrs. Ramsay becomes the "delicious fecundity, this fountain and
spray of life" that supplies Mr. Ramsay with the balm his wounded

ego constantly desires, his need for "sympathy" illustrates the "fatal sterility of the male," plunging itself "like a beak of brass, barren and bare" (58), into Mrs. Ramsay's life-giving force. As Woolf's extreme imagery implies, the line drawn between the genders at once ensures that each sex feels it is incomplete without the other (without Mrs. Ramsay's nourishment, Mr. Ramsay will perish of aridity, etc. [59]) and simultaneously dismantles itself by proving these distinctions to be unfixed after all: thus it is Mrs. Ramsay's "masculine" spray, ironically, that metaphorically fertilizes her husband, he who is "femininely" barren.

This pattern of sexual categorization and reversal also permeates the series of images inserted throughout the text to illustrate the limitations that these accepted roles impose on the Ramsays' personal identities. For the sexual and marital hierarchy implicit in Mr. Ramsay's "reason" and Mrs. Ramsay's "emotiveness" turns out to be as deceptive as the slippery boundaries of their professed sexual identities. Despite Mr. Ramsay's belief that he, as the husband, is his wife's gallant protector, it is actually Mrs. Ramsay's understood duty as "wife" to shield *him* from the paucity of his accomplishments; in compensation, he maintains (and Mrs. Ramsay abets) the illusion of her inferior, trivializing mind, disregarding the fact that only she of the two can truthfully and ruthlessly look reality in the eye.[78] One result of this deception is to force Mrs. Ramsay into becoming a backstage manipulator, working to arrange the appearance of Mr. Ramsay's superiority while repressing the discontents that follow from her often greater self-awareness. Like Maggie Verver's, the mission inscribed by her wifely role is not to veer by a hair's breadth—to paraphrase James—into the truth. Another inevitable result of this masquerade is that it facilitates Mr. Ramsay's practical supremacy in the relationship. "He is petty, selfish, vain, egotistical," Lily complains in a prophetic diatribe, "he is spoilt; he is a tyrant; he wears Mrs. Ramsay to death" (40).

The duplicities involved in the wedlock ideal are nowhere clearer than in Mrs. Ramsay's investment in the institution of marriage itself. "What was this mania of hers for marriage?" (261), Lily will ask years later, and rightly wonder whether Mrs. Ramsay's admonitions that "an unmarried woman has missed the best of life" (77), like her compulsive attempts at matchmaking, betray an unconscious self-defensiveness. Although it also flashes across Mrs. Ramsay's mind that it may be "an escape for her too, to say that people must marry; people must have children" (92–93), she cannot stop herself. Thus, in a wishful projection similar to the romantic denouements that Nelly Dean and Sir Hugo unsuccessfully plot for their charges in *Wuthering Heights* and *Daniel Deronda*, Mrs. Ramsay fantasizes a highly unlikely marriage between William Bankes and Lily. While some of Mrs. Ramsay's fantasies, such as the lighthouse trip, are affirmative ways of giving shape to her world, this particular projection reveals a negative need (again, like Maggie Verver's) to justify the form of her own married life, even at the expense of lying to herself about its content. Such acts of self-deception do not define the whole of Mrs. Ramsay, as any reader knows. One of the most memorable things about Mrs. Ramsay, indeed, is that against her often conventional public facade she also maintains a hidden inner life that—complementing the generally positive identity she feels in relation to her children—is real, essential, unconventional. If the marital state demands of Catherine and Gwendolen and Maggie a bifurcation of wifely role and private self that is finally inwardly deadening, in ironic contrast such a separation becomes Mrs. Ramsay's means of inner survival, allowing her the illusions that make female subordination in marriage bearable while preserving for her own peace of mind a private, untouched interior life.[79]

Flashes of this other self—silent, beautiful, remote, and stern— briefly surface when Mrs. Ramsay does not think she is being watched, "as if she had been pretending [to this point] and for a moment let herself be now" (25). The reader's first truly privileged view of Mrs. Ramsay alone, released from external constraints, occurs in the eleventh subsection as she shrinks into the "wedge-shaped core of darkness" that is her most fully aware self: "She could be herself, by herself" (95). Mrs. Ramsay's desire for privacy is, of course, a facet of the universal human condition. But as part of the text's pervasive and profound questioning of wedlock, the devastating significance of this moment is quite clear: an essential part of Mrs. Ramsay's identity cannot exist *with* her husband, and this is a truth that she will die without facing. Structural repetition, as we shall see, reinforces this fact, for each of Mrs. Ramsay's moments of vision in which she achieves a sense of inner coherence is broken by Mr. Ramsay's demand for attention. Thus, rather than providing the avenue to identity promised in traditional fictions of female maturation, marriage fosters the split between wifely role and inner essence that, in a vicious circle, necessitates the prevarications and manipulations needed to maintain the illusion of complementary union as a state of "balance" or "harmony." The lack of meaningful communication between the Ramsays takes on a new significance in this light, emerging as Mrs. Ramsay's unconscious strategy for preserving her independence in confinement. Yet whether an inviolable self "invisible to others" (95) can ever compensate for an unfulfilling union only serves to open to question the necessity of such a compromise and, with it, the central tenets upon which the Victorian ideal of marriage rests.

II

The manner in which this disturbing portrait of a marriage provides a focus for Woolf's innovations in form can be seen both in the specific techniques underlying the immediacy of the text's narrative flow of consciousness and in the larger structural design that links its time-divided parts. The interplay of subjective perspectives that characterizes "The Window," for instance, comprises a succession of "random" moments that have meaning only insofar as they reveal various aspects of the Ramsays' marriage. Woolf moves the reader in and out of the interior perspectives of husband and wife, then from their viewpoints to those of the houseguests who observe them (both as a pair and separately), as if offering pieces of a puzzle that the reader is to assemble: that puzzle is the question formed by the Ramsays' wedded life. In contrast to this constant flux of events, the duality of the overall structure of the novel—two specific moments in time separated by the passing of ten years—calls forth a different kind of marital commentary as Mrs. Ramsay's haunting presence in death in the final section throws into relief her earlier *absence* in life. Comparable to Brontë's technique in *Wuthering Heights*, structural repetition-with-a-difference (the same place, the same unfinished events, with the heroine's death in the space between) creates a destabilizing variant of double plot that does not permit the questions raised by the Ramsays' marriage in the first part to rest easily. Moreover, this diptych-like structure raises as a crucial issue the question "whether to paint or to marry,"[80] for the juxtaposition between Lily and Mrs. Ramsay as central figures in these sections externalizes the specifically female conflict between marital role and independent fulfillment that we have already seen to exist at the heart of Mrs. Ramsay's divided identity.

Moreover, the generative nexus of plot in both halves of the novel—the prospect of taking the trip to the lighthouse—is pivotally related to the problematic status of the Ramsays' marriage. Their opposing views on whether the next day's weather will permit the voyage, introduced in the text's first scene, becomes the emblem of a silent, unending war of perspectives: Mrs. Ramsay's opening "Yes," an affirmation of imaginative possibility that flies in the face of probability, stands irrevocably against Mr. Ramsay's immediate, practical-minded, and "masculine" negation. Thomas Matro has noted how the grammatical structure of such sequences—"Yes . . . But . . . But . . . ." (9–11)—creates a series of infinite qualifications mirroring the novel's thematic inconclusiveness;[81] I would suggest that this unending oscillation of viewpoint extends to the novel's larger units of structure as well. For the argument over the trip continues to shape the Ramsays' day and to order the text; it moves from subtle disagreement to outright confrontation as Mr. Ramsay verbally "damns" the "extraordinary irrationality" and "folly of women's minds" (50) that leads Mrs. Ramsay to encourage James's hopes of the trip. The final scene of the section returns to this same conflict. Mr. Ramsay implicitly raises the challenge by saying, "You won't finish that stocking [for the lighthouse keeper's son] tonight" (184), and Mrs. Ramsay, in her final lines, abdicates by affirming *his* view: "Yes, you were right. . . . You won't be able to go" (186). Against this reality of "fact," however, the reemergence of plot in the third section will depend upon the poetic truth of Mrs. Ramsay's original affirmation: ten years deferred, the trip is finally made.

If "The Window" incorporates the traditional war of the sexes into its narrative arrangement via the Ramsays' continuing debate over the lighthouse trip, the section's repeating structural rhythms also encode the theme of marital self-division in its representation of Mrs. Ramsay's three moments of vision. The sense of oneness and piercing self-knowledge that Mrs. Ramsay achieves, for example, in a moment of privacy after sending James off to bed—culminating in her epiphanic realization that "It is enough!" (100)—is abruptly terminated, one paragraph later, by Mr. Ramsay's selfish desire that she relinquish her private ecstasy (threatening because it attests to her ability to exist without him) and return to his illusory sphere of control: "For he wished, she knew, to protect her" (100). A similar capitulation is demanded in the famous dinner party sequence, as Mrs. Ramsay creates a sense of "the whole held together" (160), not just for herself but for the entire group. For the "coherence in things" (158) that she has summoned forth begins to dissipate, once again, under her growing consciousness of Mr. Ramsay's competing demand for support: "It was as if she had antennae . . . which, intercepting certain sentences, forced them upon her attention. . . . She scented danger for her husband" (161). This pattern recurs a third time in the climactic scene of "The Window" section. Alone with her husband, Mrs. Ramsay sinks into herself as she reads a sonnet, approaching another transcendent moment of vision as she cradles the "essence" of life, "suddenly entire" and complete, in her hands (181). In a telling juxtaposition, however, the first sentence of the immediately following paragraph indicates the dissolution of the moment and its familiar source: "But she was becoming conscious of her husband looking at her" (182). As always, the demands imposed by Mr. Ramsay and dictated by Mrs. Ramsay's conception of wifely duty stand in the way of her autonomy.

The open-ended structure of this entire scene—forming the reader's last glimpse of the Ramsay's married life—also plays a crucial role in the text's dismantling of the Victorian marital ideal; like the tableau ending *The Golden Bowl*, the ambiguities pervading the scene hold husband and wife in an uneasy and unspoken tension that, despite their mutual affection, leaves the quality of their marriage open to speculation. In the lull that follows Mrs. Ramsay's reading of the poem, each partner *waits*, in silence, for the other to fill a specific need: the vague "something" (176) Mrs. Ramsay "wants" from her husband is most simply a confirmation that their traditional relationship has some "value" (183), in face of her rising doubts about all marriage; the "something" (184) Mr. Ramsay in turn "wants" from his wife is an avowal of love, the ultimate sign of her dependence on him. Mrs. Ramsay believes her wish has been granted, ironically enough, when Mr. Ramsay antagonizes her: "That was what she wanted—the asperity in his voice reproving her" (184). So "put in place" by her supposed opposite and superior, Mrs. Ramsay can renew her delusive belief in the fiction of the total sufficiency of their relation; in an ironic twist of illogic, she feels as if his exercise of authority and her subsequent acquiescence "proves" that the hierarchical balance in their marriage has been right all along.

However, as Mrs. Ramsay becomes aware of Mr. Ramsay's reciprocal needs, a new level of silent confrontation surfaces to unsettle this easy resolution: "And what then? For she felt that he was still looking at her, but that his look had changed. He wanted something—wanted the thing she always found it so difficult to give him; wanted her to tell him that she loved him. *And that, no, she could not do*" (184; emphasis added). Refusing to admit the implications of her reticence, Mrs. Ramsay hides behind the excuse that she cannot express feelings in words; in the place of words, she creates an illusion of assent by smiling at Mr. Ramsay—a manipulation of silence as timely as Maggie Verver' pregnant pauses—and, instead of saying what he wants her to say, states that he has been right about the impossibility of the lighthouse trip. By giving in to Mr. Ramsay on *this* front, she indeed demonstrates wifely "love" as it is defined in traditional wedlock (bowing to his superior knowledge), and thus exclaims to herself that "Nothing on earth can equal this happiness" (186). Yet, in withholding a spoken declaration, Mrs. Ramsay simultaneously withholds part of herself. Refusing to share herself, her thoughts, with her husband, she unconsciously rebels against and helps disprove the idealized image of wedlock as an all-encompassing and self-sufficient entity —an image that she consciously upholds. And if Mrs. Ramsay pridefully considers her feat of "not say[ing] it" (185) a "triumph," the section's final line reminds us that this silent "communication" of love is, at its base, a disturbing act of combat in a war of gains and losses that has gone on for years: "And she looked at him smiling. For she had triumphed again. She had not said it: yet he knew" (186). With this carefully placed colon, holding the pronouns "she" and "he" in an indefinite suspension, Woolf leaves us with a powerfully resonant grammatical sign of the psychological stalemate that is wedlock.

The destabilizing impact of cutting the narrative off at this critical juncture becomes obvious in the immediately following section, "Time Passes." Not only is the previously intimate focus on the

Ramsays' marriage jarringly truncated by the narration of this in-terlude, the marriage itself is just as violently terminated by Mrs. Ramsay's death, reported in a parenthetical aside. Both these de-flating structural effects participate in the text's critique of wedlock by forcing the reader to experience a sense of frustration and in-completion analogous to the frustrations and incompleteness hid-den within the Ramsays' marriage. At the same time, the loss of Mrs. Ramsay's unifying presence, radically decentering the re-maining narrative, paradoxically keeps the novel's counter-tradi-tional investigation of wedlock alive by raising the questions with which the dual plots of "The Lighthouse" must come to grips: what has Mrs. Ramsay's life meant? will the future show her vision to have been as empty as her death or will it last?

Against the enormous narrative and temporal gap opened up by the "Time Passes" section, the eerie repetition in "The Lighthouse" of actions begun but never completed ten years before, almost as if nothing has changed, ushers into the present-time of the novel the unresolved reverberations of the past. Narrated in an alternating sequence, Lily's attempt to finish her painting forms one line of development, Mr. Ramsay's pilgrimage to the lighthouse, after all these years, the other; and both plots vividly attest to the prob-lematic past of the Ramsays' marriage. In the case of Mr. Ramsay's trip, love and guilt, not necessarily a better understanding of Mrs. Ramsay, inspire his effort. While for the reader the voyage vindi-cates Mrs. Ramsay's affirming imagination, Mr. Ramsay remains locked in a solipsistic, "masculine" notion of reality that, while touching on one level, renders his final gesture ambiguous and delusive on another. Reaching the lighthouse and thinking, "I have found it," he ignores the silent pleas of both James and Cam to let them love him ("but he said nothing"), and in leaping out of the landing boat "as if . . . into space" (308), he continues to play out the role of the alienated quester facing the void alone.

The counter-balancing series of scenes depicting Lily's attempt to finish her long-abandoned painting creates its own dialogue with the past. For Lily the act of painting is synonymous with the act of remembering Mrs. Ramsay and acknowledging the pain of her ab-sence; hence, the unresolved "relation between . . . masses" (221) that her canvas poses is inextricably linked in Lily's mind to the "centre of complete emptiness" (266) that Mrs. Ramsay's death has left behind. In an inspired moment of letting go, Lily turns from her painting and imaginatively *reinvents,* then empathetically *enters* into, the flawed married life of the Ramsays in the eleventh subsection, an unconscious and poignant act of artistry that metaphorically "solves" the mystery of their relation by recreating it from their perspectives. Reaching into a past earlier than the text's beginning, Lily's vision novelistically portrays their courtship as an "old-fashioned scene" (295) played out in the polarized roles of gentleman and lady; her mental narrative then relives the tensions, the hidden arguments, the slammed doors, of the Ramsays' private married life that refute the general impression of their union as a "monotony of bliss" (296). This imaginative reconstruction of the Ramsays' marriage as a war of wills and opposing needs begins uncannily to echo *the very day* Woolf has just recorded in "The Window": Lily's "marriage fiction," in effect replicating Woolf's marriage plot, brings the Ramsays of ten years ago back to life.

Appropriately, then, Lily's vision reaches a climax in an image of unresolved marital impasse as powerful as that ending section one. For the result of Mrs. Ramsay's "hang[ing] stealthily about" to "win" his wife's attention and her "hold[ing] off" time and again, in Lily's imagined narrative, is always Mrs. Ramsay's acquiescence, "go[ing] to him" in the end; away from the guests, "they would have it out together," Lily supposes, but "with what attitudes and what words?" And the ambiguous, unknowable quality of such moments is reinforced by the public selves the Ramsays quickly reassemble before meeting their guests for dinner—where, in Lily's tableau, they remain frozen in a figure of unresolved opposition that mirrors the tension pervading the library scene in "The Window": "and there they were, he at one end of the table, she at the other, as usual" (296–97). As usual; that is, suspended in an eternal opposition "without any possible conclusion."

This "return" of the Ramsays in Lily's memory triggers a crucial, closely linked sequence of actions bringing Woolf's novel to its climax: it occasions the magical return of the "ghost" of Mrs. Ramsay in the present, which in turn brings on the epiphany that enables Lily to complete her painting. For as the flicker of "white" in the window where Mrs. Ramsay sat ten years before casts a shadow that alters Lily's composition, the artist realizes that her canvas must incorporate both the "objective" and "subjective" perspectives di-

vided between the Ramsays in life; the miracle of unity and difference must be recognized with the single frame, not parceled out
into falsely externalized, gender-associated oppositions: "One wanted, she thought, dipping her brush deliberately . . . to feel simply
that's a chair, that's a table, and yet at the same time, It's a miracle, it's
an ecstasy. The problem might be solved after all" (299–300). While
the appearance of Mrs. Ramsay's ghost ("There she sat") adds one
component, Lily also knows "she wanted him," Mr. Ramsay, too
(300), and thus in looking to the sea and visualizing his landing at the
lighthouse adds the stroke that finishes her painting and completes
her vision.[82] Combining and balancing within one frame elements
and perspectives unnaturally distributed among the sexes, Lily's
painting symbolically resolves—but *only* symbolically—the issues
raised by the Ramsays' marriage; it is a crucial aspect of Woolf's plot
that the Ramsays themselves have resolved nothing. Indeed, the
schism between the realms of the living and the nonliving that now
separates the Ramsays only repeats, on another level, the division
that has always existed between them ("he at one end of the table,
she at the other"), and the hope of imaginatively bridging this gap
remains a task for autonomous souls like Lily. Thus the finality of
Lily's last stroke, like Woolf's own aesthetically crafted end, becomes
a visionary projection of future possibility that simultaneously reopens, rather than resolves, the questions inherent in the preceding
narrative of uneasy wedlock.

There is, moreover, another dimension to Lily's effort that
sheds light on the special nature of the dual movements ending the
text. As Lily recognizes, Mrs. Ramsay's special talent, the mark of a
true artist, was that of "giving [things] a wholeness not theirs in
life" (286); this task Lily now attempts to emulate, using her painting to give Mrs. Ramsay back to her children "whole" in a way "not
[hers] in life." Analogously, although *To the Lighthouse* ends with the
simultaneous completion of two actions, the coherence or "wholeness" that ensues from this aesthetic gesture does not attempt to
cover over the unresolved tensions and the limited choices of the
past, nor does it deny the world of differences of which all lives are
composed. For nothing really ends, as Lily knows; life goes on, and
the attempt to make connections—internally and externally, as Lily
and Mrs. Ramsay both do—defines the only grounds on which reality can truly be *lived*. Woolf's narrative structure embodies this

vision of the openness of life by showing how two moments, widely separated by time and death, create an ongoing dialogue in which the ghosts of the past continue to haunt the present, at the same time that the present looks toward an unknown, visionary future— a double movement that parallels Brontë's suspension of plots at the end of *Wuthering Heights*. In the unstable textual world that follows upon Woolf's breaks with traditional novelistic continuity and containment, the Victorian marital ideal proves equally unstable, deconstructing itself from within while making room, by the very void its absence leaves, for a vision of a different story—perhaps Mary Carmichael's narrative, or Lily's future paintings—that, in reaching beyond the division of sexual constructions, would render the narrative disturbances wrought by uneasy wedlock obsolete.

Conclusion: Continuing Conjugal Concerns

The preceding analyses of *Wuthering Heights, Daniel Deronda, The Golden Bowl,* and *To the Lighthouse* should give us some sense of the daring, even potentially revolutionary, project in which these texts were engaged. In an effort to counter society's dominant mythology of wedlock, these novels pitted their intrinsic power as works of the imagination against the authority inherent in cultural norms; significantly, their dissenting message found a vehicle for expression in the disruptive and destabilizing tendencies inherent in the dialogical form of prose fiction itself. However indirectly, the result attests to a unique capacity of literature if not directly to incite social change, at least subtly to alter perceptions of social reality by exposing the latter's own fictions. For the very fact that there was another story to tell, as the counter-narrative of wedlock-gone-wrong made clear, gave the lie to the ubiquity of the romantic wedlock ideal, revealing its actual status as a cultural artifact, a historically specific construction of people's desires, rather than as an innate or natural law. Refusing to simplify, ignore, or erase the contradictions embedded in the sexual order underlying the myth of marital happiness, the trajectories of these uneasy narratives resist the very process of ideological formation by making visible ideology's concealments, elisions, and resolutions.

Despite their inception in differing time periods, social contexts, and authorial predispositions, the novels studied in this chapter converge in their methodology: all four attempt to defuse the precepts governing standard love fiction by translating the unresolved tensions of conjugal warfare into principles of narrative structure. The open-ended, decentered plots ensuing from this effort contribute to what might be called a revisionary erotics of the text, a reshaping of the very dynamics of narrative and human desire. The difference that these revisionary efforts have made is palpable on a number of interconnected thematic levels. First, the representation of marriage as "a battle which must always be going forward" consistently grounds itself in the conflict between personal identity and marital role, a conflict primarily inscribed in the narrative of the female protagonist's self-diminishment and psychological constriction. While the male counterparts in these novels may also find their identities compromised in marriage, such losses generally occur within and from a position of social and psychological power. Modes of characterization attest to this distinction as well. It is no coincidence that husbands from Grandcourt to Adam Verver and Mr. Ramsay are defined by an interior emptiness, blankness, and inscrutability so extreme as to make them appear one-dimensional; what might at first glance pass for unrealistic "flatness" in these figures strategically evokes their ability and privilege, as men, to remove themselves from the immediacy of domestic warfare, hence from the immediacy of textual representation. Conversely, it is the female character, her sense of identity inseparable from the concrete realities of conjugal impasse, who emerges as the more self-divided, hence more "rounded" figure in these novels.

Second, these texts consistently chip away at socially and fictionally sanctioned gender polarities by creating male and female characters whose behavior disproves such arbitrary boundaries. Catherine's sense of command, Gwendolen's desire not to "do as other women did," and Lily Briscoe's dedication to her career all demystify cultural assumptions of femininity, no less than Deronda's empathetic compassion or the young Heathcliff's marginality belie myths of masculine hardness and automatic power. These individual instances of acting subjects who do not conform to stereotype are tied to a third feature of these novels: the promotion of relationships, both romantic and nonromantic, that serve as alternative models to the hierarchy and polarity prevailing in marital ideology. Hence Brontë's striking use of the sibling metaphor for a heterosexual passion rooted in affinity, as well as Eliot's depiction of male–female friendship that need not be sexual to be fulfilling—a description that also holds true of the same-sex bond connecting Mrs. Ramsay and Lily in what is perhaps the most deeply felt relationship in *To the Lighthouse*. Fourth, and finally, the way in which Lily becomes Mrs. Ramsay's surrogate daughter indicates the degree to which these texts create new models of extended "family"; the abuses inherent in the conjugal ideal are contiguous with the failure of the traditional family of Oedipal romance to provide sustenance to its individual members.

We have already seen how these thematic resonances find expression in several formal equivalents. As if in anticipation of Woolf's injunction to break the sequence, these works strategically displace, reverse, and rewrite the crises, thresholds, and climaxes associated with marriage fiction, an act which bestows on their trajectories the possibility of signifying differently. Likewise, these novels tamper with conventional perspectival structures, using narrative viewpoint, spatiality, and distance to create eerie overlappings and repetitions that, in breaking narrative linearity, instill new genealogies of meaning and of relation. The novel of uneasy wedlock also frequently makes use of dual or multiple plot structures whose decentering energies strip the conjugal ideal of its primacy as a univocal end for marriage or marriage plots. The complex interweaving of subgeneric modes, styles, and voices in these counter-traditional novels, moreover, creates further levels of ongoing dialogue that work against traditional resolution. Although all novels are multivocal and polyphonic, containing a range of competing languages and genres, it is telling that conventional love fiction has generally pretended to one dominant mode, whereas the texts under discussion here more self-consciously flaunt their generic modalities in order to heighten the tensions residing in their content; thus the challenging combination of the gothic, realistic, metaphysical, and folktale in *Wuthering Heights* or the competing narrative logic of quest romance, realistic causation, and the melodramatic in *Daniel Deronda*.

Setting oneself in opposition to a social myth as pervasive and influential as that of patriarchal wedlock is, of course, never an easy task, never "finished business," as the degrees of ambivalence coex-

CONTINUING CONJUGAL CONCERNS

isting with rebellion in these texts attest. The cynical observer could argue that the denouements of some of these novels offer up marriages that, on the surface, may not seem strikingly different from examples of the conventional ideal—the endings of *Wuthering Heights* and *Daniel Deronda* include hopeful marriages, after all, and *The Golden Bowl* ends, for better or worse, with a reunion. The point needs to be made, however, that rebelling against the sexual politics of heterosexual coupling does not necessarily mean the wholesale repudiation of *all* ideals of marital happiness (hence Brontë's vision of a new paradigm of loving in my reading of the Cathy-Hareton alliance); nor does it ensure against the intrusion of some lingering nostalgia, on the author's part, for a form of relation he or she is otherwise committed to overthrowing (hence Eliot's sentimental projections onto the Daniel-Mirah union). The blind spots that remain in any attempt to break from tradition also help explain the occasional instances of sexual stereotyping that crop up in these otherwise unconventional texts. But while none of these works is uniformly free of sexual biases, as entire organizations their plots move beyond such lapses, in my view, by incorporating into their uneasy forms the more all-encompassing problematic represented by marital deadlock. By focusing on issues that simultaneously overlap personal and public desires, male and female spheres, these texts make room for ambiguity at the same time that their organization deflects attention away from whatever private ideal of love or whatever internal conflicts the writer might unconsciously harbor, and point toward the ascertainable, disruptive contradictions welling up within patriarchal ideology.

Both to explain and offset these traces of ambivalence, it is fitting to consider, at least briefly, the biographical elements contributing to these writers' rebellions against the romantic norm. Despite the fact that the causal connection of real-life "evidence" to the fictional text must always remain hypothetical, it is certainly suggestive that all four of these writers occupied, both by choice and by circumstance, extremely peripheral positions in society at large, and it could be argued that their marginality allowed them, in highly individual ways, the psychological and critical distance from which to judge the inadequacies of a male-dominated sexual code more objectively than those inside the system could. For instance, the dynamics of Emily Brontë's "outsider" status—as a single woman, an unknown writer, and a mystic living in the relative isolation of Haworth—certainly contributed to her unconventional vision of human wholeness and passion; moreover, as the comments of Brontë's few associates reveal, her proud self-sufficiency and quietly formidable inner strength suggest a personality that transcended traditional sexual categorization.[83] Considerably more conflict marks Eliot's personal rebellion against social norms of womanhood, but nonetheless it is clear that her minority status as a female intellectual and writer, coupled with her painful defiance of sexual convention by living as Lewes's common-law wife and being ostracized from polite society, lies behind the often radical impulse, as well as the ambivalences, that fire her fictional criticism of the marriage tradition. We can locate the same dynamic working itself out in another vein in James's case. Although his homosexuality was not consciously acknowledged until late in life, this mark of difference must have early on exacerbated James's anxious sense of not-belonging vis-à-vis the heterosexual world whose romantic transactions he recorded with a mixture of attraction and disdain; in turn, such intuited feelings of marginality may well have increased James's imaginative sympathies for his female protagonists as victims, not unlike himself, of an oppressively male-dominated system. Woolf's life, in contrast, was filled with much more explicit reminders of her exclusion from the dominant order from her youth onward. Educationally deprived by her father, haunted by the cultural image of the "angel in the house" she had rejected, prey to isolating bouts of mental illness, Woolf learned to convert marginality into an alternative, self-affirming lifestyle—evidence of which we can see in her association with the fringe world of Bloomsbury, her marriage to a Jew, and her determined rise as a woman writer. To a great degree, then, since their investment in perpetuating the patriarchal values of a status quo from which they were to some degree already excluded was minimal, all these writers forged in their own lives a "counter-traditional" reality whose impress can be felt in their imaginative responsiveness to issues of love and marriage.

While the achievements of *Wuthering Heights*, *Daniel Deronda*, *The Golden Bowl*, and *To the Lighthouse* are considerable, these were not the only texts written between 1848 and 1929 to mount an effective critique of sexual relationship through an undermining of narrative expectations and conventional formats. Several other fictions at least approach this chapter's description of the open-ended plot of uneasy wedlock, but, before listing some of them, I would like to draw attention to a related novelistic category: texts whose attack upon the romantic marital ideal is embedded in plots or subplots of *uneasy courtship* rather than of uneasy wedlock—a strategic countermove opening the love-making process itself up to ambiguity and question.

One of the more famous demonstrations of this approach occurs in James's *The Bostonians* (1886). Despite the ambivalence the text displays toward feminist activism, James quite clearly uses its courtship structure to dismantle the whole notion that sexual opposition and male mastery in love will lead to ever-after happiness. His critique reaches its climax, appropriately, in the satiric last lines, which deliver up a quintessentially unhappy union in the language of its happy opposite: "'Ah, now I am glad!' said Verena, when they reached the street. But though she was glad, [Ransom] presently discovered that, beneath her hood, she was in tears. It is to be feared that with the union, so far from brilliant, into which she was about to enter, these were not the last she was destined to shed."[84] The moment of romantic closure (signified by an ominous embrace evocative of the Prince and Maggie's in *The Golden Bowl*) is simultaneously a reopening of all the narrative's prior disturbances: any prognosis of wedded life beyond Verena's tears is bound to be uneasy and unfulfilling, given Ransom's avowedly misogynistic views and his reclamation of Verena as a triumph in the war of the sexes.

The Rhoda-Everard sections of Gissing's *The Odd Women* (1893) similarly turn the Austenian courtship format inside-out. As in *The Bostonians,* the plot revolves around the erotic war a threatened male supremacist wages against an emancipated New Woman who disdains marriage because of her dedication to her work and the feminist cause—the difference being that Rhoda, unlike Verena, is a committed feminist whose strength of mind is, ironically, the very quality that becomes increasingly attractive to Everard. The two tentatively draw together, only to be propelled apart, in a series of inconclusive proposal scenes that, as in the Austenian pattern, are marked by mistaken and mismatched viewpoints, external obstructions, and surprising reversals of attitude. But this is "Austen" with a crucial difference. For the self-knowledge that finally brings

Everard and Rhoda's maturing perspectives into correct alignment—the pivotal turn that makes union possible in Austen's plot—is precisely the understanding that renders marriage between Gissing's protagonists impossible: despite the fact that they *do* love each other, the process of courtship has taught Rhoda, in a neat reversal, that she cannot sacrifice her autonomous selfhood and her work for Everard's terms of love, which, given his desire to dominate, must always be possessive and hence self-diminishing.[85] At text's end Rhoda rejoins her original society of "odd women," the feminist sisterhood that Verena rejects, in an affirmation of self and solidarity verging on a visionary openness: "We flourish like the green bay-tree. . . . The world is moving!" (336). The sense of hope embodied in the unknown future recalls, in part, the closural strategies of *Wuthering Heights* and *Daniel Deronda*.

A more convoluted example of the subversive function that the courtship plot can serve exists in Charlotte Brontë's profoundly ambiguous and deeply psychological *Villette* (1853). On one level, as I have argued in chapter 3, Lucy's personal growth is measured, as in any courtship plot, by her relationships with unworthy and worthy objects of desire. Within this double-suitor format, the hinted-at death of M. Paul, cutting short the possibility of romantic fulfillment, marks a sobering but (Brontë implies) realistic end to the trajectory of Lucy's stoical experience. Beneath this tragic love-plot, however, the text encodes another, more devious counter-narrative through the enigmatic voice and unsettling personality of its first-person narrator. The frequently commented-upon gaps in Lucy's narrative, which include her withholding of textual knowledge from the reader (and sometimes from herself) and the blurring of the line between narrating and experiencing selves, initially signal a neurotic unwillingness to write herself into her text; but by its end they become the conscious manipulations of a narrator whose mental and autoerotic health depends on her refusal to be pinned down, either by possessive men or prying readers. Continually swerving out of our grasp just when we think we "have" her, Lucy paradoxically creates a space both within and outside her text that allows her to become an autonomous self, one who escapes traditional female choices and confinement within traditional categories of the Victorian heroine. In the process, the elliptical, teasing shape of Lucy's "interior" story, calling into question the linearity of the overt courtship structure, creates a circuitous trajectory of narrative desire, a particularly female narrative erotics. The ambiguous openness of this subtext competes with the tragic closure of the love-plot, balancing the loss of M. Paul with a diffuse autoerotic gain.

However subversive this underlying narrative may be, Brontë's closural manipulations allow her to sidestep the difficulties of representing Lucy as an independently spirited but married woman, and this conflict is precisely the subject taken up by a group of other narratives with counter-traditional affinities. Here it is appropriate to turn back to Gissing's *The Odd Women*. For the questioning of the unequal dynamics of sexual polarity in the Rhoda-Everard plot is heightened by the bald unmasking of the sentimental Victorian ideal in the simultaneous story of Monica and Edmund Widdowson's disastrous marriage. As Gissing notes, the despotic Widdowson is "a monument of male autocracy" to whom it has never occurred "that a wife remains an individual, with rights . . . independent of her wifely condition. Everything he said presupposed his own supremacy; he took for granted that it was his to direct, hers to be guided" (152). An admittedly traditional resolution concludes the devastating representation of marital warfare that unfolds from Widdowson's tyranny (Monica dies in childbirth after an ineffectual rebellion, a near affair, and immense suffering), but the closural repose attained here is qualified by the events that have occurred in the other "half" of the novel's dialogical structure; indeed, it is Monica's child—a daughter—who becomes the future hope of Rhoda's community of odd women in the visionary final scene.

We have seen how Woolf used modernist innovations in narrative form to dismantle patriarchal marriage in *To the Lighthouse*, a maneuver echoed in other early twentieth-century works, including E. M. Forster's *Howards End* (1910), D. H. Lawrence's *The Rainbow* (1915) and *Women in Love* (1920), and her own *Mrs. Dalloway* (1925). *Howards End*, in particular, is a superb example of the way in which principles of open form can embody a critique of the uneasy tensions of conjugal warfare. While Forster's epigraph, "Only connect," foreshadows his major theme, Margaret Schlegel's dawning realization that "actual life is full of false clues and sign-posts that lead nowhere" points to his narrative method. The entire plot is predicated on a series of "false clues" and "innumerable false starts" which generate a textual openness that confutes any easy possibility of relation, whether textual or interpersonal.[86] If the narrative seems continually to be escaping the reader's determinations by splintering into unresolved subplots (a tactic recalling the swerving trajectory of *Villette*), a comparable element of surprise and inconsistency colors Forster's method of characterization. This method is most vividly represented in Margaret's unexpected eagerness to marry Henry Wilcox, whose values oppose her own in nearly every way: Forster's decentering strategies of plot and of characterization thus dovetail with particular force in dramatizing the destabilizing effects wrought by this union. For as the "astonishing glass shade" (174) of marriage cuts Margaret off from her prior sufficiency, she undergoes a by-now-familiar awakening to the abuses built into marital hierarchy and into the social order lying behind it: "Ladies sheltering behind men, men sheltering behind servants—the whole system was wrong, and she must challenge it" (214). The "wrongness," more specifically, lies in what the narrator labels "man's deft assertion of his superiority" (303), and the consequence is a marital war in which, as Margaret realizes, "she was fighting for women against men" (290).

The unexpected turns of Forster's plotting, it becomes clear, serve a double signifying function. First, the continual breaking of narrative relation reinforces the theme of failed heterosexual relation. "Cause and effect would go jangling forward to some goal doubtless," Margaret thinks in the aftermath of the events that have separated her from Henry, "but to none that she could imagine" (332). The unpredictability of such a future, however, points to the second function of Forster's narrative technique: continually splintering one's plot not only breaks expected sequences but opens up new and multiple avenues of possible connection. Throughout the text, gleanings of "truer relationship," of "hope on this side of the grave" (103, 206, 330), have marked the epiphanic thresholds of Margaret's journey toward self-knowledge— moments that have occurred as expansions outward and that, significantly, have always involved other women: Mrs. Wilcox, Miss Avery, Helen. The final unexpected "turn" of the plot becomes a vindication of this hope, as the text's severed narrative and human relations are reassembled in the new and visionary regrouping toward which events have been jangling all along: the instatement of matriarchal community at Howards End, in which the reaffirmed sisterhood of Margaret and Helen, presided over by the ghost of the original matriarch, Mrs. Wilcox, is joined by the reformed, now docile Henry, and is granted hope in Helen's illegitimate child (who serves, like Monica's child in *The Odd Women,* as a closural emblem of futurity). These multiple relations replacing the traditional dyad of novelistic heritage, Forster's unconventional community becomes a celebration of the "eternal differences" making up the human "family" (338). It also triumphantly exemplifies Margaret's observation that "one's hope was in the weakness of logic" (339). Indeed, exposing the illogic of the marriage plot has also been Forster's strategy for opening a narrative space in which his vision of future possibility for the sexes and for the entire human race can find expression.

Forster's final scene, with its focus on the unknown future, is matched by the ambiguity concluding the open-ended examinations of marriage in *Mrs. Dalloway* and *Women in Love.* Given the oppositional nature of Clarissa Dalloway's choices (self without passion with Richard, passion without self with Peter), the question of what her marriage has meant remains open to conjecture, like the final image of Clarissa herself: "For there she was." And, in Lawrence's case, even the positive model of marriage with which his text's monumental examination of sexual and marital relationship ends cannot contain the uneasy questionings that have pervaded its double plots. In the final lines of the text, the intensity of Birkin's unsatisfied yearning for a male as well as female companion provokes Ursula's exasperated retort, "You can't have two kinds of love. Why should you!" Birkin's counter-response, "I don't believe that," with which the novel ends, indicates how far this exchange is from being a final word on the subject: the tension hanging fire in the refusal to agree becomes, in effect, the threshold to a yet untold story, the story Lawrence cannot tell.[87] The unfulfilled, nonheterosexual alternatives to wedlock that haunt both of these texts—epitomized in Clarissa's memory of Sally's transfiguring kiss and Birkin's love for the now-dead Gerald—point us to fictional realms where men and women find emotional satisfaction outside of wedlock with members of their own sex.

The titles I have listed above by no means exhaust the list of modern form-breaking representations of uneasy wedlock that could be analyzed within this chapter's framework: Charlotte Perkins Gilman's "The Yellow Wallpaper" (1899), Kate Chopin's *The Awakening* (1899), Zora Neale Hurston's *Their Eyes Were Watching God* (1937), Christina Stead's *The Man Who Loved Children* (1940), Tillie Olsen's "Tell Me a Riddle" (1956), and Doris Lessing's *The Golden Notebook* (1962), among many others. In splendid but different ways, all these texts carry on the counter-traditional task of making their formal innovations a means, in DuPlessis's phrase, of "writing beyond the ending" of the traditional love-plot. That all the writers I have just mentioned are women, moreover, underlines the fact that although men may and do critique marriage with acuity and sensitivity (I would argue that Richardson and James and Forster do so particularly well), the inequities of wedlock have been most frequently dramatized on women's behalf, even when the writer is male, in Anglo-American fiction; because women stand to benefit most immediately from the demystification of a system—and a story—that has worked to the benefit of men at their expense, it also makes sense that more women than men have actively engaged in a revision of the marriage plot.

In the following chapters, we will be looking at some of the additional motivations that may inspire a counter-traditional narrative: in the case of the male quest novel, the impulse to discover worlds without women, and, in the case of the novel of female community, to celebrate worlds (metaphorically) without men. The parenthetical qualification inserted here, however, should stand as a warning that the content of these chapters is not nearly so symmetrical as their twin foci on unmarried protagonists might first suggest. It will pay to remain sensitive to the varying motivations underlying these accounts of male and female separatisms, as well as to their implications for effecting social change.

Certain issues that have dominated, even motivated, the narrative of uneasy wedlock may simply be absent from one or the other of these two modes, given the differing angles of vision and personal investments their protagonists bring to the institution of marriage. The most striking change of focus between this chapter and the next, indeed, is the fact that the quest romance has little to say directly about women's position within the marital order—*the* central issue in the text of uneasy wedlock—because its critique

begins at another point altogether, in the service of its male protagonists' quests for identity. Whether such omissions qualify the
counter-traditional power of such articulations, or simply shift it to
new and different grounds, remains to be seen. Suffice it to say, at
this point, that these texts, being less immediately entangled in the
knots of marital tradition, have found it easier to forego its fictional
conventions; with surprising ease and dexterity they have projected into fictional life a silent minority of men and women who
have always existed outside the strictures of the marriage tradition
and its preordained plots.

Chapter Five

Male Independence and the American Quest Romance as Counter-Traditional Genre

Hidden Sexual Politics in the Male Worlds of *Moby-Dick, Huckleberry Finn, Billy Budd,* and *The Sea Wolf*

> Could I remake me! or set free
> This sexless bound in sex, then plunge
> Deeper than Sappho, in a lunge
> Piercing Pan's paramount mystery!
> For, Nature, in no shallow surge
> Against thee either sex may urge,
> Why hast thou made us but in halves—
> Co-relatives? This makes us slaves.
> If these co-relatives never meet
> Self-hood itself seems incomplete.
>   Herman Melville, "After the Pleasure Party"[1]

> projected romance [is] . . . experience liberated, so to speak;
> experience disengaged, disembroiled, disencumbered,
> exempt from the conditions [of everyday life] that we usually
> know to attach to it.
>   Henry James, Preface to *The American*[2]

As the subject matter of the previous chapter has demonstrated, the most direct way to subvert the ideological values associated with wedlock was to attack the marriage tradition from within; representations of domestic life as unhappy and open-ended exposed the myth of final happiness as, at best, an incomplete truth, a half-told tale. A less direct but equally subversive challenge to courtship and wedlock plotting issued from novelists choosing to depict a wholly different story—that of the single or unattached protagonist existing outside the boundaries of matrimonial definition or familial expectation. We have already seen how one of the less popular truths to emerge from the counter-tradition's focus on deadlocked marriage was that of a sense of self crippled, if not destroyed, by the oppressive gender roles embedded in the conjugal ideal; from Catherine Linton's agonizing descent into schizophrenia to the Ramsays' acceptance of their marital status as half-selves, the conflict between marital and individual identity repeats itself. To avoid this seeming inevitability, the writers addressed in this and the following chapter chose to explore the possibilities of male or female subjectivity attained outside of wedded life and roles—most often a matter of choice and escape for the single male protagonist, one of circumstance and constriction for the unmarried or widowed woman. By definition, such fantasies of freedom have not only worked to expose the dialectic of sexual power underlying social assumptions about identity and gender in marital relationship, but have also demanded alternative modes of expression.

The absence of women, courtship, and marriage in classic American fiction has been a critical commonplace since the 1960 publication of Leslie Fiedler's equally classic *Love and Death in the American Novel*. In truth, however, as recent feminist criticism has reminded us, the canonized text of men-without-women represents a minority tradition deviating from a popular one in which women, courtship, and marriage are very much in evidence. While such critics are correctly wary of any artistic expression that claims an exemption from sexual bias while excluding the representation of women, the status of quest romance as a literature written by and about men does not invariably mean—as we too often assume—that it exclusively valorizes ideological concerns that our culture has designated "masculine" or "patriarchal."[3] Rather, concealed beneath the male-defined exterior of a few important examples of the genre, there exists a fascinating if sometimes ambivalent exploration of sexual politics, including a *potentially* radical critique of the marital norms, restrictive sexual roles, and imbalances of power underlying nineteenth-century American familial and social life. And in such texts, as those of Melville, Twain, and London will variously illustrate, the degree to which such a hidden agenda is present often corresponds to the experimental daring of this "aberrant" narrative mode.

In this regard, Fiedler's explanation of the quest's adversarial relation to its parent tradition, the English novel, is most illuminating. For he sees what he calls the American gothic-romance originating not merely in self-conscious reaction to the formal realism of early English fiction but also in unconscious rebellion against the ethos of sexual polarity pervading the sentimental treatments of love and seduction that had followed in the wake of Richardson's achievement. Transplanted to American soil, this literary ethos of "debased Richardsonism," according to Fiedler, sent the serious American writer scurrying in pursuit of less puerile subject matters and modes—whence the accomplishments of authors ranging from Cooper and Hawthorne to Melville and Twain. Fiedler argues that the mutual bonding of males repeated throughout the American canon thus came into being as an alternative to the antagonistic heterosexual relationships emanating from the novel's "sentimental love religion." However, in tracing the paradigmatic movement of the male quester away from societal structures—including marriage—Fiedler often betrays a biased view of "normal" or "correct" male development, one rooted in the psychoanalytic milieu of America in the 1950s: for, in his eyes, the freedom sought by the male protagonist "on the run" from society *necessarily* constitutes an arrested adolescent avoidance of adult identity and hence of the mature love embodied in marital responsibility.[4] Despite the partial truth of this view when applied, for instance, to such figures as Rip Van Winkle and Natty Bumppo, it does not follow that every unattached or independent quester lacks personal fulfillment—or is caught in a "regressive" homosexual phase of development—simply because he avoids the constraints of patriarchally conceived marriage or traditionally defined manhood.

Indeed, several examples of the quest genre—*Moby-Dick* (1851), *The Adventures of Huckleberry Finn* (1884), *Billy Budd* (c. 1891), and *The Sea Wolf* (1904)—point in a different direction: the quester's linear projection outward from the closed circle of society into undefined geographic and textual space "liberate[s] him," to paraphrase Henry James's definition of American romance, "from the conditions that we usually know to attach to [experience]." And the consequence of that liberation, for a handful of these unconventional protagonists, is the discovery of an affirming, multiform self that has begun to break through the strictures traditionally imposed on male social identity. Thus, the outward voyage to confront the unknown that by definition constitutes quest narrative simultaneously traces an inner journey toward a redefinition, a "remaking," of self that defies, at least partially, social convention and sexual categorization. The lines from Melville's poem "After the Pleasure Party," used as an epigraph to this chapter, eloquently evoke the hidden or unconscious goal of many such quests: "Could I remake me! or set free / This sexless bound in sex . . ." Adopting Melville's terminology, we might say that the yearning to be "set free" from those inner and outer "bound[s] in sex" which threaten to stultify the self leads to a "plunge" into the "mystery" of sexual identity, the psychological terrain of Pan, that is analogous to the physical act of questing itself.

This goal, moreover, helps distinguish the American genre from the archetypal pattern of quest romance described by Northrop Frye. For in the traditional model the mythic wanderer most often returns from his perilous journeys to the world of the known as a culture hero, his discovery of identity serving a *social* good that heals the wasted kingdom.[5] In spirit if not always in reality, the prototypical American quester remains a rebel figure or social out-cast whose true self can only exist *outside* the parameters of his culture, in a "wild zone" analogous to Catherine and Heathcliff's moors in *Wuthering Heights;* unlike the hero of the mythic pattern, he strives not so much for reintegration into society as for rein-tegration of his often fragmented identity, a leveling of the reduc-tively constructed hierarchies of heart and mind as well as those severed "halves" of personality associated in "After the Pleasure Party" with the two sexes:

> Why hast thou made us but in halves . . .
> If these co-relatives never meet
> Self-hood itself seems incomplete.[6]

The following pages will attempt to measure the radical implica-tions—and psychic dangers—of the questing figure's departure from prescribed sexual norms by examining four fantasies of male freedom and escape in which the format's provisional, "unfixed" organization facilitates an unusually probing inquiry into the social and psychological problematic of masculine identity. Instead of un-covering a univocal paean to traditional norms of manhood, we will find inscribed in the trajectories of these specific American quest narratives visions of selfhood and mutual relationship that attempt to break down conventional sexual categorization by breaking through the limiting forms of culture and the conventions of love literature at once. In a sense, the questing vision was ultimately limited by its chosen field of representation; for the decision to forego the world of male–female relations necessarily involved an absence of female reality that, in replicating women's metaphoric invisibility in patriarchy, could be manipulated to support a misogynistic worldview, as we will be seeing in twentieth-century manifestations of the genre. Nonetheless, the early *potential* of the mode was immense, for by presenting the figuratively all-male world as an *imaginative* alternative to existing social and literary constructs, the quest writer—like the solitary Melvillean quester whose removal from society has "led [him] to think untraditionally and independently"—found himself empowered to express in "a bold and nervous lofty language" (*Moby-Dick* 71), perhaps for the first time, a questioning of the dominant sexual order within which he too was trapped.

The male quest in American fiction represents only one branch, of course, of the larger fictional category labeled the "Romance" by early advocates of the form. The quest formula shared with American romance the latter's repudiation of the strictly realistic methods associated with conventional English fiction;[7] but the quest variant went further in also repudiating the love emphases of traditional fiction—an inheritance from which very few general American romancers were exempt, as the stereotypical images of women, high degrees of etherealized eroticism, and reliance upon conventional love-plot mechanisms in writers as diverse as Cooper, Poe, and Hawthorne indicate. The case of Cooper is particularly relevant, since his "romances" of the American wilderness and sea share some affinities with the quest but ultimately diverge in regard to their sexual politics; hence his exclusion from this chapter's grouping of male quest fiction. For despite memories we may have of the Leatherstocking Tales occurring in a "world without women," Cooper's sagas of male bonding are actually shot through with courtship subplots in which the protection of frail maidenhood provides the underlying structure—and offers a clue to the author's true allegiances. Indeed, as Nina Baym has demonstrated, marriage is essential to each of the tales, its function that of validating an essentially conservative social message—and ensuring a

male-regulated society—by imprinting the codes of white civilization on the "virgin" face of the dark wilderness. If *The Last of the
Mohicans* (1826) is the most obvious example of the importance of
women, race, and marriage to Cooper's romances, *The Pathfinder*
(1840) is the most telling. For even as Natty Bumppo forfeits his
chance to marry Mabel Dunham in order to remain a bachelor in a
world of men, he acts in the greater service of the patriarchal
order; since Mabel's father has been suddenly killed, Natty as his
loyal friend must step in as her paternal guardian, and, as Baym
observes, it is in this fatherly role that Natty "hands Mabel over to a
younger suitor, who has been fretting impatiently in the wings
since the opening chapter" and who now steps forward to frame
the courtship action. Inscribed in Cooper's fictional mythos, then,
is an order of homosocial relations between men that, to borrow
from Eve Kosofsky Sedgwick's provocative thesis, depends upon
the real or symbolic presence of women to legitimize those bonds.[8]

The context of the quest narrative poses some significant differences. For the writer of the quest romance, in contrast to the
general romancer, dealt by definition with a world almost totally
devoid of women or heterosexual social regulations, a world in
which the exploration of sea or desert provided a fresh and alternative subject for one wishing to rebel against the thematic strictures
of the literary marriage tradition. Historically, as Frye has demonstrated, the questing hero's physical movement away from civilized
realms, often alone, has made the development of his independent,
singular identity a natural focus, and American adaptations continue this emphasis. What is different—and exciting—about American versions of the quest romance formula is the extent to which the
fair lady who typically figured as the medieval quester's goal or
reward has been displaced by the more metaphysical objects of
truth, absolute reality, the nature of authority, and similar lofty
issues. Implicit in this shift, whether of conscious or unconscious
design, are several very significant factors: first, having less occasion
to promulgate the objectification and idealization of women inherent in most other literatures of the time, the quest skirts the historical perception of woman as man's opposite, leaving the universe
instead to play the antagonistic role of "Other"; second, since the
quester's virility is therefore less dependent on genital than heroic
contact (as Fiedler puts it), his acquisition of adult male identity is

freed from usual connotations of reproductive function and social good in a marital context; and third, the "forward thrust of inquiry, the dynamic assertion of self in a progressive line of exploration" that John Seelye defines as the genre's underlying structural principle theoretically dissociates the mode from the closural constraints that the finality of return-and-marriage, if only as symbol, would impose.[9]

The quester's journey *into* the unknown simultaneously implies an escape *from* the known—that is, the context of nineteenth-century American culture. As we have seen, Fiedler argues that the quest writer's avoidance of themes of passion and marriage was a direct result of his society's extreme degree of sentimentalization and sexual bifurcation. This assumption is corroborated by Ann Douglas's *The Feminization of American Culture,* which analyzes the sentimental myth of absolute connubial love and of the wife's domestic role that took root in early nineteenth-century America and rapidly became *the* middle-class ideal;[10] the pattern is similar to that characterizing the great bourgeois upheaval in England one hundred years before. The difference was in the *extremity* of sex-role division in the States, a fact apparent to English visitors in the 1830s who, like Harriet Martineau, were taken aback by the "persuasion" current in the country "that there are virtues which are peculiarly masculine, and others which are peculiarly feminine."[11] In the years that followed, the more that the growth of capitalism encouraged "masculine" aggression and drive in its fledgling male entrepreneurs, the more society venerated traditional "feminine" values which in turn kept women in their place. This increasingly severe dichotomization of sexual spheres and roles in turn gave rise to a deceptively oppressive myth of female "authority" or "influence" in the home that overran American culture with a vengeance. It is telling that Mrs. Sarah Hale, one of the most vocal proponents of the "influence" theory, admonished her lady readers not to hold back one iota of love from their deserving husbands in nearly the same breath that she also polarized the sexes as "Man the murderer and woman the mourner," and again as "fiend and angel"[12]—terms that make one wonder on what common grounds the twain were ever to meet in felicitous union.

Given the investment of the status quo in maintaining this hierarchical division of the sexes, it is small wonder that the unmarried male, having chosen his independence (for whatever of a variety of reasons) from the "orderly state" of marriage and the blandishments of the supposedly softer sex, came under attack by the moral guardians of society. "Does not your heart become chilled," the hero of the fictionalized tract *Married and Single* (1845) warns his bachelor friend, "at the soul-revolting idea, that all the noble deeds . . . of a Washington would have been lost . . . to the world, if his father had acted the strange, unnatural, criminal part you propose to yourself?"[13] If one turns from the reality of bachelorhood, with its various causes, to fictional representations of single men, an interesting parallel emerges: like his "socially deviant" creator the antirealist writer, the solitary quester-figure was forced into an alien position by virtue of his self-definition;[14] in the eyes of a culture that valued marriage as its highest good, he was foreordained to enact a role "strange, unnatural, criminal"—and, above all, counter-traditional—in abjuring conjugal responsibilities.

If the imaginary quester sought to flee the oppressiveness of this marital ethos, the romance quest writer also sought escape from the seeming sentimental banalities of much popular "women's fiction"—literature generally written by and for women that often served as a tool of socialization into proper "feminine" roles, even as it sometimes subverted patriarchal authority.[15] Jane Tompkins has taught us to refrain from judging these works as artistic failures, but rather to see in their "sensational designs" effective and powerful expressions of a specifically cultural mission—in the case of the domestic text, the attempt to "rearrange culture from a woman's point of view" for woman's benefit.[16] However, as in Mrs. Hale's theory of women's special "influence" as spiritual exemplars, this point of view depended upon a consolidation of female power *within* the already existing structure of the Christian home, hence within marital custom. Thus, the tendency of these sentimental writers to employ pat formulas to convey their deliberately didactic messages of domestic and spiritual bliss hinged on the shared belief, as the novelist Mrs. E. D. E. N. Southworth put it, that the marriage vow was "the most sacred tie on earth," one that if unraveled would imperil "the social welfare of the whole community"[17]—and, Tompkins would add, endanger hopes of attaining the heavenly kingdom that their texts had remade in the maternal image.[18] The premise underlying this image of the sacred tie or knot, as we saw in chapter 1, is the same that the marriage tradition had raised to a theoretical justification of narrative containment. Acting from the ardent belief that they were giving testimony to the fixed order lying behind as well as within this world, domestic women writers coerced, with unabashed fervor, the structural paradigms of courtship, seduction, and marital trials inherited from English love fiction into serving their evangelical aims. Hence, as Herbert Ross Brown explains in the standard work on the sentimental tradition, "the final solution was neatly reserved for the last chapter where the punishment was made to fit the crime, and the reward to equal the virtue. To achieve it, authors subjected the long arm of coincidence to the rack of expediency where it was stretched and fractured to suit every need of the plot."[19] Coincidence-ridden scenarios and plot improbabilities become, in this view, evidence of a larger Providential order. Demonstrating the spiritual worth and influence of the virtuous heroine, these texts may have proved personally empowering for their largely female readership. Nonetheless the *earthly* order within which their heroines moved left unchanged the dichotomization of sexual roles and separate spheres, and the attendant problems of authority and submission, characterizing nineteenth-century patriarchal and sentimental culture. The overwhelming domination of the American fictional market by these single-minded tracts—inspiring Hawthorne's unkind reference to that "damned mob of scribbling women"[20]—could only intensify the sense of exclusion felt by those writers in search of nondomestic, counter-cultural themes and uncontrived forms.

Rather than directly challenge the stereotypes of the sexes promoted by this fictional system and its parent realist tradition, the prototypical romance writer simply abandoned the subject of "realistic" romantic involvement altogether; some romancers like Hawthorne and Poe turned to largely allegorical modes of narration whose dichotomized images of light/dark heroines, in particular, were as "unreal" as those mythologized by sentimental fiction, while the quest writer sidestepped the social and literary problematic of the sexes by imagining worlds without women, hence

ostensibly free of the gendered system creating a sexually bifurcated society. As we have noted, there may be at times a fine line
separating innovative and conservative impulse in the writer's
choice of the quest as narrative subject. By examining *how* the male
world is used, however, whether it gives voice to dominant values,
as in Cooper, or attempts through indirection to give voice to a
hitherto silenced reality and alternative world, as in Melville, we
can begin to filter the wishfully escapist from legitimately progressive variations within the genre. In the latter case, moreover, it
is important to realize that the socially subversive content of the
fiction is, as in much marginalized women's fiction, filtered first
through the private realm of individual desire; rather than con-
fronting the politics of sexuality head-on or in a public context,
such texts often limit their explorations of the impingements of
social and fictive structures of power to the personal level—a focus
nonetheless opening up, for the quest writer, a hitherto unexplored geography of possibility underlying social myths of male
identity and relationship.

A later and contrasting literary context that sheds light on this
aspect of quest narrative is the male adventure story of the frontier
or wild West, with its prototype in Cooper's wilderness tales. Only
superficially resembling the demystification of masculine identity
in the quest romances under investigation in the following pages,
this late-century development actually served the same ideological
function for its male readers as the sentimental treatise did for the
female audience: through its romanticized fantasies of supervirile
heroism and strength, the western novel validated accepted notions
of sexual hierarchy and male authority. Significant in this regard—
and radically at odds with the quest genre—is the fact that the
frontier hero's rough-and-ready adventures are almost always governed by a crude manifestation of the courtship pattern.[21] As we
have also seen in the Leatherstocking Tales, it is the inspiriting
presence of women—as frail vessels to rescue and protect from the
menacing wilderness environment, as signifiers of a civilization
whose values can only be maintained by male prowess—that gives
the frontier novel's hypermasculine ethos its whole point. From
opposing vantage points, then, the western and sentimental genres—along with most "Romance" narrative in general—main-

tained an essentialist myth of sexual dichotomization from which the protagonists of Melville's, Twain's, and London's quest novels attempt to escape.

While these various literary and social contexts help to explain the genesis of the quest format, certain repeating thematic and formal tropes peculiar to the genre attest to the uniqueness of its attempt to reenvision male sexual identity. Paramount among three distinguishing traits that I will mention here is the ever-present male bond in the world of the quest. Fiedler first introduced the concept that the genre's "manly friendships" represent "a kind of counter-matrimony": whence the relationships of Ishmael and Queequeg, Huck and Jim, Van Weyden and Wolf Larsen. As emotional alternative to the conventions and constrictions associated with the social ideal of wedlock, the "pure marriage of males"[22] not only is a practical alternative to loneliness but also facilitates bonds that are deeply committed, even erotic, and yet—unlike hierarchically ordered marriage—not an infringement to either partner's sense of personal freedom. Such a rejection of institutional marriage operates on several levels. At least in theory, the mutuality of gender, it would appear, facilitates a degree of equal interchange and individuality that the dualistic assumptions underlying conventional marital union automatically negate. As a result, these questing comrades often evolve multifaceted relationships that daringly blur the boundaries traditionally separating literary subject and object: their loving bonds simultaneously partake of brotherly, passionate, paternal, filial, even maternal qualities, without being restricted to one role or model alone. Even when the paired questers compose a racial duality—which Fiedler interprets as a symbolic union of the "primitive" or instinctual life and the questing ego[23]—the fact remains, first of all, that such pairings are inherently transgressive rather than conventionally polar, and, second, that the black–white opposition is frequently only "skin-deep," as it were, since the true source maintaining the male bond is its radical mutuality—of spirit, of gender, of democratic fraternity.

To recognize the counter-traditional potential invested in the relations established by these questers, it might be helpful to compare them to the male pairings generally presented in the British literary tradition. For the latter relationships often fall into a recognizable master–servant (and sometimes teacher–pupil) pattern; the " unions" struck between Crusoe and Friday, Pickwick and Sam Weller, Holmes and Watson, Kim and the lama, tend to replicate the more strictly hierarchical order of English society or Empire. Often associated with familiar domestic situations, rather than with journeys into the defamiliarizing reaches of the unknown, such relations generally occur in comedic fictional modes, unless, as in D. H. Lawrence's "The Prussian Officer" (1914), overt homosexual attraction transforms the accepted master–servant hierarchy into a sadomasochistic configuration that ends in tragedy. The division along class lines determining the flow of power within these hierarchical male bonds, moreover, hints at a metaphorically gendered division as well: it is fairly clear who is the "dominant" partner, who the more dutiful "wife," in most of these examples.[24]

As one of the foremost English authors to combine the quest into strange settings with instances of male bonding, Rudyard Kipling provides an especially useful measure of the differences separating English and American manifestations of the theme. For example, in *The Man Who Would Be King* (1899), the bonding of two scurrilous rascals—whose fraternal league is parodied in their status as Masonic "brothers"—inaugurates a fantastic quest for the hidden treasures of Kafiristan. For both men, the quest becomes an act of exploit, conquest, and hence a dream-fantasy of absolute, phallic power, a dream realized in the crowning of one of the "brothers," Dravot, as "King" of the country they discover. The stereotypically "masculine" cast of such a construction of power and desire points us, furthermore, to the misogynistic underpinnings of the bond established between these two men. For their relationship begins with the drawing up of a "contrack" in which they mutually foreswear women and alcohol in the name of the quest: their success, that is, depends on the mandatory exclusion of women. In fact, it is when Dravot decides to take a bride that the dream of unchallenged authority, or kingship, falls apart and the two are expelled from the kingdom. Dravot and Peachy's relation thus at once mirrors and parodies what we might call a patriarchally inscribed fantasy, one in which the homosocial bond becomes a way of escaping the "contamination" of women; Kipling's purpose is neither to redefine masculinity nor to explore a new emotional geography for men's friendships.

In contrast, the boy hero of *Kim* (1901) undergoes a quest of self-discovery that resembles, in some ways, the trajectory that we will be tracing in *The Adventures of Huckleberry Finn*. Like Twain's protagonist, Kim also inhabits multiple (and not specifically "masculine") roles; his white skin as ostensibly brown as an Indian's, Kipling's orphan crosses the boundaries of race with ease in the disguise of a low-caste native. And, like Huck, he is accompanied on his pilgrimage by an older man, the lama, who is on his own quest for a kind of freedom. The end that awaits Kim's quest for identity, however, is worlds removed from Twain's text. Rather than lighting out for the territory in an act of continuing nonconformity (as Huck does), Kim undergoes a discovery of origins that culminates in his assimilation into the white world of masters: with the transformation of native urchin into English sahib, the novella may safely close. Thus the quest format in *Kim* encodes an imperialist tract (Kipling had written "The White Man's Burden" two years earlier), whereby patterns of West and East, dominator and dominated, even "masculine" and "feminine," ultimately reinforce a lesson in maturation in which manhood depends on an assumption of authority over others. It is not irrelevant that the bond between Kim and the lama is entirely de-eroticized; likewise, the desexed teacher–pupil male bond in Kipling's *Captains Courageous* (1897) makes possible, as in *Kim* and *The Man Who Would Be King*, a more purely "boys' adventure" story in which the counter-traditional implications of male bonding in worlds without women can be elided.[25] Contrastingly, we can hypothesize that the less defined class system, the more democratic spirit, the sexual demographics, and the sheer newness of the American nation, its psyche forged in resistance to hierarchy and still undergoing radically destabilizing metamorphoses, all spurred the American quest writer to dream of possibilities between men hitherto unexplored in the more stratified English tradition of male friendship.

The absence of women in the American quest narrative provides a second indication of its untraditional status, although with different repercussions than one might expect. For, although the male quest by definition excludes woman as major protagonist (the second half of London's *The Sea Wolf* will prove an instructive exception), her traces nonetheless resurface in the world of the quest to play a crucial role on various levels of signification: as material representation of the domestic "scene" from which the quester flees, as cosmic symbol and image of life-affirming values traditionally associated with the maternal, as inner principle within the individual male quester, and as external role imposed on weaker or less gender-bound men by repressive figures of authority.[26] As the lines cited from Melville's "After the Pleasure Party" indicate, the quest not only reaches *beyond* for a metaphysical explanation of existence, but may also reach *within* for a psychogenic truth of sexual identity radically at odds with society's constitution of "the feminine" as a specifically female and hence "inferior" category.

Exactly what is meant by incorporating the "feminine" into the male psyche, of course, is not unproblematic, as my previous comments on the term "androgyny" have begun to indicate. Particularly when male writers have promulgated concepts of androgyny, the results, like Jungian theories of the *anima*, have frequently maintained a gynocentric bias by compartmentalizing the "feminine" as an inner, hierarchically secondary "part" of the encompassing "masculine" whole; thus the English Romantics, working within an accepted literary tradition of what might be called male-sanctioned androgyny, often tended to appropriate the so-called "feminine" in ways that simply translated the external polarity of the sexes into a dualistic model of the internal life of the psyche. This kind of male incorporation or appropriation of female "otherness" sidesteps the more radical implications of attempting to envision a male subjectivity for which the "feminine" is never "other" because it is already an intrinsic, integral aspect of a dynamically multiform self.

Something of the latter identification, I will be arguing, can be found at work in *Moby-Dick, Huckleberry Finn,* and *Billy Budd.* All to some extent participate in a dialogue between those expansive selves—like Ishmael, Huck, Billy—whose equanimity rests on an unselfconscious acceptance of the love and compassion traditionally associated with the female sphere of the heart, and those obsessed questers, filled with a will to power that blinds them to this truth. The danger besetting the man who resists traditional "masculine" self-definition is best illustrated in *Billy Budd,* where the hero's "androgynous" attributes are perceived as "feminine" weaknesses to those authorities who fear loss of their male-identified powers and thus force the "handsome sailor" to assume a subordinate role analogous to that of woman's in society. The very existence of such "female-substitute" figures in the quest genre becomes a powerful textual signifier of the oppressiveness and potential destruction associated with an ethos equating power with masculinity.

A third distinguishing trait of the American male quest—noted by Chase, Brodhead, Seelye, and others—is its unique narrative structure. What has gone unmentioned, however, is the degree to which the mode's textual organization, in replicating the quester's search for unboundaried male self-definition, evolved as an important correlative of the counter-traditional thematic potential outlined above. In essence, the rejection of restrictive cultural formats, triggering the protagonist's desire to escape society, simultaneously operates as a rejection of the concept of stable narrative centers; that is, the forward movement of the quest into unknown *geographic* space is so orchestrated as to create a linear projection into undefined *textual* space. Instead of a symmetrically unified pattern based on conflict, separation, and resolution, the structural organization of the quest novel is characterized by an open series of often jarring or startling narrative expansions and transformations. Related to Romantic theories of the organically proliferating text, the quest narrative thus has an effect of having been already always in process, of forever reaching after new and unexpected plateaus of meaning. Like the voyage of the Pequod in *Moby-Dick*, its trajectory seems to move in two directions at once, "one to mount direct to heaven, the other to drive yawingly to some horizontal goal" (200). And as Richard Brodhead has demonstrated, this effect is often achieved by the linking together of disparate representational modes of fiction, so that the reader gains the sense not merely of several types of narrative strung together, but of one mode after the other being left behind, traveled beyond, as the evolving quest carries both reader and protagonist into increasingly uncharted and heteroglossic realms of discourse and plot.[27] These transitions from one mode of narrative to the next are often marked by threshold moments that serve as springboards from which the narrative, like the quest itself, launches forward into the unknown, or by symbolic moments of rebirth that propel the protagonist into new contexts and new identities. Nothing is certain about where the direction will next move, except that there will be no regression, no real return to the familiar. As such, the narrative rhythm in itself begins to map out a counter-traditional geography of male desire in fictional form.

Typically accompanying these shifts in mode are abrupt refocusings of perspective, exemplified by the much discussed movement in *Moby-Dick* from Ishmael's narrating voice to omnisciently narrated scenes to which he has no access. This process of juxtaposing voices and viewpoints is not simply authorial idiosyncrasy or pyrotechnical display; more importantly, the technique reenacts a process happening on the psychological level as the hero's identity undergoes successive expansions toward an ideally inclusive openness. The result is an altered mode of characterization that cannot be subjected to the kind of developmental reading appropriate to a traditional bildungsroman; as "voices" and subjects of their texts' ever-shifting registers, Ishmael and Huck, for example, are both consistent and inconsistent, mature and immature, assuming a multitude of functions that, however contradictory in a dominantly realistic mode, here attest to a construction of personality that embraces the fullness of contradiction and difference. The representational and perspectival strategies structuring the quest thus function in concert with its thematic content; its innovative format embodies both the quester's fantasized escape from restrictive sexual convention and his subsequent expansion into a multiform sense of self. In the process, as the following examples of *Moby-Dick, Huckleberry Finn, Billy Budd,* and *The Sea Wolf* will show, the movement of the quest forms an emphatic rejection of the narrative stability and fortuitously merging plot lines associated with much nineteenth-century fiction and with the love-plot in particular.

·*Moby-Dick*·
The Great American Love Story

Although mention of Melville usually conjures up images of harpoons rather than marriage (a suggestive juxtaposition in itself, as we shall see), a major theme in his work concerns the sexual polarity that can render wedlock a life-denying prison and selfhood a state of inner fragmentation. This critique of wedlock ranges from the broadly satiric, as in the classic battle of the sexes enacted by the native couple Samoa and Anatoo in *Mardi,* to the truly disturbing tale of marital warfare in "I and My Chimney," the story of a husband threatened by the loss of his male-identified superiority. "If the doctrine be true that in wedlock contraries attract, by how cogent a fatality must I have been drawn to my wife!" he laments in a statement foreshadowing the stalemate that closes his narration, as he vows that he and his old-fashioned, phallic chimney, which his wife wants to remove from the house, "will never surrender" to "female jurisdiction."[28] Whatever the relation of these disquieting portraits to Melville's own ambivalent experience of wedlock, his fiction often offers for our analysis a grim picture of the married state as a battleground upon which, given conventional attitudes, there is little hope for peaceful resolution.[29] At the same time, his novels and stories stage an unremitting attack on stultifying fictional conventions, including those constraints on form inherited from the literary marriage tradition. The would-be writer and title character in *Pierre: or, The Ambiguities* acknowledges precisely these strictures when faced with the "unravel[ing] plot" of Isabel's past: "By infallible presentiment he saw, that not always doth life's beginning gloom conclude in gladness[,] that wedding-bells peal not ever in the last scene of life's fifth act," and that life's narratives "have no proper endings."[30]

Melville's evolution of the male quest narrative can be seen as a defiant response to these concerns: his strategic reformulation of the quest romance genre gave him a public forum from which he could engage in a sustained attack on the sentimental literary ideology that countenanced an unbridgeable separation of male and female roles, powers, and spheres, and from which he could express, in turn, his opposing personal vision of vital male identity. In Melville's world of quest, in fact, individual masculine authenticity depends on the effort to reconcile such false dualities, resulting in an ideal given concrete if brief representation in the avatars of the Handsome Sailor prototype that recur throughout the canon; these men (Marnoo of *Typee,* Jack Chase of *White-Jacket,* Billy Budd) are most notable for a striking combination of masculine and feminine beauty that comes to represent a psychic equilibrium within.[31] But it is in *Moby-Dick* (1851), the prototypical quest narrative, that Melville most allusively and deeply explores the psycho-sexual connection between male subjectivity and an acknowledgment of the symbolically "feminine" in man; in the process the issue of sexual identity becomes an inseparable part of the text's subject matter and narrative form. The result is a completely different mode of "love story," one in which unending quest (as pursued by Ishmael) rather than ultimate conquest (Ahab's goal) comes to define the independent self and its relationship to others.

I

Despite its lack of heterosexual romance, *Moby-Dick* exudes a powerful erotic energy that is manifested in a complex network of sexual innuendo, imagery, and mythic allusion.[32] Ever since D. H. Lawrence's identification of the White Whale as the great American phallus, numerous psychoanalytic readings have focused on the battle of Moby Dick and Ahab as an expression of the aggressive male libido. This narrow focus, however, has often tended to neglect the equally powerful symbolic significance with which Melville imbues nonphallic and female-related imagery throughout the text.[33] For example, the purportedly phallic whale is actually evoked in terms suggesting a paradoxical union of masculine and feminine principles; its deadly forehead, which may first seem a personification of masculine aggressive force, conceals an inner sanctum of femininely figured sweetness (284–85), and the dangerous "power" and "might" of its opposite anatomical member, the tail, is mitigated by its undulating grace and delicate beauty (315–16). Sea and sky, moreover, the encompassing universe of the novel, are figured in a suggestively titled chapter ("The Symphony") as a primordial wedding of "hardly separable" (442) elements iconographically represented as male and female. Nothing, including the erotic dynamic of narrative driving this story, is simply one thing or the other.

What might thus be called the polymorphous life force at work in the natural and linguistic worlds of this text becomes an especially evocative backdrop for Melville's dramatization of a similar state existing in human nature. Such a condition is best epitomized in the sporadic glimpses we are given into the narrating personality of Ishmael, who, like his biblical namesake, wanders as an exile and outcast on the margins of society; a metaphoric child of the "wild zone," he alone of the crew of the Pequod, appropriately enough, progresses toward an unbound identity that is always in motion, never fixed by conventional rules or social roles. For on a psychic level Melville figures the goal of Ishmael's inner quest as an inner resilience that can withstand the assaults of external circumstance while maintaining the "rarer virtue of interior spaciousness" (261).[34] And this elasticity, this inclusive expansiveness, is exactly the quality that Ishmael's textual presence and narrating voice will affirm time and again: it can be seen in his incorporation of contradictory viewpoints and his admission of the relativity of truth; it characterizes his passive acceptance of ultimate mystery yet active commitment to questioning (and questing); it allows room for both his transcendental flights of fancy and self-deprecating bouts of skepticism. Importantly, it also motivates the incredible succession of symbolic rebirths he undergoes from one end of the novel to the other: under Queequeg's influence, noted below, Ishmael experiences his first rebirth; after being lost and found at sea he will claim, "I survived myself" (195); a metaphoric birth from the whale skeleton-turned-temple in the Bower of the Arcasides episode is signaled in the words, "I emerged" (375); and, as we shall see, the death-dealing catastrophe ending his journey aboard the Pequod becomes the occasion for a final rebirth at novel's end: "One did survive . . . and I was he" (470). By lining up the clues scattered throughout the text's piecemeal characterization of Ishmael, one can begin to infer the extent to which the "polymorphous" elements of his life-affirming, flexible personality mirror the narrative's ongoing redefinition of the normative boundaries of masculinity and relationship.

Melville indeed opens his text with a paradigm of the means to a self-sustaining, counter-traditional identity in the extended vignette of Ishmael's developing relation to his New Bedford bed-companion, Queequeg, who himself is a model of independent wholeness, "content in his own companionship, always equal to himself" (52). Ishmael, in contrast, begins his narrative in a state of self-division, a "damp, drizzly November in [his] soul" (12), as the famous mock-suicidal opening of chapter 1 reveals. Under the restorative influence of the self-possessed and loving South Sea Islander, however, he soon undergoes a "melting in me" that heals his "splintered heart" (53). Thus the male bond opens the way to an undivided identity, once Ishmael learns to overcome his initial prejudices and recognize in this seemingly racial "other" a mutual companion, an equal spirit, and an equivalent, mirroring self. And because this bond ultimately rests on equality and a mutual recognition of independent identities, it encodes, as Baym has observed, a set of values directly "opposite . . . the usual female–male association";[35] it affirms one's individuality without halving it.

Furthermore, Melville's repeated references to the "heart's honeymoon" (54) shared by these two "Bosom Friends" (the title of chapter 10) as a kind of mock-marriage italicize the degree to which it is presented as a positive alternative to the conventional wedlock ideal. "You had almost thought I had been his wife" (32), Ishmael exclaims upon awakening in Queequeg's affectionate embrace, an action carried to its logical extreme in chapter 10 when Queequeg "pressed his forehead against mine, clasped me round the waist, and said that henceforth we were married" (53). Thus the parodic use of connubial imagery and sentimental love language, coupled with Ishmael's admission that Queequeg, despite his apparent "savage" otherness, is his spiritual equal, works to undermine the concepts of sexual polarity and hierarchy embedded in popular definitions of romance. Additionally, although this "pure marriage of males," in Fiedler's phrase, may ostensibly be sexless (hence "pure"), and thus different from heterosexual marriages, its representation is also undeniably eroticized by Melville in its own right. In effect, the homoeroticism of the men's physical intimacy serves a function parallel to the linguistic parody transpiring simultaneously: it taunts societal and sexual norms of respectability in order to suggest that the only means of achieving an independent, questing identity is through the rejection of convention.[36] Ishmael sums up the counter-traditional significance of such a stance when he identifies his bond with Queequeg, in an offhand comment, as a relationship in which "those old rules would not apply" (53).

Exactly *what* the male bond helps to unite within Ishmael is given further representation several hundred pages later in the "Grand Armada" chapter, which, as many critics have noted, presents an externalized version of the internal union already prefigured in Ishmael's bonding with Queequeg.[37] For as his whaleboat inadvertently penetrates to the "innermost heart of [a] shoal" of gallied whales (324), the young man has a revelation of the sources abiding at the secret heart, the center, of life. Within this circle of "enchanted calm," the boat is visited by sporting "cowes and calves[,] the women and children of this routed host" (324); in the translucent "watery vaults" below the craft there unfolds a "still stranger world" of "nursing mothers" (325) and of "young Leviathan amours in the deep" (326). What makes this glimpse of maternally figured love and the life processes so overpowering is Ishmael's immediate recognition of an analogous state existing within himself at this very moment: "And thus . . . did these inscrutable creatures at the centre freely and fearlessly indulge in all peaceful concernments; yea, serenely revelled in dalliance and delight. But even so, amid the tornadoed Atlantic of my being, do I myself still for ever centrally disport in mute calm . . . deep down and deep inland there I still bathe me in eternal mildness of joy" (326). In finding this vast realm of human potential "deep down and deep inland" (326), Ishmael embraces as *intrinsic* and unthreatening aspects of his own adult male identity those "rarer" virtues of "interior spaciousness"—love, peace, mildness—traditionally labeled as feminine although not exclusive to either sex; his discovery entails an identification with and passive acceptance of something that is *real* in his own being. This state of mind is far from being a simple expression of an infantile desire to return to the womb, and it is qualitatively different, I would suggest, from the male psyche's incorporation of the "feminine" in traditional literary representations. In Ishmael's case, rather, there is nothing to be incorporated or appropriated; the "feminine" values he discovers "at the centre" of his being have never been "other" but have always been part of his very sense of self.

Although the actual moment passes as the herd of whales disperses, its interiorized vision of love echoes throughout the rest of the novel, perhaps most vividly dramatized as external possibility in the famous "A Squeeze of the Hand" chapter. In this simultaneously rhapsodic and comic scene, where the crew lovingly joins hands while squeezing whale casing or sperm, the inner "mildness of joy" experienced in the Armada becomes a joyous embrace of all fellow men.[38] The male bond of two equivalent selves celebrated at the Spouter Inn is thus transformed into a communal principle of fraternal democracy shared among several dozen men. Yet pointedly enough, as Chase and Shulman note, despite its patriotic echoes this ideal of loving community exists *outside* the "settled social order," because its literally all-male constituency necessarily forms a "radically unorthodox alternative" to societal—and specifically marital—norms.[39] In this regard the deliberate eroticism that envelops the act of squeezing "sperm" (seen by some critics as homoerotic, by others as autoerotic), like Ishmael and Queequeg's "marriage," not only forms a sly joke on literary-social standards of decorum but also accentuates the essential *nonconformity* of a fantasy of society based on equality and brotherly love rather than on sexual hierarchy.

The degree to which Ishmael's always expanding identity depends upon his unquestioning acceptance of the "maternal" or "feminine" within himself is also central to the narrative's conclusion. It is the Rachel, after all, the loving mother "in her retracing search after her missing children" (470), that reclaims Ishmael from the wreck of the Pequod, just as it is Queequeg's coffin, which Fiedler calls a surrogate for Ishmael's lover/companion, that springs from the womblike vortex caused by the sinking ship to float Ishmael to the safety of this mother's embrace.[40] In this penultimate image of rebirth, Ishmael undergoes yet one more expansion of self as he survives to tell the tale. His salvation, however, is neither fixed nor permanently secured, like that of a traditional hero, at the novel's end. It will rather depend on a continuing series of "rebirths" into progressively new worlds: selfhood is realized, paradoxically, in the perpetual act of questing for it. Ishmael's diffusive textual presence and voice have reaffirmed this truth time and again, suggesting in the process his capacity for transcending socially prescribed labels and for championing a revisionary definition of his autonomous subjectivity as a man. Melville's text, it is true, never tests this ideal in a world of men and women, but within a world of men, at least, it triumphs.

II

Of course, as every reader knows, the quest for selfhood in *Moby-Dick* does not only unfold by positive example. The encompassing, fluid identity toward which Ishmael is always moving is continually counter-balanced by Ahab's rigid self-definition, as the latter character's tragically fixed purpose and fixated personality attest. Having concentrated all his energies, both emotional and libidinal, into one singularly aggressive goal, Ahab becomes the stereotype of the destructive "male" impulse, his "deepeningly contracted" (161) personality recalling the single-minded determination fueling Lovelace and Heathcliff's acts of female persecution in *Clarissa* and *Wuthering Heights;* all three men, along with *Deronda*'s Grandcourt, are obsessed by varieties of erotic domination as the only means of asserting their superiority in a world in which their identity as men depends on being recognized as separate from and above any threatening "other." In the process, Melville's mad captain has replaced the potential for human relations of love and parity with violent thrusts against an imagined foe. The aim of "quest," thus perverted by Ahab's "narrow-flowing monomania" (161), has become, simply, one of "conquest"—a conquest as sexually charged and as self-destructive as if the arena in which it were taking place were indeed that of patriarchal marriage.

Ahab's defiant posturing specifically reveals the self-hatred that is unleashed against others when the softening influences associated with the heart, the soul, the emotions, are lost to human nature. Thus, in a speech in chapter 38 that identifies the soul's gender as female, Ahab's first mate mourns that "small touch of the human mother" and "soft feeling of the human" which he feels that Ahab, through his assumption of absolute mastery, has "overmanned" both in himself and in his crew (148); a few chapters later the reader is made privy to Ahab's nightmare-ridden sleep when this very "soul" attempts to escape the "integral" of which it is part (175), an action metaphorically leaving Ahab a divided man. The incompletion that results from the triumph of will over feeling is also figured in the symbolic castration that occurs (in the narrative time prior to the novel's opening) when Ahab loses his leg in combat with Moby Dick. On the one hand precipitating the Captain's obsession with besting the whale, this loss of limb on the other ironically reveals that the aggressive ethos to which Ahab clings is his own worst enemy. For, before sailing on the Pequod, Ahab is found unconscious one night, "his ivory limb having been so violently displaced, that it had . . . all but pierced his groin" (385).[41] The implication is clear: the aggressive behavior fostered by a culture's phallocentricism is self-destructive, rendering one psychically and physically impotent—and, hence, like Ahab, incapable of initiating positive human contact.

The degree to which the values of hatred and tumult finally supplant in Ahab those of love and inner calm embraced by Ishmael reaches a narrative climax rife with sexual implications when Ahab declares his satanic allegiance and "right worship" to "my fiery father" and rejects the power of the mother ("my sweet mother, I know not") during the terrifying storm-at-sea episode near the end of the novel (416–17). As he establishes his supremacy by waving a lightning-lit harpoon—snatched from the "conspicuous crotch" (417) of his whaleboat and discharging "a levelled flame of pale, forked fire" (418)—over the heads of his terrified crew, it is obvious that phallic power has become satanic, an event clinching the psychic pattern of resemblances between Ahab and his English counterparts in "masculine" diabolism—Lovelace, Heathcliff, and Grandcourt.[42] It should come as no surprise, then, that soon afterward in the "Symphony" chapter Ahab once again rejects the momentarily softening emotions coaxed to life within him by the surrounding environment, his "hardened" resolve resurfacing "against all natural loving" (445). By the time the climactic three-day chase begins, Ahab's identity has become more contracted than ever, impervious to change or emotion—the man has become a nightmarish embodiment of the erotic compulsion to subjugate lying behind the traditional male ethos that makes heroes of conquerors and uses power to maintain its supremacy in a gender-divided world.

Ahab's external relationships, like Ishmael's, reveal much about his inner state of being. The consequences of his only two intimate bonds (with his crazed double, the cabin boy Pip, and the mysterious Parsee, Fedallah) are presented in two tellingly juxtaposed sequences in chapters 129 and 130. Pip's schizophrenia, the result of having internalized fears of displaying unmanly cowardice when abandoned during a sea chase, awakens Ahab's long-dormant compassion, and the captain's offer to make his cabin Pip's "home" is a symbolic drawing together, a momentary act of union, signaling his unconscious recognition that Pip's presence evokes a missing part of his own identity. But the very feelings awakened by Pip lead the captain to sever the bond because "there is that in thee, poor lad, which I feel too curing to my malady . . . and for this hunt, my malady becomes my most desired health" (430). In contrast to the healing that Queequeg's similarly generous love brings to Ishmael's splintered heart, Ahab's diseased drive for conquest demands the expulsion of the weaker or unmanly impulse of love that Pip's presence has inspired in him. The price of Ahab's decision, however, as Pip's reply makes clear, is a denial of wholeness. "Ye have not a whole body, sir," the boy declares in one of his madly true statements that reflects on Ahab's psychic well-being as much as his physical body; "I ask no more [than that] I remain a part of ye" (436). In the immediately following chapter, Ahab's evil alter ego, the shadow-figure Fedallah, comes to the fore as his rightful mate in an antagonistic dance of polar opposites in which, at first glance, Ahab appears as the "lord . . . [and] the Parsee but his slave" (439), but in which Fedallah has actually gained ascendancy over Ahab's will. Fearful of the truth lying in the adage that "like cures like" (430), Ahab turns from Pip's benign influence to an imprisoning bond that ironically reproduces the paradigm of love relationship as a struggle of opposites, and in so doing dooms himself to a fight to the death.

III

It is part of the unfolding nature of Melville's multivalent and shifting allegory that the contrast between Ishmael's acquisition of an open perspective that might be called androgynous and Ahab's imprisonment within a limited role only surfaces in bits and pieces; their characters are never frozen into absolute antitheses but emerge through the dynamic and dramatic interchanges within the narrative itself. The result, nonetheless, is a powerful critique of the male ethos ruling American society, one that is extended, to a significant degree, by Melville's unconventional manipulation of formal structure throughout *Moby-Dick*. In defining the quester's pursuit of "open independence" as a rejection of the finality of port or harbor, the "safety" of home or hearthstone (97), Melville suggests the manner in which the very trajectory of his text, a linear projection into the unknown, breaks not only from the closed world of shore values but also from the self-contained design and narrative ends of classic prose fiction. But the structure of this quest narrative is not linear in a simply descriptive fashion. As Brodhead has perceived, the novel's sense of irrevocable forward motion results from the strategic arrangement of a series of continually transforming narrative modes and extending perspectival structures.[43] As a result, the reader's sensation of traveling through and beyond a succession of texts and superimposed views of reality replicates that of the quester plunging into the unknown in search of a new identity.

The tendency of the narrative to "take off" into the unknown is promoted on several technical levels: it typifies the "tendency . . . for facts, events, and images," as Walter Bezanson has shown, "to become [multivalent] symbols";[44] it characterizes the mode by which discrete sentences, paragraphs, and chapters trigger metaphysical flights of imagination; and it governs entire developmental sequences of action and information. Thus, the predominantly comedic mode of the initial shore chapters, climaxing in the "marriage" of Ishmael and Queequeg, gives way to a new form and a new realm, that of supernatural romance, as the Pequod launches its mysterious quest into the "lone Atlantic" (p. 97). The world of romance is in turn interrupted and extended by a variety of representational modes—stage-drama, monologues, Montaigne-like essays, interpolated tales, and more—whose shifts in format are accompanied by modulations in points of view. This organicism engenders an expansive textuality appropriate to the recording of Ishmael's growth toward inclusive, unlimited identity; for his chameleon shifts of tone, style, and role—matching and accommodating these various structural modulations—attest to what Brodhead calls a "mazy dance of mind" capable of activating "a whole range of emotional, intellectual, and imaginative potentials within."[45] Structure, in effect, becomes as instrumental as characterization in conferring on Ishmael an identity that breaks from traditionally static norms.

The open pattern that Ishmael comes to view as more true to life and to the human personality ("There is no steady unretracing progress in this life; we do not advance through fixed gradations, and at the last one pause," he states in a famous passage [406]) also becomes descriptive of Melville's textual enterprise; through Ishmael's narrating voice he constantly emphasizes the openness of a narrative technique that "promise[s] nothing complete" (118) or final. In juxtaposition to Ahab's enunciation of his madly fixed purpose in chapter 44, Ishmael declares at the beginning of chapter 45 that his own direction as narrator will be determined by impression and indirection rather than straightforward movement, and he thus voices an aesthetic credo that corresponds to the inconclusive openness of his own personality: "I care not to perform my task methodically" (175).[46] Nothing could be more removed from Ahab's desire for absolute finality—an "end" ironically attained when the captain's corpse, tied forever in deathly "reunion" to his undefeated antagonist, the White Whale, sinks into the depths of the mystery that Ahab could never fathom alive.

Although the literal action of the hunt thus draws to a close, it is significant that the novel's meaning remains deliberately open. The final lines before the Epilogue signal this inconclusiveness as linear time itself "collapse[s]" and as "the great shroud of the sea," covering the Pequod and thus obliterating traces of Ahab's aggressive assault, returns to a primordial, undifferentiated world (already heralded in "The Symphony") in which the sea "roll[s] on as it rolled five thousand years ago" (469). The open mystery of the whale, moreover, is recapitulated in the openness concluding Ishmael's story. His symbolic rebirth and rescue from the wreckage of the Pequod ("one did survive the wreck . . . and I was he" [470]), reactivating the continuing possibilities of self-discovery, moves Ishmael toward an open future and unknown point in time from which he narrates the Epilogue. The "portrait" of Ishmael, therefore, resists a final framing, just as his identity has to this point escaped restrictive definitions of "masculine" behavior. Melville's break from fictional tradition in evolving the quest narrative, it becomes clear, has helped give voice to an imaginative vision and an alternative version of male reality that eludes the impositions of social and sexual conformity.

·The Adventures of Huckleberry Finn·
Searching for a Male Eden

Variations on the interfused themes of autonomous selfhood, less constricting gender roles, and counter-traditional male bonds also figure prominently in the voyage of self-discovery charted by Mark Twain in *The Adventures of Huckleberry Finn* (1884). A paradoxical man, forever attempting to straddle several worlds at once, Twain in his domestic life seems at first glance the prototype of Victorian sentimentality, extolling his wife's restraining influence and preaching the sanctity of marriage as a regaining of the heavenly paradise.[47] In truth, however, as much of his better fiction betrays, Twain's imagination insistently turned to the boys' world of childhood as the true, lost Eden for which neither marriage nor modern life could compensate. The deceptive simplicity of this shift from the literary ideal of marriage to an ideal of childhood has worked both in its time and our own to disguise the intensity of the subversions, both conscious and unconscious, that underlie this beguiling yet horrifying text. The degree to which Twain's "innocent" account of "boyhood" actually undermines the status quo has been thoroughly analyzed in terms of nineteenth-century racist beliefs and politics; Huck's quest through the contrasting worlds of shore and river provides a devastating commentary on the confrontation between enslavement and freedom in American life, race, and culture. Huck's unending search, however, is also a response to another facet of his society's bankrupt structure of power: its bifurcated sexual ethos and sexual stereotypes that impede self-expression. In rejecting the shore world's negative models of masculine aggression and feminine piety alike, Huck pursues an elusive independence of self, rooted in an ethos of compassionate love, that runs counter to traditional social, sexual, and familial hierarchies. Above all else, it is Huck's loving relationship with the slave, Jim, that measures his status as a cultural misfit and his unretraceable deviation from a traditional standard of manhood.

As the traces of incomprehension and prejudice that recur throughout Huck's textual representation suggest, his transformation into an exemplar of ideal independence is never complete, and this is of course part of the point. But, in contrast to a world enslaved to custom, Huck shares with Ishmael an innate flexibility and receptivity in face of the unknown that is ultimately saving. The multiple roles, identities, and fabricated biographies he invents during the course of his quest give him the figurative space within which to develop a more complete sense of self.[48] When Mrs. Loftis discovers he isn't "Sarah Williams," Huck becomes "George Peters," and when that fails, "Sarah Mary Williams George Alexander Peters";[49] in the raftsmen passage he proclaims himself the "Charles William Albright" of Ed's ghost tale, then admits he is "really" only "Alex James Hopkins" (240). The Grangerfords know him as "George

Jackson," he parades as the English valet "Adolphus" in the Wilks home, and Tom's rescue scheme calls for him again to impersonate a woman as the "yaller" servant-girl (210). Whereas the disguises donned by the charlatan Duke and Dauphin simply make clear their parasitic relationship to society, Huck's sometimes facile, sometimes uneasy, movement among multiple identities attests to his desire for freedom from *all* fixed roles: whether or not his masks succeed, he is ever willing to transgress boundaries of class, race, and sex in order to follow the path of his desires.

Like a younger Ishmael, Huck also undergoes a series of symbolic deaths and rebirths that, analogous to the various identities he assumes, illustrate his continually expanding personality. From the staging of his own "death" as an escape from Pap in chapter 7 to his reincarnation as "Tom Sawyer" in chapter 32 ("for it was like being born again, I was so glad to find out who I was" [177]), Huck's various avatars imply an unending evolution away from fixity toward an integral aliveness. These rebirths, not coincidentally, mark progressive stages in the novel's structure, for its organization is predicated upon a series of modal and tonal shifts tracing Huck's geographic, then psychological, removal from societal structures that impede personal development.

The two initial stages of Huck's removal from the known define sentimental repression and brute force as the seemingly dual sources of his oppression, only to reveal that both are part of the same institutionalized system of American patriarchy. In an opening self-consciously represented as an organic extension of the child's novel, *The Adventures of Tom Sawyer* (1876), Huck finds himself trapped in the "feminized" world, to borrow Ann Douglas's phrase, of the Widow Douglas and Miss Watson, "respectable" women who ply the tools of conventional morality and religious piety in an attempt to sanitize the boy's rebellious strain and thereby "fix" him within a norm of childhood predictability. The internal bifurcation between private and public realms that domestic "sivilization" creates in Huck can be measured in his only escape from the daytime world of decorum—his nocturnal participation in Tom Sawyer's unreal and childish fictions of adventure.[50] The imaginary terrors of Tom's games become very real, however, with Pap's kidnaping of Huck, which inaugurates a new stage in the evolving narrative. Accordingly, the novel shifts from the genre of adolescent escape fiction to that of backwards melodrama. Imprisoned in the cabin in the woods at one remove from the decorous social order of St. Petersburg, Huck finds himself once again psychologically circumscribed—now by stupidly "masculine" force rather than "feminine" threats of conscience. But in both cases the power structure sanctioning Huck's oppression remains the same. For, antisocial as Pap may seem, he shares with the Widow Douglas a belief in familial and social hierachy that justifies his parental brutality as well as his racial bigotry.

Staging his "death" to escape Pap's tyranny, the "reborn" Huck begins an odyssey—first to Jackson Island, then down-river with the runaway Jim—that initiates yet another mode of narrative, the quest proper. The diametric opposition between Huck's values and the world he is attempting to elude becomes the text's basic structural principle from this point to the end of the river voyage in chapter 31. For the geographically linear projection of the quest is periodically interrupted by digressive shore episodes and picaresque adventures that expose, time and again, the cooperation of patriarchal and sentimental norms in corrupting American culture: the feud waged by the Grangerford-Shepherdson men, for example, exposes the meaningless aggression inherent in Southern patriarchy, while their womenfolk illustrate lives of domestic triviality; the corrupt Duke and Dauphin exemplify the ominous power that resides in self-conscious manipulation of the social forms upon which their existence nonetheless depends; the Pokeville revival scheme, like Peter Wilks's funeral, ridicules the sentimental piety of the indiscriminately sobbing crowd which can just as easily become the senseless mob howling for blood and vengeance, as in the Colonel Sherburne incident.

Juxtaposed with the power of oppression, however, is the potential power of love residing in the river idyll itself, an wishful oasis of freedom to which Huck repeatedly returns after his disastrous adventures on shore.[51] As the one constant element in the fluid down-river movement, the raft comes to represent a more stable concept of "home" than its sentimentalized Victorian counterpart: "We said there warn't no home like a raft, after all," Huck comments upon escaping the gruesome aftermath of the Grangerford-Shepherdson family feud, happy to feel "free and safe once more" (95–96). The freedom momentarily grasped from restrictive social codes and identities is symbolized in the companions' shucking of the clothes of society for naked ease; as Huck later observes of one of the Dauphin's disguises, "I never knowed how clothes could change a body before" (127).

And if this momentary paradise comprises an unconventional definition of home, its two members form an equally counter-traditional example of "family," constructed as it is of two races and one sex. Similar to the bond shared by Ishmael and Queequeg, Huck and Jim's attachment is forged in a mutuality of spirit that, over time, becomes genuine, reciprocal, and nonpossessive: as such it at least partially transcends the hierarchies defining the relation of man and wife, parent and child, white and black, in American society. If Huck's identity cannot be fitted to one role, neither does this bond conform to a single need; rather it simultaneously embodies multiple dimensions. Fiedler rightly observes of this "counter-marriage of males" that "Jim is all things to [Huck]: father and mother and playmate and beloved, appearing naked and begowned and bewhiskered . . . and calling Huck by names appropriate to their multiform relationship: 'Huck' or 'honey' or 'chile' or 'boss,' and just once 'white genleman.'"[52] In other words, Jim is about all a loving mate can be, *yet also himself:* as he pronounces early in the novel, "I owns myself" (42), his words calling to mind the self-possession of Queequeg, "always equal to himself" (*Moby-Dick* 52). Thus, in sharing with Huck a mutual companionship, Jim also provides the boy with a model of the independent integrity that is the ideal goal of the quest.

For in Twain as in Melville the path to individuality lies through heartfelt compassion, and the stages by which Huck discovers the worth of his attachment to Jim simultaneously chart his progress towards a nonconforming identity that depends on *not* being "man enough" (75) to participate in society's legalized structures of oppression. Such an epiphany characterizes the river episode of chapter 16 in which Huck proves his loyalty to Jim (whom he shamefully realizes he has earlier abused) by lying to a group of slave hunters about the race of his raft companion.[53] The terminology used to express this snap decision suggests the unconscious extent to which Huck's nonconformity has at this moment become a disavowal of traditional norms of masculinity: *"I warn't man enough*—hadn't the spunk of a rabbit. I see *I was weakening;* so I just give up trying, and up and says—'He's white'" (75; emphasis added). A "real man," one infers, doesn't save "niggers" and thereby jeopardize the hierarchy upon which his own superiority rests. Likewise, Huck's famous decision in chapter 31 to "go to hell" rather than "pray a lie" comes as the result of being overwhelmed by a series of memories of his and Jim's idyllic and naked life together, memories that figuratively "unman" the boy: "somehow I couldn't seem to strike no places *to harden me* against [Jim]" (169; emphasis added). Again, Huck's growth toward nonconforming identity simultaneously involves a rejection of traditional masculine associations (strength, hardness) and an awareness of the subversive depth of his love for Jim. Both chapters 16 and 31 have been recognized as pivotal turning points in Huck's education into the duplicitous morality of a racially oppressive society; what also needs to be emphasized is the degree to which the very language encoding these explicit critiques of racial inequality calls forth an implicit critique of the sexual ethos abetting such a social norm.

What, then, many critics have asked, happens to Huck's gains in self-knowledge in the final escapades at Phelps Farm? In stepping off the raft in chapter 31, Huck walks into another novel—one authored, in a figurative sense, by Tom Sawyer—and accordingly his character seems to transform dramatically as he becomes a passive accomplice in Tom's sadistic rescue schemes to "free" Jim from his captivity at the Phelps's. The widespread criticism that this change in action and neglect of Huck's prior development are moral "evasions" of the novel's thematic implications, however, needs to take into consideration the modal shifts typical of the quest genre in general and to judge Huck's behavior in light of their function.[54] Seen from this perspective, one realizes that the episode at Phelps Farm, rather than marking a complete departure from the social criticism that has preceded, forms the final in a series of transforming modes of fictional representation: from its opening in a juvenile fantasy fiction that is presented as a spin-off of *Tom Sawyer* to a quest idyll punctuated by the violent, the gothic, and the picaresque, the text now evolves into a scathing social satire that works to expose the fictions of authority by which a slave-owning society operates. Throughout this evolving structure, moreover, Huck's character and "voice" have assumed any number of functions, ones that would seem contradictory in strictly realistic fiction but that in this case attest to the ever-changing contexts, the shifting textual registers, activating the organization of quest narrative. Within the final focus of the novel, the reader is asked, then, to "read" Huck the way Tom, the virtual "creator" of this ending section, envisions him—it may be Huck's voice that continues to narrate, but it temporarily adapts to the new fictional realm (satire) into which the speaker has stepped.

For Master Tom's ridiculous rescue scheme—worked out "regular" according to "what's in the books" (13)—becomes Twain's bitterly satiric comment not only on a society gone mad, but also on the puerile plot formulas underlying such a mentality—formulas that Twain himself is violating in writing a romance quest. Conventional minds like Tom's, Twain implies, incapable of seeing beyond narrow codes of social behavior that prejudge some fellow human beings as naturally inferior, are likewise incapable of breaking from narrow codes of fictional form. Hence, epitomizing the banal voice of literary decorum, Tom patiently explains to the bewildered Huck that in the absence of the obstacles typifying conventional fictive plotting, they must "invent all the . . . difficulties and dangers" (188) in arranging Jim's escape (Tom's greatest invention, of course, has been to "forget" that Jim has already been freed by Miss Watson's will), and Tom accuses Huck of not "ever seem[ing] to want to do anything that's regular; you want to be starting something fresh all the time" (189). In contrast, *rules*—of social behavior, of literary convention—are *all* to Tom: "I wouldn't stand by and see the rules broke," he stubbornly says of his escape plot, "because right is right, and wrong is wrong" (194). The inadequacy of Tom's viewpoint is exposed when his regulated plot backfires— indeed, approaches tragedy—as Tom is shot and Jim recaptured to be hanged. Traditional novelistic form, Twain implies, may be the least effective way of "freeing" a subject—be that subject Jim, or be it Twain's politically subversive themes.

Yet Tom's fantasies seem to carry the day, given the neatly contrived, happy ending and last-page revelation that Jim is a free man after all. But we simultaneously learn that Huck has also been "freed"—released by the death of Pap into sole possession of his named identity. Tom's earlier gripe that Huck "want[s] to be starting something fresh all the time" (189), rather than going along with "regular" conventions, becomes a prophecy of the text's final structural turn. For in the last lines Huck announces his intention of escaping the boundaries of conventional life and the closure of Tom's imposed fiction by lighting out for the Territory. With this final gesture, Huck reaffirms both the forward-moving dynamic of the quest and his own counter-traditional opposition to growing up to fit a "sivilized" definition of manhood. One may question whether Huck will ever succeed in attaining true or total self-expression, however far west he moves, but this closing ambiguity only enhances the radical implications of Twain's social criticism and Huck's desire for personal freedom. Male Edens such as Huck dreams of do not, in fact, exist; the Territory, like the River, can never really escape the "real" world, and the fantasy of undivided freedom remains only a fantasy as long as that "real" world remains divided— whether by class, race, or sex. Thus, as Melville will demonstrate in *Billy Budd,* the underside of the all-male world, ironically, is often a microcosm of exactly those tensions from which the quester seeks to flee with his band of comrades. The ending of *Huckleberry Finn* may seem happy, but, given the larger questions that it raises, it is far from final.[55]

·*Billy Budd, Sailor (An Inside Narrative)*·
The Death of the Handsome Sailor

As the nineteenth century drew to a close, the sentimental and domestic ideology that had long dominated American culture, according to Ann Douglas, began to give way to a more overtly masculinist ethos that venerated power at the expense of almost all the values identified with woman's "sphere." These included not only what was perceived as shallow or excessive sentiment, but also those very emotions of the heart celebrated by Ishmael and Huck yet sometimes denigrated as "feminine" or "womanly." The new era, in contrast, exemplified by the growing popularity of machismo in heroes both real and mythic (the Teddy Roosevelt of Rough Rider fame, the cowboy-savior of the western novel), ushered into being a definition of culture based on physical aggression, phallic virility, and authority that has since become axiomatic of the self-image of the "normal" twentieth-century American male.[56] Melville's last and unfinished work, *Billy Budd, Sailor* (c. 1891), appraises the

effects of this burgeoning set of values in an allegory of life and
death aboard a man-of-war literally and figuratively adrift at sea.
With damningly calm, clear simplicity, this text presents the death
of Melville's personal ideal of independent manhood—the Handsome Sailor prototype embodied in the androgynous Billy—at the
hands of brute violence and unfeeling justice. In so doing, this interiorized version of the quest romance unequivocally sets itself
against a power-oriented culture whose univocal reading of "masculine" authority and "masculine" identity not only further disem-
powered women in general but also threatened to eclipse that
which specifically interested and involved Melville: the "feminine
in man."[57]

The conjunction of "masculine" and "feminine" traits in Billy's
appearance, coupled with his personality and its effect on others, is
one indication of the extent to which a probing of sexual identity
forms an important strand in this short novel's extremely complex
exploration of the problematic nature of authority and rebellion.[58]
The narrator early explains that the magnetic charm of the "Handsome Sailor" type—of which Billy becomes the exemplar—resides
in a combination of "strength and beauty . . . , comeliness and
power, always attractive in masculine conjunction" (44). On the one
hand, Billy boasts a "masculine beauty" (53) and fine physical
"mold" (51) that "in the nude might have posed for a statue of
young Adam before the Fall"(94); on the other, with a face "all but
feminine in purity" (50), Billy's shipboard status is likened to that
of a "rustic beauty" (51). Thus, for all the marks of the "heroic
strong man, Hercules," in his physical bearing, Billy also calls to
mind "something suggestive of a mother" favored by the goddess
of Love, Venus (51). And it is this latter characteristic, feminine-
associated love, that Billy's personality most abundantly conveys, as
his harmonizing role as "peacemaker" aboard the merchant ship
Rights-of-Man illustrates; Billy's unconventional presence triggers
in his fellow sailors a loving devotion that causes them also to veer
from traditional masculine norms. The result, as the captain says, is
that "it's the happy family here" (47). Billy's uniqueness and autonomy of being, furthermore, is underscored by the fact that he alone
among the impressed sailors on the Bellipotent has not "known a
hearth of some sort" or left behind "wives and children"; rather,

like the wandering Ishmael and homeless Huck, his "entire family" is "invested in himself" (50).

However, the floating, idyllic, and all-male camaraderie of the Rights-of-Man—evocative of the Edenic paradise temporarily established aboard Huck and Jim's raft—is only a memory in *Billy Budd,* for the narrative begins after the foretopman's impressment into the King's service by the officers of the Bellipotent. Billy's translation from one ship to the other, as the names "Rights-of-Man" and "Bellipotent" suggest, outlines a crucial rite of passage marking his growth from a youthful, idealistic state of freedom to an imprisoned adult life in which martial power stands as the controlling metaphor for a state of domination; the shipboard world of the male quest, hitherto represented as an escape from social circumscription, has become a microcosm of the hierarchical world left behind. Thus the impressing officer, in a flashback to the impressment scene, sardonically notes that this "Apollo" must now become "the man-of-war's man" (48)—and this, Melville later adds, in a malevolent "world not without some mantraps" (70). It is telling that the imagery Melville uses to convey Billy's impressment— "a goldfinch popped into a cage" for whom any demur would have been useless (45)—recalls the entrapments that the transition to adulthood, and to object status, brings to female protagonists from Catherine Earnshaw to Gwendolen Harleth and Charlotte Verver. Billy, that is, symbolically plays out the fate of woman in the ship's masculinist society because he, as a less easily classifiable man among men, becomes the "other" or "alien" whose presence, like that of women in patriarchy, at once exposes its elisions and yet becomes the ironic justification of its structure of power, since threatening "others" must, according to such logic, be suppressed.

The psychological action culminating in the eclipse of Melville's male ideal unfolds, appropriately, as a series of confrontations between the untraditional Billy and the Bellipotent's two representatives of entrenched power, the bullying "master-at-arms," Claggart, and the authoritarian captain, Edward Fairfax Vere. Both men perceive Billy as a threat because his presence subconsciously reminds them of the loving faculty within themselves—which they associate with the feminine—that they have suppressed to ensure their superiority over and control of others. Claggart's dual feelings of attraction for and subsequent hatred of Billy's physical beauty, for instance, amount to a profound "envy" (78) of the young sailor's sensed difference, and it is this inner conflict that initiates the action of the narrative. The master-at-arms, the narrator tells the reader, "could have loved Billy if but for fate and ban"—and if part of that "ban" is the nineteenth-century taboo placed on homosexual desire, part of that "fate" is Claggart's recognition that Billy embodies exactly that wholeness that he himself lacks.[59]

Thus, the master-at-arms' attraction becomes a smoldering "passion" of hatred (77) that renders any mutual love on the order of that experienced by Huck and Jim, or Ishmael and Queequeg, impossible. As Georges-Michel Sarotte and E. Grant Watson have realized, Claggart's ensuing attempt to dominate Billy through persecution—precipitating the plot of Billy's tragedy—is both a displacement of erotic desire and a defensive mechanism to protect himself against love, that very *nonaggressive* force embodied in Billy that Claggart at once desires and fears.[60] In the sadomasochistic configuration that Claggart and Billy form—a perverse parody of the romantic ideal of complementary opposition—it is inevitable that words be replaced by physical aggression as the only "sexual" mode of communication possible between the two men, for these are the terms that the "master" Claggart has imposed on his victim. "I could only say it with a blow" (106), Billy thus testifies of his spontaneous rebellion against this tyranny, which results in Claggart's death; he actualizes, in a sense, the murderous thoughts that Gwendolen Harleth's experience of marriage as an act of unending psychological violence has provoked in her subconscious.

At this crucial threshold point the narrative focus shifts to Vere, who despite his attempts at fairness embodies an intellectualized version of the impulses underlying Claggart's impassioned hatred. For Vere's is a "resolute nature" (60) founded on a degree of self-control as extreme and as crippling as Claggart's repressed passions; his reasoned deliberations leave him "the most undemonstrative of men" (60), an incomplete self "lack[ing] in the companionable quality" (63). Only in response to Billy's crime does the extent of Vere's allegiance to authoritarian norms surface, however, and then in a very telling substitution of terms: "The father in him, manifested toward Billy thus far . . . was replaced by the military disciplinarian" (100). Although Vere may be justified in fearing mutiny, given the politically unstable climate of the times, the extreme "prudence and rigor" (103) that he chooses to exercise in summoning the drumhead court indicates an anxiety that is inwardly as well as outwardly motivated. For as his amazingly explicit summary speech at Billy's trial indicates, his hardness and rejection of mercy are directly linked to a fear of the "feminine in man," and all that term connotes, as dangerously subversive of his authority. First, warning the jury not to be unduly swayed by compassion, Vere sets himself up as the correct model of one who "strive[s] against scruples that may tend to enervate decision" (110); implicit in Vere's use of the word "enervate" is the effeminacy that nineteenth-century cultural ideology associated with a lack of strength and draining of vitality. The compassionate "scruples" (another telling word choice) that would pardon Billy, it follows, must then be a product of womanly weakness unsuited to manly decisions. Thus Vere leads up to a condemnation of the "feminine in man," as he calls it, by conjuring forth a false analogy between the head and heart as gendered components of the human personality: "But let not warm hearts betray heads that should be cool. . . . Well, the heart here, sometimes *the feminine in man,* is as that piteous woman, and hard though it be, *she must here be ruled out*" (111; emphasis added). Not only is the jury being told to rule out "that piteous woman" in themselves, but they are implicitly being directed to "rule out" Billy, who has come to represent the "feminine in man," the androgynous possibility and signifier of difference that must be expelled if the hierarchical supremacy of men is to be maintained in the world of which the Bellipotent is a microcosm. For Vere also stresses that Billy's crime has been to violate the whole concept of traditional hierarchy by "strik[ing] his superior in grade" (111). In a man-of-war world, as well as in society, disciplinary action for this infraction of order must "[take] after the father"—that is, the destructive principle Vere identifies as "War" itself (112). The purpose, then, toward which Vere drives as "steadfastly" (113) as Ahab in *Moby-Dick* is nothing less than a violent erasure of the "feminine," hence radically insubordinate, impulse embodied in Billy. In commenting on Vere's judgment as a covertly political act, Barbara Johnson correctly notes that "the legal order, which attempts to submit 'brute force' to 'forms, measured forms,' can only eliminate violence by transforming violence into the final authority."[61] On the extratextual level, this denial of the reality of Billy's possibility, one realizes, also renders invisible the reality of women in the larger world that these authority figures control, the world that Melville has chosen not to represent.

While patriarchal rule superficially triumphs in this confrontation—for Billy is hanged—the male world without his harmonizing presence is left more incomplete than ever, a fact simultaneously registered in the "ragged edges" (128) of the novella's narrative structure. Melville spells out his narrative technique in a self-reflexive passage at the beginning of chapter 4 whose facetious tone is a challenge *not* to take the organization of *Billy Budd* seriously: "In this manner of writing, resolve as one may to keep to the main road, some bypaths have an enticement not readily to be withstood. I am going to err into such a bypath . . . ; a literary sin the divergence will be" (56). The tone may be Fieldingesque, but the meaning is not: for as our previous readings of *Moby-Dick* and *Huckleberry Finn* have shown, the bypaths of indirection form the true trajectory of quest romance, providing an impressionistic means of rendering truths otherwise obscured by the unrealistically streamlined contours of conventional fictional form. Melville again drives this lesson home as the narrative begins to taper off inconclusively after Billy's execution for what might analogously be called his "sin" of "divergence" from the "main road" of convention: "The symmetry of form attainable in pure fiction cannot be so readily achieved in a narration essentially having less to do with fable than with fact. Truth uncompromisingly told will always have its ragged edges; hence the conclusion of such a narration is apt to be less finished than an architectural finial" (128). Throughout the text Melville has made its "asymmetrical" attributes of form suggestive of an ever-deepening inquiry into the contradictory nature of male authority and identity. Hence, the "voyage into the unknown" format of the quest genre is depicted here less as an external than psychological event, as the absence of all but minimal physical action in this narrative suggests. Instead, the "movement" characteristic of the mode occurs as an intellectual or textual activity: one chapter will become an opening up, rather than linear extension, of the information conveyed in its predecessor; seeming digressions turn out to be the main trajectory of the narrative; the shifting of focus from Billy to Vere, then to Claggart and back to Vere, abets the disorienting sensation of an evolving movement whose destination is uncertain; Melville's use of a conjecture-filled narrative voice which can only hypothesize about, but never penetrate, the various characters' states of consciousness heightens the reader's experience of plunging blindly into a mystery—Billy's martyrdom—for which there is no final explanation.

The purposefully "ragged edges" (128) of Melville's conclusion—a series of digressive "sequel[s]" (128) that follow upon Billy's execution—therefore introduce several divergent impressions of Billy and his story in order to continue the questioning raised by the prior events; issues are refused the simplification inherent in a closed plot format. These "sequels" not only precipitate a series of modal transformations (from quasi-scientific explication to newspaper account to verse ballad) typical of quest structure, but also underscore the issues of sexual identity and authoritarian power raised throughout the text. As Johnson remarks, "The ending not only lacks special authority, it problematizes the very *idea* of authority" by "fearlessly fraying its own symmetry."[62] Thus, the subtext of the inconclusive debate in chapter 26 waged by the ship's purser and surgeon over Billy's uncommon *lack* of involuntary "muscular spasm" (or ejaculation) at the moment of hanging returns us indirectly, but unmistakably, to the issue of phallic power opposing Billy's difference throughout the text; the flashback to the scene of the hanging in chapter 27, elaborating on Vere's strategic use of martial discipline to quell the crew's restlessness, like chapter 28's flash-forward to describe the fall of the supposedly indominable Belli-*potent*, again suggests the immediate and long-range effects of male authority.[63] As if in imitation of these themes, the dynamic hitherto driving the text figuratively defuses itself, peters out, without a single explosion.

In sum, the result of the inconclusive quest narrative utilized in *Billy Budd*—epitomized by the disturbingly falsifying rewriting and inversion of Billy's story in historical record (the newspaper report in chapter 29) and in legend (the ballad that ends the novel)—constitutes a disturbing exploration into the far reaches of patriarchal power and its ability to erase the difference of its opponents. In *Moby-Dick* Melville shows how the all-male world of quest could presage either the egalitarian fraternity of comrades, such as that envisioned in "A Squeeze of the Hand," or the "indissoluble league" (146) linked together by Ahab's lust for dominion over all external objects. Intuitively aware of the shift taking place in his culture from a blatantly sentimental to masculinist ethos that was its inverse, Melville here reveals the all-male world to be an inferno of violence, domination, and repression when the powers of authority are allowed to stamp out the "feminine in man"; simultaneously, the narrative of women's fate, their suppression, is implicit, if only as a shadow, in the fate of Billy's difference in this microcosmic universe. And the outcome of the confrontation between self-sufficiency and limited sexual roles, played out as psychodrama in this "inside narrative" (the novella's subtitle), foreshadows the advent of the male-oriented novel of the twentieth century, in which men bond together not to escape sexual dichotomization but to perpetuate its stranglehold on norms of identity.

·*The Sea Wolf*·
In Search of the Perfect "Man-Type"

The status of Jack London's *The Sea Wolf* as a quest novel falls somewhere between the extremes of male fiction staked out, at the one end, by the Melvillean quest narrative and, at the other, by the machismo of Hemingway and his imitators. On one level London seems as vitally concerned with issues of sexual identity as Melville; yet his attempt to chart a more positive ideal through male bonding is fraught with ambiguities that become not only thematically but textually problematic when, at novel's end, the format of the quest dissolves into that of sentimental romance. The conflicting allegiances of *The Sea Wolf* (1904) offer an excellent opportunity to assess the potentialities and liabilities inherent in using the quest romance mode as an expression of rebellion against literary and sexual norms.

London's novel shares with other male quest narratives a sea journey into the literal and metaphysical reaches of the unknown, experienced by reader and protagonist alike as a process of defamiliarization. Opening with the shipwrecked Humphrey Van Weyden stranded "in the midst of a gray primordial vastness," the action shifts to Wolf Larsen's seal hunter whose plunging movement "into the heart of the Pacific" seems, like Ahab's Pequod, to near the "bounds" of "the universe itself."[64] Simultaneous with this geographic removal, Humphrey is gradually divorced from the realm of the psychologically familiar as the increasing outbreaks of violence aboard the renegade ship transform it into a nightmarish inferno. This process of removal from the known is matched by another element common to quest narrative—Humphrey's immersion in an all-male environment that inspires a redefinition of his own manhood and subsequent realization of a supposedly more well-rounded identity.

But here we can pinpoint an important difference between London's purpose and that of the preceding works. Whereas Billy's identity has always been what might be called unselfconsciously "androgynous," and whereas both Ishmael and Huck grow to recognize as part of their intrinsic natures values traditionally deemed feminine or maternal, Humphrey's task is strikingly reversed: he must learn, rather, to incorporate into his essentially "effeminate" being the manly element missing in his dilettantish upbringing. "My muscles were small and soft, like a woman's" (30), he confesses to the reader, explaining that "I had not been called 'Sissy' Van Weyden all my days without reason" (64). Thus, while Melville and Twain at least in part reclaim the feminine from stereotypical associations in order to revitalize it as a symbol of a positive loving capacity that includes men as well as women, London continues to link femininity with negative associations (weakness, passivity, inertia), at least as long as they predominate in a man. On a thematic level, the goal of Humphrey's quest for identity is a blending of his initially "feminine" sensibility with virile "masculine" strength, but London's valorization of the latter, it will become clear, ultimately circles back to a dualistic view of the sexes, despite his efforts to expand the parameters of male sexual identity. In the process, London goes far beyond the genre's inherent focus on maleness to deify phallic power.

Fished from the sea and rubbed back to life aboard Larsen's "brute-ship" in a ritual as liminal as any of Ishmael's and Huck's rebirths, Humphrey is quickly initiated into a totally alien, all-male world where "force, nothing but force obtained" (32) and where all "weakness is wrong" (55). The hierarchy of domination that arises from this ethos of brute strength—an anarchic version of the ironclad authoritarianism represented in *Billy Budd*—is embodied in Wolf Larsen, captain of the Ghost and Humphrey's immediate model for the elemental "potency" (13) and "virility of spirit" (16) characterizing the perfect "man-type" (99). Sarotte notes that "with an interesting regularity, Jack London introduces some feminine feature here and there in his hypervirile hero,"[65] and in Wolf's case this includes satiny fair skin which Richardson's Pamela might well have coveted. Despite Wolf's unfeeling cruelty, he is also characterized as a brooding thinker haunted by "that questing, that everlasting query . . . as to what it was all about" (59). Hence he becomes Humphrey's emblem of the archetypal romantic quester (a figure that we have already encountered in Mr. Ramsay's fantasized self-image) as well as virile superman: "I could see him only as living always, and dominating always, fighting and destroying, himself surviving" (120).

Although Humphrey's prognosis of Wolf's future turns out to be wrong, his relationship with Wolf provides the necessary spur to the young man's growth and survival. In a telling metaphoric reversal, Wolf's manly presence—with its faint hint of the feminine— becomes the "virgin" territory or wilderness into which Humphrey's quest for "manhood" must penetrate: "I felt an elation of spirit," Humphrey says when in the Captain's presence, "I was groping into his soul-stuff . . . , I was exploring virgin territory. A strange, a terribly strange, region was unrolling itself before my eyes" (56). So intimate a drawing together may seem to echo the affirming bonds of Ishmael and Queequeg, or Huck and Jim, but in fact Humphrey and Wolf's gravitation to each other is based on an antithetical norm of polarity and hierarchy. For Wolf not only provides the visible text or subject-matter of Humphrey's lessons, but he is also his teacher and complete master in an arrangement closer to marital conventions than London realizes: "And thus it was that I passed into a state of involuntary servitude," Humphrey reports of the role he assumes in response to Wolf's domination, "He was stronger than I, *that was all*" (23; emphasis added). The sexual undercurrents always present in Humphrey's physical attraction to Wolf and Wolf's selective preference for Humphrey also expose the conventional dynamics implicit in their master-slave relationship. When Humphrey first sees Wolf in the nude, for instance, he is instantly mesmerized by his "masculine" beauty, a feeling which London captures in a linguistic equivalent of sexual climax: "I could not take my eyes from him. I stood motionless, a roll of antiseptic cotton in my hand unwinding and spilling itself down to the floor" (99). Wolf's "command" that the awed Humphrey feel "the great muscles [that] leapt and moved under [his] satiny skin" (99) becomes an act of deliberate, teasingly coy provocation; such manipulation of sexual appeal establishes Wolf's power at the same time that it valorizes male virility above any other erotic expression; on a more overt level, Wolf demonstrates the same kind of manipulation of sexual attraction that gives Prince Amerigo emotional control over Maggie and Charlotte in *The Golden Bowl*. Simultaneously, the homoeroticism that Melville makes a positive symbol for unconventionality in *Moby-Dick* becomes, unconsciously for London, an extension of the destructive male–female dialectic from which Melville's questers flee.

The disquieting resonances of such a relationship inevitably mark Humphrey's development, calling into question the ideal of manhood that London has set up as the proper end of his protagonist's quest. As in the preceding quest narratives, personal growth is measured in a succession of newly acquired identities and roles, a process initiated when the nearly drowned Humphrey is renamed "Hump" by Wolf and made to assume the role of cabin-boy with the promise that "it will be the making of you" (18). Having plummeted from a position of elite but effete worldly status (as literary critic and reviewer) to the lowest position in the shipboard hierarchy, Hump undergoes his first rite of passage when he beats up the bully Cooky, a man even more effeminate than—and hence in this hierarchical world inferior to—himself. For this exercise of physical force, Hump earns Wolf's approbation, "You've got spunk" (65)—that very quality, ironically, which Huck feels guilty for lacking when he does not betray Jim to the slave hunters (*Huckleberry Finn* 75) and which, in the colloquial sense of the word, is the substance that Billy's hanged corpse refuses to produce in involuntary "muscular spasm" (*Billy Budd* 124). Progressing up the ladder of manhood to the coveted rank of Wolf's "mate" in a bond as nearly romantic as nautical, Hump becomes "aware of a toughening or hardening I was undergoing" (108). While he maintains enough of his former values to realize that brutality alone is wrong, he welcomes the fact that he can "never again be quite the same man" because he feels that in touching upon his masculinity (i.e., his toughness and hardness) he is encountering "the world of the real" for the first time (108).

But simultaneous with this process is Hump's awareness of the inadequacies of Wolf's world and creed—namely, its "unnatural" exclusion of women and the crew's lack of any capacity for "softness, and tenderness, and sympathy" (89). However, unlike the texts of Melville and Twain, which advocate a realization *within men them-selves* of emotions and values traditionally associated with women, Hump means his solution literally: it is the *actual presence* of women in their symbolic role as spiritual exemplars that is needed, without which the inherent "brute" in man cannot be tamed nor a "balance to their lives" restored (89). What is problematic is not so much Hump's desire for female companionship as the stereotypical manner in which he imagines their function in relation to men. Moreover, his conservative estimation of male and female nature as hierarchical opposites, brutes versus angels, anticipates the next turn of plot as the shipwrecked Maud Brewster enters the hitherto all-male world of the Ghost and irrevocably upsets its psychological dynamics. The modal shift from quest format to erotic-seduction narrative accompanying Maud's arrival serves to underscore London's vision of "correct" male development for Hump. For by becoming the "willing slave" (133) of Maud rather than Wolf, Hump redirects his newly acquired "masculine" energy into the chivalric service of fragile womanhood—a sacred duty successfully carried out when he strikes a blow to Wolf, his former master, to keep him from raping Maud; here we have Billy's climactic "blow" of self-declaration ("I could only say it with a blow") being rewritten as a sign of male heroics and female subordination. Tellingly, Hump's chivalrous love comes into being the very instant he becomes aware of Wolf's sexual desire for Maud. That is, Wolf's cruder lust awakens Hump's purer erotic love in a paradigmatic situation of triangular desire that fixes the woman as mediator between men; Hump gets his real desire—figuratively, to have and to be Wolf—in a socially acceptable way by usurping his master's place in falling in love with Maud.[66]

Following Hump's strategically "positive" exertion of male strength in saving Maud from rape, the narrative undergoes yet another modal shift as Hump engineers his and Maud's escape from

THE SEA WOLF

Wolf's ship; a kind of New World narrative now evolves as the two set up house on a deserted island, Maud playing Friday to Hump's increasingly resourceful Crusoe in a primitive version of the traditional domestic plot. Hump's successes in sheltering and protecting the physically less competent Maud, confirming his new "masculine" identity, precipitate an inner recognition of his undying love for Maud and of his natural ascendancy in the conventional sexual order: "Instantly conscious I became of my manhood," Hump lyricizes upon embracing Maud for the first time, "I felt myself masculine, the protector of the weak, the fighting male. And, best of all, I felt myself the protector of my loved one" (201). Hump's last rite of passage is accomplished when he defeats the now weakened and blinded, hence symbolically castrated, Wolf—who has coincidentally drifted to the same island—and prepares to sail back to civilization with Maud. With this imminent return to social order, the rhetoric of the last pages of the novel, in which the lovers exchange declarations, becomes a replica of standard sentimental romance, the very fiction early American romancers attempted to repudiate:

> "My woman, my one *small* woman," I said, my free hand petting her shoulder in the way all lovers know though never learn in school.
> "My man," she said, looking at me for an instant with tremulous lids which fluttered down and veiled her eyes as she snuggled her head against my breast with a happy *little* sigh. (252; emphasis added)

It is telling that neither Hump's sense of himself as a "man" nor Maud's as a diminutive "woman" stands alone; the identity of each depends on the concept of a complementary other who is to be possessed rather than appreciated for his or her individuality— "my" man, "my" woman. Unlike the self-possession characterizing the independent identities of Ishmael or Huck or Billy, the "new" definition of "the great Man Comrade"[67] toward which London has directed his quest novel becomes, in Hump's case, evidence supporting an already existing ethos. The "feminine" side of the male protagonist, represented by Hump's initial effeminacy and aesthetic capacities as a critic of poetry, is deflected to the female "half" of a literal conjunction of male and female—for Maud, conveniently, is no less than a poet by profession. The union that takes place within Ishmael has once again become the union that takes place externally, and in being made simultaneous with the ending of London's novel, it brings to a halt the fictional movement and meaning synonymous with quest.

Conclusion: The Capitulation of Twentieth-Century Quest Fiction

The imminent return of Hump and Maud to civilization—transforming the text's infinity-bound quest into a circular voyage of return and a recuperation of the familiar—serves to remind us of the potential of earlier quest narrative to move in the opposite direction—into unknown spheres where a realm of "interior spaciousness" awaits discovery. For, at its most psychologically adventurous, the quest as conceived by Melville or Twain activates a vision of male subjectivity and autonomy that engages in a quietly but covertly revolutionary sexual politics of its time, abjuring traditionally masculine terms of domination in its effort to break out of constricting sexual categories. Looking back on these four texts, we can begin to sum up the positive and negative valences accruing to the literary attempt to inscribe the trajectory of the male quest in a world without women. The counter-traditional possibilities of the questing hero's escape from a marriage-oriented culture appear threefold. First, his removal from social and sexual expectations makes possible a more inclusive and transgressive sense of identity that, like Ishmael's or Huck's, is multiform, fluid, and affirming in its integrity—characteristics that also typify the personal and collective identities established in the female communities explored in the next chapter. Second, the elevation of mutuality—rather than polarity—in the male bond presents a conceptual alternative to the gender inequality institutionalized by marriage in heterosexual relationships. And, third, an understated but powerful critique of the dominant sexual order often lingers in image, symbol, and situation in the all-male world; thus, as in *Billy Budd*, the degree to which the world of quest is self-consciously used to replicate the negative aspects of the society from which the quester has flown can become the vehicle for acute social criticism of the male-dominated structures of power responsible for American sentimentalism as well as aggressive expansionism. As all these analyses have indicated, furthermore, the genre's potential for exploring the various implications of male independence exists in proportion to the "unfixed," provisional status of its narrative form. Hence, *The Sea Wolf*'s lack of success in maintaining the open-ended imperatives of the mode—signaled in its return to the happy ending of conventional romance—also becomes a sign of its abandonment of the untraditional themes developed in earlier examples of the quest narrative.

London's confused alliances—holding to both a "progressive" sexual ethic and an overtly masculinist creed—help explain the failure, by and large, of modern quest fiction to continue the unorthodox explorations into the male psyche begun by some of its predecessors, and in the process, his example glosses some of the potential liabilities and contradictions in the mode. For twentieth-century versions of the male quest—and here I largely agree with Fiedler's analysis of modern American fiction—have become increasingly ambiguous and self-deceiving as escape into a womanless world has become only a metaphoric rather than actual possibility; in a chiasmic reversal, the counter-traditional *fantasy* of escape from self-negating marital convention, which I have been metaphorically describing as an escape into "a world without women," has become the *literal* desire of many modern American male writers who have made women the scapegoat for their (the men's) dissatisfaction with the institution of marriage. And, as part of this reverse movement, literary evocations of the male bond have ceased to function as positive expressions of alternative relationship; rather, the depiction of camaraderie among men more frequently disguises the author's profound desire to avoid female reality altogether, while the fantasy of escaping society with one's comrades becomes the protagonist's ultimate excuse for misogynistic exclusivity. The underlying fear of losing power that motivates such attitudes—so well dramatized in the pathological cases of Ahab, Claggart, and Wolf—has led not only to a new and destructive stereotype of femininity (the "castrating bitch" syndrome) but also to a new archetype of phallic manhood, epitomized in the supervirile and silent western hero impervious to overt displays of emotion but swift to take violent action.[68]

These negative manifestations of the modern-day quest, emerging from what was initially a movement away from stereotype, have been complicated by another factor: the distrust, in a more self-conscious age, of the homosexual implications of relationships between men who metaphorically flee women. The result has often been an increased representation of machismo in male relations, as if mere muscle would allay such fears, and a shying away from the ideal embodied in Billy, as if representing the "feminine in man" would constitute an admission of sexual "deviance." Ironically, the natural and unconscious celebration of homoeroticism in traditional quest narrative becomes the ultimate taboo in most contemporary renderings of the form, unless, as in some beat literature, sex between men becomes a mode of consolidating their power and mobility at the expense of women.[69]

It is illuminating to trace these various ambivalences at work in Hemingway's *The Sun Also Rises* (1926) and Mailer's *The Naked and the Dead* (1948), two modern adaptations of the genre obsessed with issues of sexual identity and independence from women. The fragmented postwar world of *The Sun Also Rises* provides the setting in which Jake Barnes's aimless quest for self-renewal unfolds. His sexual war-wound, the modern day equivalent of Ahab's maiming, leaves Jake literally a man without women despite the hovering presence of Brett; Jake's sexual lack thus becomes the symbol of a personal inner void as well as the sign of the impotence of the world at large. Counterpoised with this despairing vision, however, is the center of values residing in the reduced, modern-day version of male quest—Jake's spiritually purifying fishing trip to Spain with Bill Gordon, which lies at the heart of the novel. Yet the negative effect of this necessarily momentary retreat is that it reinforces the men's tendency to see *all* the world as an exclusively male domain; Brett, indeed, can only participate in this world by playing (unsuccessfully) at being "one of the boys." Her "masculine" rakishness and costuming are ultimately less a violation of her world's gender standards than a carefully circumscribed male fantasy of phallic, yet feminine, womanhood. The irony is that in such a misogynist universe, any even slightly independent woman like Brett, because of the threat she ultimately poses to male superiority, is doomed to personal failure (thus Brett will penitently mourn her loss of femininity at text's end) and authorial erasure (thus Hemingway strips Brett of the charms with which his imagination has initially invested her as an all-powerful earth goddess).

Mailer's novel, on the other hand, exposes the hellish underside of Hemingway's nostalgic dream of an untroubled male Eden. Set in the all-male environment of a Pacific war zone, its central action a monomaniacal quest through the defamiliarizing reaches of the island Anopopei's jungles and mountains, *The Naked and the Dead* uses conventions of the quest format to show that there is *no escape*, however far one journeys, from the power structures that rule society and dictate human behavior. All of Mailer's characters, having left behind them personally disastrous relationships with women, only find in war another battleground on which to vent their sexual frustrations and inadequacies; even the men's own in-group relationships are power plays, demonstrating a "universal" compulsion to dominate and control others through acts of meaningless aggression. Thus, Mailer makes the quest into war—and his inquiry into the psychology of power—a scorching indictment of a destructive ethos associated with masculine aggression. But, at the same time, he seems to view the urge to fight and conquer as an inescapable aspect of maleness, and in the process he denigrates the alternative value of what we have been calling the "feminine" as a saving inner principle or outer reality. The women of the novel, present only in the "Time Machine" flashbacks, are almost always seen as antagonistic "Others" who are stereotypically naive, frigid, lascivious, or conniving, and all of whom Mailer seems to hold responsible for the inherent sexual warfare that drives men to violent extremes. And the one male character explicitly linked with "feminine" feelings, General Cummings (whose father used to beat him for acting "like a goddam woman")[70] is depicted as a homosexual fascist whose closeted desires are directly responsible for the doomed mission on which he sends the reconnaissance team. The "villain" wrecking the quest, that is, is the "feminine" in man, personified by Mailer as homosexual and thus antithetical to his "heterosexual" conception of masculinity. The novel's "strongest" point, so to speak, is at once its true weakness: for the oppressive vision of aggressive force that Mailer discloses simultaneously eclipses his perception of other, less "strong," possibilities.

These modern versions of the quest formula would seem to confirm Sedgwick's thesis in *Between Men: English Literature and Male Homosocial Desire* that men form socially permissible bonds in order to perpetuate patriarchy.[71] The patriarchal order, that is, carries on its functions as if it were a "world without women," whether or not women are actually present to participate in its transactive desires. In a sense, then, even the earliest imaginings of the world of male quest are not without a certain potential ambiguity; by limiting their explorations to the "feminine in man," they unconsciously perpetuate the dominant order's excision of women in the real world. But this is where it becomes crucial for us to distinguish between, say, the pairing of Natty-Chingachgook, who recuperate the wilderness for the white man, and that of Ishmael-Queequeg, who plunge into its mystery in search of their own untapped potential. For as long as the possibility of breaking completely with the world of the known could be imagined *as actuality* by the nineteenth-century quest writer, the symbolic value of venturing into the unknown with other men held the power of meaning *differently,* as against the pattern that Sedgwick sees as pervasive. Indeed, the unlikely heroes that we find in Ishmael, Billy, and Huckleberry attest to the fact that outside the boundaries of social constriction there exists for such men the possibility of reimagining male identity; outside the boundaries of social discourse, an innovative language of the masculine self; outside the boundaries of conventional literary texts, the forward momentum of an ever-unfolding narrative form that we now call the "quest."

By way of conclusion, I would like to anticipate the subject matter of the following chapter—female communities in fiction—by turning to a fictional model that we might not suspect of drawing on the American male quest: Charlotte Perkins Gilman's account of a feminist utopia, *Herland,* written in 1915. For in the parodic narrative action framing this fantasy of an *all-female* world, three male explorers inadvertently dash headlong through the circumference of a hidden Amazonian kingdom; their act of discovery simultaneously triggers an opposing form of narration, which absorbs all forward motion and reformulates it in the nonlinear patterns that constitute the Herlanders' non-patriarchal way of life. This brilliantly arranged opening sequence, of course, deliberately appropriates the linear movement associated with the quest in order to debunk the aggressive ethos that Gilman categorically equates with it. But the trajectory that these opening chapters inscribe, fascinatingly enough, is mirrored, on a smaller scale, in the reversal of perspectives used to evoke the movement of Ishmael's whaleboat in the Grand Armada chapters of *Moby-Dick*—a deathly plunging movement forward that is magically transformed into a magnetic drawing inward, into the "enchanted circle" within which the feminine secrets of life and ongoing creation unfold. It is this prospect of interior recovery, this wedding-within of those socially designated "co-relatives" without which "self-hood itself seems incomplete," then, that forms the wishful goal and unorthodox "love story" of those quest romances which made of the symbolic act of questing a modus vivendi and of its literary method a counter-traditional genre.

Chapter Six

Centered Lives and Centric Structures in the Novel of Female Community

Counterplotting New Realities in *Millenium Hall, Cranford, The Country of the Pointed Firs,* and *Herland*

> We women can't go in search of adventures—to find out the North-West Passage or the source of the Nile, or to hunt tigers in the East. We must stay where we grow, or where the gardeners like to transplant us.
>
> Gwendolen to Grandcourt, in George Eliot's
> *Daniel Deronda*[1]

> Women have no wilderness in them,
> They are provident instead
> Content in the tight hot cell of their hearts
> To eat dusty bread.
>
> Louise Bogan, "Women"[2]

In psychological as well as geographical terms, the place allotted to women—married or single—in nineteenth-century English and American patriarchy was essentially static. As Gwendolen implies during her courtship in *Daniel Deronda,* the single action or "movement" permitted women is marriage, and to facilitate this end, her sex must paradoxically "stay where we grow," that is, must remain an object of another's approach, and hence forfeit traveling "in search of adventures" as men do—adventures that may, as the experience of the American quester has indicated, become a means of escaping the confines of wedlock altogether. This basic historical differentiation between male mobility and female stasis has helped shape the narrative responses of those authors attempting to fantasize the trajectory of experience for the protagonist of either sex who achieves self-definition outside of marital life and roles. For men, the choice not only of whom to marry but whether to marry at all has been a traditional privilege, serving as an implicit control over female destiny. Thus, bachelorhood in nineteenth-century life, although discouraged, was ultimately (if sometimes reluctantly) accepted as a measure of man's relative freedom to go and do as he liked, a fact inscribed in the outward-bound trajectory of the quest.

In contrast, what was viewed as a matter of choice and escape for men was transformed into a condition of unfortunate circumstance and constriction for women: to remain unmarried was to be classified as one of the unchosen, to forfeit one's "natural" biological destiny, and hence, to lose one's claim to social utility as mother of the nation, all in one fell swoop.[3] Worse, remaining single was to incur the derisive naming feared by Charlotte Stant in *The Golden Bowl:* "'Miss,' among us all is too dreadful. . . . I don't want to be a horrible English old-maid" (1:219). On the one hand, Victorian society could excuse its disappointed old maids their status under the assumption that these "redundant women" (so the phrase went) would have married if given half a chance; on the other hand, it had little pity and few kind words for the woman who claimed her independence from men and marriage as a personal right. Relevant in this regard is Ruth Perry's comment on the singleness of the eighteenth-century feminist Mary Astell: "To a historian considering women's alternatives in that era, the choice of celibacy—however repressive it may seem to post-Freudians—has the ring of emancipation."[4] Such, perhaps, was also the Victorians' fear; for the public condemnation of female autonomy increased in proportion to the growth of late nineteenth-century women's movements that advocated emancipation. This hostility can also be linked to the rise of the masculinist culture traced at the end of the last chapter; as one famous representative of the new status quo, Theodore Roosevelt, put it, "the woman who deliberately avoids marriage . . . is in effect a criminal against the race, and should be an object of contemptuous abhorrence by all healthy people."[5] What the mid-nineteenth-century author of *Married and Single* called the "strange, unnatural, criminal" deed of bachelorhood[6] was thus transformed, through rhetoric like Roosevelt's, into the "crime" of the (would-be) emancipated woman. It is no wonder that a majority of Victorian women—assaulted by external pressures to conform and having internalized social opinion in the mode of Charlotte Stant—learned to abhor the fate of the old maid and, for a combination of reasons both pragmatic and romantic, actively sought out the alternate status of wifehood. Whatever their potential doubts about the marriage state itself, those thoughts often waxed pale before the alternative.

Yet despite these pressures and desires, the reality of a dramatically increasing spinster population in both England and America characterized the second half of the nineteenth and beginning of the twentieth centuries, a development due less to significant increases in the number of emancipated "New Women" (although the movement had its impact) than to the rising spiral of female births, the removal of marriageable men to industrial centers, and the slow increase in modes of employment open to women.[7] We have already noted two testimonies to this social phenomenon, James's *The Bostonians* (1886) and Gissing's *The Odd Women* (1893), both of which took as their foci the hitherto ignored political and economic realities of the aggregates of unmarried women now amassed at the very center of Victorian society. In Britain and America, these underground networks of single and widowed women were coalescing into substantive communities hidden *within* a world that considered them superfluous or redundant. Yet, ironically, to join the ranks of this socially invisible sorority was to find oneself more "fixed," more circumscribed, than ever in a limited and limiting social position, a situation quite opposed to that escape into the metaphoric wilderness of possibility which the male's disavowal of a marital role ostensibly freed him to explore. The countertraditionally spirited novelist could not ignore the fact that any fictionalized "liberation" of the female protagonist from the prison of matrimonial destiny marked, at least in the eyes of society, her enclosure within a more imprisoning role as "old maid," condemned to solitary survival within, as Louise Bogan puts it in the poem cited at the beginning of this chapter, "the tight hot cell" of her heart.

For these reasons, the socially enforced immobility of the single heroine—living, typically, among a community of other unmarried or widowed women that is in turn girded by conventional society— has become a central metaphor and structural principle in novels attempting to counterplot paths of possibility for women who have foregone the usual fictional denouement of marriage. This chapter will focus on four texts in which the marginality of the female community becomes a metaphoric center, providing an alternative environment where protagonists learn to sustain themselves through mutual bonds that look beyond men and marriage. In Sarah Scott's *Millenium Hall* (1762), Gaskell's *Cranford* (1853), Jewett's *The Country of the Pointed Firs* (1896), and Gilman's *Herland* (1915), the situational stasis of the unmarried female protagonist(s), while calling attention to the stifling effect of society's sexual and marital norms, is transformed into a positive emblem of the woman's existential *status*, of a hard-earned inner freedom wrested from patriarchal control. Likewise, the narrative organization of these novels mirrors yet simultaneously refutes the protagonist's societal circumscription: its transformation of her circular entrapment into nonlinear rather than causally ordered patterns of narrative quietly undermines the tradition of logocentrism that has governed Western thought and shaped its standard fictions of sex, love, and marriage since the rise of the novel.

In imagining the possible contours of the yet "untold" story of Chloe and Olivia in *A Room of One's Own,* Virginia Woolf became the first important critic to address the potentially innovative consequences of using women's personal relationships as a literary model for narrative relations; in recent years, this subject has resurfaced as the focus of much feminist critical theory. Woolf, pointing out the limitations of a literary tradition that "almost without exception" has shown its fictional heroines only "in their relation to men" (86), suggests that the depiction of women like Chloe and Olivia without men could (1) free the representation of female identity from the conventional iconography fantasized by men, substituting in its place the reality of "women as they are" (92); (2) pioneer structural innovations by "tampering with the expected sequence" (85) associated with conventional male-female plot dynamics; and (3) insert into the literary canon a female style capable of expressing, perhaps for the first time, "those unrecorded gestures, those unsaid or half-said words, which form themselves, no more palpably than the shadows of moths on the ceiling, when women are alone" (88).

Woolf only erred in assuming that in 1929 such a vision of female independence and relationship was yet to be realized. For, as Nina Auerbach has brilliantly demonstrated in *Communities of Women: An Idea in Fiction,* there has always existed in the Anglo-

American novel a submerged tradition "allowing women an independent life beyond the saga of courtship and the settlement of
marriage."[8] Auerbach summarizes several characteristics of these
"furtive, unofficial, often underground" sororities that will recur
in various guises—as ordered estate, primly Victorian village, is-
lands in the sea, mythical Amazonian kingdom—in the novels encompassed by this chapter's focus. Hidden within the social fabric
yet psychologically excluded from participation in its functions—
and thus in a sense metaphorically recapitulating the contradictory
position of all female subjects within the dominant order—these
communities, Auerbach suggests, have transformed their isolation
into a "self-sustaining power" that allows them to transcend "male-
defined reality." In so doing, they are often rewarded with "the
invisible and often partial gain of a possession that is also self-possession." Rooted in a single, static setting—in stark relief to the
ever-changing terrain of the male quest—the female enclave gains
strength from its corporate (rather than merely individual) completeness, its communal powers of imaginative self-creation and recreation, and its possession of a shared, buried language or code of
beliefs that is empathetically communicated, as Woolf intimates, in
those "unsaid or half-said words" that thus escape patriarchal
censure.[9]

In another relevant study that focuses on interpersonal rather
than communal female relationships in fiction, Elizabeth Abel outlines what she calls the "(e)mergence" of individual female autonomy or wholeness through the psychological dynamics of female
bonding and its recapitulation in women's literature. Grounding
her literary analyses in Nancy Chodorow's psychoanalytic revisions
of Freudian theory, Abel hypothesizes that women's adult relationships, psychically modeled after the infant daughter's bond
with the mother, are potentially "fluid, open, and nonhierarchi-
cal," unlike the differentiation characterizing mother-son and
male-female relationships. By serving as mirrors of each other,
women friends can thus facilitate a shared self-recognition rooted
in biological and psychological likeness and in a merger of personality that opens the way to an integrated identity, in contrast to the
fragmentation of self experienced in conventional paradigms of
heterosexual union based on polarity.[10] "To study the relation of
mother and daughter," Marianne Hirsch has commented, "is to

find continuity and relationship where one expects to find difference and autonomy. This basic and continued relatedness and
multiplicity, this mirroring . . . have to be factors in any study of
female development in fiction."[11] Something of the difference that
a writing daughter's relation to her mother makes, not only to the
basic grammar of her life but to her art, can be inferred from the
opposing scenario that Mary E. Wilkins Freeman depicts in *Madelon* (1896), in which a father's incomprehension of his daughter's
developing personality is cast in intriguingly literary terms: "He
could not comprehend womankind. His sons were to him as words
of one syllable in straight lines; his daughter was written in com-
pound and involved sentences, as her mother had been before
her."[12] Because the adult female self that emerges from these
bondings with the mother and other women follows a path quite
distinct from institutionalized models of male development, Judith
Kegan Gardiner also argues that literary definitions of female
identity should not be fitted to the fixed modes of characterization
that reflect male psychoanalytic perceptions of normative, mature
identity as something stable and irreversible, words "in straight
lines," as Freeman puts it. Rather, the female psyche remains relational and fluid in definition throughout the course of the women's
life, cyclical as well as progressive in orientation, and generally "less
fixed, less unitary, and more flexible" than the traditional personality patterns ascribed to men.[13]

One consequence is that we will find the emergence of female
autonomy more likely to be represented as a collective rather than
solely individual accomplishment in these novels, a fact to which
the lack of a clearly dominant, central protagonist in several of
them attests. *Millenium Hall* and *Herland,* for example, portray
their respectively philanthropic and Amazonian communities *only*
collectively. Likewise, the gradual emergence of Matty and Mrs.
Todd as "central" figures in *Cranford* and *The Country of the Pointed
Firs* depends on their larger representative function; the highly
empathetic personality of each, tending to merge with her
surrounding female community, becomes symbolic of the whole
enclave's communal characteristics, values, and self-definition.
Similarly, the first-person onlooker/narrators of these latter two
works—both unmarried women—manifest unprepossessing and
nearly anonymous personalities that refuse to stamp the narrative

with their individuality. Instead, they interfuse with their subject matter until it defines them reciprocally. At the same time, these representations of the female community do not ignore the dangers of female collectivity—the fear, as Jane Gallop puts it, of the "monstrous" engulfment of the individual psyche in the all-encompassing "mother."[14] But the most striking fact about such texts is the degree to which traditionally understood subject-object relations (the source of psychoanalytical definitions of differentiation from the mother as the cause of future antagonism) is subverted by the *unantagonistic* rhythms of narrator and subject, of narration and reading, established in their structures.

Along with these literary observations, there have recently evolved valid historical and anthropological justifications for examining female relationships and women's communities as contexts for the development of self-sufficient female identity. Dismantling the twentieth-century stereotype of woman-to-woman rivalry and disloyalty as the norm, Carroll Smith-Rosenberg's essay, "The Female World of Love and Ritual," has most notably advanced the theory that same-sex friendships were an institutionalized, socially viable aspect of the nineteenth-century American woman's life, often parallel to but separate from her marital relationship, a conclusion that Lillian Faderman's full-length study, *Surpassing the Love of Men*, corroborates for her English sisters.[15] Indeed, as Smith-Rosenberg's exhaustive review of Victorian women's letters and diaries makes clear, it was heterosexual marriage, not the homosocial tie, that women (and men as well) considered "unnatural." Attributing this "emotional segregation of men and women" to the "rigid gender-role differentiation" in those familial and social structures whose rise we traced in chapter 2, Smith-Rosenberg concludes that the feminine sphere became a source of "essential integrity and dignity," and the lifelong bonds formed between its married as well as unmarried participants allowed them to develop an "inner security and self-esteem" denied in "the larger world of male concerns."[16]

Extending Smith-Rosenberg's analysis of the historicity of an exclusively female sphere as the result of sexual dichotomization, Gerda Lerner also argues that the "female culture [resulting] *within* the general culture shared by men and women" has constituted an autonomous counterforce, not merely a subculture, transforming its enforced segregation (whose purpose has been subordination) into a complementary assertion of "the importance of woman's function, even in its 'superiority,'" to the public world of the male.[17] A similar theory has emerged in recent cultural anthropology, suggesting, in Showalter's summary of the movement, "that women constitute a muted group, the boundaries of whose culture and reality overlap, *but are not wholly contained by,* the dominant (male) group."[18] In other words, there is that exclusive aspect of the world of ideas, ritual, and difference shared by women that always remains *outside* the dominant boundary; Edwin Ardener labels this zone "wild," an image I have borrowed for my discussion of the moors in *Wuthering Heights,* and one that is evocative, as well, of the land of adventure that Gwendolen Harleth complains is closed to women.[19]

But as Ardener's formulation intimates, there is also a possibility of escape and adventure for women lying in the interstices of patriarchy, where women's communities of spirit coalesce and find freeplay in imaginative expression. This theoretical realm, indeed, is Hélène Cixous's "moving, open, transitional space" to which French feminist theorists look for the emergence of a truly distinctive *écriture féminine,* a female poetics liberated from the masculine tradition of logocentrism; from this territory, Monique Wittig has drawn the revolutionary themes and form of her utopian anti-novel, *Les Guérillères.*[20] But whereas the emphasis in contemporary (and particularly French) feminist literary criticism has been largely to uncover the subversions wrought by *linguistic* traces of female "difference," this chapter proposes that the *structural* formulations of these four differing accounts of the wild zone equally encode the disruptive power of women's writing: in this case, the power to plot alternative existences for those rare protagonists who elude the self-containment of marriage and marriage plotting.

In this regard, Joanna Russ's comments on plot structure offer some helpful support. Expressing her belief that women writers in particular should be obliged to represent their heroines in formats other than love-plots, Russ proposes as an alternative the "lyric" mode, in which discrete elements circle around "an unspoken or thematic or emotional center"; its principle of organization would be associatively rather than chronologically or causally dictated. "A writer who employs the lyric structure is setting various images, events, scenes, or memories to circling around an unspoken, invisible center. The invisible center is what the novel . . . is about; it is also unsayable in available dramatic and narrative terms."[21] Russ here describes a format very close to that which this chapter identifies as operative in many novels of female community. However, since the term "lyric," as applied both to poetry and to poetically textured novels, has more frequently been used to describe associative patterns of imagery, metaphor, and symbol than applied to the relation of concrete units of narrative organization, I have chosen the word "centric"—variations of which are also often used in relation to female art forms[22]—to epitomize the generic qualities contributing to the counter-traditional status of such texts.

As their titles indicate, the centric structures of *Millenium Hall, Cranford, The Country of the Pointed Firs,* and *Herland* are all predicated upon static loci or settings that become emblematic of the rooted values and outwardly "still" lives of their female protagonists. Not only the seeming timelessness of these locations, but the reduction therein of all significant action to a minimum ("significant," that is, as measured by the external world), militates against a driving narrative impulse or strictly linear development toward crisis, climax, and resolution such as characterizes the closed trajectories of much romantic and seduction fiction. Instead, the structures of these novels pivot upon and centralize the very stasis that appears to hold the single female protagonist "captive" within her environment, only to reveal that her stationary confinement is a cache of freedom, integrity, and power invisible in the external world of love and marriage. To effect this centricity of form, the logic of incremental repetition rather than the causality of linear narration is made to govern loose, episodic arrangements in which seemingly disconnected or random events "circle" around unchanging truths. Therefore, meanings only gradually tend to accumulate as narrative doubles back on itself, indirectly implying its message in differing registers or vignettes (as in *Cranford* and *The Country of the Pointed Firs*), or as chapter upon chapter becomes an extended illustration of the same central utopian precept (as in *Millenium Hall* and *Herland*). The nonlinear order produced by such layering and accretion of both event and exposition "interrupts" or "breaks," as Woolf says of the hypothetical story of Olivia and Chloe, the "expected" order of things—that is, the progressive order toward the fixed end enshrined in traditional theories of narrative desire. To the contrary, Woolf hypothesizes in her fantasized reading of Chloe and Olivia's story that "one could not see a wave heaping itself, a crisis coming around the next corner" (95). Indeed, novels of female community often maximize upon a number of consecutive minor crises, rather than a linear buildup to one significant crisis, in order to create a continual rhythm of flux and reflux around their dramatic events.

Consequently, the temporal component of narrative in these novels often shifts to reflect its centric structuring. The interjection of continually reviving memories into present narrative time, for example, creates a sense of both circularity and stasis in these isolated worlds where all time except the repeating natural cycles seems to have stopped. Not only is the logic of "man-made" time overwhelmed by and encompassed within this larger, nonlinear view by the structural interlacing of past memory and present event, but so too is the logic of men and "man-made" events such as marriage. Neither the advent of men nor the occurrence of marriage is restricted from the metaphorically all-female worlds of these novels. Either event, however, when it does occur, is so placed within the general structural movement that it is absorbed into or made subordinate to the dictates of the text and the desires of the female enclave.[23] As Scott, Gaskell, and Gilman's texts particularly illustrate, both men and marriage lose their power to control women or author the plots of their lives; instead they become friendly tools in the hands of the community to secure its perpetuation or protection.

In repeatedly illustrating the collective power of the female community to expel or incorporate male reality according to its needs, the centric structures of these four novels thus reflect the hard-earned autonomy, the centered lives, of its time-battered yet self-sustaining members. The very fact that the unmarried protagonist and her all-female world successfully *endure*, both spiritually and physically, at the conclusions of these novels implies a quiet but devastating criticism of the conventional structures of relationship to satisfy—or be unconditionally necessary to—all human needs. Hence the appropriateness of including these fictional worlds of female community as counter-traditional testimony of the continuing struggle to subvert the ideological values of the novelistic marriage tradition by overturning its form.

·Millenium Hall·
The Hidden Fruits of Pastoral Retirement

The thematic and formal traits typifying the novel of female community are abundantly present in this unsung and early critique of the marriage tradition by Sarah Scott, a largely forgotten contemporary of the first generation of great English novelists.[24] Part of the marvel of A Description of Millenium Hall (1762) is its ability to present its often subversive messages in socially acceptable terms. Because its subject, a "female Arcadia" (178), is imbued with such virtues as reason, piety, and charity, the novel invites approval as an embodiment of the best of eighteenth-century ideals; the fact that the genteel ladies of Millenium Hall can be made to fit conventional wisdom as "disappointed" women, furthermore, serves to excuse their "retirement" from the active world of men and marriage. Yet the very existence of this Utopian enclave of independent—and independently wealthy—women simultaneously refutes many of the most basic tenets of the English social structure: its basis is entirely collective; its operation daily extends beyond class and economic boundaries; its educational system produces women intellectually equal to men and economically capable of living alone; its circle of intimate friendships raises the ideal of sisterhood to a self-sufficient law. What makes this thematic duplicity all the more fascinating is that the novel's form embodies the same doubleness: its series of inset tales about the women's pasts combines what seems to be every possible variation on the traditional love-plot with an essentially nonlinear organization that mirrors the harmonious stasis that has been created within this all-female world.

The frame situation and opening sequence of the text illustrate Scott's talent at bending literary conventions to suit her own strategic purposes. Superficially working within a time-honored topos of Utopian fiction, the novel takes the form of a letter written by a gentleman traveler on tour of southern England (accompanied, not coincidentally, by a youthful coxcomb whose ideas of womanhood are in need of much amendment). Halted by a broken chaise and forced to take shelter from a storm at an estate named Millenium Hall, the narrator and his companion are startled to find "the Primum Mobile" residing at the center of "this earthly paradise" (33) to be an exclusively feminine society. This discovery becomes the pretext for the gentleman's novel-length letter detailing the Utopian charms of this hidden world. By making the spokesperson for "so uncommon a society" of women (34) an outsider who just happens to be male, Scott has subtly appropriated a standard device in Utopian travel narrative—the first-person observer—to articulate an essentially alien feminist vision and render it accessible to her audience (a manipulation of perspective we will see Gilman using to a similar effect a century and a half later in *Herland*).

This simultaneous overturning of conventional expectations and fictional conventions continues in the opening sequence as the visitors meet the inhabitants of the Hall. The narrator notes that one lady's complexion is "agreeable, though brown" (34), another's "features . . . too irregular to be handsome, but . . . engaging" (34), yet another's countenance "rather pleasing than beautiful" (35). The unconventional realism of such descriptions anticipates the series of other deflations of "feminine" stereotypes that soon follow. Foremost, the men's initial impression that such a community must be "rusticated" and "antiquated . . . by having lived so long out of the great world" (38) is forced to yield to the realization that these women have not simply secluded themselves from the world. Rather, as the narrator admits, they have made "as it were *a new one* for themselves, constituted on such very different principles from that [we] had hitherto lived in" (48; emphasis added). This difference is the key to Scott's feminism and her counter-traditional plotting. For the rest of the novel is a careful demonstration of the fact that the very marginality of these protagonists as unmarried women, paradoxically, has made possible their creation of a better, alternative world that stands as a judgment on the one from which their unexpected guests have arrived and the one where the reader uncomfortably remains.

After this opening sequence, the remaining text becomes a series of loosely connected episodes—organized according to a principle that is essentially accretive rather than causal—illustrating this "new" world's "different principles." Thus the present-time action revolves around the ladies' exhibition of their many charitable and educative projects, tours punctuated by discussions of their lives and social, economic, political, and religious values. The central principle governing these activities and beliefs, the men discover, is one common to the other novels in this chapter: that of generosity, which the ladies of Millenium Hall define as the "reciprocal communication of benefits" among "friends" (80). If generosity seems a stereotypically "feminine" attribute, these women have transformed it into a powerful means of taking concretely "nonfeminine" action to better the social lot of others less fortunate than they. The three charitable institutions they have established under the aegis of the estate make clear the potency of the women's ideal of giving. First, the men are taken to the colony of old-lady cottagers whom the ladies have taken off the hands of the parish and usefully employed as caretakers of the younger children of the poorer women villagers. It is women who benefit, all the way around, from this arrangement, and the cottagers, following the example of their benefactors, attest that "now we love one another like sisters, or indeed better" (40). Second, the men discover the asylum established for deformed outcasts, physical "freaks" whom the ladies protect from the world's cruelty by allowing them to create their own world in which "natural deficienc[ies]" (44) cease to be important. The implied analogy between this marginal community and the self-sustaining world created by the single women—"cripples" in society's eyes—offers moving testimony to both these women's deprivations and their triumphant survival. The charity of the estate extends to the upper class as well, as the men learn when they are shown a third project: a nearby mansion maintained for indigent gentlewomen. The result, as with the cottagers, is a spiritual "sisterhood" based on practical principles of collective sharing that not only "preserve an exact equality between them" (83) but grant to each an "equality" of being that an otherwise slavish "dependance" (82) on wealthy relations would deny.

Interspersed episodes, exposing the men to the community's woman-centered educational system, underscore the feminist basis of Scott's Utopian vision. Since founding Millenium Hall, its residents have established within its walls an ongoing school to help orphaned young girls "left destitute of provision" (122) by discriminatory inheritance laws. Themselves having benefited from exceptional educations, the founding ladies supervise the general liberal education of these pupils, schooling them to enter the few professions open to "accomplished women of an humble rank" (122); in the meantime, they have also established a cottage school for fifty village girls, training them in domestic skills "that they may have various means of gaining their subsistence" (154) other than the surety of marriage. In both endeavors the ladies' mission anticipates that of Gissing's "odd women" of a century and a half later, Mary Barfoot and Rhoda Nunn, who also view economic independence as the first and necessary step to women's larger personal freedom. The economic ramifications of this female-centered estate, moreover, extend into the general life of the parish, for the addition of Mrs. Trentham's fortune to the community has been used to invest in a neighborhood carpeting industry, which draws upon hundreds of formerly unemployed villagers. What is striking in this capitalistic enterprise is the untraditional role the women assume as stewards of the business in order to "prevent the poor from being oppressed by their superiors" (196).

In sum, by withdrawing from the world of fashionable society and selfish competition, the owners of Millenium Hall have not only ensured an emotionally and economically prosperous future for themselves by setting into operation a world that stands on its own; in the process they have communally fostered their own autonomy. Their success is registered in the narrator's representation of the community as a pastoral utopia—though one with a difference: "All that romance ever represented in the plains of Arcadia, are much inferior to the charms of Millenium Hall; except the want of shepherds be judged a deficiency, that nothing else can compensate; there indeed they fall short of what romance writers represent, and have formed a female Arcadia" (177–78). The *fruitful* stasis that typifies this paradise (as if the "millenium" of the estate's title has indeed arrived but without putting an end to progress) becomes a testament to the seemingly "feminine," maternal principle of sheer giving that these independent women have successfully transformed into a whole mode of well-being.

Moreover, the spirit that has brought this gathering of women together has been "maternal" from the beginning, as the history of their personal bonds with each other demonstrates. The four inset narratives recounting the past lives of Louisa Mancel and Mrs. Morgan, Lady Mary Jones, Mrs. Selvyn, and Mrs. Trentham, interspersed among the episodic glimpses into present life at the Hall, first appear to index conventional fictional trajectories of female experience: tragically thwarted love, near seduction, miserable marriage. But in an uncanny foreshadowing of Chodorow's psychoanalytic theories of mother-daughter bonding, all of these women's unsatisfactory experiences in the realm of heterosexual desire have been offset by their saving bonds with women who function as both friends and mother surrogates; in eventually forming a female collective they are acknowledging the sororal forces that have helped them to survive the conclusion of the traditional love-plot, figuratively speaking, and to enter a new realm of fictional possibility.

A summary of the double plot of the first inset biography, "The History of Mrs. Mancel and Mrs. Morgan," illustrates this central truth. Orphaned in childhood, Louisa Mancel enters a boarding school, where she comes under the loving care of the slightly older Miss Melvyn (the future Mrs. Morgan), who feels for her "an affection quite maternal" (58). The roots of Miss Melvyn's feelings are not hard to trace: her own superior education and sense of self-worth are the legacy of her dead mother, an extremely strong and intellectual woman whose mental gifts made a mockery of the role she was forced to play in her married life as her husband's "inferior" (54). The perils of female maturation begin in earnest for Miss Melvyn when her spiteful stepmother withdraws her from school and forces her to marry a man repugnant to her whole being. The "severest affliction" of her marriage, interestingly, is the "cruel separation" (96) it enforces between her and Louisa; the two women's "romantic friendship," to use Faderman's term, has begun to assume the shape of a traditional courtship plot. The subsequent narrative of Mrs. Morgan's wedlock is an uneasy as any described in chapter 4 above; her husband's denigration of her mind is nothing compared to the "uneasiness" she suffers "from his nauseous fondness" for "her person" (100). Her friend Louisa's experience, in the meantime, first assumes the shape of near seduction (when her trusted male guardian attempts to assault her), then of tragic romance. Having become an elderly woman's companion to place herself beyond the reach of the sexual menace that her beauty inevitably occasions, she finds herself honorably wooed by her employer's noble grandson in a situation that is socially impossible because of her uncertain birthright. In a providential twist, Louisa changes jobs to resist temptation, only to discover in her next employer her long-lost *real* mother; between them springs up a bond that demonstrates that maternal love, whether literally or figuratively manifested, is the only true saving force in this world.

At this juncture, turning points occur in both plots that seem to suggest conventionally happy ends for Louisa and Mrs. Morgan alike. With her newly established identity, Louisa becomes an acceptable candidate for her beloved Sir Edward's hand, and in the adjoining narrative Mr. Morgan's sickbed awakening to his wife's virtues is followed by his death and hence her fortuitous release from marital suffering. But it is typical of Scott's counterplot that nothing goes so smoothly. In an unexpected reversal, Louisa's lover dies before he can rejoin her, and even more unconventionally she grows to accept this disappointment as a blessing in disguise, for it saves her from the constrictions she views as inherent in the wifely role: "had she married [him], her sincere affection . . . would have led her to conform implicitly to all his inclinations" (123). More than this, it would have deprived her of "all the heart-felt joys she now daily experiences" (123) in the present-time narration of Millenium Hall. The fact there there is life after love for Louisa is intimately tied to the fact that Mr. Morgan's illness has already facilitated her long-awaited reunion with Mrs. Morgan: "these ladies met after so long an enforced separation, with a joy not to be imagined by any heart less susceptible than theirs, of the tender and delicate sensations of friendship" (120). The plot of their "sensible" friendship, which structurally as well as thematically provides this tale with the its closest semblance to a happy love interest, also frees Mrs. Morgan from a conventional fictional end. For the death of her husband leads *not* to a happier second match (the conventional reward for wifely suffering) but to the financial freedom making possible the establishment of Millenium Hall for herself, Louisa, and their similarly minded female friends. The linear trajectories inscribing both women's experiences in love are consequently redirected into the greater centric pattern governing the text as a whole.

The other "biographies" trace similar escapes from the dictates of conventional love-plotting. The various love affairs of Lady Mary Jones reveal the dangers of an upbringing in fashionable "society" where flirtation can lead to seduction and tragedy; after several narrow scrapes, Lady Mary turns in relief to the nonthreatening, serious reality that Millenium Hall offers. A moral upbringing, in contrast, leads to the same end—life at the Hall—for Harriot Selyvn. Upon the death of her loving guardian, she moves in with her best friend, the older Lady Emilia Reynolds, and she later rejects the proposal of a supposedly reformed rake on the grounds that "enjoying perfect content, she had no benefit to expect from change. . . . For what reason then should she alter her state?" (163). Moreover, the "present happy situation" that she declares she will never exchange "for the uncertainties of wedlock" in a society where men treat women's honor as a "lawful prize" (165–66) turns out to be paradigmatic of the metaphoric values with which Scott invests female friendship: in a key turn of the plot, Lady Emilia reveals herself as Harriot's actual mother. Again, intimate female friendship is portrayed as a logical extension of the mother-daughter bond. Upon Lady Emilia's death, Harriot finds a new, collective "mother" in her companions at the Hall. Scott's final portrait frames its critique of the marriage tradition in yet another way, detailing an ideal friendship between male and female cousins—figured in terms of sibling likeness recalling *Wuthering Heights*—who are pressured by society into believing that they must be in love. After an uneasy engagement and its disruption, they forego their "hopeless passion" (194) and return to their original, "untainted" friendship. The woman earns her recompense when her cousin gives her permission to raise the only child of the unhappy marriage he eventually makes: instead of a husband, she gains a daughter, who lives with her at Millenium Hall. What might appear a tragically abortive romance to outsiders—or to writers of conventional fiction—has instead been reformulated as a hidden blessing in the economy of this fictional world, yielding the literal fruit of matrimony, a daughter who promises to be brilliant, without the dangers and abuses of wedlock.

In all these "biographies," then, a traditional fictional trajectory of female experience is transformed into something altogether different. A striking parallel uniting these stories is that four of these women grow up as orphans (and the fifth, Miss Melvyn, is cast out of her home by her stepmother). Beginning life, that is, as "dispossessed" members of society, they not only learn the hardships of being outsiders but *choose*, finally, to remain outsiders by refusing to define themselves in terms of men or marriage; foregoing the assumed rewards of matrimony, they have converted dispossession, as Auerbach might put it, into a state of self-possession. Finding emotional satisfaction in their individual bonds with each other and in their collective acts of charity, this female enclave remains on friendly enough terms with the male world from which it has covertly seceded; the women enjoy being hospitable to the narrator and his friend, largely because men in general have ceased to pose any kind of threat to their present stability. There are limitations, however, to the feminism of Scott's Utopianists. Partly as a strategy to ensure their own survival, partly as a mechanism of psychological accommodation, these unmarried women laud "matrimony," for example, "as *absolutely necessary* to the good of society" (125; emphasis added), and they do not appear to be aware of any irony in their doing so. In addition, what might be called a patriarchal "Authority" creeps into their otherwise feminine circle in the form of the one force, the masculine deity, to whom they constantly refer and defer. But these degrees of external socialization do not detract from the important difference their personal rebellion against conventional female destiny has made. A subtle but telling indication of this quiet revolution occurs in the wedding celebration of a former pupil that the narrator witnesses. The girl is given a small fortune to mark this threshold, but so are *all* the young women the ladies of the Hall have brought up, whether single or married—everything is equal in this new world. Likewise, Scott has structured a novel whose critique of the sexual norms underlying marriage and marriage-plots is hidden, like this "amiable family" (38) itself, within a society and a textual form it appropriates for its own ends. "Retirement" from one world allows the self-generation of another realm, one whose Utopian vision its male observers will carry back into a society yet in need of reform.

·Cranford·
The "Elegant Economy" of Female Fortitude

Unlike *Millenium Hall*, Elizabeth Gaskell's account of old maids and widows in *Cranford* (1853) was early incorporated into the canon as a classic of sorts—but only at the expense of being known as a volume of "lavender and lace" sketches. Praised for an artless charm and pastoral delicacy implicitly associated with "feminine" artistry, the collection's episodic recounting of visitors' arrivals, tea parties, magic shows, old stories, and shopping sprees led earlier scholars to discount its artistic coherence and declare the text "practically structureless; this is part of its charm. The successive scenes pass before the reader as easily as if he were slipping different colored beads along a string."[25] As opposed to this appreciative rather than analytic view, a group of critics in the 1960s, motivated by New Critical imperatives, began to search for a linear "novelistic" unity in *Cranford*. But their efforts to discover traditionally developmental structures within its characters, plot, or themes shared an unquestioned assumption: namely, the belief that the all-female community at Cranford *had* to begin in a state of abnormality. Otherwise, according to the formalist logic of novelistic unities, there would be no "problem" for the remaining plot to resolve. And yet, tellingly, all these New Critical analyses posit exceptionally contradictory answers to the question of what a "normalization" of the community's original status would mean. These diverse opinions of *Cranford*'s artistic merits should awaken our suspicions that something about Cranford's apparently innocuous content, as well as its form, has never been all that it appears.[26]

Indeed, it might rather be argued that the sequence of events composing Gaskell's "plot" accrues meaning not because of any strictly causal arrangement—many of the episodes could be rearranged without disturbing the text's essential meaning—but because it continually repeats, in differing registers and recurring rhythms, the quiet victory over circumstance that has been achieved by this timid but self-possessed community of survivors. Rather than presenting a negative ideal in need of immediate reform, the "elegant economy" embraced by *Cranford*'s genteel spinsters from the text's beginning is less an appearance-saving device than a meaningful expression of the central truth around which they have organized their lives: namely, that having sustained an "elegant" dignity of spirit in the face of social deprivation and disapprobation, the "economy" of their marginal lives has even before the text's opening been rewarded with a communal resilience in surviving independently of the dominant social order. If *Cranford*'s narrative structure is cohesive, its unifying principles derive more from the circumscribed stasis associated with spinsterhood than from precepts of conventional narrative linearity.

The modal difference between *Cranford*'s centric structure and the developmental stages characterizing the standard love-plot also lies behind Gaskell's creation of Mary Smith as her first-person narrator. A frequent visitor from the neighboring industrial city of Drumble, Mary bridges the gap between the seemingly "static" world of the nearly all-female Cranford, where time seems to stand still ("There had been neither births, deaths, nor marriages since I was there last" [52], she jokes), and the "progressive" world of Drumble, where the values of her "manly" father ("clear-headed and decisive and a capital man of business' [195]) hold sway. The two towns thus become geographic embodiments of the doctrine of "separate spheres" regulating the sexes in mid-century England, and the narrator's mobility between the two introduces an implicit sexual dialectic into the text, but as subtle commentary rather than contentious plot. The manifold consequences for *Cranford*'s organization can be seen, once again, in Mary's function as the recorder of life in the village. While Scott's Utopian fantasy makes strategic use of a male narrator to validate its vision, Gaskell's strategy in choosing a woman narrator affirms the life of the Cranford society from an insider's angle of vision. For despite Mary's relative youth and sometimes ironic reflections on the anachronistic aspects of the lives of her Cranford friends, she too is an unmarried woman, and her spinster status leaves her entirely empathetic toward her subject matter; spiritually she is one of the Cranford single women, never an entirely objective commentator. As a consequence of this "inner view" into what might be her own future, Mary Smith's relationship to the material she narrates replicates the psychological dynamics of intimacy and mirroring that Chodorow and Abel theorize as an intrinsic aspect of female bonds. Thus her self-effacing participation in the textual action—she goes without being named up to three chapters from the end—allows her presence to merge almost completely with those she observes. One result of so intimately entering into and identifying with the timeless rhythms of this world is that Mary's narrative takes on a similarly circular quality, as we shall see.

Within this intimate alignment of narrator and subject, Gaskell's text repeatedly demonstrates that Cranford deserves to be considered a "world" in its own right, serving not so much as an *escape* from the "masculine" world of Mr. Smith and heterosexual couplings, as some critics have suggested,[27] as an *alternative* reality in itself. Unlike the parallel enclaves of women confined within the male-defined reality of the Drumbles of England, Cranford's society commands geographic and economic as well as psychological space; like the community of *Millenium Hall,* it thus has the power to enforce its alternative system of values. This fact the opening sentence of the text announces in a tone both whimsical and triumphant: "In the first place, Cranford is in possession of the Amazons; all the holders of houses, above a certain rent, are women" (39). The community's power of material "possession," one immediately learns, is the direct consequence of its Amazonian—that is, manless—status: "If a married couple come to settle in the town, somehow the gentleman disappears; he is either fairly frightened to death by being the only man in the Cranford evening parties, or he is accounted for by being with his regiment, his ship, or closely engaged in business all the week in the great neighbouring commercial town of Drumble. . . . In short, whatever does become of the gentlemen, they are not at Cranford"(39). Although Gaskell's tone is gently humorous, the incidents that follow illustrate precisely this fact, as Nina Auerbach has shown: as if by magic, threatening males are either made to "disappear" or are absorbed into the feminine structures of Cranford's reality.[28] The subsequent absence of male domination, in turn, insures the relative autonomy of Cranford's women. "What could they [men] do if they were there?" Mary Smith rhetorically asks, providing her own rejoinder: ". . . the ladies of Cranford are quite sufficient" (39).[29]

The self-suffiency of the female community, also mirrored in its geographic and situational insularity, is not without its adverse effects, a fact the text candidly acknowledges. Entrapment in stasis, among mirroring selves, can at one extreme become narcissistic and self-indulgent. Thus the ladies of Cranford pride themselves on being sublimely out-of-date, and they stubbornly claim allegiance to all things "traditional," even while their independent lives constitute a quiet breaking of tradition. The fears of loneliness, recurring memories of lost loves, and the unfulfilled maternal yearnings that punctuate their lives also evince the degree to which these single women have internalized society's devaluation of spinsterhood, despite their protestations of relief. But, in fact, the silently endured sufferings of the women of Cranford—the source of their various personal inadequacies and comic eccentricities—

become a further sign of their present equanimity and self-possession: this is one of the central meanings of the key metaphoric value, "elegant economy," practiced by the community. Introduced in
the opening chapter and echoing throughout almost all of the subsequent episodes, the motto becomes one of the symbolic "centers"
giving structure to a series of events that exist primarily to amplify
some aspect of its muted meaning.

On the surface the motto "elegant economy" refers to the verbal
subterfuge by which the ladies decorously avoid mentioning the
reality of their penury. Unlike the women of Millenium Hall, Cranford's genteel spinsters do not possess independent wealth with
which to facilitate their dreams. On one level an economic signifier,
on another the phrase evokes the moral superiority and psychological integrity of the spinsters' having maintained a code of "good-
will" (40) and "kind feelings" (155) in face of social stigmatization.
These interlocking meanings come together in Mary's seemingly
casual observation that these impoverished ladies have, Spartan-
like, "concealed their smart under a smiling face" (41). Not only a
pinched purse, but all the hardships and emotional pain accruing
to the spinster's lot lie behind that "smart," an attitude summed up
in one character's confession that her life has not "been sad, only so
very different to what I expected" (158). It is in part this overcoming of circumstance that has as its reward what another old maid
calls the "delicate independence existing in the mind of every refined female" of Cranford's circle (191).

The doctrine of "elegant economy" is most fully embodied in
Matty Jenkyn's achievement of such "delicate independence" after
her elder sister Deborah's death. Having always lived in the shadow
of her more outspoken sister, the reticent Miss Matty distrusts her
own inner strengths—strengths always present but in need of
awakening. Glimpses of Matty's potential firmness of character surface in the chapters 4 and 8. But the real catalyst setting her underlying Amazonian generosity of spirit into motion is the failure of
the bank of which she is a stockholder, inspiring her sense of communal responsibility to its distraught working-class noteholders. At
once steeling herself with "that self-control which seemed habitual
to ladies of [her] standing in Cranford" (178) yet assuming a "soft
dignified manner peculiar to her, rarely used, and yet which became her so well" (176), Matty begins to command the combination

of firmness and softness essential to the doctrine of "elegant econo-my." It is "*our* bank," Matty reminds the narrator; "if honest people are to lose their money because they have taken *our* notes," she declares it is only "common honesty" to stand by them, whatever one's personal loss (176–77; emphasis added).[30] The communal spirit that has permeated Cranford's daily life and been the subject of others' ridicule turns out to be the basis of an encompassing ethical perspective reaching into the economic spheres of life.

Matty's willingness to forego her own meager annuity to help the shareholders in turn unlocks her friends' ever-present reserve of strength and generosity. Impoverished themselves, these wom-en agree in secret to pledge an annual fund to go toward Matty's rent. As Miss Pole proudly (if a bit stiltedly, having trouble reading from her prepared prompt cards) announces to the group, "*We, the ladies of Cranford . . . can resolve* upon something" (191; em-phasis added). For by "resolving" to ensure Matty's self-sufficiency, the female community is in effect ensuring its own perpetuity. The diffusive example of such "elegant economy" also extends to the lower rungs of Cranford's social classes. Martha, Matty's faithful servant, refuses to leave her mistress—indeed, she coerces her fi-ancé into looking for a house into which they can take Matty as a permanent boarder. Nor, once Matty is set up in her own business of selling teas and comfits, can the dire warning of Mary Smith's father about Matty's overly generous—that is, non-Drumble—han-dling of her trade have any meaning in a community where every-one actively conspires to make her brave business a success; Mr. Smith's mercantile verities simply do not carry weight in this covertly communal enterprise.

Along with the structural accretion of events giving voice to the principle of elegant economy, patterns of male intruders form an-other incremental rhythm that circles around and animates the central truth of this text's alternative reality. The first two episodes, for instance, record the advent of the blustering but kind-hearted Captain Brown and his daughters. Just as the overbearing reality of his "masculine gender" (42) and "manly frankness" (43) threatens to swamp the ladies' slender authority and make their hard-earned verities appear mere fancies, he is killed off by a passing train. In an unintentionally ironic reversal, it is the "unreal" community that survives in "real" time; the Captain's manly bluster, however well intended, turns out to be the more ephemeral modus vivendi. A second invasion of masculine "presence" immediately follows in chapters 3 and 4, as Mary learns of Matty's youthful courtship with the farmer Holbrook; typifying the circular sense of time permeating both town and text, the past becomes present as Holbrook and Matty accidentally meet for the first time in forty years. But as there was no fulfillment of romance in the past, Gaskell makes clear that romance is not her present subject when Mary's "castle building" dream of "sentimental romance" is blown "into small fragments," first by learning Mr. Holbrook's age, then by meeting him in his dotage (70). Although he lingers long enough to invite Matty, Miss Pole, and Mary to dinner, his exit from the narrative is almost as abrupt as was his entrance—he goes the way of Captain Brown, dying without time for an adieu.[31]

The pattern of male intruders resumes three chapters later when Signor Brunoni, a magician whose sleights of hand seem at first a personification of "masculine" power and mystery, descends upon the female community. Brunoni's magic involves more than his performing tricks; his very aura of unassailable, foreign vigor turns out to be an illusion. For the ladies' spellbound awe and admiration is decisively shattered several weeks later when they discover Brunoni laid low by illness at a nearby country inn and in dire need of all the "feminine" help they can offer; they, in effect, now wield the power of life and death over this "poor man" as they engineer his recovery. Brunoni's financial straits, moreover, give the community an occasion to practice its collective generosity: "it was wonderful to see what kind feelings were called out by this poor man's coming amongst us" (p. 155). Once the women effect his recuperation, Brunoni is quickly ushered out of the narrative; only at the female community's express command does he reappear at novel's end to provide a summer evening's entertainment.[32]

The surprise arrival of Peter Jenkyns, Matty's "long-lost" brother, in the final chapters repeats Brunoni's example of a male whose presence can be safely harnessed for the continuing benefit and entertainment of the community. Unlike the other Cranford intruders, however, Peter does not need to undergo trials of rebirth to insure his harmlessness. For, as Matty's earlier stories of his youth have already demonstrated, he has always been a foe of male

privilege and a willing accomplice of female harmony. His trans-
vestite capers, recounted by Matty to Mary, not only establish his
youthful flaunting of masculine norms of behavior, but also set him
against his father's merciless authoritarianism and lead to his deliberate removal to the margins of English society as sojourner in In-
dia. Like the young Heathcliff in *Wuthering Heights*, Peter has too
quickly been pigeonholed by critics as an embodiment of traditional masculinity, the ruling "patriarch" among a covey of women,
simply because he is male. Rather, joining his sister upon his return
in the gentle arts learned from their mother's example,[33] he readily *unites with* the ladies of Cranford in the cause of perpetuating
peace and harmony; it is he who effects a reconciliation between
the feuding Mrs. Jamieson and Mrs. Hoggins because he wants
"everybody to be friends, for it harasses Matty so much to hear
these quarrels" (217). And as a sojourner in foreign lands, Peter
introduces a cultural relativity into Cranford's society that widens
its imaginative circumference without disturbing its geographic
containment.

Peter's return, it is true, does provide Gaskell with a providential
means of rescuing Matty from poverty, and as such his idealized
role as brother-savior is reminiscent of the role played in Gaskell's
North and South by Margaret Hale's long-absent brother Frederick.
But the very displacement of this sentiment onto a sibling configuration—similar to those in *Wuthering Heights* and *Daniel Deronda* (to
the extent that Gwendolen and Daniel's bond is siblinglike)—enhances *Cranford*'s counter-traditional thematics. The proof of Peter's filial allegiance is humorously rendered in his adroit handling
of the rumor that the widowed Mrs. Jameison is casting an amorous eye in his direction. Drawing on his Indian tall tales, Peter lulls
her into a forgetfulness that diffuses any romantic "threat." As
Auerbach puts it, "Marriage succumbs to a wonderful lie" with Peter's fabrications, leaving Cranford "at one with itself. . . . At the
end of the novel the natives of Cranford have achieved beati-
tude . . . without the usual novelistic sacrament of marriage."[34]

The three marriages that *do* take place in the novel—thus creating yet another of its incremental patterns—are made to serve the
specific needs of the community rather than provide the text with a
traditional ending. For instance, the death of Captain Brown,
rapidly followed by that of his oldest daughter, leaves a second

daughter alone in the world. A sweet, dimpled ingenue who seems to have wandered out the pages of a Dickens novel, she clearly does not belong among the hardier Cranford spinsters and widows. Thus it is with a communal sigh of relief that a former suitor, Major Gordon, fortuitously appears on scene to sweep her away; the conventional Victorian heroine finds her way back into a conventionally Victorian love-plot and is removed, except as grateful visitor, from the text. The event hence leaves the stasis of the community undisturbed, with the beneficial exception of its having gained allies in the outside world via the Gordons. Marriage is again deflected from the center of Cranford society to the fringes after the brief reappearance of Matty's old suitor, Holbrook; the upshot is that Matty generously encourages her servant Martha to take up a follower and in the process wins for herself the unexpected boon of *two* faithful retainers during the bank crisis. And when the couple names their first daughter after Matty, they symbolically secure her future perpetuation; a continuing lineage of names has been provided without labor, as it were, on Matty's part. The third marriage to punctuate the text, reversing the formula of *Pamela,* is a triumph of class democratization, uniting the wholesomely unpretentious, older Lady Glenmire, a visitor to the community, and its respected but non-aristocratic doctor, Mr. Hoggins. Marriage, then, forms an unobtrusive rhythm in the centric patterning of the novel. As in *Millenium Hall* it is present, it is celebrated, and yet it never really threatens the rooted independence of Cranford's spinsters and widows. By way of contrast, it illuminates their self-sustaining and provident existences.

The circling and incremental patterns lending coherence to *Cranford*'s episodic structure thus imprint, from beginning to end, a message of the hard-won harmony that exists at the static heart of the supposedly deprived but unexpectedly full lives of these husbandless women. It is appropriate that Gaskell ends with the ceremonial epilogue titled "Peace to Cranford," in which the dramatis personae of all ranks are gathered together, from the now-married Mrs. Gordon to Signor Brunoni, to celebrate the community's continuity. Divorced from the context of patriarchal marriage, those so-called "feminine" virtues of charity, kindliness, and trust—also intrinsic to life in Scott's female Utopia—can exist as primary rather than segregated aspects of reality, precisely because their bearers have learned to abjure traditionally "feminine" dependence for communal interdependence and the saving economy of elegant, individual fortitude.

·The Country of the Pointed Firs·
Matriarchs in Maine

Before the advent of feminist literary criticism in the 1970s, many scholars tended to characterize Sarah Orne Jewett as if she were an American version of one of *Cranford*'s old maids, making her single status the basis of a misleading estimate of her art as desexed and conservative: even today she remains "Miss" Jewett to many readers, much as Elizabeth Gaskell, of major nineteenth-century women writers, has been categorized as "Mrs."[35] Recently, however, Josephine Donovan has intelligently argued that the author's lifelong awareness of women's limited opportunities shaped her entire literary output: that awareness underlies the elegiac tone of missed or lost opportunity and the theme of isolation running throughout her stories of remote New England and Maine life.[36] And it is certainly the impulse that inspired her only full-length novel, *A Country Doctor* (1884), the story of a self-reliant New Woman who does *not* abdicate her career for marriage, unlike the women physicians in Howells's *Dr. Breen's Practice* (1881) and Elizabeth Stuart Phelps Ward's *Doctor Zay* (1882).[37]

Likewise, the vital emotional core of Jewett's most famous work, *The Country of the Pointed Firs* (1896), is located in its representation of an extensive web of female bonds that render the romantic expectations of conventional love fiction unimportant. Jewett once advised the aspiring writer Willa Cather to "find your own quiet center of life, and write from that"[38]—and this philosophy is central to the rendering in *Pointed Firs* of a matriarchal world in which time exists chiefly in the external cycle of the seasons and the internal cycle of memory. Narrating her tale in lyrically short, episodic, and numbered sections whose major force is accumulative rather than sequential, Jewett creates a counter-traditional text about primarily single and widowed women who, having long since centered their lives in communal stasis, have in turn become the creators of a counter-traditional reality in which emotional commitment and autonomy harmoniously coexist.

The symbolic "center" occupied by this female-populated reality is suggested by the text's narrative frame. In the opening sequence the narrator—a self-reliant, unmarried, and unnamed woman writer—journeys by water to spend her summer at Dunnet Landing, a timeless speck of village on the "unchanged shores"[39] of Maine; the text ends with her steamboat departure from this hidden enclave. But this "corner of the world" (15), located at the margins of modernity, turns out to be a vital "centre of civilization" (13) for its inhabitants, containing an infinitely expansive system of "feminine" values and relationships that, as the narrator announces in recounting a return voyage, make her "feel solid and definite again, instead of a poor, incoherent being. Life was resumed" (147). Solid Dunnet thus comes to represent an inner stability essential to living, and this truth forms the thematic core around which the subsequent layers of episode and events recounting the narrator's stay are arranged.

In contrast to Gaskell's proper village, stasis in Jewett's community is not just a function of physical insularity. The town of Dunnet rather serves as a hub connecting a larger network of outlying island communities and inland farms among which movement is both frequent and welcome; together these pockets of community form the abstract "region" of values symbolized by "the country of the pointed firs." Stasis in this work thus becomes more a function of the immemorial timelessness of its setting than of geographic or mental constriction: to be rooted in this timeless region is to make possible an *expansion* of self. This truth is conveyed in an epiphanic scene where the narrator, from the vantage point of a high promontory on an island in the bay, finds herself in the center of a series of concentric rings, enclosed by "the circle of pointed firs" below her and then by "the ocean that circled this . . . and all the far horizons." Rather than feeling constricted (as Eliot's Gwendolen does) by such far-reaching vistas, she experiences "a sudden sense of space . . . that sense of liberty in space and time" (46). Hence, her entrance into the remote but central world of Dunnet signaled at the narrative's opening may also be seen as a metaphoric opening into that "wild zone" or free space belonging to women otherwise trapped in patriarchy; enclosure within the ring of values guarding Dunnet's female enclave becomes the precondition of freedom and self-possession.

And self-possession is the key trait shared by the inhabitants of Dunnet's world. For what the narrator finds abiding at the heart of life represented by this geographic and narrative center is a fiercely independent culture kept alive by an extended community of individualistic women who have survived, along with the weather, the vicissitudes of marriage and the deprivations of spinsterhood. The description of the herb tansy, which grows like "folks that had it hard in their youth, and were bound to make the most of themselves before they died" (19), provides an apt emblem of the hardy and hard-earned selfhood of all these women. Even more strongly than in *Cranford*, one consequence of such independence is a benign indifference to male presence or support. The few elderly men who dot the landscape are either harmless eccentrics, relegated to the fringes of its society, or willing adjuncts like Peter Jenkyns of *Cranford* in maintaining its matriarchal order. Mrs. Todd, the narrator's landlady, "mateless and appealing" (159), "great and self-possessed" (139), sums up a general attitude as she and the writer prepare to sail to Green Island, her mother's home: "We don't want to carry no men folks havin' to be considered every minute an' takin' up all our time. No, you let me do; we'll just slip out an' see mother by ourselves" (35). Similarly, Mrs. Todd's matter-of-fact assessment of her marriage—"'t wa'n't what either one of us wanted most" (17)—also appears representative of the surviving women; she tells the narrator that she appreciated her departed husband most for his benevolent noninterference in her daily pursuits (94). On the other hand, like Matty Jenkyns, Mrs. Todd carries in her heart the vestiges of an unrealized love affair. But her pangs, like Matty's, have safely been stabilized as past event, and their periodic resurgence as memory serves mainly to enhance the mythic heroism of Mrs. Todd's present-day survival.

Beyond the rejection of marriage as a woman's sole basis for self-definition, Jewett's female community is united by a shared set of values emanating from a matriarchal worldview akin to Scott's emphasis on mothers in *Millenium Hall*. Foremost among these "feminine" values—and echoing the goal sought in many of the quest narratives examined in the previous chapter—is that of the heart: love pure and simple. The narrator, for one, comes to the realization that she has "never found love in its simplicity as I . . . found it at Dunnet Landing" (151). Such elemental feeling, untainted by superficial social codes or sexual menace, creates the pervading mood of "peace and harmony" that characterizes the relationships among these women. Their sense of loving community, furthermore, is tied to a related value, "hospitality," which is defined as the art of giving oneself over to others in "perfect self-forgetfulness" (46–47); the result—unlikely in a more competitive environment where passivity is considered a weakness—is an interfusing of selves that yields the harmony of the communal whole. The women's continual exchange of visits, providing the text with its basic structure, becomes the occasion for the practice of such hospitality. The shared reminiscences and exchanged information about absent friends that result from these instances of personal contact keep alive a spirit of community that sustains its members when each finds herself alone.

The communal values of Dunnet's female population are best summed up in the characterization of Mrs. Todd, whose spirit pervades the text even when she is offstage. Like her home, which first appears "to be retired and sheltered enough from the busy world" (14) but in fact turns out to be a bustling center of commerce and an informal "school" (18) for other women in the herbal arts, Mrs. Todd commands existence from its heart. Appropriately, the narrator first characterizes Mrs. Todd as "a huge sibyl," dispensing the secrets of life and death from the darkened interior of her living room, where she stands at "the centre of a braided rug" whose rings "circle about her feet in the dim light" (17). The sense of arrested motion in this passage, transforming Mrs. Todd into an immemorial image of female wisdom, summons forth her related symbolic functions as herb gatherer and all-powerful mythic force. As an herbalist, Mrs. Todd demonstrates a closeness to nature and a power of healing traditionally associated with the "wise women" of folklore. Using the seasons as her guide to make herb-hunting forays into the countryside that forms her second "home," Mrs. Todd is so attuned to natural rhythms as to strike the narrator as "some force of Nature" personified, with "cousinship to the ancient deities" (137). Such references, evoking the ancient rule of the mother goddess, transform Mrs. Todd into a present-day *magna mater* whose presence attests to the covert survival of a matriarchal order in the remote reaches of Maine. One of Jewett's most effective structural devices for conveying this sense of mythic

THE NOVEL OF FEMALE COMMUNITY

timelessness involves the repetition, with only slightly varying set-tings and allusions, of tableaus involving Mrs. Todd in an arrested pose—usually outlined against the sky—that momentarily stop the narrative.[40] The still-life effect of these inserted moments marks the text's structure with a rhythm that keeps circling back on itself, like the natural cycle, thus abetting Jewett's plotting of an essen-tially static, nonlinear reality.

The mythically powerful and mothering figure of Mrs. Todd, moreover, becomes the narrator's creative muse; for in learning the nonverbal "language" of Mrs. Todd's natural rhythms, the narrator learns the structural and verbal rhythms appropriate to her textual representation of Dunnet's centric world. But the relationship of the two women does not limit itself to the dichotomous paradigm of artist/muse characterizing the traditional iconography of male au-thorship and female inspiration. To the contrary, the narrator and Mrs. Todd merge in a mutually constructive alliance which, like that of Mary Smith and her friends, confirms recent theories of the psychological dynamics of female bonding. For the initial cordiality of landlady and boarder quickly dissolves into "a deeper intimacy" as Mrs. Todd unburdens her "heart" to the narrator under the spell of quiet summer evenings (16–17); in a reciprocal gesture, Mrs. Todd undertakes to initiate this "humble follower" (137) into the secrets of Dunnet life. Returning to Mrs. Todd's door after a long separation, the narrator finds her "heart . . . beating like a lover's" (148), for she is no longer the outsider but an integral part of the "chain of love and dependence" that links "far island . . . and scat-tered farms" (82) in a sphere of intimacy.

The bond uniting Mrs. Todd and the narrator is also integral to the structural dynamic of *Pointed Firs*. As the younger woman's passport to the inner world of Dunnet, Mrs. Todd leads her on the herb-hunting excursions and neighborly visits that at once intro-duce her to the countryside and also make her privy to its citizens' conversations and recollections. Such visits, excursions, and ex-changes, recounted in the narrative's sequentially numbered, seemingly random episodes, make up the bulk of the text. Al-though each individual fragment is relatively self-contained, the episodic journeys of the two women, like radii reaching out into the region encircling Dunnet, create a repeating rhythm of extension and return to an unchanging center of calm. The meaning of such

journeying, whose pattern Marjorie Pryse has described as one of
"invagination,"[41] differs radically from those voyages inscribed in
the trajectory of the male quest. For, in contrast to the quest's persistent "thrusts" into the *unknown,* the sallying forth of Mrs. Todd
and the narrator is always circular in its structure, an affirmation of
the *known* that leads back to familiar and abiding truths; such pil-
grimages serve to keep open those channels of communication essential to the spirit of the extended community.[42]

One such exemplary journey occurs exactly mid-narrative when
Mrs. Todd takes the narrator to visit her mother, Mrs. Blackett,
whose island home, "a complete and tiny continent" (40) in itself,
mirrors the elderly lady's self-sustaining independence. "Solidly
fixed into the still foundations of the world" (120), Green Island
becomes another of the text's emblems of static centricity, as does
the eighty-six-year-old widow herself, whose years seem to defy the
forward progression of time: "she took on a sudden look of youth;
you felt as if she promised a great future, and was beginning, not
ending, her summers and their happy toils" (41). The fiercely
strong bond between mother and daughter forms a matrilineal line
to which the narrator becomes the adoptive heir. This triumvirate
of women is reunited in the text's penultimate journey, an inland—
as contrasted to island—pilgrimage to the Bowden family reunion.
The long episode (which forms the last episode before the concluding frame in the original edition) demonstrates that if Mrs. Todd is
the region's most active matriarch, her mother remains its un-
disputed sovereign. Mrs. Todd's triumphant proclamation that
"Mother's always the queen" (89) of such festivities thus has its general as well as specific meaning: not merely Mrs. Blackett, but the
larger idea of matriarchy, reigns supreme in this world.

A related structural function of the narrator's continuing visits is
that of contrasting the lot of those who have successfully established communal roots to those who abjure meaningful ties. Two of
the text's most memorable isolates, revealingly, are men. Captain
Littlepage's crazed certainty that he has discovered a sea route to
"eternity," almost a parody of Ahab's obsession with the ultimate in
Moby-Dick, ironically alienates him from the life that lies all around
him. The bravado of this retired sea captain is, however, calmly
viewed by the feminine community as harmlessly eccentric, not a
real threat. Also suffering from a solitude bordering on the unreal

is another of the narrator's acquaintances, Elijah Tilley. Having insulated himself within his marriage as the whole of life, he decides to "tough it out alone" (106) after his wife dies, and, shutting out external reality, pathetically lives in memories of the dead past. The implicit commentary on the hazards of isolation for both these men finds its parallel in the inserted tale of "poor Joanna" that Mrs. Todd narrates. "Crossed in love" (61), Joanna masochistically punishes herself by withdrawing from society—and symbolically from life itself—to become a hermit on Shellheap Island. Not only does Joanna's case illustrate the dangers of placing "all [one's] hopes . . . on marryin'" (61), but for the narrator she becomes an especially poignant symbol of a solitary woman lacking the community that the Dunnet women have established: "My thoughts flew back to the lonely woman on her outer island; what separation from humankind she must have felt, what terror and sadness" (67).[43]

Three other inserted tales merit attention—those segments posthumously interpolated into the 1910 edition of *Pointed Firs*. Technically speaking, Warner Berthoff is quite right when he argues that their addition destroys the narrative unity of the teller's summer stay and thus should be dropped from the collection.[44] However, given the fact that the structural precepts underlying the narrative of female community encourage a certain accumulation of noncausally related scenes, the extent to which these episodes incrementally repeat previously established themes make them of critical interest. In "The Queen's Twin," for example, the ability of female friendship to ward off isolation is thematically explored from yet another angle in the case of Mis' Abby Martin, an eccentric who fancies herself the spiritual twin and sister of Queen Victoria. As Mrs. Todd suggests, Abby has in effect fabricated this imaginary sisterhood to fill the lonely void left by a hard life and a bad marriage. The "Dunnet Shepherdess" episode, centering on Esther Hight, is another in Jewett's series of portraits of strong women who have "managed to succeed" (126) independently of men and gained "a lovely self-possession" (127) as the result; when she finally marries Mrs. Todd's femininely mild and equally aged brother in the third of the interpolated segments, "William's Wedding," her chosen mate seems more brother than lover, a substitution of roles that makes their union analogous to that established by

Miss Matty and her actual brother at the end of *Cranford*. Most importantly, their autumnal union becomes the occasion for an affirmation of the power of loving community advocated throughout the text by its circle of women. All three interpolations, then, extend the length of *Pointed Firs* through added illustration rather than through "forward" motion.

Both in the original edition and the editorially revised 1910 edition, the narrator's leavetaking from this inner realm forms the final episode. Her departure by water—as indicated in the section's title, "The Backward View"—serves to enclose the story of Dunnet within narrative brackets that at once epitomize its stasis and hidden centrality. The emphasis of the brief scene is the heartfelt parting of Mrs. Todd and the narrator, whose bond has come to exemplify the quality of female lives rooted in natural time, as opposed to "the thick of battle" (158) that the narrator knows awaits her in the world-at-large. As the framed inner story or "heart" of this text suggests, the narrator must now transform the lessons of its matriarchal circle into an inner principle, a central truth upon whose foundation she can build the "coherence" of her outer life. It is appropriate that as the narration draws to its close, so too the season, summer, "com[es] to its lovely end" (157); the repeating narrative rhythms of *The Country of the Pointed Firs* merge with the natural cycles in inscribing its matriarchs within a timeless circle of harmonious stasis. Not only in terms of characterization, but also in regard to narrative format, Jewett has created a text written from a "center of life," to paraphrase her advice to Cather, that counters the fictional linearity of romantic alignment as it upholds the stationary truths and eternal natural rhythms embedded in the Dunnet way of life.

·*Herland*·
Feminist Fantasies of Utopia

While Scott, Gaskell, and Jewett contented themselves with quiet subversions of male hierarchy, the turn-of-the-century writer Charlotte Perkins Gilman threw herself into the midst of public controversy as an unabashed advocate of radical social change for women. Promulgating in her fiction as well as nonfiction (including the classic *Women and Economics* and the journal *The Forerunner*) a vision of nonpatriarchal, collectively organized society, this feminist-socialist thinker repeatedly pointed to her culture's sentimental myth of wedlock as the product not of disinterested love but of individual, selfish need. Most readers today know Gilman as the author of the haunting, powerful short story "The Yellow Wallpaper" (1899), whose relentless attack on the abuses of power and gender in marriage calls to mind many of the features I have associated with the counter-traditional representation of "uneasy wedlock."[45] In contrast to this grim portrait, Gilman's Utopian-feminist *Herland* (1915) approaches similar issues through a very different fictional tack: this fantasy of an all-female kingdom uses humor, positive example, and gentle satire, rather than gothic horror, to undermine the Victorian ideology of love and marriage. In this joyful celebration of female selfhood and community, the microscopic enclaves of permanence and peace sketched by Scott, Gaskell, and Jewett have been expanded by Gilman into an entire, self-regulating nation. Yet its geography of possibility remains as invisible to the known world as England's Cranfords or America's Dunnets until three male explorers—like the travelers in *Millenium Hall*—stumble across its circumference, their subsequent movement absorbed into a nonlinear narrative pattern that reflects the Herland way of life. What they find in Herland and report back to the "real" world in the form of a first-person text touches on most of the traits we have thus far identified with the "centric" plot of female community: in this truly Amazonian kingdom peace and progress coexist, "mothering" forms the central religion, and a collective spirit of sisterhood has replaced the ill effects of competitive individualism and industrialization. Above all else, it is the absence of patriarchy that makes possible this nearly perfect kingdom; gender has absolutely ceased to make a difference because for nearly two thousand years no men have been present to impose a male perspective of femininity on these self-sufficient women. And the result, logically enough, is a feminist dream of Utopia.

From Peter Jenkyn's stories of travel in the Orient to Captain Littlepage's reminiscences of "voyages of discovery" at sea, references to questlike exploits have been incorporated into the narrative of female community as reminders of the relative stasis of its female constituents. *Herland* goes a step further in constructing a

frame situation that spoofs the American quest archetype, as pointed out at the end of chapter 5 above. On one level, of course, opening with a male's narrative "perspective" is, as in *Millenium Hall*, a
strategic decision; the "objective" yet sympathetic voice of Van Jen-
ning validates the unfamiliar world he uncovers for the reader. But
the situation itself becomes a humorous critique of the fate of the
twentieth-century quest narrative. As avid members of a fact-find-
ing expedition in an unspecified hinterland, Gilman's triad of male
explorers entertains an exaggerated notion of heroic fulfillment in
braving the unknown that owes more to the virile ethos of writers
like London than the introspection of Melville. Of these boon companions, Terry in particular embodies the attitude that transformed the expression of quest into one of conquest around the
turn of the century: always in need of an object "to oppose, to
struggle with, to conquer" (99), his great frustration is that there
was nothing left to explore now, only patchwork and filling in" (1–
2)—actual patchwork, ironically enough, being an age-old expression of female creativity. Rumor of a forbidden kingdom, "a
strange and terrible Woman Land in the high distance" (2), comes
as the perfect answer to Terry's dissatisfaction, and thus he fi-
nances with delight the scientific exploration that becomes more of
a Melvillean descent into (or, in this case, ascent to) a "sacred center" than he or his companions bargained for.[46] For the immediate
end that the three men have in mind—"penetrating" the mountain
ridges that gird and protect the secret interior of this kingdom—
turns out to be merely the *beginning* of Gilman's feminist narrative;
at this point, ironically, the quest format almost immediately gives
way to a different narrative principle, one which appropriates and
radically redefines the hitherto linear momentum of the explorers'
enterprise.

For, once having broken into the circle of Herland's boundaries,
the men are lured into the heart of the kingdom, where their "Rash
Advances" (the punning title of chapter 2) lead them to "A Peculiar
Imprisonment" (chapter 3)—they suddenly find themselves surrounded by an impenetrable wall of matronly but impassive fe-
males. From this point forward, their quest's "advance" is
determined by this encompassing ring of women: "they motioned
us to advance, standing so packed . . . that there remained but the
one straight path open . . . ; there was simply nothing to do but go

forward—or fight" (22). As the men are subsequently herded down this human "cattle chute" to imprisonment in stasis, Van ruefully reports, "We were borne inside, struggling manfully, but held secure most womanfully, in spite of our best endeavors" (23). Thus begins the next stage of Gilman's narrative format, for where the quest movement ends, a new story, both in its content and structure, unfolds.

Having been physically "borne" over the threshold into captivity, the men are now reborn into the reality of Herland's nonpatriarchal society, as the imagery of rebirth used at the beginning of chapter 3 signifies. Awakening as if "coming back to life" (24), the prisoners discover that they have been stripped of civilization's old clothes and, to their manly dismay, "washed and put to bed like so many yearling babies" (25) in flowing unisex garments that leave them "feeling like a lot of neuters" (26). Virtually every chapter after the third and fourth centers around the reeducative process for which this reclothing has been mere preparation. The narrative sequence, hereafter, thus consists of the layering, the accumulation, of scenes, passages, and actions that amplify the nonsexist philosophy abiding at the core of the Herlanders' lives. Consequently, in place of the inward or centripetal momentum traced by the first three chapters, the text now institutes an outward-reaching movement from the symbolic center into which the men's original trajectory has been redirected. The symbolic reverberations of this structural pattern-ing are self-evident: captivity within a static world—fixing these male questers, in a neat reversal, in a position analogous to women's in patriarchy—becomes a liberating expansion once the "prisoner of gender" learns to renounce his or her learned biases about the sexes and heterosexual relationship. Hence it is appropriate that as the men undergo their lessons, their perceptions are metaphorically depicted as "deepening and widening" (95) in circles of understand-ing; reciprocally, as the wonders of the country "[open] up" (90) before their eyes, they begin to see that all life in this female Utopia is interconnected in an ever-encompassing network: "The things they learned were *related*, from the first; related to one another, and to the national prosperity" (100).

Paralleling the process of the men's widening mental horizons during their "classroom lessons" in chapters 5 and 6, their intro-duction to the actual kingdom in chapters 7 and 8 roughly pro-

ceeds from the kingdom's heart to the cultivated, gardenlike forests that form its natural circumference. Along the way they are
exposed to the country's history, scope, inhabitants, and customs.
In making the primary function of these events an amplification of
Herland's model way of life, Gilman like Scott before her revises
the episodic format of Utopian narrative to suit a specifically feminist task, and in the process creates a nonlinear, cyclical structure
similar to those in other novels of female community. The static
formal quality that readers often perceive in *Herland* thus reflects
the collective serenity of *a life without strife* that has taken root in this
female world. As Van warns the reader, his tale will contain "no
adventures" of the sort that fiction usually involves, "because there
was nothing to fight" (49). With the masculine worldview of Terry
absent, the momentum driving conventionally linear plots has simply become irrelevant, leaving narrative desire free to reformulate
itself in new patterns.

Within the centric structure that follows from this radically different perspective, the men's lessons in Herland's nonlinear world
order involve the repeated overturning of their socialized perceptions about sex roles and sexual power. The extent to which an
asymmetrical dichotomization of gender has permeated and shaped
Western culture becomes evident to Van as he contrasts the two
cultures: "We have two life cycles," he says of America, "the man's
and the woman's. To the man there is growth, struggle, conquest. . . . To the woman, growth, the securing of a husband, the
subordinate activities of family life. . . . Here was but one cycle, and
that a large one" (101). Balancing the men's gradual loss of a sense of
innate superiority is the deflation of their expectations of female
inferiority. Because there is "no accepted standard of what [is] 'manly' and what . . . 'womanly'" (92) in this kingdom, its self-sufficent
women manifest a fullness that sets them figuratively as well as
literally worlds apart from the helpless, weeping heroines of sentimental fiction. Thus, by degrees Van is led "to the conviction that
those 'feminine charms' we are so fond of are not feminine at all, but
mere reflected masculinity—developed to please us because they
had to please us" (59). That is, the assumed polarity of the sexes is
revealed as an artificially imposed social construct whose purpose is
to support a male-identified order.

The lack of sex role differentiation in Herland also renders inoperable the pervasive Western archetype, traced at length in chapter 2 above, of love union as a coming together of opposites in which each partner contributes "half" (presumably his "masculinity" and her "femininity") to make up a whole existence. Because his society has associated power with men, as Van explains to the Herlanders, "the marriage tradition of our general history . . . relates the woman to the man." "He goes on with his business, and she adapts herself to him and to it" (122), Van continues, unconsciously echoing Blackstone's legal definition of "husband and wife [as] one person in law," that person being "the husband." To avert such hierarchical control of one sex over the other, Gilman offers a new model of heterosexual relationship in the experimental "courtships" (arranged by the nation's ruling council) that form a unifying thread in chapters 8 through 12. Whereas the tales of bygone courtship and seduction punctuating the Utopian format of *Millenium Hall* highlight the present-day equanimity of the women, the romances between Herlanders and captives look toward a future reconciliation of the sexes. Terry, of course, fails to establish a relationship of parity since his entire identity depends on a traditional belief in sexual polarity, and Jeff becomes too idealistic a votary of Herland womanhood. But the romance of Elladore and the narrator Van, who has all along struck the Herlanders "more like us . . . like People" (89), offers a paradigm of the new hope that Gilman sees as truly natural. Because friendship—or "higher comradeship" (90)—precedes the passionate feeling that Van later develops for Elladore, mutuality replaces polarity as the basis for their bond and helps to ensure an equality based on each partner's separate sense of identity. The untraditional implications of such a model of loving are paralleled by Gilman's transformation of the traditional "declaration" scene of fiction into an avowal of individual identity and vocation. "I ceased to feel a stranger, a prisoner," Van reports of Elladore's company; "there was a sense of understanding, of identity, of purpose" (90). That "purpose," appropriately, emerges in Van's realization of his desire to reform the world outside Herland; his mission coalesces with Gilman's reformist spirit as his proposal of marriage becomes, in effect, "Will you be my comrade in this cause?"[47]

In addition to overturning accepted sexual roles and paradigms of heterosexual love, the example of this feminist Utopia chal-

lenges the individualistic ideal of perfect, transcendent love enshrined in the Victorian conceit of hearth and home as man's
refuge from the world. Terry voices the egocentric desire of the
prototypical Victorian paterfamilias: "A man wants a home of his
own, with his wife and family in it." The perspective in Herland,
however, is obviously different, making literal what has been implicit in the other novels of female community in this chapter: "to
these large-minded women whose mental outlook was so collective,
the limitations of a wholly personal life were inconceivable" (97).
This communality supplants the traditional function of the nuclear
unit, for "All the loyalty and service men expect of wives, they gave,
not singly to men, but collectively to one another" (95). The result
is a united sisterhood. willingly cooperating—much like the microcosm of society gathered around Millenium Hall—for the best of
the nation. Within this revisionary perspective, the *whole* nation becomes a "home," a fact intuitively gleaned by the explorers the moment they arrived within its boundaries: "Everything was beauty,
order, perfect cleanness, and the pleasantest sense of home over it
all" (19). Later, when Terry sneers that "there isn't a home in the
whole pitiful place," Jeff retorts, quite accurately, that "There isn't
anything else, and you know it" (98).

It is Herland's matriarchal view of life that is responsible for the
"quiet potency" (18) that pervades this paradise and secures its future, and this view is epitomized in the art of "mothering"—the
central fact as well as religion of the nation. Since the miracle of
parthenogenesis that occurred two thousand years ago, guaranteeing the kingdom's perpetuation through female progeny, mothering has been reconceived as a collective enterprise; one needn't be a
childbearer to be a mother, for the children are communally
shared—they are "our" children. In addition, removed from a
male-identified context, "motherly love" has lost its limited domestic
connotations and has been elevated to a ruling ethical model of right
behavior and interaction, one that lies behind the social and economic innovations characterizing this feminist Utopia; its matriarchal governance lacks the competitive destructiveness of the
male world because all phases of Herland life are linked in the
progressive cause of betterment for all.

But the essential harmony abiding in Herland and the nonlinear
patterning that encodes it are finally shattered. The cause of this

rupture, Terry's attempted rape of his "girlfriend," Alima, is iron-ically appropriate from both a thematic and a formal point of view. By replicating the violence of the archetypal rake of the seduction plot, Terry at once breaks the nonsexist faith of the Herlanders and introduces into the centric narration the combative forward motion that culminates in the men's expulsion from Herland's magical zone and, therewith, brings an end to the novel. What actu-ally happens when the sexually frustrated Terry hides in Alima's bedroom (an echo of Lovelace in Clarissa's closet) and attempts to use "sheer brute force" to "master this woman" (132) is quite liter-ally another story. For Alima does not submit—or faint away like Clarissa—but rises up, calls for aid, and masters Terry in turn. Van makes the literary as well as social implications of Alima's revolu-tionary action explicit: "Come to think of it, I do not recall a similar case in all history or fiction. Women have killed themselves rather than submit to outrage; they have killed the outrager; they have escaped; or they have submitted—sometimes seeming to get on very well with the victor afterward. . . . the point is Lucrese submit-ted, and Alima didn't" (143). In breaking the format of the pro-totypical seduction plot, this text preserves, as it were, its essential centricity by expelling the outrager, Terry, from its midst.

The last line of the novel, "we at last left Herland" (146), hence revives the outward-turning movement of quest, bracketing the central truths of Herland as a cyclic eternity, "overlooked and for-gotten" (143) but nonetheless existing in the interstices of man-made time. Does *Herland,* then, lament the passing of an Amazo-nian fantasy of power, or does it celebrate the incipient renewal of its values in the real world? On the one hand, Van and Elladore have accompanied Terry back to the outside world in order to be-gin the task of public reform, carried on in Gilman's sequel, *With Her in Ourland* (1916); on the other, Terry's act of outrage within the sphere of Herland perhaps foreshadows the fragility of its met-aphoric survival in the real world of men and women, where the problematic relation of male power and heterosexual desire re-mains unresolved. What is clear, in the end, is that by employing a fantastical Utopian format as the vehicle for her rhetorical feminist message, Gilman has unfolded an attack on her age's assumptions about gender and its relation to love, courtship, and marriage that becomes, by implication, an attack on the form of fiction itself: the

TOWARD AN ECRITURE FÉMININE

effort to reform public opinion, Gilman learns, must also re-form the text.

Conclusion: Toward an *Ecriture Féminine*

Lying forgotten in bound copies of *The Forerunner* for more than half a century, *Herland* (1915) and its fate vividly illustrate the fact that the effort to reform public opinion through re-forming the text, as I have just described Gilman's mission, does not necessarily guarantee a work of fiction a place in literary history, especially when its subject revolves around groups of unmarried, older women. The marginality encoded in the themes and structures of these fictions is repeated, tellingly, in the scholarly neglect that has either buried these works beneath the weight of literary tradition or, at best, recuperated them as examples of an essentially "feminine" craft—delicate but trivial, small-scale rather than grand. Such strategies of exclusion ironically suggest the counter-traditional *effectiveness* of these texts: to someone somewhere, their difference from the conventional love-plots of Anglo-American tradition has loomed as a threat worth repressing.

Given the relative neglect of these novels compared to the "classic" status that American quest narrative has attained, the juxtaposition in chapters 5 and 6 of these two bodies of fiction raises some potentially troubling questions about the relation of counter-tradition to the process of canon formation. Of course, the quest narrative was also once considered peripheral to the literary mainstream, merely boy's adventure fiction; but the belated recovery of Melville and the transformation of Twain from humorist to highbrow artist in the first half of this century have catapulted their works into some of the most widely read and taught examples of nineteenth-century American literature. One might plausibly ask whether it is possible that the same texts taken to define the tradition could also be so counter-traditional, while the parallel subversion of love-fiction in novels about separate communities of women seems intrinsic to their exclusion from all but feminist canons. Is the problem merely that critics of the male quest have failed to see what is "really" going on in its pages all along?

What these questions point out, in the first place, is the constructed nature of all literary canons, and the instances of willed and unconscious blindness among those who make them in the second. As Tompkins has noted, "the rhetoric of American criticism habitually invokes democratic values as a hallmark of greatness in American authors,"[48] and when the American quest novel was resuscitated between the world wars (and into the period of the cold war), it was praised for its bold championing of individual freedom and the rights of common man—issues equally pertinent to the critics writing about them in a world that seemed on the brink of totalitarian overthrow. I do not mean to imply that the quest narrative does not encode a powerful political message radically connected to the founding spirit of the country and opposed to any perceived betrayal of these ideals. The point, rather, is that just as the critical acclaim gathering for these novels focused on qualities pertinent to the contemporary scene, these same critics were as apt *not* to see aspects of these texts inimical to their values, even when these features stemmed from the same egalitarian ideal. Once admitted to the canon on "democratic" grounds, the genre was secured from accusations of (un-American) sexual nonconformity, at least until Fiedler appeared on the scene. The reason for any fiction's canonical status, Tompkins would remind us, is a complex product of the milieu in which it is read and critiqued, not necessarily the final word on its contents.

What I have been calling the quest's counter-traditional potential for undermining patriarchal norms, moreover, has managed to slip into the ranks of the "accepted" for a variety of related reasons. The most basic is that male critics have not in general expected to find male prerogatives disputed by members of their own sex, especially in literary works otherwise congenial to their sympathies; men generally "pass" with other men, whatever their degrees of hidden difference or opposition to norms. Second, the sexual politics of the quest narrative are rendered less threatening by the fact that the mode does not explicitly take up the cause of women's oppression in its critique of the sex system. (For the same reason, many feminist critics have automatically assumed the genre to be inherently sexist, and taken its canonical status as sufficient reason to dismiss it from feminist scrutiny.) Third, the very fact that these novels represent "worlds without women," it would seem, taps into so deeply rooted a male fantasy of escaping "the other sex" altogether—a fantasy inscribed in innumerable American institutions ranging from politics to recreation—that its (male) readers and critics have not always stopped to consider that this escape may signify differently for the quest writer than for themselves.

The lack of attention paid to texts generated around the subject of women living separately from men can be explained in similar terms. The critical tendency to assume that male-oriented texts do not subvert male norms has been paralleled by a widespread blindness to the possibility that the female-oriented text could be other than "feminine" in the most pejorative sense; the predisposition has been to judge the events and habits of female daily life as inherently nondramatic, static, and hence lacking in representational significance. Moreover, since its subject does not invite male participation, we may hypothesize that such texts arouse men's worst fears of exclusion, on the one hand, and of engulfment in difference, on the other; here are novels with no place, as it were, for men to occupy. Equally alienating is the fact that the discourse of these female communities is not one of power, especially as constituted in a masculine view of reality, but a discourse of the mother—the original "other" from which men presumably spend their lives trying to differentiate in order to define their separate identities.

In addition, certain aspects of characterization in these female fictions have exacerbated their poor critical reception. The spinster figure, for example, if examined from an unsympathetic point of view, may seem to reproduce demeaning stereotypes of behavior—a squeamish avoidance of sexuality; telltale regrets about forfeited motherhood; meddling or busybody tendencies; a sentimental outlook on the world. While these questionable traits—to the degree that they are actually present—occasionally betray the author's unresolved feelings about the female character's single status, more often they are the consequence of the author's realistic awareness of the fact that circumscription *within* a patriarchal world inevitably leads to some internalization of the dominant culture's definition of spinsterhood. Whatever their origin, these "cues" have hitherto provided the literary establishment with an excuse to judge these works as stereotypical, of interest only to a small class of women, and hence of negligible interest to the world at large. The irony is that the quest novel is also filled with ambivalent cues, ones that in contrast have given various critics license to read into the entire genre the "he-man" ethos embodied in London's Wolf Larsen and parodied in the figure of Gilman's Terry.

In taking measure of the asymmetrical reception of these two modes, finally, it is also useful to remember that both came into being in eras that embraced the doctrine of separate spheres as the inevitable consequence of an innate difference between the sexes, and for all the counter-traditional integrity of these two categories of texts, implicitly they too uphold this sexual division by virtue of their subject matter. More to the point, when the sexes are segregated in a culture that is patriarchal, as history has so often demonstrated, the male sphere is going to be valorized—no matter how radical its "hidden" sexual politics—and the female sphere—no matter how conformist *or* nonconformist—is going to be shunted aside. The critical reception of the male quest and female community, along with the canon-making process that has elevated the one mode and sidelined the other, has echoed this historical segregation, reviving the distinction between "masculine" and "feminine" as literary value.

Nonetheless, as this chapter has repeatedly demonstrated, the process of marginalization has hardly interfered with the rich imagining of female solidarity in worlds existing outside of marriage. From the early accomplishments of English novelists like Clara Reeve in *The School for Widows* (1791), to the international and postmodernist scope of Monique Wittig's acclaimed *Les Guérillères* (1969), experimentations with centric narrative structures have accompanied the articulation of the story of women's relationships with each other rather than with men. In addition to those texts which assume a circular form and a communal subject, a lively and unexpectedly sympathetic tradition foregrounding the life of the single woman has also persisted in the novel; numbering among such protagonists are Brontë's Lucy Snowe, Trollope's Lily Dale in *The Last Chronicle of Barset* (1867), James's Olive Chancellor (who, after all, does survive the break with Verena to address the waiting public in the Music Hall), Gissing's several "odd women," Cather's Thea Kronberg in *The Song of the Lark* (1915), and Wharton's Charlotte Lovell in "The Old Maid" in *Old New York* (1924).[49] In face of the assumption, parodied by Forster, that when one thinks in the vague of a novel, one imagines a linear trajectory consisting of "a man and a woman who want to be united and perhaps succeed," the history of the novel has often told another story.

Then, again, there are those texts which in significant ways have drawn upon elements of the text of female community without entirely fitting the definitions presented in this chapter. The narratives of Mary E. Wilkins Freeman, for example, often pivot upon the psychological dynamics of mother-daughter bonding, illustrating the viability of unions other than marriage to satisfy basic human desires for intimacy (less positively, the success of these mother-daughter bonds usually depends on a symbolic division into traditional male-female roles). In Ellen Glasgow's *Barren Ground* (1925), Dorinda Oakley's struggle to establish an independent life against marital norms also conforms to several of the patterns this chapter has associated with the novel of female community, not so much on structural as on imagistic and psychological levels. The dominant force in a female triad including her mother and a black woman servant, Dorinda takes over her family farm and achieves success in a "man's role" by rooting herself to the land and the natural cycles which her life and the three sections of the text come to replicate: by triumphing over the "barren ground" of romantic illusion, she gains an old-age equanimity that is depicted as continually radiating inward to her truest self, rippling outward to encompass the landscape that has given her life meaning and identity—an inner state of being captured in the external imagistic pattern of endless concentric circles. Like *Barren Ground*, Willa Cather's *Sapphira and the Slave Girl* (1940) tells a straightforward story on the surface: the jealousy of a pre–Civil War matron toward her husband's favorite slave-girl, Nancy. But Cather undermines both the stereotypical dimension of this tale (woman-against-woman) and its overt linearity in two ways: by focusing on the problematic relations of mothers and daughters in two parallel matriarchal lines, one black and one white, that extend from grandmother to grandchild, and by augmenting Sapphira and Nancy's conflict with inset stories, memories, and digressive meanderings that enhance the narrative's aura of a female-oriented reality repeating itself endlessly (this cyclical quality becomes even more apparent at text's end, where we learn for the first time that the narrator has spent her childhood with these older women, listening to the stories that she now weaves for us). Like

THE NOVEL OF FEMALE COMMUNITY

Wilkins and Glasgow, Cather dips into the storehouse of themes and strategies developed in the counter-traditional novel of female solidarity, hinting at a subversion of the marriage plot without fully exploring the implications of her narrative experiments.

Djuna Barnes's *Ladies Almanack* (1928), Gloria Naylor's *The Women of Brewster Place* (1982), and Pat Barker's *Union Street* (1982), however, are texts that triumphantly exemplify the (counter-)tradition explored in this chapter. Not only do all three works represent collective communities of women in narrative organizations whose logic is cumulative and cyclical rather than linear, but they all force the reader to perceive differences within difference. For each of these accounts, written from the marginal perspective of the woman's community, also explores the added difference that sexual preference, racial heritage, or class background may create for the already marginalized woman—Barnes by depicting the lesbian demimonde abroad, Naylor by showing the ostracization at work within the already ostracized black slum of her title, Barker by evoking the impoverished lives of working-class women in a depressed industrial town in northern England.

Ladies Almanack, only in private print until 1972, forms a particularly modernist summation to many of the issues raised in this chapter. With virtuoso skill, Barnes appropriates the ribaldry of the masculine novelistic tradition associated with Fielding, the diction of eighteenth-century chapbooks, and the obfuscations of modernist indirection, Joycean wordplay, and self-reflexivity to encode within her "almanack" format a ringingly defiant celebration of lesbian love; situating itself "Neaptide to the Proustian chronicle," the Preface punningly promises "gleanings from the shores of Mytilene [the isle of Lesbos], glimpses of its novitiates" to the attentive or initiated reader.[50] At the center of this female cosmography is the saint of woman-woman love, the insatiable Dame Evangeline Musset (a thinly veiled portrait of Nathalie Barney), who preaches to all young women "the Consolation every Woman has at her Finger Tips, or at the very Hang of her Tongue" (6). The sexuality hitherto repressed in the representation of female enclaves from *Millenium Hall* to *Herland*—and the homoeroticism implicit in the romantic friendships in some of these texts—wells forth as frankly physical desire in a community whose self-definition depends on an acknowledgment of sexual preference. Dame Musset's presid-

ing presence, threading its way through the loosely connected, elliptical vignettes attached to each of the twelve months into which
this *Almanack* is divided, provides the text with its basic thematic
unity. If it is obvious to "all Society" that fate "would by no Road,
lead [Dame Musset] to the Altar" (8), it is also true that her refusal
of conjugal destiny opens the way to *all* roads: the entire world
becomes a geography of possibility for the woman who loves wom-
en. "There is no Land so uncharterd of Trails" (38) as will not yield
amorous success, we learn in May, and August ends with a prophetic vision of women from all ranks merging into a veritable
army on the march, "some of all sorts, to swarm in that wide Acre"
(54) where female values triumph over man's.

By making the cyclical progress of the calendar months her text's
only absolute ordering principle, moreover, Barnes deliberately attempts to write into narrative form a "woman's time" that subverts
the linearity Western culture has associated with masculine logocentrism. This breaking out of a conventional temporal framework—with its implicit analogy to lesbianism as a subject that
necessarily shatters boundaries when admitted into the dominant
discourse—is repeated in Barnes's disregard of generic boundaries,
indeed her disregard of the very boundaries of the printed page.
For the *Almanack* combines prose passages with examples of poetry,
song, engravings that often continue or extend the text, and annota-
tions. In February, for example, the "Saints Days" listed in smaller
script in the right column offer a miniature biography of Dame
Musset's whole life, thus glossing the "Love Letter" forming the
primary text to the left; toward the end of March a zodiac is inserted
in the margin of the main text to reveal a myth of lesbian origin, of
"the first Woman born with a difference" [26]. Monthly subsec-
tions, furthermore, cover topics as various as "DISTEMPERS," "HER
TIDES AND MOONS," and "SPRING FEVERS, LOVE PHILTERS AND WINTER
FEASTS." Spilling over the margins of the traditional text, these
narrative improvisations convert the marginality and invisibility of
the lesbian into a profoundly visible network of signs that the reader cannot ignore. As one character says of the woman-identified
woman, "Is she not the spinning Centre of a spinning World?"
(51), and in structuring her revisionary counterplot around such a
transformed perspective, Barnes triumphantly presses the tradition pioneered by Scott, Gaskell, Jewett, and Gilman to new limits.

In contrast to Barnes's modernist pyrotechnics, Naylor and Barker ground their fictions—each a mixture of story collection and novel—in the mimesis of everyday detail. Nonetheless, their structural formats explicitly mirror the narrative strategies of Barnes and her predecessors. A static place—Brewster Place, Union Street— becomes the center around which the author weaves a series of accretive, interconnected but independent stories of female fortitude and bonding; in each, an ostensibly entrapping environment is transformed by the collective strength of the women into a spiritual source of endurance and the will to change. *The Women of Brewster Place*, aptly subtitled "A Novel in Seven Stories," details the process by which seven black women of widely differing ages, backgrounds, and personalities have ended up in this walled-in street; the tribulations of poverty and racism, of lovers who never stayed and husbands who have run away, of pampered children too weak to support their mother's dreams, are mitigated by the support these women offer each other. Paradigmatic of this sustaining love is the bond that immediately forms the evening Miss Eva takes the homeless, husbandless Mattie and her baby into her home: "The young black woman and the old yellow woman sat in the kitchen for hours, blending their lives so that what lay behind one and ahead of the other become indistinguishable."[51] Nearly each segment ends with an affirmation of the power of the female bond to transcend, if not avert, tragedy; one of the most memorable minor climaxes involves the much older Mattie, now the matriarch of Brewster Place, as she ritualistically bathes a stunned young mother whose daughter has accidentally been electrocuted. In effect Mattie reawakens the bereaved mother to life by reconnecting her, inch by inch, to the materiality of her flesh: "And slowly she bathed her. . . . Making Ciel rise and kneel in the tub, she cleaned the crack in her behind, soaped her pubic hair, and gently washed the creases in her vagina —slowly, reverently, as if handling a newborn" (104). Simultaneous with Ciel's rebirth, an image of woman's body as her own is born from the printed page, breaking a literary tradition of representational prohibitions (for the woman writer) and appropriations (by the male writer).

To assert that female networks are intrinsically or unproblematically supportive and nurturing is to skirt the dangers of cliché and politicized rhetoric. Naylor, however, daringly moves beyond any such oversimplification by introducing in the next to last story a lesbian couple, Lorraine and Theresa, whose difference challenges the other Brewster women to question the intensity of their own loving bonds. "But I've loved some women deeper than I ever loved any man," Mattie admits, pondering the ironies of the heterosexual black woman's experience; "Maybe it's not so different. . . . Maybe that's why some women get so riled up about [lesbianism], 'cause they know deep down it's not so different after all. . . . It kinda of gives you a funny feeling when you think about it that way, though" (141). (Even more complexly, Naylor makes the imperfection in Lorraine and Theresa's relationship their own inability to accept each other's differences.) Ultimately, the commonality *in* difference that connects the lesbian couple to each other and to their female neighbors as equally marginalized victims of a patriarchal world emerges in Naylor's conclusion. In a horrifically visceral scene that presents the act that Richardson and Hardy omit from direct representation, a gang of black youths rape Lorraine—whose preference denies them their one perceived power in a white man's world that otherwise castrates them—and shatters her mind forever. The women of Brewster Place intuitively understand this act of violence for what it is, an act against female self-possession, and in the apocalyptic final story, they attempt to expunge the horror by ripping down the brick wall that has separated their street from the adjoining white community. When women and other minority groups stand to be counted, Naylor implies, their communal strength becomes a political force that changes history.

The empathetic bond between narrator and text pervading Naylor's *Brewster Place* is also a pronounced characteristic of Barker's *Union Street,* which intimately and compassionately enters into the lives of its working-class Englishwomen through a series of (again) seven interconnected stories. While in Naylor's fiction black men are generally peripheral to the main lines of action, except as shadowy lovers (or rapists) who disappear in the light of day, Barker's community of women is pervaded by the immediate presence of the men; because all her female characters are married, recently widowed, or sexually involved, the stories in *Union Street* repeatedly dramatize the difficulties of heterosexual bonding in a patriarchal system, and Barker takes care to portray the problems of her male characters with the same depth she accords her women. Despite this male presence—and the corollary fact that none of Barker's female characters thus qualify as "women without men" in the sense of *Cranford*'s spinsters, for instance—her primary object remains that of examining the common ties, bonds, and experiences that knit these women, on both realistic and metaphoric levels, into a sisterhood that helps them survive in an embattled, usually sexually bifurcated world. Like the lives of these women themselves, therefore, Barker has designed each of the seven stories to stand on its own, as an individual statement of a specific dilemma of womanhood (rape, marriage, pregnancy, abortion, prostitution), yet simultaneously to contribute to the collective whole—the whole that is at once the text itself, *Union Street,* and the community of women that lives on Union Street.

Viewed individually, these stories and these histories seem filled with desparation and the sheer monotony of lives spent fighting poverty; viewed as a whole, however, a more hopeful story of communal resilience begins to emerge. Barker fits this dual vision into a structure that is centric as well. The sequence of the stories, arranged to form a cycle illuminating the stages common to women's experience by moving from an adolescent girl's coming of age to the death of a old woman, invites the reader to view all these women, on a symbolic level, as aspects of the same person; the final thoughts of the dying Alice Bell, fragments of memory overwhelming her consciousness, suggest exactly such a perspective: "Were they the debris of her own or other's lives? She had been so many women in her time."[52] Concurrently Barker makes the reader gradually aware, through subtly plotted intersections between the stories, that all these lives are unfolding simultaneously, not sequentially. Thus, from one perspective, all time collapses into one archetypal person; from another, into one crystallized moment. And this simultaneity ultimately makes a crucial difference in the overall effect of Barker's nonlinear organization. For *Union Street* begins with the violence that ends *Brewster Place*, depicting in excruciating detail the rape (again, in a blind alley) and subsequent psychosis of twelve-year-old Kelly Brown; at the end of this opening sequence, as Kelly meets an anonymous, dying bag lady in the park, one senses a possible turn in the girl's mental state, but without knowing for sure. In the final story, Alice Bell plans her own death rather than be committed to a nursing home, and when she leaves her flat to freeze to death in the park, we realize that we have returned to the scene presented in Kelly's section two hundred pages before. This time around, as many of the same words and phrases of the earlier scene return intact, it becomes clear that the momentary bond forged between equally victimized old lady and young girl creates an epiphanic moment triggering Kelly's mental recovery: "The girl held out her hand. The withered hand and the strong young hand met and joined. Silence. Then it was time for them both to go" (245)—Alice toward death, Kelly toward life. As age and youth have joined hands, so too the cycle of stories comes full circle at this moment: in collapsing the temporal frame of the narrative to make Kelly's tentative rebirth the ending of the whole book rather than merely of the first section, Barker suggests that the girl may escape the repeating cycle of victimization pervading Union Street. Appropriately, Barker's final image is not of circles, then, but of the spiralizing flight of birds: "So that in the end there were only the birds, soaring, swooping, gliding, moving in a never-ending spiral about the withered and unwithering tree" (245).

Even more than the scene in *Brewster Place* where Mattie washes Ciel's body, the sheer physicality of language and image in *Union Street*—particularly as it relates to the minutiae of female experience—results in a text that is achingly palpable; in effect, the materiality of woman's existence, so long denied in literature, becomes the material of the text itself. Echoing Cixous's call for women's texts to "write the body," this act embodies a distinctively feminine *jouissance* in discourse—the goal, consciously or unconsciously, toward which all the novels discussed in this chapter have been moving. The structural formats of these texts, in attempting to replicate the nontraditional nature of experience being expressed in their contents, have created a narrative erotics that, like Luce Irigaray's description of the plurality of women's libidinal economy, "upsets the linearity of a project, undermines the goal-object of a desire, diffuses the polarization toward a single pleasure, disconcerts fidelity to a single discourse."[53] In this light, the thematic and formal difference that results from the literary foregrounding of the female community, reaching from the present obscurity of Sarah Scott to the critical and popular acclaim that has greeted Naylor and Barker, has created a distinctive genre of counter-traditional

The Novel of Female Community

fiction of which Woolf's Chloe and Olivia would have been proud. "Oh, I've finished with all that . . . I am thankful to have finished with all that," Glasgow's Dorinda Oakley says of marriage at the end of *Barren Ground*,[54] and her statement—even with its touch of irony—provides an apt metaphor for the fate of the novelistic marriage tradition, and the sexual ideology embedded within it, when challenged by the transforming presence of the counter-traditional text. Be it the undermining dialogue of uneasy wedlock, the male quest into a world of alternate possibilities, or the sustaining fiction of female community, another story has always been present, muted but available, awaiting its chance to rewrite the official history of the novel and to transform its future forms.

Notes

Chapter 1

1. George Gissing, *The Odd Women* (1893; New York: Norton, 1977), p. 58. All further references to this work appear in the text.

2. Henry James, "The Future of the Novel" (1899), quoted in *Theory of Fiction: Henry James*, ed. James E. Miller, Jr. (Lincoln: University of Nebraska Press, 1972), p. 340.

3. M. M. Bakhtin, "Epic and Novel: Toward a Methodology for the Study of the Novel," pp. 11 and 7, respectively; and "Discourse in the Novel," p. 367; both in *The Dialogic Imagination: Four Essays*, trans. Caryl Emerson and Michael Holquist (Austin: University of Texas Press, 1981).

4. Ibid., p. 39.

5. Virginia Woolf, *A Room of One's Own* (New York: Harcourt, Brace, 1929), p. 80. All further references to this work appear in the text. Woolf, like Bakhtin, notes on the same page that "The novel alone was young enough to be soft in her [the woman writer's] hands," as opposed to "all the older forms of literature [that] were hardened and set by the time she became a writer."

6. See E. M. Forster, *Aspects of the Novel* (1927; rpt. New York: Harcourt, Brace, World, 1954); Leslie Fiedler, *Love and Death in the American Novel* (New York: Stein and Day, 1966); Evelyn J. Hinz, "Hierogamy versus Wedlock: Types of Marriage Plots and Their Relationships to Genres of Prose Fiction," *PMLA* 91 (1976): 900–913; Sandra M. Gilbert and Susan Gubar's discussion of images of female confinement often lead them to address the issue of closure in *The Madwoman in the Attic: The Woman Writer and the Nineteenth-Century Literary Imagination* (New Haven: Yale University Press, 1979); Nancy K. Miller argues for the specificity of "irregular" female form in "Emphasis Added: Plots and Plausibilities in Women's Fiction," *PMLA* 96 (1981): 36–48, and postulates "euphoric" and "dysphoric" trajectories to the heroine's experiences in love in texts by men, in *The Heroine's Text: Readings in the French and English Novel, 1722–1782* (New York: Columbia University Press, 1980); Lee R. Edwards talks about open and closed trajectories, though often in a more mythical and experiential than structurally specific sense, in *Psyche as Hero: Female Heroism and Fic-*

tional Form (Middletown CT: Wesleyan University Press, 1984); Rachel Blau DuPlessis's *Writing Beyond the Ending: Narrative Strategies of Twentieth-Century Women Writers* (Bloomington: Indiana University Press, 1985), which appeared after I finished this book, details the many ways in which twentieth-century women writers have manipulated love-plot conventions to "write beyond the ending."

To this list could also be added Nina Baym's examination of sentimental paradigms in *Woman's Fiction: A Guide to Novels by and about Women in America, 1820–1870* (Ithaca NY: Cornell University Press, 1978); Jean E. Kennard's analysis of the double-suitor convention in the female bildungsroman genre in *Victims of Convention* (Hamden CT: Archon, 1978); Rachel M. Brownstein's focus on heroines created by men and women alike in *Becoming a Heroine: Reading about Women in Novels* (1982; rpt. Harmondsworth: Penguin, 1984); and, in a more limited sense, Alfred Habegger's discussion of marriage themes in male and female American writers in *Gender, Fantasy, and Realism in American Literature* (New York: Columbia University Press, 1982). Two studies of marriage in fiction less relevant to my purposes are A. O. J. Cockshut, *Man and Woman: A Study of Love and the Novel, 1740–1940* (New York: Oxford University Press, 1978), which divides texts into optimistic and pessimistic varieties; and Laurence Lerner, *Love and Marriage: Literature and Its Social Context* (London: Collins, 1977), which mixes sociological and literary observations with a variety of genres.

7. Tony Tanner, *Adultery in the Novel: Contract and Transgression* (Baltimore: Johns Hopkins University Press, 1979), p. 15.

8. William Makepeace Thackeray, *The History of Henry Esmond, Esq.* (1852; rpt. New York: Holt, Rinehart, 1962), pp. 491–92.

9. Lawrence Stone lists most of these traits in *The Family, Sex, and Marriage in England 1500–1800* (New York: Harper and Row, 1977), p. 282.

10. See Terry Eagleton, *Criticism and Ideology: A Study in Marxist Literary Theory* (1976; rpt. London: Verso, 1978), on the liberal sense of overt political beliefs (70), on naive historicist conceptions (32), on the Lukácsian interventionist fallacy (69), and on the inadequacy of a macro/micro "deep structure" model (97–98).

11. Penny Boumelha, *Thomas Hardy and Women: Sexual Ideology and Narrative Form* (1982; rpt. Madison: University of Wisconsin Press, 1985), p. 5. Boumelha's synthesis of Marxist trends, like Eagleton's, cited above, has been enormously helpful to me; for other influences, see Louis Althusser, *Lenin and Philosophy and Other Essays*, trans. Ben Brewster (London: New Left Books, 1971); Pierre Macherey, *A Theory of Literary Production*, trans. Geoffrey Wall (1974; rpt. Boston: Routledge and Kegan Paul, 1978); and Fredric Jameson, *Marxism and Form* (Princeton: Princeton University Press, 1971).

12. Alain Robbe-Grillet, *For a New Novel. Essays in Fiction*, trans. Richard Howard (New York: Grove Press, 1965), p. 32.

13. See, for example, the parallels and divergences between Marxism and feminism that Catherine A. MacKinnon sets up in "Feminism, Marxism, Method, and the State: An Agenda for Theory," *Signs: Journal of Women in Culture and Society* 7 (1982): 515–44.

14. "The Difference of View," in *Women Writing and Writing about Women,* ed. Mary Jacobus (New York: Barnes and Noble, 1979), p. 12.

15. I follow the lead of most feminist critics in using the term "patriarchal" in this general sense, as contrasted to its more historically precise usage, which refers to a precapitalist mode of social organization.

16. Robert A. Padgug, "Sexual Matters: On Conceptualizing Sexuality in History," *Radical History Review* 20 (1979): 9.

17. George Eliot, *The Mill on the Floss* (1860; rpt. New York: Oxford World Classic, 1981), p. 75.

18. Dinah Mulock Craik, "Something to Do" (1858), excerpted in *The Norton Anthology of English Literature,* 4th. ed. (New York: Norton, 1979), 2:1661; emphasis added.

19. Charlotte Brontë, *Shirley* (1849; rpt. Harmondsworth: Penguin, 1974), p. 367; emphasis added. All further references to this work appear in the text.

20. George Meredith, *The Egoist* (1879; rpt. New York: Norton, 1979), p. 28.

21. *The Awakening and Selected Stories of Kate Chopin* (1899; rpt. New York: Norton, 1976), p. 56.

22. Sir Walter Scott, *Waverley; or, 'Tis Sixty Years Since* (1814; rpt. Harmondsworth: Penguin, 1972), p. 183.

23. Herman Melville, *Moby-Dick* (1851; rpt. New York: Norton, 1967), p. 271. All further references to this work appear in the text.

24. Particularly illuminating on this double critical standard is Elaine Showalter, *A Literature of Their Own: British Women Novelists from Brontë to Lessing* (Princeton: Princeton University Press, 1977), pp. 73–99.

25. It is not irrelevant that the dog's name is Phoebe, the Greek goddess of the hunt and virginity associated with Diana in the Roman pantheon. In light of the Dianic associations of the virgin sylvan chase that provides the two women a private space emblematic both of their friendship and of their freedom to form identities separate from men, the fact that this Diana-Phoebe should now turn up as a maddened creature who threatens death is disturbingly appropriate to the shift in the plot's emphasis from female freedom to heterosexual courtship.

26. Mrs. E. D. E. N. Southworth, *The Mother-in-Law* (New York, 1851), p. 167, quoted in Herbert Ross Brown, *The Sentimental Novel in America, 1789–1860* (Durham NC: Duke University Press, 1940), p. 285.

27. Anthony Trollope, *The Warden,* (1855; rpt. New York: Oxford University Press, 1952), p. 278, quoted in J. Hillis Miller, "The Problematic of Ending in Narrative," *Nineteenth Century Fiction,* 33 (1978): 5. I am indebt-

ed to Miller's use of the knotting/unknotting metaphor in this short piece, pp. 3–7, which I have appropriated for my different "ends" in these paragraphs.

28. Tobias Smollett, *The Expedition of Humphry Clinker* (1771; rpt. Harmondsworth: Penguin, 1967), p. 388.

29. Charles Dickens, *Oliver Twist* (1837–38; rpt. New York: New American Library, 1961), p. 480.

30. James, "The Future of the Novel," pp. 341–43.

31. *The Newcomes* (1853–55), vol. 8 of *The Works of William Makepeace Thackeray*, The Biographical Edition (New York: Harper and Brothers, 1898–99), p. 805.

32. Quoted in Winifred Gérin, *Charlotte Brontë: The Evolution of Genius* (New York: Oxford University Press, 1967), p. 510.

33. Nina Auerbach, *Communities of Women: An Idea in Fiction* (Cambridge MA: Harvard University Press, 1978).

34. Boumelha, p. 5.

35. See, for example, Jeffrey Weeks, *Sex, Politics, and Society: The Regulation of Sexuality since 1800* (London: Longman, 1981), pp. 96–121.

36. Toril Moi, *Sexual/Textual Politics: Feminist Literary Theory* (London: Methuen, 1985), p. 14.

37. René Girard, *Deceit, Desire and the Novel*, trans. Yvonne Freccero (1961; rpt. Baltimore MD: Johns Hopkins University Press, 1965); Leo Bersani, *A Future for Astyanax: Character and Desire in Literature* (1976; rpt. New York: Columbia University Press, 1984), p. 60; Peter Brooks, *Reading for the Plot: Design and Intention in Narrative* (New York: Knopf, 1984).

38. N. Miller "Emphasis Added," p. 46. Miller acknowledges the influence of Peter Brooks, "Freud's Masterplots," *Yale French Studies*, 55–56 (1977): 280, on her formulation.

Chapter 2

1. Andreas Capellanus, *The Art of Courtly Love*, trans. and intro. John Jay Parry (New York: Columbia University Press, 1941), Seventh Dialogue, p. 100.

2. William Whately, *The Bride-bush; or, A direction for married Persons. Plainely describing the duties common to both, and peculiar to each of them* (London, 1619), p. 31.

3. [John Dunton], *The Athenian Mercury*, 1:13 (May 5, 1691), n.p.

4. A similar comparison appears in Fiedler, p. 47, and is intimated in Jean Hagstrum, *Sex and Sensibility: Ideal and Erotic Love from Milton to Mozart* (Chicago: University of Chicago Press, 1980), pp. 31–32. The term "courtly love" (or *amour courtois*) is a nineteenth-century construct, coined by the late nineteenth-century medievalist Gaston Paris in his article, "Lancelot du Lac, II. *Le Conte de la Charrette*," *Romania* 12 (1883): 459–534, and it has come under considerable attack in recent years by one school of medievalists claiming Paris in effect "created" a myth of courtly love which has no corre-

spondence in reality or literature; see especially Peter Dronke, *Medieval Latin and the Rise of European Love Lyric* (Oxford: Clarendon, 1968), xvii and passim. A more sensible middle ground can be found in Roger Boase, *The Origin and Meaning of Courtly Love: A Critical Study of European Scholarship* (Manchester: Manchester University Press, 1977), who after meticulously collating the entire body of scholarship on the subject defends both the critical pertinence of the term "courtly love" and the significance of its literary and social manifestations in late twelfth-century Provence.

5. A. B. Taylor, *An Introduction to Medieval Romance* (London: Heath Cranton, 1930), p. 235; the statistics are from L. T. Topsfield, *Troubadours and Love* (Cambridge: Cambridge University Press, 1975), pp. 2–5. Of these 460-odd poets, 20 are known to be women, as Meg Bogin reports in *The Women Troubadours* (1976; rpt. New York: Norton, 1980), p. 11. Whether or not the male troubadour actually did have a "beloved," as Taylor claims, one can see the mythologizing of the convention at work in the thirteenth–fourteenth-century "vidas" and "razos" popularizing the lives of the troubadours, many of which are reprinted in *Proensa: An Anthology of Troubadour Poetry*, ed. George Economou, trans. Paul Blackburn (Berkeley: University of California Press, 1978), pp. 67, 72–73, 88–89, 95, 189.

6. Bernart de Ventadorn, "Can vei la lauzeta mover," trans. Blackburn, *Proensa*, lines 13–24, 17–19, p. 76.

7. For the diffusion of the courtly ethos across Europe, traditionally attributed to the influence of Eleanor of Aquitaine and her daughter the Countess Marie of Champagne, see Taylor, pp. 235–36; Robert S. Briffault, *The Troubadours* (Bloomington: Indiana University Press, 1965), p. 5; and Parry, Intro. to *The Art of Courtly Love*, pp. 13–15; John Benton, however, rejects the theory that Marie's court served as the point of transmission of the Provençal love ethos northward, in "The Court of Champagne as a Literary Center," *Speculum: A Journal of Mediaeval Studies* 36 (1961): 551–91.

8. E. Talbot Donaldson, "The Myth of Courtly Love," in *Speaking of Chaucer* (London: Athlone Press, 1970), p. 157. C. S. Lewis's *The Allegory of Love* (New York: Oxford University Press, 1938) is largely responsible for early theories of adultery as a foregone conclusion in courtly society; taking Capellanus's distinction between *amor* and *affectio maritalis* at face value, Lewis concluded that "any idealization of sexual love, in a society where marriage is purely utilitarian, must begin by being an idealization of adultery" (p. 13). Among those who have since attacked this famous overgeneralization are D. W. Robertson, Jr. in *A Preface to Chaucer* (Princeton: Princeton University Press, 1962), pp. 84–85, 393–96, and Henry Ansgar Kelly in *Love and Marriage in the Age of Chaucer* (Ithaca: Cornell University Press, 1975), p. 20.

9. Denis de Rougemont, *Love in the Western World*, trans. Montgomery Belgion (1940; rev. New York: Pantheon, 1956), pp. 118–19.

10. The antisocial and potentially disruptive implications of courtly love

are especially reflected in its implicit challenge to the feudal hierarchy; its subconscious discontent with the Church's long-standing diatribes against sex and advocacy of celibacy as the supreme human good; and its tendency to elevate private experience over communal well-being. Theories of courtly love as antireligious "heresy" can be found in Lewis, pp. 14–18; A. J. Demony, *The Heresy of Courtly Love* (New York: McMullen, 1947), pp. 18–19; and, from a different perspective, De Rougement, p. 72–91. Theories of its origins as the expression of a repressed matriarchal past or as "the psychic reaction against [feudalism's] cult of paternalism" are found in Robert S. Briffault, *The Mothers: A Study of the Origins of Sentiments and Institutions* (1927; abr. London: Allen and Unwin, 1959), 3:505, and in Maurice Jacques Valency, *In Praise of Love: An Introduction to the Love-Poetry of the Renaissance* (New York: Macmillan, 1958), p. 35, respectively. For pertinent data on cultural-sociological fluctations—large numbers of single men, a new class of knightly retainers, the rising practice of primogeniture—making the feudal system susceptible to this new ideology, see Boase, p. 91.

11. Robertson, pp. 374–75. In citing these symbolic meanings, Robertson tends to overidealize the actual status of marriage itself. It is precisely such contradictions between theory and actual practice that Shulamith Shahar finds characteristic of the "realities" of medieval women's married lives in *The Fourth Estate: A History of Women in the Middle Ages,* trans. Chaya Galai (London: Methuen, 1983), esp. chap. 4, "Married Women," pp. 65–125, and chap. 5, "Women in the Nobility," pp. 126–73. See John T. Noonan, Jr., *Contraception: A History of Its Treatment by the Catholic Theologians and Canonists* (Cambridge MA: Harvard University Press, 1965), pp. 143–300, for medieval attitudes on marriage.

12. As G. P. Murdock comments, "Marriage exists only when the economic and the sexual are united into one relationship, and this combination occurs only in marriage." See "The Universality of the Nuclear Family," in *A Modern Introduction to the Family,* ed. Norman W. Bell and Ezra F. Vogel (Glencoe IL: Free Press, 1960), p. 42.

13. Claude Lévi-Strauss, *The Savage Mind* (Chicago: University of Chicago Press, 1966), pp. 123–26.

14. See Gayle Rubin, "The Traffic in Women: Notes on the 'Political Economy' of Sex," in *Toward an Anthropology of Women,* ed. Rayna R. Reiter (New York: Monthly Review Press, 1975), pp. 157–210. Her source in Claude Lévi-Strauss is *The Elementary Structures of Kinship* (Boston: Beacon, 1969), p. 115: "The total relationship of exchange which constitutes marriage is not established between a man and a woman, but between two groups of men, and the woman figures only as one of the objects in the exchange, not as one of the partners."

15. See J. Huizinga, *The Waning of the Middle Ages* (1948; rpt. New York: Doubleday, 1954), pp. 108–9; Boase, p. 92.

16. Lewis, p. 8; De Rougement, p. 111. For a thorough overview, see

Hilda Graef, *Mary: A History of Doctrine and Devotion* (New York: Sheed and Ward, 1963), vol. 1.

17. Susan B. Winnett, "Terrible Sociability: The Text of Manners in Laclos, Goethe, and Henry James" (Ph.D. Diss., Yale University 1982), p. 7.

18. John Stevens, *Medieval Romance: Themes and Approaches* (New York: Norton, 1973), p. 40.

19. *The Works of Plato,* ed. Irwin Edman (New York: Simon and Schuster, 1928), p. 339.

20. *Tristan and Isolde,* trans. A. T. Hatto (London: Penguin, 1960), p. 195. See Jakobson's comments in "Two Aspects of Language and Two Types of Aphasic Disturbances," in *Fundamentals of Language,* with Morris Halle (The Hague: Mouton, 1956), pp. 77–78, and Brooks's extrapolations thereupon, pp. 56, 90–92.

21. *The Works of Geoffrey Chaucer,* ed. F. N. Robinson, 2d ed. (Boston: Houghton Mifflin, 1957), "Troilus and Criseyde," 3:1405-8, p. 436.

22. Johann Wolfgang von Goethe, *The Sorrows of Young Werther and Selected Writings,* trans. Catherine Hutter (New York: Signet, 1962), p. 108. All further references to this work appear in the text.

23. Richard of St. Victor [d. 1173], *Tractatus de quatuor gradibus violentae charitatis,* quoted in Boase, p. 134, from Dronke, 1:65n. On the treacherous role of mediation in the production of insatiable desire, see Girard, pp. 42–43; on the sadistic and masochistic sides of internally suppressed repeating desires, and on the fantasy of death as the absolute pleasure, see Bersani, pp. 6–7, in a section appropriately titled "Murderous Lovers."

24. Joseph Campbell's *The Masks of God: Occidental Mythology* (New York: Viking, 1968) traces the origins of duality in ancient myth in its first several chapters. For the relation of the body/soul dualism to the Christian concept of marriage, see Irving Singer, *The Nature of Love: Plato to Luther* (New York: Random House, 1966), pp. 204–6, 221–22.

25. Guillaume de Lorris and Jean de Meung, *The Romance of the Rose,* trans. Charles Dahlberg (Princeton: Princeton University Press, 1971), lines 21617–8, p. 352, and 4293–4, pp. 94–95, respectively.

26. Guilhem IX, "Farai chansoneta nueva," in *Proensa,* lines 39–40, p. 18; Arnaut Daniel, "En cest sonet coind' a leri," lines 22–25, ibid., p. 97. As Valency says, "The Provençal *chanson,* as we might expect in the poetry of a male society, directed itself to the female, but it focused interest unequivocally on the male. The song was in praise of the lady, but the voice, the heart, and the soul of the chanson were the the voice, the heart, and the soul of the knight" (p. 37). For differences in troubadour verse by women overlooked by Valency, however, see Bogin, p. 68.

28. Jean-Jacques Rousseau, *La nouvelle Héloïse,* trans. Judith H. McDowell (University Park: Pennsylvania State University Press, 1968), p. 92. All further references to this work appear in the text.

29. Tanner's extended analysis of this novel in *Adultery in the Novel*

focuses on the "Power of the Father" as the book's tension-giving theme; see also Miller, *Heroine's Text*, pp. 96–115, which links Julie's fear of desire and her security within *la maison paternelle*.

30. Julie has earlier defended traditional constructions of sexual difference-as-opposition with a passion: "The attack and defense, the audacity of men, the modesty of women—these are by no means conventions, as your philosophers think, but natural institutions" (p. 108).

31. McDowell, Intro., p. 3.

32. De Rougement, p. 221.

33. Choderlos de Laclos, *Les liaisons dangereuses,* trans. Richard Aldington (New York: Signet, 1962), p. 29. All further references to this work appear in the text.

34. Gustave Flaubert, *Madame Bovary,* trans. Paul de Man (New York: Norton, 1965), p. 26. Bersani also quotes this passage, in a somewhat similar context, in his chapter on "Emma Bovary and the Sense of Sex," p. 96. All further references to Flaubert appear in the text.

35. Tanner, pp. 13–14.

36. See the excessive number of "failed" affairs catalogued by Judith Armstrong in *The Novel of Adultery* (New York: Harper and Row, 1976), esp. chap. 4, "The Order Vindicated: The End of the Affair," pp. 126–46.

37. Thomas Becon, Preface to Bullinger's *Der Christlich Eestand* (The Christian State of Matrimony) in *Worckes I* (London, 1560–64), DCXvii, quoted in William and Malleville Haller, "The Puritan Art of Love," *The Huntington Library Quarterly* 5 (1941–42): 244–45. I am indebted to this excellent article for directing me to most of the Puritan manuals and sermon collections cited in this section.

38. William Perkins, *Christian Oeconomie: or, A short survey of the right manner of erecting and ordering a familie, according to the Scriptures. First written in Latine by the Author M. W. Perkins, and now set forth in the vulgar tongue . . . by Thomas Pickering* (London, 1609), p. 11.

39. Stone, p. 216. See also Louis B. Wright, *Middle-Class Culture in Elizabethan England* (Chapel Hill: University of North Carolina Press, 1935), esp. chap. 7, "Instruction in Domestic Relations," pp. 201–27, and Christopher Hill, *Society and Puritanism in Pre-Revolutionary England* (New York: Schocken, 1964), chap. 13, "The Spiritualization of the Household," pp. 443–81.

40. Henrie Smith, "Preparative to Mariage," in *The Sermons of Maister Henrie Smith, gathered into one volume. Printed according to his corrected copies in his life time* (London, 1593), p. 40. As the Hallers report, "Puritan churchmen in heeding the injunction to marry did not merely lay aside their clerical celibacy. They stretched their souls to love their wives in the spirit of godliness; they suffused marital relations afresh with religious emotion—which is to say with imaginative significance deeply felt" (p. 254). See also Stone, p. 180.

41. Smith, pp. 35–36; Whately, *The Bride-bush*, p. 31.

42. William Gouge, *Of Domesticall Duties* (London, 1622), p. 272.

43. See the "Homily on Marriage," quoted in Stone, p. 198; and William Blackstone, *Commentaries on the Laws of England*, 4 vol. (1765–69; rpt. Chicago: University of Chicago Press facsimile edit., 1979), 1:430. Yet, as many historians have pointed out, the frequency of the cry for female obedience and submission implies that not all women and wives were living up to the Puritan ideal: as in the life of medieval women, there was a severe disjunction between theory and reality. The Hallers claim that one major reason the Puritan dogmatists insisted so strongly on female subordination was that they intuitively realized how *small* the degree of inequality was between man and woman—so small as (God forbid) to be taken for equality (p. 249). This narrowing gap between the sexes also involved an economic dimension, given the increased wage-earning opportunities for women in shopkeeping trades during the general period. For additional background on women's place in the Renaissance, see also Wright, chap. 13, "The Popular Controversy over Woman," pp. 465–507; and Chilton L. Powell, *English Domestic Relations, 1487–1653* (New York, 1917), chap. 5, "Contemporary Attitudes towards Woman," pp. 147–78.

44. Gouge, pp. 16–17; emphasis added. See Stone, chap. 5, "The Reinforcement of Patriarchy," esp. pp. 151–55, 216–18, on the effects of the nuclear family on marital dynamics.

45. Baldasaare Castiglione, *The Book of the Courtier*, trans. George Bull (Harmondsworth: Penguin, 1967), pp. 211, 220–21; emphasis added.

46. Sir Thomas Elyot, *The Book Named the Governor*, ed. S. E. Lehmberg (London: Dent, 1962), pp. 77–78, emphasis added.

47. "Marsilio Ficino's Commentary on Plato's Symposium: The Text and a Translation," trans. Sears Reynolds Jayne, *University of Missouri Studies* 19 (1944): 146.

48. Ficino, pp. 144–45; emphasis added.

49. "The Relic," *The Poetry of John Donne* (New York: Norton, 1966), p. 38. See also "The Extasie," "Valediction Forbidding Mourning," and "The Canonization."

50. See A. R. Cirillo, "The Fair Hermaphrodite: Love-Union in the Poetry of Donne and Spenser," *Studies in English Literature* 9 (1969): 81–95.

51. See J. B. Broadbent, *Poetic Love* (London: Chatto and Windus, 1964), on continuities between late medieval and metaphysical lyric; and Kelly, on anticipations in the Chaucerian ethic of marriage of the ideology promulgated in Renaissance England.

52. Donald Cheney, "Spenser's Hermaphrodite and the 1590 *Faerie Queene*," *PMLA* 87 (1972): 198. With a touch of his usual hyperbole, C. S. Lewis credits Spenser with inaugurating the "defeat of courtly love by the romantic conception of marriage" (p. 298). A much longer explication of *The Faerie Queene* in context of Spenser's other poetic works would only

begin to reveal the complex and perhaps ultimately contradictory views of love held within the narrative poem: Spenser espouses a vision of psychic androgyny in Britomart, yet demeans Artegall for cross-dressing in book 5; he suggests (after Ficino) that love begins in likeness, yet populates his poem with various explicit images of *discordia concors* and ambivalent unities.

53. *King John*, 2.1. 437–42. Quoted from *The Complete Pelican Shakespeare* (Baltimore MD: Penguin, 1969). All other quotations from the plays throughout this book are from this edition and appear in the text.

54. Madeleine Doran, Intro. to *A Midsummer Night's Dream*, in the Pelican Shakespeare, p. 146.

55. See Hagstrum, p. 26, and William Haller, "Hail Wedded Love," *ELH: A Journal of English Literary History* 13 (1946): 79–97. Hagstrum's analysis of sentimental love in the Enlightenment is predicated on the influence of the Milton archetype.

56. *John Milton: Complete Poems and Major Prose*, ed. Merritt Y. Hughes (New York: Odyssey Press, 1957), bk. 4, lines 750–52. All further references to *Paradise Lost* appear in the text according to book and line.

57. In *Complete Prose Works of John Milton*, ed. Ernest Sirluck (London: Oxford University Press, 1959), 2:246.

58. David J. Latt argues a similar point in "Praising Virtuous Ladies: The Literary Image and Historical Reality of Women in Seventeenth Century England," in *What Manner of Woman: Essays on English and American Life and Literature*, ed. Marlene Springer (New York: New York University Press, 1977), p. 52.

59. "The Hypochondriak: On Marriage," in *The London Magazine* 41 (Feb. 1781), rpt. in *Boswell's Column*, ed. Margery Bailey (London: William Kimber, 1951), p. 215, also quoted in Hagstrum, pp. 274–75.

60. Wetenhall Wilkes, *A Letter of Genteel and Moral Advice to a Young Lady* (1740; rpt. London, 1766), p. 186.

61. In Stone, see ch. 7, "The Companionate Marriage," esp. pp. 325–60. See also note 3 to this chapter.

62. Following the Civil Marriage Act of 1653 during the Puritan Reformation, the civil appropriation of marriage reached a climax in the passage of Lord Hardwicke's Marriage Bill of 1753–54; by specifying the necessary conditions for legal marriage, the latter act effectually rendered the officiating clergy agents of state. An especially helpful source on the legalistic correlatives of authority in marriage from a literary perspective can be found in Susan Staves, *Players' Scepters: Fictions of Authority in the Restoration* (Lincoln: University of Nebraska Press, 1979), pp. 14, 116, 149–51.

63. Mary Astell, *Some Reflections Upon Marriage*, 4th ed. (1730; rpt. New York: Source Book Press, 1970), p. 106.

64. See, for example, Richard Allestree's widely read manual, *The Ladies Calling* (Oxford, 1673), pt. 2, which argues that marriage without love is "only a Bargain and Compact, a Tyranny perhaps on the mans part, and a

slavery on the womans. 'Tis love only that cements the hearts, and where that union is wanting, 'tis but a shadow, a carcass of marriage" (pp. 23–24).

65. Hester Chapone, *Posthumous Works* (London, 1807), 2:151, 149; my emphases substituted for Chapone's. Quoted in Stone, p. 327.

66. Hagstrum, p. 10.

67. See Hagstrum, pp. 163–64; Christopher Hill, "Clarissa Harlowe and her Times," *Essays in Criticism* 5 (1955): 334; Stone, p. 352.

68. Ian Watt, *The Rise of the Novel: Studies in Defoe, Richardson, and Fielding* (Berkeley: University of California Press, 1964), pp. 160–61.

69. The "transfer of heroism from the military camp to the hearth" in redefining male success is described in Hagstrum, p. 162.

70. *The Rash Resolve; or, The Untimely Discovery* (London, 1724; rpt. New York: Garland, 1973; facsimile ed.), n.p.

71. Hill, "Clarissa Harlowe and her Times," p. 331. Mary Poovey explores the economic imperatives and social contradictions embodied in the ethos of female chastity throughout the eighteenth and into the beginning of the nineteenth century in *The Proper Lady and the Woman Writer: Ideology as Style in the Works of Mary Wollstonecraft, Mary Shelley, and Jane Austen* (Chicago: University of Chicago Press, 1984), pp. 5–30.

72. *Moll Flanders*, ed. G. A. Starr (New York: New American Library, 1964), p. 62. On the marriage crisis, see Watt, pp. 138–47, and Poovey, pp. 12–13.

73. Joseph Addison, *The Spectator* (1711), no. 261, quoted in Stone, p. 276. See also Daniel Defoe's *Conjugal Lewdness; or, Matrimonial Whoredom: A Treatise Concerning the Use and Abuse of the Marriage Bed* (1727; rpt. Gainesville FL: Scholars' Facsimiles and Reprints, 1967), esp. chap. 4, "Of the absolute Necessity of a mutual Affection before Matrimony, in order to the Happiness of a married State, and of the Scandal of marrying without it" (pp. 95–122).

74. That the freely chosen marriage for love continued to form a central ideal in these dramas is evident in the fifth-act repentance overtaking the prototypical rake, Dorimant, in Etheredge's *The Man of Mode* (1676), as well as in the climactic rescue of the virtuous heroine from the grasp of arranged marriage, as in Wycherley's *The Country Wife* (1675). Later sentimental comedy, like Steele's *The Conscious Lovers* (1722), continued to advocate the cause of true love over parental influence, while reform plays like Cibber's *Love's Last Shift* (1696) promoted the myth of the saving power of connubial love, and mid-century world-weary comedies like Fielding's *Rape upon Rape* or *The Modern Husband* (1732) derided the hypocritical forces of sexual and economic opportunism that paid lip service to the ideal they were busily attempting to subvert. As Robert Hume states in his excellent article, "Marital Discord in English Comedy from Dryden to Fielding," *Modern Philology* 74 (1977): 248–72, "Almost all of the witty anti-matrimonialist protagonists . . . really protest not marriage but marriage of economic convenience" (p. 253). See also Staves's theatrical examples in

chap. 5, "Sovereignty in the Family," pp. 111–89, and P. F. Vernon's "Marriage of Convenience and the Moral Code of Restoration Comedy," *Essays in Criticism* 12 (1962): 370–87.

75. See Stone, on right of choice, pp. 272–73; on philosophical concepts of autonomy, pp. 223–24. On the situation of the aristocracy, see Hill, "Clarissa Harlowe in her Times," pp. 315–19.

76. Stone, p. 286.

77. Mary Wollstonecraft, *A Vindication of the Rights of Women* (1792; rpt. Troy NY: Whitston Publishing Co., 1982), p. 163.

78. As Stone, p. 284, puts it, "For the first time in history, romantic love became a respectable motive for marriage among the propertied classes."

Chapter 3

1. Forster, *Aspects of the Novel*, pp. 54, 55.

2. Susanna Rowson, *The Inquisitor* (1788; rpt. Philadelphia: Matthew Carey, 1794), p. 189.

3. John J. Richetti, *Popular Fiction before Richardson: Narrative Patterns, 1700–1739* (Oxford: Clarendon, 1969), pp. 124–26, 149, 151–52; Watt, p. 142. On pre-Richardsonian epistolary fiction by women, see Ruth Perry, *Women, Letters, and the Novel* (New York: AMS Press, 1980). Perry reports that 54 pre-Richardsonian epistolary novellas were by women (29 by Eliza Haywood alone) and 72 by men; many others were published anonymously (p. 17).

4. Richetti, p. 208; see also pp. 151, 167. As Richetti aptly sums up the ethos at work here, "She vibrates, he controls" (p. 187).

5. Ibid., p. 198.

6. Ibid., pp. 221–35; the quotation is from p. 220.

7. Ibid., p. 208.

8. Robert Kiely, *Beyond Egotism: The Fiction of James Joyce, Virginia Woolf, and D. H. Lawrence* (Cambridge MA: Harvard University Press, 1980), p. 164.

9. Terry Eagleton, *Literary Theory: An Introduction* (Minneapolis: University of Minnesota Press, 1983), p. 185; see also Tzvetan Todorov, "The Grammar of Narrative," on the transformation from beginning to end that constitutes narrative, in *The Poetics of Prose*, trans. Richard Howard (1971; rpt. Ithaca NY: Cornell University Press, 1977), pp. 108–19.

10. Brooks, pp. 101–3; and Eagleton, *Literary Theory*, p. 186.

11. Conversations with Susan B. Winnett on this topic have significantly expanded my own hypotheses about such "ejaculatory" narrative models.

12. Robert Scholes and Robert Kellogg, *The Nature of Narrative* (New York: Oxford University Press, 1966), p. 212; emphasis added. Teresa De Lauretis, in *Alice Doesn't: Feminism, Semiotics, Cinema* (Bloomington: Indiana University Press, 1984), p. 108, also launches a similar critique of Scholes's masculine sexualization of narrative metaphor, quoting from the even

more blatant examples that occur in his *Fabulation and Metafiction* (1979), p. 26.

13. See Monroe Beardsley, *Aesthetics: Problems in the Philosophy of Criticism* (New York: Harcourt, Brace, 1958), pp. 251–53, on dramatic or kinetic structure and the "coherence" of literary structure; Sheldon Sacks, *Fiction and the Shape of Belief: A Study of Henry Fielding (with Glances at Swift, Johnson, and Richardson)* (Berkeley: University of California Press, 1964), p. 15, on the necessary movement from "unstable relationships" to the "complete removal" of complications; and Frank Kermode, *The Sense of an Ending* (New York: Oxford University Press, 1967), p. 18.

14. Beardsley, pp. 247–48; see Gérard Genette's chapters on "Mood" and "Voice" in *Narrative Discourse* (1972; rpt. Ithaca NY: Cornell University Press, 1980).

15. For an overview of fictional bildungsroman, see Jerome Buckley, *Seasons of Youth: The Bildungsroman from Dickens to Golding* (Cambridge MA: Harvard University Press, 1974), esp. p. 17; for feminist reworkings of these patterns, see the essays in *The Voyage In: Fictions of Female Development*, ed. Elizabeth Abel, Marianne Hirsch, and Elizabeth Langland (Hanover NH: University Press of New England, 1983).

16. N. Miller, *The Heroine's Text*, xi.

17. Nathaniel Hawthorne, *The Blithedale Romance* (1912; rpt. New York: Dutton, 1926), p. 60.

18. Lionel Casson, *Masters of Ancient Comedy*, ed. Lionel Casson (New York: Macmillan, 1960), p. 66.

19. The prose romance elements of the plot in *Tom Jones* are enumerated by Sheridan Baker in "Fielding's Comic Epic-in-Prose Romances Again," *Philological Quarterly* 58 (1980): 63–81.

20. Kennard, *Victims of Convention*, pp. 10–11.

21. Hinz, "Hierogamy versus Wedlock," pp. 903–04.

22. N. Miller, xi. Miller labels the trajectories of these two female-centered textual patterns "euphoric" and "dysphoric."

23. Fiedler, p. 60; De Rougement, p. 221.

24. Hagstrum, p. 274.

25. Samuel Richardson, *Clarissa, or the History of a Young Lady*, 4 vols. Everyman Edition (New York: Dutton, 1932), 3:281 (I have deleted Richardson's italics). All further references to this work appear in the text.

26. Brooks, pp. 98–102, elaborates on the psychologically "conservative" implications of repetition and the "binding" of textual pleasure by using Freud's *Beyond the Pleasure Principle* as a model of narrative production.

27. Coleridge to Joseph Cottle, 7 March 1815, in *Collected Letters of S. T. Coleridge*, ed. E. L. Griggs (Oxford: Clarendon Press, 1959), 4:545.

28. Eagleton, *Criticism and Ideology*, pp. 83–85; see also Althusser, "Ideology and Ideological State Apparatuses," pp. 152–59, 163–64.

29. Annette Niemtzow, "Marriage and the New Woman in *The Portrait of a Lady*," *American Literature* 47 (1975–76): 394.

30. Arthur Blackamore, *Luck at Last*, in *Four Before Richardson: Selected English Novels, 1720–27*, ed. William Harlin McBurney (Lincoln: University of Nebraska Press, 1963), p. 80; emphasis added. All further references to this work appear in the text.

31. Bersani, p. 55.

32. On this subject, see Margaret Kenda, "Poetic Justice and the Ending Trick in the Victorian Novel," *Genre* 8 (1975): 336–51.

33. Marianna Torgovnick, *Closure in the Novel* (Princeton: Princeton University Press, 1981), p. 11. See George Kennedy on verb tense use, in "Dickens's Endings," *Studies in the Novel* 6 (1974): 280–87.

34. Tanner, p. 15.

35. On the Greek New Comedy and Alexandrian Romance paradigms, see Casson, ed., *Masters of Ancient Comedy*, cited above; Moses Hadas, Intro., *Three Greek Romances* (1953; rpt. New York: Bobbs-Merrill, 1964), pp. vii–xiii; Northrop Frye, *Anatomy of Criticism: Four Essays* (1957; rpt. New York: Atheneum, 1968) pp. 43–45, 163–71; and Samuel Lee Wolff, *The Greek Romances in Elizabethan Prose Fiction* (1912; rpt. New York: Burt Franklin, 1961), pp. 135–37 and passim.

36. Longus, *Daphnis and Chloe*, in *Three Greek Romances*, p. 3. All further references to this work appear in the text.

37. See Michel Foucault, *The History of Sexuality*, vol. 1: *An Introduction* (1976; rpt. New York: Vintage, 1980); see esp. chap. 1, "The Incitement to Discourse," pp. 17–35, for more on the way discourse reveals as it conceals.

38. *Pamela or Virtue Rewarded* (New York: Norton, 1958), p. 26. All further references to this work appear in the text.

39. Perry, p. 159.

40. *Love in Excess; or, The Fatal Inquiry* (London: J. Roberts, 1719–20), 1:39. All further references to this work appear in the text.

41. Richetti, p. 207. I am indebted to Richetti's excellent analysis of this novella, pp. 179–207.

42. Watt, pp. 158–62.

43. Opening her chapter on *Pamela* in a similar vein by quoting Huysmans's statement, "Tombera? tombera pas?," N. Miller, *Heroine's Text*, notes that the plot can only retroactively be seen as an unqualified "courtship" narrative: "to call the relationship between Mr. B. and Pamela *as it unfolds* a courtship, is to empty the text of its implicit violence" (p. 165, n. 2).

44. See Jessica Benjamin, "Master and Slave: The Fantasy of Erotic Domination," in *Powers of Desire: The Politics of Sexuality*, ed. Ann Snitow, Christine Stansell, and Sharon Thompson (New York: Monthly Review Press, 1983), pp. 281–99.

45. N. Miller, *Heroine's Text*, p. 49.

46. Jane Austen, *Pride and Prejudice* (Boston: Houghton Mifflin, 1956), Riverside Edition, p. 201. All further references to this edition appear in the text. I am indebted to Joseph Wiesenfarth for much of my Austen analysis.

47. Kennard, p. 23.

48. Gilbert and Gubar, p. 121.

49. See Auerbach's interesting argument in *Communities of Women*, pp. 35–55, that the Bennet sisters are "waiting women" held in limbo in a drawing room world where all movement and initiation belongs to men.

50. Gilbert and Gubar make a fine case for both *Jane Eyre* and *Middlemarch* as courtship narratives that succeed in presenting final models of equitable union. In their eyes the Jane-Rochester relationship is an example of a nonexploitative, mutual dependence that does not negate the individual power of each of these strong characters (pp. 336–74; esp. pp. 368–69); in the case of Eliot's novel, they see Will Ladislaw as the author's "radically anti-patriarchal attempt to create an image of masculinity attractive to women" (528–29) and thus a worthy mate of Dorothea.

51. Peter K. Garrett, *The Victorian Multiplot Novel: Studies in Dialogical Form* (New Haven: Yale University Press, 1980), see note 41, p. 20.

52. Gérin, pp. 510–13.

53. For a few of many perspectives on the parameters of renunciation, rebellion, and feminism in this novel, see Gilbert and Gubar, chap. 12, "The Buried Life of Lucy Snowe," pp. 399–440; Mary Jacobus, "The Buried Letter: Feminism and Romanticism in *Villette*," in *Women Writing*, pp. 42–60; and Robert Bernard Martin, *Charlotte Brontë: The Accents of Persuasion* (New York: Norton, 1966), pp. 143–86.

54. Kennard, pp. 63–79, for example, points out that the premature death of a young heroine may actually be a way of subverting the usual equation in the female bildungsroman of female maturity with the hero's virtues.

55. William Gilmore Simms, *Charlemont* (1856), quoted in Fiedler, p. 220.

56. As such the seducer perpetuates the fantasy of erotic domination through violence described by Benjamin in "Master and Slave," cited in note 44 above. The impulse to erotic domination—most typically of woman as other—is tied, Benjamin forcefully argues, to our culture's stress on male individualism and hence to the sadist-seducer's "need to establish autonomous identity and the need to be recognized by the other" as superior (p. 282). Yet the latter desire for recognition tacitly reveals a contradictory *dependence* on the other, the object, for which the subject devises a psychic defense—sadistic domination—which finds its outlet in violent sexual mastery (pp. 283–85).

57. An exception would be those female libertines, such as Moll Flanders and Fanny Hill, whose sexual careers form *euphoric* rather than tragic trajectories. I would argue, however, that their successes owe more to their

assimilation of male modes of enacting their desires and to their existence as their author's (male) fantasies of the sexualized woman than to their own sexual autonomy.

58. See Raymond Hilliard's insightful essay, "Desire and the Structure of Eighteenth Century Fiction," *Studies in Eighteenth Century Culture* 9 (1979), esp. pp. 362–64. Bersani also discusses the ideology of a "coherent, hierarchical wholeness" of personality as a defense against the deconstructive force of unbounded desire (p. 56).

59. Perry comes to similar conclusions about the reader's position in the eighteenth-century epistolary fictions of sex she analyzes: "the reader, who has all along been reading the letters which tell the story, cannot help but be implicated in the exposure, the mind-rape, which is being acted out at the center of the book" (p. 135).

60. Eliza Haywood, *The Mercenary Lover; or, The Unfortunate Heiresses* (London, 1726; facsimile edition), p. 24. All further references to this work appear in the text.

61. Such a lurid commingling of seduction and incest themes foreshadows later gothic seduction fictions ranging from Horace Walpole's *The Castle of Otranto*, Matthew G. Lewis's *The Monk,* and W. B. Brown's *The Power of Sympathy* to much of William Faulkner's canon.

62. Fiedler, p. 71, subscribes to such a view himself. The sexual assumptions underlying influential readings of the novel from Dorothy Van Ghent's essay in *The English Novel: Form and Function* (New York: Harper and Rowe, 1953), pp. 45–63, to William Beatty Warner's deconstructive *Reading Clarissa: The Struggles of Interpretation* (New Haven: Yale University Press, 1979), have also perpetuated a similar dualism, unconsciously advocating something akin to a rape mentality, in positing oppositions between Lovelace and Clarissa based on his Daemonic/Nietzschean "power" and her repressive "prudery." Readings more congenial to my own begin with Watt and include Terry Eagleton, *The Rape of Clarissa: Writing, Sexuality, and Class Struggle in Samuel Richardson* (Oxford: Basil Blackwell, 1982), and Terry Castle, *Clarissa's Ciphers: Meaning and Disruption in Richardson's Clarissa* (Ithaca NY: Cornell University Press, 1982).

63. See Benjamin's psychoanalytic schema sketched in note 56 above. Eagleton in *Rape* is quite precise on the related fallacies involved in the critical promotion of the "myth" of Lovelace's prowess: "Thoroughly narcissistic and regressive, Lovelace's 'rakishness,' for all its virile panache, is nothing less than a crippling incapacity for adult sexual relationship. His misogyny and infantile sadism achieve their appropriate expression in the virulently anti-sexual act of rape. It is this pathetic character who has been celebrated by the critics as Byronic hero, Satanic vitalist or post-modernist artist" (p. 63).

64. Judith Wilt, "He Could Go No Farther: A Modest Proposal about Lovelace and Clarissa," *PMLA,* 92 (1977): 19–32, ingeniously argues for Lovelace's impotence at the moment of crisis.

65. Thomas Hardy, *Tess of the D'Urbervilles* (Boston: Houghton Mifflin, 1960), p. 24. All further references to this work appear in the text.

66. Boumelha, *Thomas Hardy and Women*, p. 122.

67. Boumelha, p. 120.

68. Alan Friedman, *The Turn of the Novel* (New York: Oxford University Press, 1966), pp. 62–63.

69. It was the male author, interestingly, who placed in the female victim's hands the means of avenging her wrong; hence, in England, Holcroft's eponymous heroine successfully fights against her would-be seducer in *Anna St. Ives* (1792), and, in America, the feminist C. B. Brown has his heroine stab her would-be rapist in *Ormond; or, The Secret Witness* (1799) as does Simms in *Charlemont* (1856).

70. Jane Evans, *St. Elmo* (New York: G. W. Dillingham, 1866), p. 564.

71. William Makepeace Thackeray, *Vanity Fair* (Harmondsworth: Penguin, 1968), p. 310. All further references to this work appear in the text.

72. See Heilbrun's "Marriage Perceived: English Literature 1873–1941," in *What Manner of Woman*, ed. Springer, pp. 163, 168, 174–75. One might modify Heilbrun's assertion by noting not only the attempts to represent married life in *Pamela II* and *Amelia* but also those in Sarah Scott's *Millenium Hall* (1762), which I discuss in chapter 6, Elizabeth Griffith's *Delicate Distress* (1769) and *The History of Lady Burton* (1771), Susan Ferrier's *Marriage* (1818), Emily Eden's *The Semi-Attached Couple* (written 1830; published 1860), Dickens's *Dombey and Son* (1846–48), Thackeray's *The Newcomes* (1855), Anne Brontë's *The Tenant of Wildfell Hall* (1848), and Emily Brontë's *Wuthering Heights* (1848), discussed in chapter 4, as well as in scores of popular domestic fictions written in England and America, such as E. D. E. N. Southworth's *The Curse of Clifton* (1852), Dinah Mulock Craik's *Agatha's Husband* (1853), and Elizabeth Stuart Phelps Ward's *The Story of Avis* (1877).

73. Hinz, pp. 903–4.

74. Kiely, p. 86.

75. Penelope Aubin, *The Life and Adventures of the Lady Lucy* (London, 1726; rpt. New York: Garland, 1973; facsimile ed.), dedication, p. vii. All further references to this work appear in the text.

76. See Lévi-Strauss and Rubin, cited in chapter 2.

77. See Hilliard, pp. 361–62, on the transposition of secular themes (such as wedlock) onto the providential plot (of fall and restoration to grace) in eighteenth-century fiction.

78. Henry Fielding, *Amelia* (New York: Harper, 1902), 1:13. All further references to this work appear in the text.

79. Review of *Amelia*, unsigned, *Monthly Review* 5 (1751): 510–12.

80. On the Restoration's new heroic type, see Hagstrum, p. 162; on the pious novella, Richetti, p. 221–35 and this chapter's section on "Pre-Richardsonian Models," above; on the feminine hero, Showalter, pp. 133–52.

81. A. R. Towers, *"Amelia* and the State of Matrimony," *Review of English Studies* 5 (1954): 156. The entire article, pp. 144–57, provides an excellent overview of the "conventional but enlightened opinion of the age" embodied in Amelia and Booth's "idealized conjugal behavior" (p. 156).

82. It should be pointed out that some critics argue for a much less "innocent" and disinterested reading of Mrs. Bennet's history; such a possibility, however, does not detract from the role the interpolation plays as a repetition of the Booths' history and a warning for Amelia.

83. Among the many critics who have explored the novel in terms of the Providence/Chance topos, see George Sherburn, "Fielding's *Amelia:* An Interpretation," *ELH* 3 (1936): 1–14.

84. This "personal revelation of order" becomes all the more ironic in light of what Eric Rothstein, *Systems of Order and Inquiry in Later Eighteenth Century Fiction* (Berkeley: University of California Press, 1975), terms "the general instability of the world of *Amelia,*" an effect that results from Fielding's having created an authorial narrator, much the opposite of the all-knowing author of *Tom Jones,* one whose "words seem to pretend to a universality they do not have within the novel itself"; occupying the same epistemological level available to the characters, he at no moment knows any more than the readers who therefore must accept the final decrees of Providence as "unauthored," in a sense, and as an article of faith. See esp. pp. 157, 166–67, and 203.

85. William Dean Howells, *A Modern Instance* (New York: Signet, 1964), p. 307. All further references to this work appear in the text.

86. Marcia temporarily breaks her engagement with Bartley in a fit of jealousy over his possible flirtation with one of his vivacious employees, Hannah Morrison (pp. 76–77); Hannah turns up in Boston as a prostitute at the very moment Bartley decides to ask Marcia's forgiveness for their worsening married life, an event sparking Marcia's hysterical refusal to listen and Bartley's decision to desert her (pp. 320–23).

87. To cite only two examples, Marcia decides she is a widow on the very day that the news that Bartley is suing for divorce reaches Boston (p. 383); on her subsequent journey to fight the suit in Indiana, she decides to turn back when, out of nowhere, an old friend of Bartley's appears in the train station with the news that Bartley lied and told him she was dead (p. 402)— the perfect stimulus to renew Marcia's vindictive fighting spirit.

88. So William Gibson identifies the ending in his introduction to the Riverside edition (Boston: Houghton Mifflin, 1957), p. xv.

89. Henry James, *The Portrait of a Lady* (Boston: Houghton Mifflin, 1963), p. 412. For an excellent reading of Isabel's final freedom in somewhat similar terms, see Donald Stone's assessment of the ending in *Novelists in a Changing World: Meredith, James, and the Transformation of English Fiction in the 1880s* (Cambridge MA: Harvard University Press, 1972), pp. 225–28.

90. Cockshut, p. 126.

91. "Postscript" (1912), in *Jude the Obscure* (1895, rpt. New York: Harper and Row, 1966), p. 49.

92. Lloyd Fernando, *"New Women" in the Late Victorian Novel* (University Park: Pennsylvania State University Press, 1977), p. 20. For summaries of the New Woman movement and its influence on literature, see Showalter, chap. 8, "The Feminist Novelists," pp. 182–215; Jenni Calder, *Women and Marriage in Victorian Fiction* (London: Thames and Hudson, 1976), chap. 15: "The Case Against Marriage," pp. 194–204; Fernando, Intro., pp. 1–23; Boumelha, chap. 4: "Women and the New Fiction 1880–1900," pp. 63–97. For a historical overview, see William Leach, *True Love and Perfect Union: The Feminist Reform of Sex and Society* (New York: Basic Books, 1980), pp. 99–129.

93. The formal innovations attempted especially in Schreiner and George Egerton (author of *Keynotes*) are interestingly explored by Boumelha, pp. 66–67, 88–93; see also Patricia Stubbs, *Women and Fiction: Feminism and the Novel 1880–1920* (New York: Harper and Row, 1979), chap. 7: "Feminist Fiction and the Rejection of Realism," pp. 109–21.

94. Boumelha, p. 84.

95. Olive Schreiner, *The Story of an African Farm* (Harmondsworth: Penguin, 1971), p. 199. All further references to this work appear in the text.

96. Grant Allen, *The Woman Who Did* (Boston: Roberts Bros., 1895) p. 37. All further references to this work appear in the text.

97. On the ideology of motherhood as a historically necessary but ultimately subversive element of late nineteenth-century feminism, see Weeks, pp. 126ff, 160–67; Boumelha, chap. 1, "Sexual Ideology and the 'Nature' of Woman, 1880–1900," pp. 11–27, and chap. 4, esp. pp. 85–88.

98. Sarah Grand, *The Beth Book* (New York: Dial, 1980), p. 527.

99. Larzer Ziff, *The American 1890s: Life and Times of a Lost Generation* (New York: Viking, 1966), p. 285. Ziff cites as examples Constance Cary Harrison's *A Bachelor Maid* (1894) and Gertrude Atherton's *Patience Sparhawk and Her Times* (1895); his entire chapter 13, "An Abyss of Inequality," is helpful on the feminist themes entering American fiction in this period.

100. Cockshut, p. 159.

101. Weeks, p. 12.

102. Fiedler, p. 317.

103. Kennard, pp. 19–20, 158–67; Heilbrun, "Marriage and Contemporary Fiction," *Critical Inquiry* 5 (1978): 309–22; the quoted material is Heilbrun's, p. 309.

Chapter 4

1. George Eliot, *Middlemarch* (Harmondsworth: Penguin, 1965), p. 890. All further references to this work appear in the text.

2. James, *Portrait*, p. 349.

3. *Twelfth Night*, 2.2.40.

4. Mrs. Oliphant, "Modern Novelists—Great and Small," review article in *Blackwood's* (May 1855), rpt. in *The Brontës: The Critical Heritage*, ed. Miriam Allott (Boston: Routledge and Kegan Paul, 1974), p. 313.

5. Thomas Hardy, *Far From the Madding Crowd* (1874; rpt. Harmondsworth: Penguin, 1978), p. 241.

6. *Diana of the Crossways*, vol. 16 of *The Works of George Meredith* (1885; rpt. London: Constable [Standard Edition], 1915), p. 156.

7. All Barthes quotations in this paragraph are from *Roland Barthes by Roland Barthes*, trans. Richard Howard (New York: Hill and Wang, 1977), p. 156; emphasis added. Marcus is quoted by Heilbrun in "Marriage Perceived," in Springer, *What Manner of Woman*, p. 162.

8. See the discussion in the previous chapter. The theory of "unstable relationships" is from Sacks, p. 15; the movement toward the "resolution a plot demands," from Scholes and Kellogg, p. 212.

9. Robert Adams, *Strains of Discord: Studies in Literary Openness* (Ithaca NY: Cornell University Press, 1958), p. 13.

10. See Friedman, pp. 26–37.

11. For analyses of the practical techniques used to accomplish these "ends," see Friedman on the expanding "stream of conscience," pp. 26–37; Beverly Gross, "Narrative Time and the Open-ended Novel," *Criticism* 8 (1966): 362–76; Torgovnick on the scenic ending, pp. 121–42; Culler on textual "recuperation," *Structuralist Poetics* (Ithaca NY: Cornell University Press, 1975), p. 137; Garrett on double-plotting, discussed below.

12. See especially J. Hillis Miller, "The Problematic of Ending in Narrative," pp. 3–7; and D. A. Miller, *Narrative and Its Discontents: Problems of Closure in the Traditional Novel* (Princeton: Princeton University Press, 1981), pp. ix–xv.

13. Garrett, p. 11.

14. On the evolution of the scenic ending, see Kenda, pp. 336–51, and Torgovnick, pp. 121–42.

15. See, respectively, the reviews in the *Examiner*, January 1848, and in the *Britannia*, January 1848, rpt. in Allott, pp. 220, 223.

16. Review, *Britannia*, rpt. in Allott, p. 225.

17. Emily Brontë, *Wuthering Heights*, Norton Critical Edition (New York: W. W. Norton, 1972), p. 41. All further references to this work appear in the text.

18. Young Cathy's statement, significantly, is made in response to her cousin Linton Heathcliff's possessive desire to make her his wife in order to ensure himself of her total loving devotion. Hypotheses of Heathcliff and Catherine's passion as incestuous hinge on interpretations of Heathcliff as Mr. Earnshaw's bastard (and hence given the name of an Earnshaw son who died in infancy).

19. Émile Montégut, Review, *Revue des deux mondes*, 1 July 1857, rpt. in

Allott, pp. 377–78. For contemporary echoes, see Adrienne Rich, "Jane Eyre: The Temptations of a Motherless Woman," *Ms.*, October 1973, p. 68, and Heilbrun, *Toward a Recognition of Androgyny* (New York: Harper Colophon, 1973), p. 80.

20. Patricia Spacks, *The Female Imagination* (New York: Avon, 1972) p. 171; Gilbert and Gubar, p. 293.

21. A similar point is made by Arnold Kettle, *An Introduction to the English Novel* (New York: Harper and Row, 1967), pp. 135, 143, and Inga-Stina Ewbank, *Their Proper Sphere: A Study of the Brontë Sisters as Early Victorian Female Novelists* (Cambridge MA: Harvard University Press, 1966), pp. 88–89.

22. See Showalter's use of these terms in "Criticism in the Wilderness," in *Writing and Sexual Difference*, special issue of *Critical Inquiry* 8 (1981): 199–201. She adapts them from Edwin Ardener, who derives the term "the wild" from his analysis of Bakweri tribal customs involving rites of female maturation in "Belief and the Problem of Women," pp. 6–7, and "The 'Problem' Revisited," p. 23, both in *Perceiving Women: The Nature of Woman in Society*, ed. Shirley Ardener (New York: Oxford University Press, 1977).

23. Garrett insightfully summarizes several of these versions of viewing the text's doubleness on pp. 18–19.

24. See Gilbert and Gubar, p. 265.

25. The significance of this moment can be measured in its uncanny repetition at several other crucial junctures in the plot structure. A close reading reveals that it has *already* been anticipated in the diary entry that Lockwood reads in the pivotal chapter 3, where Catherine announces her and Heathcliff's intention to rebel against Hindley's tyranny by escaping to the moors under the dairymaid's cloak. Heathcliff's reference to the same cloak in his account of the evening's outcome to Nelly, in chapter 6, becomes the reader's one clue linking the two accounts as parts of the same evening's sequence. Catherine indirectly returns to this moment in the pivotal mad scene of chapter 12, as we shall also see.

26. See Gilbert and Gubar on Catherine's Satanic "fall" from a patriarchal heaven, pp. 271–78.

27. T. E. Apter points to the critique of the *Liebestod* theme in "Romanticism and Romantic Love in *Wuthering Heights*," in *The Art of Emily Brontë*, ed. Anne Smith (New York: Barnes and Noble, 1976), p. 209, as do Gilbert and Gubar, p. 284.

28. Heilbrun, *Androgyny*, p. 81.

29. These points are echoed in Carol Ohmann, "Emily Brontë in the Hands of Male Critics," *College English* 32 (1971): 913, and Carolyn V. Platt, "'Their Eyes are Precisely Similar': Androgyny in *Wuthering Heights*," unpublished article (written while author was with the Women's Studies Program, San Diego State University, 1977), p. 12.

30. In turn, this revelation displaces Isabella's version of Heathcliff's

brutish behavior on the evening of Catherine's burial (an inserted narrative flashback occurring in chapter 17). In "The Place of Love in *Jane Eyre* and *Wuthering Heights*," *The Brontës: A Collection of Critical Essays,* ed. Ian Gregor (Englewood Cliffs NJ: Prentice-Hall, 1970), pp. 90–92, Mark Kinkead-Weekes demonstrates how these deliberately juxtaposed accounts form a "radical reinterpretation of the whole story," throwing new light on Heathcliff's suffering.

31. With Catherine's death there ensues another fissure in the temporal structure as Nelly muses to Lockwood about Catherine's heavenly reward. Her wishful impression at the time—"I see a repose that neither earth nor hell can break"—gives way to a direct question to Lockwood: "Do you believe such people *are* happy in the other world, sir? . . . I fear we have no right to think she is" (pp. 137–38). A disturbing enough reflection by itself, the remark is immediately juxtaposed with Heathcliff's reaction at the (past) time of Catherine's death, "May she wake in torment!" (p. 139). Again, the superimposition of perspectives transports the unresolved disturbances of the past into the present.

32. See, for example, Ewbank's assertion that "We are left at the end with . . . two movements [that] are not at any point fused, but remain counterpointed" (p. 126), and Alan Loxterman's argument for "two distinct endings . . . which result from contradictory types of love" that create an "ambiguous suspension" at the text's end, in "*Wuthering Heights* as Romantic Poem and Victorian Novel," in *A Festschrift for Professor Marguerite Roberts,* ed. Freida Elaine Penniger (Richmond VA: University of Richmond Press, 1976), p. 97. Critics typically attempt to assert the priority of one event over the other, sometimes suggesting that they represent antithetical comedic and tragic patterns, at other times suggesting that the one is conventionally "closed" but the other less so.

33. Peter Grudin, "*Wuthering Heights:* The Question of Unquiet Slumbers," *Studies in the Novel* 6 (1974): 396, and Thomas Moser, "Whatever is the Matter with Emily Jane? Conflicting Impulses in *Wuthering Heights*," *Nineteenth Century Fiction* 17 (1962): 15, respectively. Ironically, several feminist critics have joined Moser in reviling the ending, but for opposite reasons: where he sees a symbolic castration of "masculine" creative energy at work, they have criticized the Hareton-Cathy union for emulating Victorian patriarchal values (see Spacks, p. 172, Gilbert and Gubar, pp. 299–301, and Heilbrun, *Androgyny,* p. 82). In counterpoint to both these extremes, Q. D. Leavis in *Lectures in America* (London: Chatto and Windus, 1969), pp. 119, 130, *praises* the ending for normalizing the relation of the sexes by returning male power to Hareton. All these critics err, I believe, in taking Nelly's word at face value. Readings more congenial to my own include Platt, above, whose viewpoint has greatly influenced my own, and, from a less specifically gendered viewpoint, Arnold Shapiro, "*Wuthering Heights* as Victorian Novel," *Studies in the Novel* 1 (1969): 285.

34. On Hareton's symbolic emasculation by "civilization," see Moser, p.

15; Van Ghent, pp. 169–70; and Richard Chase, "The Brontës or Myth Domesticated," in *Forms of Modern Fiction,* ed. William Van O'Connor (Minneapolis: Uniersity of Minnesota Press, 1948), p. 108.

35. Platt, p. 22, also makes this point.

36. See Grudin's careful summary, pp. 389, 404, of these folkloric signifiers.

37. Barbara Hardy, intro. to George Eliot, *Daniel Deronda* (Harmondsworth: Penguin, 1967), pp. 22, 8. All further references to this work appear in the text.

38. Fernando, p. 62.

39. Review of Cross's *Life* of Eliot, *Atlantic Monthly* 60 (May 1885): 668–78, item 69 in *George Eliot: The Critical Heritage,* ed. David Carroll (New York: Barnes and Noble, 1971), p. 499.

40. These references occur in letters to her publisher, John Blackwood, near the beginning of her career (1 May 1857) and while readying to conclude *Deronda* (18 April 1876). See *The George Eliot Letters,* ed. Gordon S. Haight (New Haven: Yale University Press, 1955), 2:324 and 6:242, respectively. Eliot's theory of the web of "inner relations" constituting narrative form is cited directly below.

41. "Notes on Form in Art" (written in 1868 but unpublished in Eliot's lifetime), in *Essays of George Eliot,* ed. Thomas Pinney (New York: Columbia University Press, 1963), pp. 431–36. See Darrell Mansell's analysis of this essay's significance in "George Eliot's Conception of Form," *Studies in the English Language* 5 (1965): 651–52.

42. George Eliot, "Art and Belles Lettres," *Westminister Review* 65 (1 April 1856): 639.

43. As Blackwood wrote to George Henry Lewes, 18 April 1876, "There is immense puzzlement as to what the author is going to make of Gwendolen . . . , especially among the newspaper critics" (see *Letters* 6:242). The range of opinions quoted in *George Eliot and Her Readers: A Selection of Contemporary Reviews,* ed. John Holmstrom and Lawrence Lerner (London: Bodley Head, 1966), confirms Blackwood's fears: some critics were tantalized by what they saw as Gwendolen's sexual appeal, others felt she deserved the "retribution" undergone in the last book for her "sins" against "pure womanly instincts" (see, for example, *The Spectator,* 29 July 1876, pp. 135–36), and still others felt she was not punished enough (see, for example, *The Examiner,* 2 September 1876, pp. 137–38).

44. Although its implications are ultimately moral and spiritual, the novel's opening sentence, "Was she beautiful or not beautiful?" (35), indicates the physical dimension of the disturbing "questions" that Gwendolen's appearance immediately raises "in Daniel's mind" (35); nor do these questions cease. At the very moment that the narrator deflects any romantic connotations to Daniel and Gwendolen's friendship by explaining that "there is a feeling distinct from [an] exclusive passionate love . . . which yet is not the same with friendship," nonetheless Daniel is simultaneously

shown suffering "from the nervous consciousness that there *was* something to guard against not only on her account *but on his own*" (683; emphasis added).

45. Mansell, p. 659, argues similarly. In contrast, see F. R. Leavis's comment in *The Great Tradition* (1948; rpt. New York: New York University Press, 1963), pp. 79–80, that the "good half" of the novel might be extracted from the "bad," leaving intact the novel he renames *Gwendolen Harleth*.

46. In the process of responding to Gwendolen's pleas for advice on how to assuage her guilt over having married Grandcourt, Daniel finds himself in the "superior" position of being Gwendolen's mentor; however, the fact that he does not willingly accept (and in fact rebels against) this role, finding its power a thankless burden, tied to the significant fact that he is not her lover, keeps their relationship from manifesting the negative imbalance of sexual power that Kennard sees as inherent in traditional uses of the mentor-pupil paradigm in stories of female development. Although such an explanation does not excuse Daniel's occasional officiousness, it is crucial that Eliot depicts Daniel's superiority as of an ethical, not sexual, order. And it is equally significant that Daniel is not only Gwendolen's mentor but becomes a pupil himself, in relation to *his* mentor, Mordecai.

47. Leon Gottfried, "Structure and Genre in *Daniel Deronda*," in *The English Novel in the Nineteenth Century: Essays in the Literary Mediation of Human Values*, ed. George Goodin (Urbana: University of Illinois Press, 1972), p. 171.

48. On this modal distinction, see Gottfried, pp. 168–69, and Garrett, p. 168.

49. See Eliot's letter to Blackwood of 10 November 1875, *Letters* 6:182–84, on rearranging the ending of book 1 to highlight this moment. All eight books, in fact, end on a significant threshold moment. Each climax, therefore, becomes a simultaneous *entrance* or *opening* into an unknown, unexpected, and expansive world, in Eliot's much-pondered organizational scheme, anticipating the ending.

50. *North American Review*, January 1877, quoted at the beginning of *Gwendolen: A Sequel to George Eliot's Daniel Deronda; Reclaimed* (Boston, 1878), p. 6, as its preface. The quotation from the novel is from pp. 311–12.

51. Blackwood to Lewes, 11 May 1876, and Blackwood to Eliot, 12 July 1876, *Letters* 6:250 and 272 respectively. See also Blackwood's letter to Eliot of 10 June 1876, written after "reaching 'The End' today," in which he cautiously comments, "The situation of Gwendolen and Deronda is so new too and oh so delicately handled," before quickly changing the subject (p. 250).

52. Brownstein aptly characterizes this letter as a "benediction," a reversal of the epistolary curse Gwendolen was sent on *her* wedding day by Mrs. Glasher (p. 233).

53. See, for example B. Hardy, p. 29; Kenda, p. 348.

54. See Brownstein on the two men's spiritual consummation as a closural pairing, p. 234.

55. Calder, p. 142.

56. James's complaint about Eliot's concluding marriage devices occurs in a review of George Eliot's *Felix Holt* in *The Nation*, 16 August 1866, quoted in Carroll, item 43, p. 275. He speaks of the "region of virtuous love" and "rigour of convention" in his essays on "George Sand" (1877) and "Matilda Serao" (1901), respectively, quoted in J. E. Miller, pp. 130 and 154. The reference to the "fatal Conclusion" of the "old tradition" occurs in the summary review, "The Novels of George Eliot," in the *Atlantic Monthly*, October 1866, quoted in Holmstrom and Lerner, p. 164.

57. For the view that Jamesian marriages "exist as ideas—as aesthetic arrangements, not physical unions," see David Craig, "The Indeterminacy of the End: Maggie Verver and the Limits of the Imagination," *Henry James Review* 3 (1982): 136. In contrast to this viewpoint are the numerous feminist perspectives that have emerged since Judith Fetterley's brilliantly radical rereading of *The Bostonians* in *The Resisting Reader: A Feminist Approach to American Fiction* (Bloomington: Indiana University Press, 1978), pp. 101–53—perspectives that document the social influences on James's form. Niemtzow, for example, concludes that public fervor over "the new woman led James on a new path to modernism as he systematically unmade the marriage novel" (p. 395); Sara Desaussure Davis offers substantive biographical evidence of James's sympathetic awareness of the historical context of feminism lying behind the inception of *The Bostonians* in "Feminist Sources in *The Bostonians*," *American Literature* 50 (1978–79): 570–87; Nina Baym's analysis of James's revisions of *The Portrait of a Lady* in "Revision and Thematic Change in *The Portrait of a Lady*," *Modern Fiction Studies* 22 (1976): 183–200, also reveals the degree to which the first edition, in particular, is a deliberate response to the fictional conventions arising from most New Woman fiction. Also relevant is Habegger's argument, in *Gender, Fantasy, and Realism in American Literature*, p. 64, that James's achievement arose from a "deep opposition to [his] culture's central gender roles"; and Donald Stone's demonstration, pp. 204 and 259–60, of the links between James's aesthetic output, his social awareness, and his times.

58. "The Future of the Novel," quoted in J. E. Miller, p. 343.

59. Niemtzow, p. 394.

60. See James's appreciative, and creatively involved, review, "Daniel Deronda: A Conversation," in the *Atlantic Monthly* 38 (December 1876): 684–94. See Leavis, pp. 85–86, for an analysis of the links between *Deronda* and James's *Portrait*.

61. The famous articulation of Isabel's being left *"en l'air"* and of the "whole" of what "groups together" (see the next sentence of my text) appears in *The Notebooks of Henry James*, ed. F. O. Matthiessen and Kenneth B. Murdock (New York: Oxford University Press, 1947), p. 18. James restates

the problem as a discrepancy between the closed form of art and the open course of reality in the Preface to *Roderick Hudson*, rpt. in *The Art of the Novel*, ed. R. P. Blackmur (New York: Scribner, 1962), p. 5.

62. Conrad, *Notes on Life and Letters* (London: Dent, 1924), pp. 18–19. Two helpful critics on James's development of open form are J. A. Ward, *The Search for Form: Studies in the Structure of James's Fiction* (Chapel Hill: University of North Carolina Press, 1967), p. 26; and Torgovnick, pp. 122–23.

63. In his 21 December 1895 entry in the *Notebooks*, p. 233, James expresses regret that he has already used this title for one of his short stories.

64. Ruth Yeazell, *Language and Knowledge in the Late Novels of Henry James* (Chicago: University of Chicago Press, 1976), pp. 125, 127.

65. Letter to Henry James, March 1868, quoted in *Henry James: The Critical Heritage*, ed. Roger Gard (New York: Barnes and Noble, 1968), p. 24.

66. Henry James, *The Golden Bowl* (New York: Scribner, 1922), 2:360. All further references to this work appear in the text.

67. See, for example, Leon Edel, in *The Life of Henry James: The Master (1901–1916)* (Philadelphia: Lippincott, 1972), 5: 214. Those critics who have seen Maggie's action as less saintly and more diabolic have generally relied on a parallel "feminine" stereotype—that of the wife as conniving shrew. These opposing schools of interpretation are summed up by Walter Wright, "Maggie Verver: Neither Saint nor Witch," *Nineteenth Century Fiction*, 12 (1957): 59–71.

68. The Prince's complaisant sexism is reflected in the approval he has won from critics who like F. W. Dupee in *Henry James* (Garden City NY: Doubleday, 1951), pp. 229–30, have praised Amerigo as a "man distinctly worth the battle" who turns to *"the next most natural thing,* a mistress," when the "order" of marriage proves unsatisfying (emphasis added).

69. See Sallie Sears, *The Negative Imagination: Form and Perspective in the Novels of Henry James* (Ithaca NY: Cornell University Press, 1963), pp. 173–75, for a somewhat similar reading of the two perspectives. It should be noted that the first book, although primarily centered on the Prince's consciousness, veers in its middle section to Adam's point of view. But because Adam's perspective is also representatively "masculine," his section forms an overall piece with the Prince's viewpoint to convey the "masculine" side of the unfolding marital war of husband and wife.

70. Dupee, p. 231.

71. Critics agreeing on the closural ambiguity welling from this scene and casting grave doubt on Maggie's enterprise include Torgovnick, pp. 154–55, in her chapter on the ambiguous gestural cues planted in this scene; Sears, pp. 192–93; and Carol J. Sklenicka, "Henry James's Evasion of Ending in *The Golden Bowl,*" *Henry James Review* 4 (1982): 60.

72. Virginia Woolf, *To the Lighthouse* (New York: Harcourt, Brace, and

World, 1927), p. 268. All further references to this work appear in the text.

73. See, for example, many of the essays in *New Feminist Essays on Virginia Woolf*, ed. Jane Marcus (Lincoln: University of Nebraska Press, 1981).

74. See the entry for 26 January 1920 in *A Writer's Diary*, ed. Leonard Woolf (London: Hogarth, 1953), p. 23; and in particular the conclusion of the essay "Mr. Bennett and Mrs. Brown," in *Collected Essays* (London: Hogarth Press, 1966), 1:319–37. These generic issues are developed in light of Woolf's views on female "difference" in an unpublished honors thesis, Jennifer L. Kapuscik, "Female Identity and the 'Unwritten Novel': Virginia Woolf's Innovative Modernism" (Harvard, 1984), whose many insights have influenced my own reading of Woolf.

75. DuPlessis's chapter, "Modifications of Romance in Woolf," in *Writing Beyond the Ending*, pp. 47–65, very clearly illustrates the degree to which Woolf's earliest fictional efforts, *The Voyage Out* (1915) and *Night and Day* (1919), attempt to óverturn the conventions of the nineteenth-century love-plot through narrative strategies similar to those noted above in Brontë, Eliot, and James.

76. For a summary of these critical viewpoints, see Jane Lilienfeld, "Where the Spear Plants Grew: The Ramsays' Marriage in *To the Lighthouse*," in Marcus, pp. 148–49. Critics approvingly inclined toward Mrs. Ramsay's "feminine" because maternal virtues include Lord David Cecil, *Poets and Story Tellers: A Book of Critical Essays* (London: Constable, 1949), and David Daiches, *Virginia Woolf* (New York: New Directions, 1963). Mitchell Leaska, in *Virginia Woolf's Lighthouse: A Study in Critical Method* (New York: Columbia University Press, 1970), represents the opposing trend, calling attention to the problematic nature of the Ramsay marriage without noting how Woolf makes this specific instance of wedlock critical of the institution itself. For Woolf's repeated fears of the novel's elegiac quality leading to its "being pronounced soft, shallow, insipid, sentimental," see the *Diary* entries for 20 July 1925, p. 80; 3 September 1926, p. 100; 13 September 1926, p. 101; and 5 May 1927, p. 107 (from which I quote in this note).

77. See Lilienfeld, in Marcus, pp. 148–65, on these specifically Victorian traits.

78. "What saves [Mrs. Ramsay] from triviality, is her steady awareness of death in every moment . . . , of life itself as 'terrible, hostile, and quick to pounce,'" observes Kiely (p. 72). The incongruity between Mrs. Ramsay's great self-knowledge and the falsifications she must resort to in order to fulfill her marital role is the subject of Judith Little's "Heroism in *To the Lighthouse*," in *Images of Women in Fiction: Feminist Perspectives*, ed. Susan Koppelman Cornillon (Bowling Green OH: Bowling Green University Press, 1972); see esp. pp. 237–38 and 240.

79. See Little, p. 240, on Mrs. Ramsay's "apparent doubleness."

80. Kiely, p. 68.

81. Thomas Matro, "Only Relations: Vision and Achievement in *To the Lighthouse*," *PMLA* 99 (1984): 215.

82. The incorporation of these two viewpoints into one object recalls Woolf's famous definition of androgyny as a mental state, in *Room*, p. 102.

83. "Stronger than a man, simpler than a child, her nature stood alone," Charlotte eulogized her sister, and her Brussels professor, M. Heger, echoing Charlotte's sentiment, wrote that Emily "should have been a man—a great navigator." Heger is quoted in C. Day Lewis, "Emily Brontë and Freedom," rpt. in the 1963 Norton Critical Edition, p. 374. Charlotte's comment occurs in the "Biographical Notice of Ellis and Acton Bell" (1850), p. 7, appended to *Wuthering Heights* after Emily's death.

84. Henry James, *The Bostonians* (New York: Modern Library, 1956), p. 464.

85. Slowly beginning to love Rhoda for the right reasons, Everard however needs to feel he is still master of the situation, and thus he devises his great test of Rhoda's devotion: he wishes to win her assent to a free union, and upon "see[ing] her in complete subjugation to him" then to propose marriage after all. In the reversals of the final proposal scene in chapter 30, it is Rhoda who stipulates that their union take place without legal bonds to test Everard's sincerity—upon which both discover the hold that convention ironically yet retains for him. He must have the superiority of social forms, if not mastery over Rhoda herself, in order to be happy.

86. E. M. Forster, *Howards End* (New York: Vintage, 1921), pp. 106, 209. All further references to this work will appear in the text. The disorienting opening moves of the novel make particularly clear the connection between formal indeterminacy and a dismantling of traditional love fiction: one assumes that Helen Schlegel's abrupt announcement of her beginning love affair in chapter 1 is going to provide a central focus, only to have this expectation immediately dispelled by the equally abrupt announcement in chapter 2 that it is "*all over*" (13) and by a rapid shift of focus to the London life of the unmarried Schlegel sisters. Similarly, Margaret Schlegel's relationship with Mrs. Wilcox promises to provide continuity, only to be cut short by the authorial narrator's matter-of-fact announcement of the latter woman's sudden death; just as abruptly the narrative breaks off and picks up two years later with the events surrounding Margaret's courtship by the now widowed Mr. Wilcox.

87. Virginia Woolf, *Mrs. Dalloway* (New York: Harvest, 1925), p. 296; D. H. Lawrence, *Women in Love* (Harmondsworth: Penguin, 1976), pp. 473. Woolf's title, of course, also suggests the degree to which her novel is about marriage and its effects on a married woman's identity. As Elizabeth Abel has demonstrated, the novel's stream-of-consciousness technique fluidly interweaves fragmented bits of what would otherwise be traditional love-plot options by agency of Clarissa's memories of Richard, Peter, and Sally at Bourton; see Abel's "Narrative Structure(s) and Female Development:

The Case of *Mrs. Dalloway*," in *The Voyage In*, pp. 161–85. The relation of Lawrence's form to his sexual ethos is extremely complex; his probing into sexuality and sexual relations in *Women in Love* indeed yields, in structural terms, an open-ended plot of uneasy wedlock, an accomplishment that would seemingly align him with the counter-traditional authors I discuss. However, his actual representation and thematic theorization of the sexes often betrays a less than counter-traditional bias—hence the exclusion of an extended discussion of Lawrence from this chapter. For instance, although Lawrence sets up the relationship of Birkin and Ursula in *Women in Love* as a direct counter to the destructive sexual polarity uniting Gerald and Gudrun in a literal fight to the death, the celebrated "star-equilibrium" of the former relationship conceals an opposition based on asymmetrical definitions of power that belie its espousal of sexual equality: "The wish for harmony [often] appears to be confused with the will to dominate," Kiely says of the novel, proceeding to identify this latter urge as "also one of [Lawrence's] problems as a writer"; see Robert Kiely's "Accident and Purpose: 'Bad Form' in Lawrence's Fiction," in *D. H. Lawrence: A Centenary Consideration*, ed. Peter Balbert and Phillip L. Marcus (Ithaca NY: Cornell University Press, 1985), p. 97.

Chapter 5

1. *Selected Poems of Herman Melville*, ed. Henig Cohen (Carbondale: Southern Illinois University Press, 1964), p. 134.

2. *The Art of the Novel: Critical Prefaces*, ed. Richard P. Blackmur (1907, rpt. New York: Scribner, 1962), p. 33.

3. On the minority status of these male fictions as compared to the popularity of women's domestic fiction, see Nina Baym's *Woman's Fiction*, pp. 11–15, as well as her article, "Melodramas of Beset Manhood: How Theories of American Fiction Exclude Women Authors," *American Quarterly* 33 (1981): 123–39. Fetterley's *Resisting Reader* epitomizes the viewpoint that the imagination informing "classic" male American fiction is narrowly limited by its patriarchal biases (p. xxvi); not only is it incapable of addressing any issues of concern to women, it also fails to "provide [any] alternative vision of being male" (p. xiv). While I admit the validity of Fetterley's observations when applied to the texts she has chosen, I would argue it does not account for the very different accomplishments of the novels included in this chapter (Melville's subversions of masculinity, for instance, are mentioned by Fetterley only in a footnote [p. 14]).

4. For Fiedler's description of the sexual combat or polarity inherent in sentimental ideology, see pp. 62–73; for his summary of the effect of its "debasement" on the so-called "anti-bourgeois" American novelist, see pp. 74–93. Fiedler's assumptions about the immaturity of the American writer/quester's attitude toward women and sex echo throughout his entire

analysis, reflected in generalizations such as "It is maturity above all things that the American writer fears, and marriage seems to him its essential sign" (p. 338).

5. Northrop Frye, *Anatomy of Criticism: Four Essays;* see "The Mythos of Summer: Romance," pp. 186–296, and especially pp. 189, 193–94.

6. This is not to suggest that such balanced "halves" are somehow equal, symmetrical in reality, or even specifically identifiable as "masculine" and "feminine" in human nature. Rather, I am borrowing the terms current in the nineteenth-century dialogue of heart and mind, emotion and reason, to analyze the reintegration that Melville—the product of such a dualistically minded culture—saw as essential for psychic well-being.

7. The antirealist aspects of American "Romance" are presented by Richard Chase in *The American Novel and Its Tradition* (Garden City NY: Doubleday, 1957), pp. 12–13; and Richard Brodhead in *Hawthorne, Melville, and the Novel* (Chicago: University of Chicago Press, 1973), pp. 18–24. Brodhead argues that Chase's categorical separation of (English) novel from (American) romance is too extreme, since one of the strategic disunities characterizing American romance is its *inclusion* of "realism," but as only one mode and angle of vision among many.

8. See Nina Baym, "The Women of Cooper's *Leatherstocking* Tales," in Cornillon, pp. 135–54 (the quotation is from p. 145), and Sedgwick, *Between Men: English Literature and Male Homosocial Desire* (New York: Columbia University Press, 1985). Another illuminating Cooper text is his sea quest tale, *The Sea Lions* (1849), in which a psychological level of male "bonding" is formed between the protagonist and his "double" as they dog each other in identically named ships across the Antartic seas; regularly punctuating this male-male psychodrama, however, are shore episodes involving the hero's fiancée, Mary, from whom he has separated at journey's beginning and to whom he will return at its very end, his inner spiritual crisis resolved, as a true Christian: the marital order signals the proper spiritual order. As Melville mockingly but accurately observed in his review of the novel, "The reader will perceive, the moist, rosy hand of our Mary is the rewards of [Roswell's] orthodoxy. Somewhat in the pleasant spirit of the Mahometan, this: who rewards all the believers with a houri." In commenting on the sentimental terms of Cooper's ending ("the action . . . is crowned by the nuptials of Roswell . . . [whom] we admire for a noble fellow; and Mary [whom] we love for a fine example of womanly affection, earnestness, and constancy"), Melville could not help but have been taking measure of his own difference in conceiving of the quest's unending nature. See *Literary World,* 28 April 1849, p. 370.

9. John Seelye, *Melville: The Ironic Diagram* (Evanston, IL: Northwestern University Press, 1970), p. 5.

10. Ann Douglas, *The Feminization of American Culture* (New York: Knopf, 1977), pp. 10–13, and 44–48. Nancy F. Cott in *The Bonds of Womanhood: "Woman's Sphere" in New England, 1780–1835* (New Haven: Yale

University Press, 1977) documents a similar process occurring in the earliest years of the century, while Habegger's study focuses on its later entrenchment.

11. Harriet Martineau, *Society in America* (New York: Saunders and Otley, 1837), 2: 233; also quoted in Habegger, p. 23.

12. *Ladies' Magazine* 8 (1835): 186; quoted in Douglas, p. 48.

13. T. S. Arthur, *Married and Single* (New York: Harper and Brothers, 1845), pp. 12–13.

14. The term "socially deviant" for the romance writer is that of Michael Davitt Bell in *The Development of American Romance: The Sacrifice of Relation* (Chicago: University of Chicago Press, 1980), who theorizes that the "Romancers," by selfconsciously identifying themselves as such, knew that they were sacrificing their relation to social norms (p. 35).

15. Some critics of the sentimental genre besides Douglas include Herbert Ross Brown, *The Sentimental Novel in America, 1789–1860* (Durham NC: Duke University Press, 1940); Henri Petter, *The Early American Novel* (Columbus: Ohio State University Press, 1971); Henry Nash Smith, "The Scribbling Women and the Cosmic Success Story," *Critical Inquiry* 1 (1974): 47–70; and Baym, *Women's Fiction*, which argues for the genre's positive influence upon its readers; in Baym's view, the heroine achieves a relative degree of autonomy, signified by the "successful accomplishment" of marriage, that presented its female audience with an enabling model of individual development (pp. 12, 17–19).

16. Jane Tompkins, *Sensational Designs: The Cultural Work of American Fiction 1790–1860* (New York: Oxford University Press, 1985), pp. 124, 160–65. Chapters 6, "Sentimental Power," and 7, "The Other American Renaissance," are especially relevant.

17. Southworth, *The Mother-in-Law*, p. 167, quoted in Brown, p. 285.

18. Tompkins, p. 163.

19. Brown, p. 176.

20. Letter, dated 19 January 1855, Liverpool, in *Letters of Hawthorne to William D. Ticknor* (Newark NJ: Canteret Book Club, 1910), 1:75.

21. For descriptions of the frontier or western genre, see Ann-Janine Morey-Gaines, "Of Menace and Men: The Sexual Tensions of the American Frontier Metaphor," *Soundings* 4 (1981): 132–48, and Fritz H. Oehlschlaeger, "Civilization as Emasculation: The Threatening Role of Women in the Frontier Fiction of Harold Bell Wright and Zane Grey," *Midwest Quarterly* 22 (1981): 346–60.

22. Fiedler, pp. 211 and 267–68.

23. Ibid., pp. 365–66.

24. See, in this vein, Rex Stout's parody, "Watson Was a Woman" (1941), rpt. in *The Art of the Mystery Story*, ed. Howard Haycraft (New York: Simon and Schuster, 1946), pp. 311–18. For an insightful overview of the rise of the character typology of the domesticized, de-eroticized "urban bachelor" in Victorian fiction (including Thackeray, Barrie, Du Maurier,

and James) and the relation of this character type to a patriarchically en-
forced system of (at once) homosocial bonding and homosexual panic, see
Eve Kosofsky Sedgwick, "The Beast in the Closet: James and the Writing
of Homosexual Panic," in *Sex, Politics, and Science in the Nineteenth-Century
Novel,* ed. Ruth Bernard Yeazell (Baltimore: Johns Hopkins University
Press, 1986), pp. 148–86.

25. Auerbach, pp. 7–9, offers some interesting comments on Kipling in
contrasting her literary communities of women to those of men. Another
major English writer using the male quest format is Joseph Conrad, of
course. If we take the example of *Heart of Darkness,* however, it becomes
clear that Conrad is using the male bond in a highly specific, symbolic way:
Kurtz is more Marlow's psychological double, his dark "other" self, than a
man to whom Marlow has bonded, as a man, in a relation of relative parity
and mutual enrichment. Moreover, the gender alignments in this novel
reveal a network of homosocial relations more akin to Kipling's *The Man
Who Would Be King* than to the American quest romance. For Marlow and
Kurtz only come together in a triangle formed, on the one hand, by the
Intended, Conrad's feminized embodiment of "the lie" of Western civilization, and, on the other hand, by the mirroring reverse of the Intended, the
colossal native woman at the outpost, emblem of the mysterious, fecund,
and dangerous lure of the "dark continent," Africa (and female sexuality,
to recall Freud's famous formulation).

26. I owe the concept of the role played by the "missing woman" in the
all-male world to Robert H. Vorlicky's suggestive study of all-male casts in
drama, "America's Power Plays: The Traditional Hero in Male Cast
Drama" (diss. University of Wisconsin, 1981); see esp. chap. 2, "The Power
of the Invisible Woman."

27. Brodhead, pp. 18–22.

28. "I and My Chimney" (1856), in *Selected Writings of Herman Melville*
(New York: Modern Library, 1952), pp. 385–86, 408, 387. Another of
Melville's works of interest in this regard is the story, "The Paradise of
Bachelors and the Tartarus of Maids"; as the opposing halves of its
diptych-like structure reveal, Melville's purpose is again to expose the destructive consequences of a social ethos that sets the sexes and their worlds
in absolute opposition. In the first half, Melville derides the static lives of
these sequestered English bachelors—not to be confused with the active,
independent, Ishmaelian quester—for their essential uselessness and re-
moteness from engagement in life. The crippling self-division that ensues
from the social dichotomization of the sexes also underlies the Juam episode of *Mardi: and a Voyage Thither* (1849; rpt. Evanston IL: Northwestern
University Press and Newberry Library, 1970). It is the custom of this
kingdom that its ruler must voluntarily accept lifelong imprisonment in a
mountain glen "cut in twain" (217) by extremes of shadow and light. The
pleasure-palaces on either side of the glen between which the king must
schizophrenically split his days are described in explicit male and female

imagery (a tower, a grotto), and he thus becomes an emblem of the psychically imprisoned, divided self torn between imposed, competitive "categories" of human nature, "his mind . . . continually passing and repassing between opposite extremes" (224).

29. Charles Haberstroh, Jr., in "Melville, Marriage, and *Mardi*," *Studies in the Novel* 9 (1977): 247–60, feels that *Mardi*, written the year of Melville's marriage, offers ample evidence that the author on some level of consciousness found his marriage claustrophobic and in conflict with his ideals of male identity. And without doubt Melville's unresolved sexual feelings toward men added to the unease of his marital state—although, as in Henry James's case, to some degree his unconsciously homosexual temperament may have given him a clearer insight into the debilitating effects of sexual marginalization within marriage and society. See also Edwin Haviland Miller, *Melville* (New York: George Braziller, 1975), p. 149, and Newton Arvin, *Herman Melville* (New York: William Sloane, 1950), p. 128.

30. Herman Melville, *Pierre; or, The Ambiguities* (1852; rpt. Evanston IL: Northwestern University Press and the Newberry Library, 1971), p. 141. Robert K. Martin's *Hero, Captain, and Stranger: Male Friendship, Social Critique, and Literary Form in the Sea Novels of Herman Melville* (Chapel Hill: University of North Carolina Press, 1986), which only came to my attention as my book went to press, superbly links issues of gender, sexuality, and genre in these novels.

31. Richard Chase elaborates on this point in *Herman Melville: A Critical Study* (New York: Macmillan, 1949), p. 33.

32. The pioneering study of sexual reference in the novel is that of Robert Shulman, "The Serious Functions of Melville's Phallic Jokes," *American Literature* 33 (1961): 179–94.

33. For representative psychological readings, see Lawrence, *Studies in Classic American Literature* (1923; rpt. New York: Anchor, 1951), pp. 156–74; Newton Arvin, *Herman Melville*, pp. 143–93; and Henry A. Murray, "In Nomine Diaboli," *Moby-Dick: Centennial Essays*, ed. Tyrus Hillway and Luther S. Mansfield (Dallas: Southern Methodist University Press, 1953), pp. 3–21. Three Freudian critics focusing on the "feminine" as well as the "phallic" in Melville are Fiedler; Harry Slochower, "Freudian Motifs in *Moby-Dick*," *Complex* 3 (1950): 16–25, and "The White Whale: The Parental Sex-Mystery," in *Mythopoesis* (Detroit: Wayne State University Press, 1970), pp. 232–41; and Mark Hennelly, "Ishmael's Nightmare and the American Eve," *American Imago* 30 (1973): 274–93.

34. This model of selfhood is implicit in a metaphoric description of the whale's thick outer walls made by Ishmael: "herein we see the rare virtue of a strong individual vitality, and the rare virtue of thick walls, and the rarer virtue of interior spaciousness. Oh, man! admire and model thyself after the whale!"

35. Nina Baym, "Portrayals of Women in American Literature, 1790–1870," in Springer, p. 222.

36. For a similar perspective, see T. Walter Herbert, "Homosexuality

and Spiritual Aspiration in *Moby-Dick*," *Canadian Review of American Studies* 6 (1975): 50–58; see also Martin, pp. 77–78.

37. See, for example, Julian Rice, "Male Sexuality in *Moby-Dick*," *American Transcendental Quarterly* 39 (1978): 241; Fiedler, p. 382; and Martin L. Pops, *The Melville Archetype* (Kent State OH: Kent State University Press, 1970) p. 78.

38. Melville's wording creates multiple links between this scene and other key scenes in my discussion: the reference to Ishmael "bathing" his hands in the globules of sperm (348) recalls the Grand Armada epiphany, where he "bathe[s] . . . in eternal mildness of joy" (326); as he almost "melt[s]" (348) into the sperm, the action echoes the "melting in me" (53) experienced with Queequeg in chapter 10; finally, in speaking of the "rare virtue" of the sperm (348), Ishmael repeats the words he has used in praising the autonomous selfhood—"the rarer virtue of interior spaciousness" (261)—to be found within the independent quester.

39. Chase, *The American Novel*, p. 106; Shulman, p. 184.

40. Fiedler, p. 382.

41. Thus, states Arvin, is this "equivocal symbol" of the "male principle directed cripplingly against him" (p. 172).

42. Both Jung and Freud associate the destructive "masculine" principle with satanic force; see Rice, p. 244, n. 5, concerning such symbology.

43. Brodhead, p. 156. Melville's *Mardi* provides an extreme example of the technical elements of this method at work, evolving from (a seemingly reliable) adventure-escape story in the mode of *Typee* to subjective allegorical romance, then from a metaphysical quest for Truth to Swiftian satire of the world related in a seemingly omniscient travelogue format at odds with the opening first-person voice.

44. Walter Bezanson, "*Moby-Dick*: Work of Art," in *Moby-Dick: Centennial Essays*, p. 45.

45. Brodhead, p. 154, 156.

46. Melville seems to parody traditional aesthetic principles of form in having the Pequod's nondescript Carpenter define the "clean, virgin, fair-and-mathematical jobs" he likes to undertake "as something that regularly begins at the beginning and is at the middle when it is midway, and comes to an end at the conclusion" (430). This unwavering regularity, obviously, stands against the open pattern Ishmael views as more true of life and the human personality.

47. See Leland Krauth, "Mark Twain at Home in the Gilded Age," *Georgia Review* 28 (1973): 105–13.

48. Kenneth Lynn equates Huck's spontaneous fictional biographies with his search for identity in "Huck and Jim," *Yale Review* 47 (1958): 427.

49. Mark Twain, *The Adventures of Huckleberry Finn*, Norton Critical Edition, ed. Sculley Bradley (New York: Norton, 1961), p. 53. All further references to this work appear in the text.

50. So Albert von Frank also observes in "Huck Finn and the Flight from Maturity," *Studies in American Fiction* 7 (1979): 4.

51. Tom Towers in "Love and Power in *Huck Finn*," *Tulane Studies in English* 23 (1978): 17–37, makes the dialectical alternation between these two forces the subject of his study, citing Huck's exchanges with Pap, the Grangerfords, and the Duke and the Dauphin as significant markers of this rhythmical pattern.

52. See Fiedler's entire analysis of the Huck-Jim bond, esp. pp. 352–53.

53. Huck's initially condescending attitude toward Jim has reached a turning point in the preceding chapter, where he attempts to trick Jim by pretending they were never separated in the river fog. Jim's moving denunciation of this unfeeling act toward a purported "fren" whose "heart," in contrast, "wuz mos' broke bekase you wuz los'" (72) shames Huck into realizing Jim's equal claim to human dignity and humane treatment.

54. Of chapter 31, Hemingway said, "That is the real end. The rest is cheating," a view Leo Marx cites in his summary of the case against the ending, *The Machine in the Garden: Technology and the Pastoral Ideal in America* (New York: Oxford University Press, 1964), pp. 339–40.

55. An excellent article regarding the "future" growth of Huck is Paul Delaney's "You Can't Go Back to the Raft Ag'in, Huck Honey! Mark Twain's Western Sequel to *Huckleberry Finn*," *Western American Literature* 11 (1976): 215–29, which evaluates the failure of Twain to finish the "Huck Finn and Tom Sawyer among the Indians" manuscript (begun 1884) because of the particularly brutal sexual realities, along with a growingly bleak existential dilemma, that must face Huck as a maturing young adult in a vicious world.

56. See Douglas, pp. 327–29 which also cites the example of Roosevelt.

57. Herman Melville, *Billy Budd, Sailor (An Inside Narrative)*, ed. Harrison Hayford and Merton M. Sealts, Jr. (Chicago: University of Chicago Press, 1962), p. 111. All further references to this work appear in the text. Martin makes an identical point in *Hero, Captain, Stranger*, p. 124.

58. Mary E. B. Fussell's research into the novella's composition in *"Billy Budd:* Melville's Happy Ending," *Studies in Romanticism* 15 (1976): 43–57, uncovers several reasons for assuming that Melville's earlier investigations into sexual identity were on his mind during its conception. For one, the early manuscript leaf upon which Melville plotted his essential creative "breakthrough" by inventing the mediating figure of Vere ("Look at it. Look at it," Melville exclaimed in the margin) is inscribed on its reverse with the dedication to that "great heart," Jack Chase, an avatar of the Handsome Sailor apotheosized in *White Jacket* as "the man who, in a predominantly masculine world, has successfully integrated the 'female' side of his nature with his more overtly 'male' side, losing by neither, gaining by both" (Fussell, pp. 46–47). In addition, Melville composed three of the most provocative later leaves on the backs of the holograph copy pages of the poem, "After the Pleasure Party," which as we have seen contains a

crucial articulation of Melville's belief in the need to break through restrictive sexual roles in order to achieve individual harmony (pp. 45–46). Hence, it is not unreasonable to assume, along with Fussell, that the associations aroused by this poem and the memory of Chase may have helped spark Melville's creation of *Billy Budd* as an investigation into the nature of masculine identity and authority.

59. Both Fiedler, pp. 454–55, and Hayford and Sealts, eds. *Budd*, p. 155, point out that the initial description of Claggart echoes Melville's earlier association of a character in *Redburn* with Tiberius, whose bust Melville viewed in Rome and described in his journal as evincing "intellect *without manliness* & sadness without goodness" (26 February 1857; emphasis added). This description of Tiberius's bust may thus be taken as a clue to Melville's attitude toward Claggart's own tragic incompletion (Hayford and Sealts, p. 155).

60. Georges-Michel Sarotte, *Like a Brother, Like a Lover: Male Homosexuality in the American Novel and Theatre from Herman Melville to James Baldwin*, trans. Richard Miller (New York: Anchor-Doubleday, 1978), pp. 78–85, and E. Grant Watson, "Melville's Testament of Acceptance," *New England Quarterly* 6 (1933): 324–25.

61. Barbara Johnson, *The Critical Difference: Essays in the Contemporary Rhetoric of Reading* (Baltimore: Johns Hopkins University Press, 1980), pp. 108–9.

62. Ibid., p. 81. In "The Impure Fiction of *Billy Budd*," *Studies in the Novel* 6 (1974): 318–26, Robert T. Eberwein makes a highly suggestive link between the authoritarian rigidity of Vere and conventional fictional form: "Vere thinks life can duplicate the closed world of pure fiction in its order and coherence" (p. 323). As Vere says at the close of Billy's execution, "With mankind, forms, measured forms, are everything" (128).

63. This series of sequels has been analyzed well by Mary Foley in "The Digressions in *Billy Budd*," in *Melville's Billy Budd and the Critics*, ed. William T. Stafford (San Francisco: Wadsworth, 1961), pp. 161–64.

64. Jack London, *The Sea Wolf* (New York: Bantam, 1963), pp. 7, 30, and 166. All further references to this work appear in the text.

65. Sarotte, p. 242.

66. A parallel for Hump's desire to "be" Wolf can be located in London's life, for the author's nickname, even before he wrote *The Sea Wolf*, was "Wolf." See Andrew Sinclair, *Jack: A Biography of Jack London* (New York: Harper and Row, 1977), p. 69. Even more telling in regard to the triangular aspects of Hump's desire, Jack claimed that his own love affair with Charmian Kittredge, who was to become his ideal wife-comrade, arose because his intense homoerotic friendship with George Sterling taught him of his own need for love (Sinclair, p. 97).

67. See London to Charmian, July 1903, in a letter lamenting "this great thing I had looked for, looked for vainly, and the quest of which I had at last abandoned . . . For I had dreamed of the great Man Comrade."

Quoted by Charmian London in *The Book of Jack London* (New York: Century Co., 1921), 2:82.

68. See the examples cited by Morey-Gaines, p. 140.

69. On the coexistence of male bonding and homosexuality in the "on the road" quests in beat writers like Kerouac and Burroughs, see Catharine Stimpson's enlightening "The Beat Generation and the Trials of Homosexual Liberation," *Salmagundi* 58–59 (1982–83): 373–92. The more usual response of the modern quest writer, however, is the tendency to make the "villain" in the all-male world a homosexual; hence General Cummings's repressed homosexual yearnings in *The Naked and the Dead*, as we shall see. The modern writer's fear of the homosexual implications of the male bond is tied to a larger narrative problem, namely, the limited fictional possibilities of representing men together in interpersonal situations other than those traditionally "male" ones of exploration, sports, or war. As Kiely insightfully notes of *Women in Love* in *Beyond Egotism*, pp. 156–68, the narrative simply stops, has no place to go, when Gerald and Rupert find themselves alone together. The generic implications of this spatial issue are fascinating when we note that the two fictional subgenres overwhelmingly concerned with relationships between men—the American quest romance and twentieth-century gay fiction—inscribe totally opposite trajectories; for the soaring movement of quest narrative contrasts vividly to the symbolic center of much gay fiction—the room or circumscribed space where all important action takes place (see, for example, James Baldwin's *Giovanni's Room* (1956), the prison cell of Manuel Puig's *The Kiss of the Spiderwoman* (1976), and the largely interior scenes of Mary Renault's "war" novel, *The Charioteer* (1953), from which the battlefields are never glimpsed).

70. Norman Mailer, *The Naked and the Dead* (New York: Signet, 1948), p. 318.

71. See *Between Men*, passim.

Chapter 6

1. *Deronda*, p. 171.

2. Showalter uses these lines as an epigraph to her lead essay, "Feminist Criticism in the Wilderness," in *Critical Inquiry* 8 (1981): 179.

3. The status of the single woman or "old maid" worsened throughout the eighteenth and nineteenth centuries as industrial development removed production from the home; there is ample evidence to suggest that unmarried female relations were considered integral and beneficial members of the extended family group as long as households produced most of their own goods. Ian Watt, pp. 144–46, notes the less favorable connotations accruing to the phrase "old maid" as her numbers soared in the late eighteenth century in England. See Douglas and Cott, cited in chap. 5, note 10; and Carl Degler, *At Odds: Woman and the Family in America from the Revolution to the Present* (New York: Oxford University Press, 1980), for

detailed discussions of early nineteenth-century American household production and its changing status; for effects of industrialism on the lot of the nineteenth-century English spinster, see Auerbach, pp. 15–23, and her *Woman and the Demon: The Life of a Victorian Myth* (Cambridge MA: Harvard University Press, 1982), chap. 4, "Old Maids and the Wish for Wings," pp. 109–49. Also illuminating is Martha Vicinus, *Independent Women: Work and Community for Single Women, 1850–1920* (Chicago: University of Chicago Press, 1985).

4. Ruth Perry, "The Veil of Chastity: Mary Astell's Feminism," *Studies in Eighteenth Century Culture* 9 (1979): 26.

5. Theodore Roosevelt to Mrs. John Van Vorst, from a letter quoted in Judith Fryer, *The Faces of Eve: Women in the Nineteenth Century American Novel* (New York: Oxford University Press, 1976), p. 15.

6. See Arthur, *Married and Single*, p. 13, quoted in the introduction to chap. 5.

7. In England for instance, from 1851 to 1871 there was a 16.8 percent increase in the single (unmarried) female population. See J. A. and Olive Banks, *Feminism and Family Planning in Victorian England* (Liverpool: Liverpool University Press, 1964), p. 27. Also quoted in a note in Auerbach, *Communities*, p. 194.

8. Auerbach, *Communities*, p. 11.

9. Ibid., pp. 6, 8–9, and *passim*.

10. Elizabeth Abel, "(E)merging Identities: The Dynamics of Female Friendship in Contemporary Fiction by Women," *Signs: Journal of Women in Culture and Society* 6 (1981): 413–35 (esp. pp. 419, 415–17, 421; the quote is from p. 419). For Nancy Chodorow's theories see *The Reproduction of Mothering: Psychoanalysis and The Sociology of Gender* (Berkeley: University of California Press, 1978), and for a summary of feminist psychoanalytic literature on mother-daughter bonding, see Marianne Hirsch, "Mothers and Daughters," *Signs* 7 (1981): 200–222.

11. Marianne Hirsch, "A Mother's Discourse: Incorporation and Repetition in *La Princesse de Clèves*," *Yale French Studies* 62 (1982): 73; also see pp. 69–73.

12. Mary E. Wilkins Freeman, *Madelon: A Novel* (New York: Harper and Brothers, 1896), p. 55.

13. Judith Kegan Gardiner, "On Female Identity and Writing by Women," *Critical Inquiry* 8 (1981): 353.

14. Jane Gallop, "The Monster in the Mirror: The Feminist Critic's Psychoanalysis," paper presented at the Harvard English Institute, September 1983.

15. Carroll Smith-Rosenberg, "The Female World of Love and Ritual: Relations between Women in Nineteenth-Century America," *Signs* 1 (1975): 1–29; Lillian Faderman, *Surpassing the Love of Men: Romantic Friendship and Love between Women from the Renaissance to the Present* (New York: William Morrow, 1981).

16. Smith-Rosenberg, pp. 9, 14.

17. Gerda Lerner, *The Majority Finds its Past: Placing Women in History* (New York: Oxford University Press, 1979), quoted in Showalter, "Feminist Criticism in the Wilderness," pp. 198–99. As the discussion of segregated spheres at the beginning of chapter 5 has already indicated, the assertion of women's superiority was not necessarily tradition-breaking (see Sarah Hale's characterization of the separate sexes, for example); the point is that such rhetoric at least helped legitimize female culture as viable, a power in itself.

18. Showalter, "Feminist Criticism in the Wilderness," p. 199; my emphasis substituted for Showalter's.

19. See chapter 4, note 22. The image of "the wild" is, in turn, extended toward women's literature by Showalter (in "Feminist Criticism," p. 200), in whose sense I use it here.

20. Hélène Cixous, "The Laugh of the Medusa," trans. Keith and Paula Cohen, *Signs* 1 (1976): 893. Cixous also advocates female bonding as the path and entrance to this territory: "Everything will be changed once woman gives to the other woman . . . [in order] to be able to love herself and return in love the body that was 'born' to her" (p. 882).

21. Joanna Russ, "What Can a Heroine Do? Or Why Women Can't Write," in *Images of Women*, ed. Cornillon, pp. 12–13 (Russ's italics omitted).

22. See, among others, Lucy Lippard, *From the Center: Feminist Essays on Women's Art* (New York: Dutton, 1976).

23. Auerbach, *Communities*, documents the thematic occurrence of this phenomenon in several texts.

24. Sarah Scott, *A Description of Millenium Hall*, ed. Walter M. Crittenden (New York: Bookman Associates, 1955). Crittenden's preface supplies biographical information that sheds light on Scott's advocacy of female bonds and support of female education. During and after her brief marriage, Scott lived with Lady Barbara Montagu (not to be confused with Scott's famous sister-in-law, the "bluestocking" Lady Elizabeth Montagu), a fact that contributed to Horace Walpole's speculation that *Millenium Hall*, published anonymously, was the work of both women; on the basis of several letters and bibliographical references, Crittenden disagrees. All further references to this work appear in the text. The novel has been reissued by Virago Press.

25. A. B. Hopkins, *Elizabeth Gaskell: Her Life and Work* (New York: John Lehmann, 1952), p. 108. Upon the favorable reception of an apparently self-contained sketch, "Our Society at Cranford," which appeared in Dickens's *Household Words* in 1851 and was to become the first two chapters of the later "novel," Gaskell produced seven additional episodes at irregular intervals over the next two years before gathering them, with slight revision, into a book-length edition named *Cranford*. See Peter Keating's introduction to Elizabeth Gaskell's *Cranford and Cousin Phillis* (New York: Penguin, 1976), p. 8. All further references to *Cranford* appear in the text.

26. For example, both Martin Dodsworth in "Women without Men at Cranford," *Essays in Criticism*, 13 (1963): 132–45, and Patricia Wolfe in "Structure and Movement in *Cranford*," *Nineteenth Century Fiction* 23 (1968–69): 161–76, identify the "feminist" isolationism of the spinsters (that is, their relative satisfaction with their independence as single women) as the abnormality and see the town moving from a rejection to acceptance of superior male presence. Dodsworth more specifically argues that the causal relationship between the novel's "halves" illustrates a *masculine* triumph over the sterile and otherwise inconsequential lives of Cranford's sexually frustrated spinsters; Wolfe, in an only apparent disagreement, argues rather that it is the emergence of true *femininity*, epitomized in Matty's growth, that reclaims the community from the "feminist" dangers of isolationism. In contrast to both of these readings, Margaret Tarratt in "*Cranford* and 'the Strict Code of Gentility,'" *Essays in Criticism* 18 (1968): 152–63, locates the text's linear development in its passage from a state of social snobbery to one of democratization. But even while Tarratt's conclusion corrects the sexual bias permeating Dodsworth's and Wolfe's attempts to "normalize" this group of "odd women," her insistence on a purely developmental framework of action aligns her with Dodsworth in judging the ladies's opening ethos of gentility as necessarily vain, trivial, and in need of drastic reform.

27. See Dodsworth, Wolfe.

28. See Auerbach, *Communities*, esp. pp. 81–85; what she demonstrates as thematically pervasive, I will attempt to show also to be a function of organizational structure. My reading of this novel is greatly indebted to Auerbach's ground-breaking analysis.

29. Indeed, the self-sufficiency of the community's old maids and widows becomes the basis of a comically exaggerated disdain of all things male. Mary reports that "we had almost persuaded ourselves that to be a man was to be 'vulgar'" (45), and Miss Deborah Jenkyns, who "altogether had the appearance of a strong-minded woman," would have "despised the modern idea of women being equal to men. Equal, indeed! she knew they were superior" (51). In this ironic turning of the tables, the degradation of masculinity mimics society's usual treatment of women as inferiors; the result is a comic, not vindictive, reversal of roles that is ultimately therapeutic.

30. Auerbach also cites the importance of this incident, p. 330.

31. Even Matty's simulated pangs of "widowhood" (one of Gaskell's comic touches) add to the deflationary, antiromantic ambience of an episode that could easily have been saccharine. For, rather than motivating a retreat into the past, the whole sequence functions to prod Matty into attending to her future, without the props of either stronger sister or illusory lover to sustain her.

32. In a deflationary stroke accompanying Brunoni's illness, his much

admired and exotic title of "Signor Brunoni" turns out to be a sham. In real life he is only Samuel Brown—a much more prosaic name that reveals his affinity with that other initially boisterous intruder into Cranford, Captain Brown, similarly laid low by "circumstances." Auerbach makes a similar connection between names, p. 84.

33. Wolfe, p. 175, provides textual evidence connecting Peter's values with his mother.

34. Auerbach, p. 88.

35. See, for example, Lord David Cecil's categorization of "Mrs." Gaskell in *Victorian Novelists* (Chicago: University of Chicago Press, 1935): "The outstanding fact about Mrs. Gaskell is her femininity" (p. 183). For comments on "Miss Jewett's maidenly bias" see the biographer Richard Cary, *Sarah Orne Jewett* (New York: Twayne, 1962), p. 141; and for a lack of erotic energy in her writing, see Ziff, p. 188.

36. Donovan, "A Woman's Vision of Transcendence: A New Interpretation of the Works of Sarah Orne Jewett," *Massachusetts Review* 21 (1980): 365–66. Attention has traditionally focused on the literary "forefathers" surrounding Jewett as a young woman; what has *not* always been noted in this welter of names is the basic fact that Jewett passed her time with the *daughters* of these noteworthies, who, together, constituted a female world, a "community of women," that was of immense insprirational value to Jewett as a single woman and as a woman writer. See Barbara A. Johns, "'Mateless and Appealing': Growing into Spinsterhood in Sarah Orne Jewett," in *Critical Essays on Sarah Orne Jewett*, ed. Gwen L. Nagel (Boston: G. K. Hall, 1984), pp. 147–65, and Glenda Hobbs, "Pure and Passionate: Female Friendship in Sarah Orne Jewett's 'Martha's Lady,'" *Studies in Short Fiction* 17 (1980): 21–29.

37. Malinda Snow addresses Jewett's consciousness of breaking the literary convention of the happy ending in "That One Talent: The Vocation as Theme in Sarah Orne Jewett's *A Country Doctor*," *Colby Library Quarterly* 16 (1980): 142–45.

38. *The Letters of Sarah Orne Jewett*, ed. Annie Fields (Boston: Houghton Mifflin, 1911), p. 249.

39. Sarah Orne Jewett, *The Country of the Pointed Firs* (Garden City NY: Doubleday, 1955), p. 13. All further references to this work appear in the text.

40. We have already noted Mrs. Todd commanding the center of her home like a huge sibyl and walking the "primeval fields of Sicily" in "cousinship with the ancient deities" (137); looking out to Green Island, she appears as a caryatid, "grand and architectural" (34); moving away from the narrator in a meadow of pennyroyal, she seems "Antigone alone on the Theban plain" (49); elsewhere she triumphantly strikes the pose of Winged Victory (41).

41. Marjorie Pryse, "Framing Modern Contexts, Regional Texts," a pa-

per presented for the Origins of American Modernism Panel of the Late Nineteenth–Early Twentieth Century American Literature Division at the 1984 Modern Language Association Convention, Washington, DC.

42. Since writing this, I have found my views of Jewett's "circular" structuring devices reflected almost exactly in Elizabeth Ammons, "Going in Circles: The Female Geography of Jewett's *Country of the Pointed Firs*," *Studies in the Literary Imagination* 16 (1983): 83–92. On the other hand, for a representative example of the attempt to read into the work a traditional kind of "novelistic" unity (bringing to mind the number of critics similarly trying to locate *Cranford*'s linear developmental mode), see Paul Voekler, "*The Country of the Pointed Firs:* A Novel by Sarah Orne Jewett," *Colby Library Quarterly* 9 (1970–71): 201–13.

43. Joanna's isolation is underlined by the community of spirit created by Mrs. Todd and Mrs. Fosdick in the event of retelling her history. "The two women had drawn closer together," the narrator observes, "and were talking on, quite unconscious of a listener" (64). Note also Jewett's deliberate choice of the word "humankind" rather than the standard "mankind" in the text above.

44. Warner Berthoff, "The Art of Jewett's *Pointed Firs*," *New England Quarterly* 32 (1959): 31–53.

45. For a review of Gilman's career as reformist and writer, see Ann J. Lane, Intro., *Herland*, by Charlotte Perkins Gilman (New York: Pantheon, 1979). Lane unearthed *Herland* from the pages of *The Forerunner;* the Pantheon edition marks its first appearance in book form. All further references to this work appear in the text.

46. Part of Gilman's strategy for reeducating the reader's perspectives on the sexes is to present stereotypical extremes of masculinity in the black-and-white characterizations of Terry and Jeff that parody the classic split perception of women in male authors from Scott and Cooper to Lawrence and Fitzgerald. Thus, Terry and Jeff illustrate two contrasting "male" perspectives used to objectify women and keep them "as different as possible and as feminine as possible" (129): Terry's supervirile pose is predicated on a belief that "there never was a woman yet that did not enjoy being mastered" (131), while Jeff's adoration of the Eternal Feminine, like the chivalric tradition noted in chapter 2 above, elevates woman to a spirituality that denies her physical reality.

47. The problem of presenting sexual passion within an equal comradeship without threatening its dynamic is one from which Gilman ultimately shies away. While Van periodically admits to feeling the desire "to lose myself in you" (126), Elladore simply cannot understand the nature of sexual desire, given her country's history. Gilman's vagueness about the sexual aspects of this "marriage" (how far *do* they go? and how often?) has disappointed some readers, for although Elladore's lack of response is understandable within the historical context that the novel establishes, the women's general sublimation of all erotic feeling into the act of mothering

and self-governance seems to reinforce the Victorian stereotype. Gilman's vagueness, however, may be part of her narrative strategy; the movement of the narrative, if not the characters, is indeed "erotic," in the sense I have been using the word here. As Lane notes, "Gilman was not alone among feminists in asserting that the strategy of sexual freedom led to another form of female subordination" (xvi).

48. Tompkins, p. xiv.

49. An informative account of Trollope's self-declared spinster, standing against earlier deprecatory evaluations, occurs in Judith Weissman's "'Old Maids Have Friends': The Unmarried Heroine of Trollope's Barsetshire Novels," *Women and Literature*, 5 (1977): 15–25.

50. Djuna Barnes, *Ladies Almanack, showing their Signs and their tides; their Moons and their Changes; the Seasons as it is with them; their Eclipses and Equinoxes; as well as a full Record of diurnal and nocturnal Distempers, Written and Illustrated BY A LADY OF FASHION* (privately printed in France, 1928; rpt. New York: Harper and Row, 1972), p. 3. All further references to this work appear in the text.

51. Gloria Naylor, *The Women of Brewster Place* (1982; rpt. Harmondsworth: Penguin, 1983), p. 34. All further references to this work appear in the text.

52. Pat Barker, *Union Street* (1982; first American edition rpt. New York: Ballantine, 1983), p. 243. All further references to this work appear in the text.

53. Cixous, pp. 880–81; Luce Irigaray, *This Sex Which Is Not One*, trans. Catherine Porter with Carolyn Burke (1977; rpt. Ithaca NY: Cornell University Press, 1985), p. 30.

54. Ellen Glasgow, *Barren Ground* (1925; rpt. New York: Hill and Wang, 1957), p. 409.

Index

INDEX

INDEX

INDEX

71, 73, 79, 82–86, 102–4, 115–18, 342n.3
Pride and Prejudice (Austen), 10, 66, 81, 89–96, 103, 179, 345n.46
"Prussian Officer, The" (Lawrence), 237
Pryse, Marjorie, 309, 371n.41
Psychoanalytic theory, and literary applications: as narrative model, 72, 343n.26; issues in differentiation, 38, 282–84, 321; masculine diabolism, 364n.42; Oedipal family romance, 216. *See also* Chodorow, Nancy; Freud, Sigmund; Jung, Carl
Puig, Manuel: *The Kiss of the Spiderwoman*, 367n.69

Quest narrative, in American literature: archetypal patterns, 229; in contrast to general "romance," 231, 234–35; in contrast to realism, 228, 241, 258; difference from bildungsroman, 241; formal innovations, 240–41, 250–51, 257–58; incorporation into women's fiction, 276–77, 312–13; indirection as technique, 252, 264–65; male-authored status, 227, 230, 235; place in canon, 319–20; potential for misogyny, 230, 235, 273–76; role of women in, 230, 239–40, 270–72, 274. *See also* American fiction; Male bonding; Masculinity

Race, issues involving, 23–24, 231, 236, 238, 245, 253, 255–57, 276, 323, 324, 326–27, 362n.25
Radcliffe, Ann: *The Mysteries of Udolpho*, 112
Rainbow, The (Lawrence), 221
Rape upon Rape (Fielding), 341n.74

Rash Resolve, The (Haywood), 61, 341n.70
Realism, quest narrative in contrast to, 228, 241, 258. *See also* English novel
Rebirth motif, 241, 244, 247, 252, 254, 314, 326, 329
Redburn (Melville), 366n.59
Reeve, Clara: *The School for Widows*, 322
Renaissance, Synthesis of Love and Marriage in: Protestant elevation of "holy matrimony," 49, 338n.40; sex-role divisions, 49–50, 339n.43; humanist and neo-Platonic influences, 51–54; literary inscriptions, 48, 54–58
Renault, Mary: *The Charioteer*, 367n.69
Rhys, Jean, 113, 136
Rice, Julian, 364n.37
Rich, Adrienne, 350n.19
Richard St. Victor, 40, 337n.23
Richardson, Samuel, 4, 46, 59, 69, 71, 108, 117, 224, 327; American heirs, 112, 228; *Clarissa*, 10, 22, 46, 66, 77, 102, 104–8, 109, 111, 248, 249, 318, 343n.25; *Clarissa* as counter-traditional paradigm, 147–48; *Pamela*, 10, 31, 61, 66, 68, 82–84, 86–89, 90, 92, 100, 104–5, 109, 112, 268, 303, 344n.38; *Pamela II*, 114
Richetti, John J., 68–70, 85, 342n.3, 342n.4
"Rip Van Winkle" (Irving), 228
Robbe-Grillet, Alain, 8, 332n.12
Robertson, D. W., 335n.8
Robinson Crusoe (Defoe), 237, 271
Roderick Hudson (James), 355–56n.61
Roman de la Rose (Guillaume de Lorris and Jean de Meung), 41–42, 337n.25
Romantic poets, English, 239